Music Education in the 21st Century in the United Kingdom

The Bedford Way Papers Series

A full list of Bedford Way Papers, including earlier books in the series, can be
requested by emailing ioepublications@ioe.ac.uk

Music Education in the 21st Century in the United Kingdom

Achievements, analysis and aspirations

Edited by Susan Hallam and Andrea Creech

Institute of Education, University of London
Bedford Way Papers

Leading education
and social research
Institute of Education
University of London

First published in 2010 by the Institute of Education,
University of London, 20 Bedford Way, London WC1H 0AL

www.ioe.ac.uk/publications

© Institute of Education, University of London 2010

British Library Cataloguing in Publication Data:
A catalogue record for this publication is available from the
British Library

ISBN 978 0 85473 899 1

Typeset by Quadrant Infotech (India) Pvt Ltd
Printed by ImageData Group

Contents

Acknowledgements

The authors would like to thank all of the contributors to this book, and also the reviewers who provided useful guidance on the proposal for this book, who include Dr Pamela Burnard, University of Cambridge; Dr Michael Fautley, Birmingham City University; Professor Peter R Webster, Northwestern University School of Music, USA; Ms Karen Brock, Tower Hamlets Arts and Music Education Service (THAMES), London Borough of Tower Hamlets; Mr Stuart Whatmore, THAMES; and David Watson, Principal, Green Templeton College, Oxford.

The author and publisher gratefully acknowledge the permission granted to reproduce copyright material in this book.

Figure 3.2 reprinted with permission from the Australian Society for Music Education Inc. (ASME) Publications: Cheng, E., Ockelford, A. and Welch, G.F. (2009) 'Researching and developing music provision in Special Schools in England for children and young people with complex needs'. *Australian Journal of Music Education*, (2), 27–48.

Figure 4.1 reprinted with permission from Professor Albert LeBlanc: 'A model of sources of variation in musical taste' (LeBlanc, 1980, © Music Educators National Conference).

Figures 8.1 and 8.2 reprinted with permission from The Associated Board of the Royal Schools of Music (ABRSM) and Soundjunction: <http://www.soundjunction.org>.

Boxes 4.1 and 4.2 reprinted with permission from Sharon Green: Green, S. (2009) 'Improving motivation for music at Key Stage 3'. In D. Bray (ed), *Creating a musical School*. Oxford: Oxford University Press (pp. 95-119).

Box 5.1 reprinted with permission from Susan Knight: Knight, S. (2010). 'A Study of Adult Non-Singers in Newfoundland'. Unpublished PhD Thesis, Institute of Education, University of London.

Boxes 7.5, 20.1, 20.2 and 20.3 reprinted with permission from Youth Music: <http://musicispower.youthmusic.org.uk/>.

Box 10.2 reprinted with permission from Live Music Now: <http://livemusicnow. org.uk/>.

Box 10.4 reprinted with permission from the authors and The Irene Taylor Trust: Cox, A. and Gelsthorpe, L. (2008) *Beats & Bars - Music in Prisons: an evaluation*. London: The Irene Taylor Trust.

Box 13.4 reprinted with permission from the publisher (Taylor & Francis Group, <http://www.informaworld.com>): Rogers, L., Hallam, S., Creech, A., and Preti, C. (2008) 'Learning about what constitutes effective training from a pilot programme to improve music education in primary schools', *Music Education Research*, 10(4), 485-497.

Box 16.3 reprinted with permission from the authors and the publisher (Taylor & Francis Group, <http://www.informaworld.com>): Papageorgi, I., Creech, A., Haddon, E., Morton, F., de Bezenac, C., Himonides, E., Potter, J., Duffy, C., Whyton, T. and Welch, G. (2010) 'Institutional culture and learning I: Inter-relationships between perceptions of the learning environment and undergraduate musicians' attitudes to learning'. *Music Education Research*, 12(2), 1-16.

Box 19.3 reprinted with permission from Sage Publications: Higgins, L. (2008) 'The creative music workshop: Event, facilitation, gift', *International Journal of Music Education*, 26(4), 326-38.

Box 19.5 reprinted with permission from the publisher (Taylor & Francis Group, <http://www.informaworld.com>): Higgins, L. (2007) 'Acts of hospitality: The community in community music', *Music Education Research*, 9(2), 281-292.

Box 20.7 printed with permission from Richard Hallam: Hallam, R. (2010) 'Effective partnership working in Music Education: an interim overview'. Paper to be presented at the 20th World ISME conference Beijing, 1-6 August.

Every effort has been made to trace copyright holders and to obtain their permission for the use of copyright material. The publisher apologises for any errors or omissions in the above list and would be grateful if notified of any corrections that should be incorporated in future reprints or editions of this book.

Preface

The development of the electronic media in the latter part of the twentieth century revolutionised access to and use of music in our everyday lives. Never before have so many different kinds of music been so easily available to so many people. We can turn on the radio, play a CD or listen to music via digital media with very little effort. This has not always been the case. In addition to our personal use, music is played in supermarkets, shopping precincts, restaurants, places of worship, schools, on the radio and television, through the medium of recordings and on the internet. Music also plays an important role in the theatre, TV, films, video and advertising. The music industry makes a substantial contribution to the economy of all developed countries. For this contribution to be sustained the music industries need a skilled workforce. Music education in its various forms supplies this workforce. Despite this, educators, worldwide, increasingly have to justify the place of music in the curriculum and battle to maintain funding for musical activities which fall outside the curriculum. This is particularly the case in times of financial restraint.

The aim of this book is to provide an overview of music education in the UK in the twenty-first century across all phases of education, celebrating achievements, identifying where there is room for improvement and setting out aspirations for the future. The first section begins by providing an up-to-date review of the wider benefits of music education, not in any way to diminish the importance of music in its own right but rather to provide evidence for music educators to justify the place of music in the school curriculum and more widely in extra-curricular and community activities throughout the life course at a time of financial constraints. This is followed by a brief overview of the historical and current context of music education, providing a framework for accessing the remainder of the book. The second section addresses issues which continue to be of interest to music educators, including the provision of music for all, the roles of listening, singing, playing an instrument, creativity, technology, performance and assessment, learning through life and the initial and ongoing training of music teachers. The final section examines music education in different contexts of learning from early years, through primary, secondary, further and higher education, in Music Services, the music studio, and in informal contexts. The final chapter sets out an agenda for consideration by music educators and policymakers which has as its aim the maintenance of high-quality provision for all, wherever they live and whatever their financial circumstances.

Susan Hallam
Andrea Creech

Notes on contributors

Pauline Adams is lecturer in Music Education, teaching on the PGCE and Master's Music Education courses at the Institute of Education, University of London (IOE). She started her career teaching in inner London schools and for some years acted in an advisory role for the Inner London Education Authority. She is the author of _Sounds Musical, a Key Stage 2 Music Scheme_ (published by Oxford University Press) and is a contributor to _The Curriculum for 7–11 year olds_ (1999; eds J. Riley and R. Prentice; published by Paul Chapman Publishing) and, more recently, _Learning to Teach Music in the Secondary School_ and _Issues in Music Teaching_ (both published in 2001 by RoutledgeFalmer). She has recently contributed a chapter to an Institute publication examining approaches to M level assignment writing for the students on the PGCE course (2010). Her research interest is currently focused on historical studies in music education.

John Conlon has over 28 years experience working within the post-compulsory education sector in a range of contexts including arts, community, theatre and adult, further and higher education. His main teaching specialisms are creative and expressive arts. He has written numerous learning programmes, has been an external examiner/verifier for examination boards and has also acted as consultant for national arts/creative lead organisations. After leaving the education sector he joined the Arts Council England where he initiated and managed research projects, including the first longitudinal study of arts interventions in English schools. He also co-initiated and became director of operations for _Creative Partnerships_, a £120 million government-funded creativity in schools programme. John is currently the pathway leader for the pre-service, post-compulsory PGCE at the IOE and divides his time between teaching and his international design business. His main education interest is creativity within teaching and learning.

Dr Andrea Creech has extensive experience as a professional musician, music teacher and researcher. She currently is Lecturer in Education at the IOE and Associate Lecturer (psychology) for the Open University. Previously she has held principal positions in orchestras in the UK and Canada and subsequently was founder and director of a Community Music School in the Republic of Ireland. Andrea has been project manager for a number of funded research projects in the areas of music education, behaviour and attendance and disaffection. Her special research interests are musical development across the lifespan, learning and teaching for older adults and the impact of interpersonal relationships on learning and teaching outcomes. Andrea has presented her work at international conferences and published widely.

Dr Colin Durrant leads the postgraduate programme in Music Education at the IOE and is conductor of the University of London Chamber Choir and Imperial College Choir. He has a wide range of choral conducting and teaching experience and is principal tutor for the Association of British Choral Directors' conducting courses in London. Following his research into the area of effective choral conducting, he designed and developed a postgraduate programme in Choral Education, the first of its kind in the UK. He has led teacher training, professional development and conducting courses and workshops in the USA, Australia, China, Hong Kong, Taiwan and Malaysia as well as in Europe and the UK and, in 2009, was one of an international panel of adjudicators and conducting master-class leaders at the Singapore Youth Music Festival. He has published numerous articles on choral conducting and music education; his seminal book, *Choral Conducting: Philosophy and Practice* appeared in 2003.

Jessica Ellison is an Australian-trained primary teacher with vast experience as a music specialist. After moving to England she increased her expertise to include early years and taught as a music specialist and classroom teacher (Early Years to Key Stage 2). She worked in both the public and private sectors, before joining a local authority Music Service where she was responsible for individual, whole class instrumental, and curriculum music lessons. Other roles included creating resources to support musical development in children and teachers, and designing and delivering continuing professional development (CPD) in music education to teachers within the borough. She teaches on the Masters level music specialism course on the PGCE at the IOE.

Dr Helena Gaunt is the Assistant Principal (Research and Academic Development) at the Guildhall School of Music and Drama in London, and a National Teaching Fellow (2009). Her current research focuses on one-to-one and small group tuition in conservatoires, orchestral musicians in the twenty-first century and the role of improvisation (verbal and musical) in developing professional expertise. Alongside research, she is a professional oboist, and has been a member of the Britten Sinfonia. She is a member of the Editorial Board of the *British Journal of Music Education*, and chairs the Research group of the Polifonia project for the Association of European Conservatoires (AEC), and the Innovative Conservatoire (ICON) group. She is also the deputy chair of a new Forum on Instrumental Teaching for the International Society of Music Education. She contributes to the specialist route for conservatoire teachers, the Professional Certificate in Teaching and Learning in Higher and Professional Education, which is run jointly between the IOE and the Guildhall School of Music and Drama.

Professor Susan Hallam is Professor of Education at the IOE and currently Dean of the Faculty of Policy and Society. She pursued careers as both a professional musician and a music educator before completing her psychology studies and becoming an academic in 1991. Her research interests include disaffection from school, ability grouping and homework and issues relating to learning in music, practising, performing, musical ability, musical understanding and the effects of music on behaviour and studying. She is the author of several books, including *Instrumental Teaching: A Practical Guide to Better Teaching and Learning* (1998), *The Power of Music* (2001) and *Music Psychology in Education* (2005). She is editor of *The Oxford Handbook of Psychology of Music* (2009) and has many other scholarly articles to her name. She is past editor of *Psychology of Music*, *Psychology of Education Review* and *Learning Matters*. She has twice been Chair of the Education Section of the British Psychological Society, and is past treasurer of the British Educational Research Association, an auditor for the Quality Assurance Agency and an Academician of the Learned Societies for the Social Sciences.

Dr Evangelos Himonides holds the University of London's first ever Lecturer in Music Technology Education position. He teaches music education, music technology and information technology, at a post-graduate level, at the IOE, and also leads the post-graduate course, 'Music Technology in Education'. He holds a Music Diploma from the Macedonian Conservatoire of Thessaloniki, Greece, a Bachelors of Science in Information Technology with Multimedia with Star First Class Honours from Middlesex University, UK, a Masters in Education with distinction from the University of Surrey, UK and a PhD in Psychoacoustics and Information Technology from the University of London. He is a Chartered IT professional with the British Computer Society. As a musician, technologist and educator, Evangelos has research interests in experimental work in the fields of psychoacoustics, music perception, music cognition, information technology, human–computer interaction, special needs, the singing voice and singing development.

Kate Laurence is Subject Leader for the Music PGCE programme at the IOE. She began her professional life as a music teacher in inner London and was Director of Music and an Advanced Skills Teacher before entering teacher education. She has held professional and advisory roles with the Specialist Schools and Academies Trust, the BBC and for Sibelius Software Ltd. Kate currently leads a number of national CPD courses for music teachers. She is the author of a number of music education resources for Rhinegold Publishing and Tribal Education. Her interests include how music teachers can develop as researchers, the personalisation of Initial Teacher Education routes for professional musicians and effective CPD in music education.

Dr Hilary McQueen studied music at Edinburgh University and trained as a teacher at St Luke's College of Education, Exeter. She has taught class music and singing, and continues to teach piano and music theory. Having developed an interest in psychology as a child, she decided to complete a degree in the subject with the Open University, followed by a Ph.D. in education at King's College, London. She was head of psychology in two institutions, taught child development for the Open University, and now combines teaching and research at the IOE. Her academic interests include the social sciences, education, music, philosophy and language.

Professor Adam Ockelford is Professor of Music at Roehampton University and has had a lifelong fascination for music, as a composer, performer, teacher and researcher. While attending the Royal Academy of Music in London, Adam started working with children with special needs, and he became interested in how we all intuitively make sense of music. Adam pursued this line of enquiry, and completed a PhD in which he set out his 'zygonic' theory of musical understanding. This theory has proved valuable in music theory and analysis, in investigating musical development and exploring interaction in music therapy and education. Adam is Secretary of the Society for Education, Music and Psychology Research (SEMPRE); Chair of Soundabout, a charity that supports music provision for young people with complex needs; and founder of The AMBER Trust, which supports visually impaired children in their pursuit of music.

Dr Ioulia Papageorgi has been a Lecturer and Coordinating Research Officer in the Department of Arts and Humanities, the Department of Psychology and Human Development and the Doctoral School at the IOE since 2006. She has also been an Associate Lecturer at the Open University in the UK since 2009. Her research interests focus on the development of expertise, the psychology of performance and performance anxiety. She has widely presented her work at international conferences and seminars. She has also published papers in international peer-reviewed journals and conference proceedings, and has authored a number of invited book chapters. Ioulia is a Fellow of the Higher Education Academy (FHEA), and a member of the Open University Psychological Society (OUPS), SEMPRE, the International Society for Music Education (ISME) and the Greek Society for Music Education (GSME).

Ross Purves is Course Manager for A level Music Technology and BTEC Music at Luton Sixth Form College, where he also teaches A Level Music and jazz improvisation. He has worked as a researcher on a series of projects in the School of Arts and Humanities, IOE and at the University of Roehampton, funded by the Economic and Social Research Council (ESRC), Youth Music and the Department for Education and Skills (DfES), among others. He is currently working on the European Union's 'Use of Music for Social Inclusion' project, based at the IOE. He contributes annual sessions on teaching A Level Music Technology to the IOE's Secondary Music PGCE and, with Evangelos Himonides, developed the IOE's Distance Learning Module in Music Technology and Education.

Dr Lynne Rogers is Senior Lecturer in Teacher Education Post-14 Sector at the IOE. She is the Director of the London Centre for Excellence in Teacher Training (LONCETT) and the Faculty Director of Initial Teacher Education. She has long-standing interests in teacher/lecturer training and learning in further and higher education and other professional settings. She has undertaken extensive research in relation to behaviour in school; disaffection from school, including the role of alternative curricula; learning, studying and homework in adolescents; and issues relating to music education. She has publications on behaviour and attendance at school, alternative curriculum, primary music education and studying.

Dr Jo Saunders is responsible for the coordination of various strands of the research evaluation of the UK government's National Singing Programme 'Sing Up' (2007–2011) at the IOE. Jo read Music and Education (BA Hons, First class) at Homerton College, University of Cambridge before completing a PGCE in Music. She was awarded a studentship (1+3) by the ESRC to complete both her M.Phil. in Educational Research (Wolfson College, University of Cambridge) and PhD (IOE). Her doctoral studies focused on the adolescent experience of the music classroom, including the formation and reformation of musical identities and engagement with the learning process. Jo has presented at national and international conferences, and published in professional journals and conference proceedings. Jo has also worked as an instrumental teacher (flute, saxophone and clarinet) as well as a music teacher in secondary schools in Cambridge and Suffolk.

Dr Maria Varvarigou has been performing as a solo singer, oboist and chorister for many years. She has participated in several recordings of Greek traditional songs and she has developed a great interest in the performance practices of traditional music. She is currently working as a researcher at an ESRC-funded project on promoting social engagement and well-being in older people through community supported participation in musical activities, and as lecturer on a module on choral conducting education at the IOE. She completed her PhD in 2009 as a scholar of the A.S. Onassis Foundation.

Professor Graham Welch holds the IOE Established Chair of Music Education and is Deputy Dean of the IOE's Faculty of Culture and Pedagogy. He is elected Chair of the internationally based SEMPRE, President Elect of ISME (becoming President in 2010) and past Co-Chair of the Research Commission of ISME. Current Visiting Professorships include the Universities of Queensland (Australia), Limerick (Eire) and Roehampton (UK). He is also a member of the UK Arts and Humanities Research Council's (AHRC) Review College for music and has been a specialist consultant for government departments and agencies in the UK, Italy, Sweden, USA, Ukraine, UAE, South Africa and Argentina. Publications number over 260 and embrace musical development and music education, teacher education, singing and voice science, and music in special education and disability.

PART 1

INTRODUCTION

The power of music: its impact on the intellectual, personal and social development of children and young people

Susan Hallam

Never before have so many different kinds of music been so easily available to so many people. The development of electronic media has revolutionised access to and use of music in our everyday lives. We can turn on the radio, play a CD, download music from the internet on to an iPod, or listen to music on video or TV with very little effort. This has not always been the case. Prior to these developments, music was only accessible for most people if they made it themselves or attended particular religious or social events. The effect of these changes has been dramatic. It is now possible for us to use music to manipulate personal moods, arousal and feelings, and to create environments which may manipulate the ways that other people feel and behave. Individuals can and do use music as an aid to relaxation, to overcome powerful emotions, to generate the right mood for social activities, to stimulate concentration – in short, to promote their well-being. It has become a tool to be used to enhance our self-presentation and promote our development. Alongside this, technological advances in research techniques have increased our understanding of the way that music can benefit the intellectual, social and personal development of children and young people. This chapter considers the evidence from that research.

Perceptual and language skills

Music has long been argued to provide effective experiences for children to develop listening skills. When we listen to music or speech we process an enormous amount of information rapidly. The ease with which we do this depends on our prior musical and linguistic experiences and the culturally determined tonal scheme or language to which we have become accustomed. This knowledge is implicit, learned through exposure to particular environments, and is applied automatically whenever we listen to music or speech. The systems which process speech are shared, in part, with those which process music. Musical experiences which enhance processing can therefore impact on the perception of language. Musical training sharpens the brain's early encoding of sounds (e.g. Patel and Iverson, 2007) impacting on the processing of pitch patterns in language (e.g. Magne et al., 2006). These changes occur relatively quickly. For instance, 4–6 year olds given music training for 25 minutes for seven weeks showed enhanced processing (Flohr et al., 2000), while with just eight weeks of musical training, 8-year-old children showed different patterns of brain activity to the control group (Moreno and Besson, 2006).

Speech makes extensive use of auditory patterns based on timbre (the distinctive character of a musical sound) which enable differentiation between phonemes (the units of sound in a word). Musical training develops skills which enhance perception of these patterns. Learning to play a musical instrument enables children to respond more quickly to the onset of a syllable, and the longer that they have been playing the sharper the responses (Musacchia et al., 2007; Peynircioglu et al., 2002). It also improves the ability to distinguish between rapidly changing sounds (Gaab et al., 2005). This is critical to developing phonological awareness, which in turn contributes to learning to read successfully. A longitudinal study of the effects of music training on brain development and cognition in young children aged 5–7, found that after one year children learning to play an instrument (mainly the piano) had improved auditory discrimination scores compared to controls (Schlaug et al., 2005). Kindergarten children also showed improved phonemic awareness compared with controls after four months of music instruction for 30 minutes a week. This included active music making and movement to emphasise steady beat, rhythm and pitch as well as the association of sounds with symbols (Gromko, 2005). Learning to discriminate differences between tonal and rhythmic patterns and to associate these perceptions with visual symbols transfers to improved phonemic awareness.

Processing of melodic contour, one of the first aspects of music to be discriminated by infants (Trehub et al., 1984), is also important in language (see Patel, 2009). Magne et al. (2006) compared 8-year-old children who had musical training with those who did not and found that the musicians performed better on music and language tests. The study showed that pitch processing seemed to take place earlier in music than in language, leading the authors to conclude that there were positive effects of music lessons on linguistic abilities.

Overall, the evidence suggests that engagement with music plays a major role in developing perceptual processing systems which facilitate the encoding and identification of speech sounds and patterns – the earlier the exposure to active music participation and the greater the length of participation, the greater the impact.

Literacy

The role of music in facilitating language skills contributes to the development of reading skills. An early study where music instruction was specifically designed to develop auditory, visual and motor skills in 7–8 year olds over a period of six months, found that the mean reading comprehension scores of the intervention group increased while those of the control group did not (Douglas and Willatts, 1994). Anvari *et al.* (2002), working with 100 pre-schoolers, found that music skills correlated significantly with both phonological awareness and reading development. Moderate relationships have also been found between memory for melody and reading age (Barwick *et al.*, 1989). Butzlaff (2000), in a meta-analysis of 24 studies, found a reliable relationship between musical instruction and standardised measures of reading ability. While, overall, the research showed a positive impact of musical engagement on reading, there were some differences. These may be explained by the kind of musical experiences with which the children were engaged and also their prior musical development. If language skills are well developed already, musical activity may need to focus on reading musical notation for transfer benefits to occur.

Some studies have focused on children who are experiencing difficulties with reading. Nicholson (1972) studied children aged 6–8 categorised as slow learners. Those receiving music instruction had significantly higher reading readiness scores than those who received no music instruction and this advantage was still in evidence a year later. Rhythmic performance seems to be an important factor in reading development. Atterbury (1985) found that children aged 7–9 with reading difficulties were poorer in rhythm performance and tonal memory than normal-achieving readers. Very brief training (10 minutes each week for six weeks) in stamping, clapping and chanting in time to a piece of music while following simple musical notation has been found to have a considerable impact on reading comprehension in children experiencing difficulties (Long, 2007). There are also indications from a range of sources that rhythmic training may help children experiencing dyslexia (Thomson, 1993; Overy, 2003).

Musical instruction can also increase verbal memory, which may support the development of reading skills (Chan *et al.*, 1998). Adult musicians have enlarged left cranial temporal regions of the brain, the area involved in processing heard information, and can typically remember 17 per cent more verbal information than those without musical training. These findings have been supported in a study of boys aged 6–15 (Ho *et al.*, 2003) and appear to be causal – the longer the duration of music training, the better the verbal memory.

Numeracy

It has long been assumed that there is a strong connection between music and mathematics, possibly because musicians are constantly required to adopt quasi-mathematical processes to subdivide beats and turn rhythmic notation into sound. Not all mathematical skills require this type of ability, which may explain why the findings from research exploring the relationship between mathematical skills and music are not always positive. Most research has supported the link between maths and music. For instance, Geoghegan and Mitchelmore (1996) investigating the impact of a music programme on the mathematics achievement of pre-school children found that the children involved in musical activities scored higher on a mathematics achievement test than a control group, although home musical background may have been a confounding factor. Gardiner *et al.* (1996), researching the impact of an arts programme, also found that participating children performed better in mathematics than those who did not, with those participating the longest having the highest scores overall. A study using a national US database also found positive effects for engagement with music. Catterall *et al.* (1999), using the NELS:88 data, compared low socioeconomic-status students who exhibited high mathematical proficiency in the twelfth grade and found that 33 per cent were involved in instrumental music, compared with 15 per cent who were not involved. Focusing on children learning to play an instrument, Haley (2001) found that those who had studied an instrument prior to fourth grade had higher scores in mathematics than those in other groups, although Rafferty (2003) found no effect of the 'Music Spatial–Temporal Maths Program' on the mathematical achievement of second graders.

The contradictory outcomes of the research might be explained by the types of musical activities engaged in and the length of time spent. Cheek and Smith (1999) found that eighth graders who had two or more years of private lessons and those learning keyboard instruments had higher scores than those learning other instruments. Focusing on the length of time engaged with music, Whitehead (2001) found that middle and high school children who were placed in high, moderate and no music instruction groups differed in mathematical gains, with the high-involvement children showing the greatest gains. Overall, the evidence suggests that active engagement with music can improve mathematical performance, but the nature of this relationship, the kinds of musical training needed to realise the effect, and the length of time required are not currently well understood.

Intellectual development

One of the first studies to consider the role of music in children's intellectual development was undertaken by Hurwitz et al. (1975) who assigned first-grade children to either an experimental group which received Kodaly music lessons for five days each week for seven months, or a control group. At the end of the study, the experimental group scored significantly higher than the control group on three of five sequencing tasks and on four of five spatial tasks. No statistically significant differences were found for verbal measures, although the children in the experimental group had higher reading achievement scores than those in the control group. These differences were maintained after two academic years.

During the 1990s there was a resurgence of interest in these issues, particularly relating to the impact of active engagement with music on spatial reasoning, an element of intelligence tests. In a typical study, Rauscher et al. (1997) assigned children from three pre-school groups to music, computer or no-instruction groups. The instruction groups received tuition in keyboard and group singing, group singing alone or computer lessons. Singing was for 30 minutes daily. The children in the keyboard group scored significantly higher in the spatial recognition test. Since then, several studies have confirmed that active engagement with music has an impact on visual–spatial intelligence. In a review of 15 studies, Hetland (2000) found a 'strong and reliable' relationship and concluded that music instruction lasting two years or less led to dramatic improvements in performance on spatial–temporal measures. She commented on the consistency of the effects and likened them to differences of one inch in height or about 84 points on standardised national tests. The consistency of these findings suggests a near transfer, automated effect, perhaps related to the skills acquired in learning to read music.

Other research has focused on more general manifestations of intelligence. Bilhartz et al. (2000) studied the relationship between participation in a structured music curriculum and cognitive development in 4–6 year olds. Half of the children participated in a 30-week, 75-minute weekly, parent-involved music curriculum. Following this, children were tested with six subtests of the Stanford–Binet Intelligence Test and the Young Child Music Skills Assessment Test. There were significant gains for the music group on the music test and the Stanford-Binet Bead Memory subtest. Adopting a cross-sectional approach, Schlaug et al. (2005) compared 9–11-year-old instrumentalists with an average of four years training and a control group. The instrumental group performed significantly better than the control group on musical audiation, left-hand index finger tapping rate, and the vocabulary subtest of the WISC–III. Strong non-significant trends were seen in the phonemic awareness test, Raven's Progressive Matrices, and the Key Math Test.

What has become a seminal study was undertaken by Schellenberg (2004) who randomly assigned a large sample of children to four different groups, two of which received music lessons (standard keyboard, Kodaly voice) for a year. The two control groups either received instruction in a non-musical artistic activity (drama) or no lessons. All four groups exhibited increases in IQ, as would be expected over the time period, but the music groups had reliably larger increases in full-scale IQ. Children in the control groups had average increases of 4.3 points while the music groups had increases of 7.0 points. On all but two of the 12 subtests the music groups had larger increases than the control groups.

A key issue arising from this research is what kinds of musical activity bring about change in particular kinds of intellectual development – and why. The research reported above was based on the implementation of a variety of musical activities, some offering a broad musical education, others focused more closely on instrumental tuition. To begin to address these questions, F.H. Rauscher, M. Lemieux and S.C. Hinton explored the impact of different types of musical activity on at-risk pre-school children ('Lasting improvement of at-risk children's cognitive abilities following music instruction', unpublished work). Five groups received piano, singing, rhythm, computer or no instruction for two years. The three music groups scored higher than the control groups on mental imagery tasks but the scores of the rhythm group were significantly higher than all other groups on tasks requiring temporal cognition and mathematical ability. The findings from this study suggest that it is rhythmic training that is important for the development of temporal cognition and mathematics (see Rauscher, 2009 for further discussion), while developing enhanced perceptual skills in relation to pitch and melody supports language development, although rhythm emerges as important in relation to literacy.

Taking these findings together, it would appear that active engagement with making music can have an impact on intellectual development. The specific types of musical participation which develop skills that transfer automatically to other areas still need to be identified, along with the common features of these skills.

General attainment

There has long been evidence that there is a relationship between general achievement and active engagement with music. However, this might have been caused by mediating factors common to both – for instance, having supportive parents and a home environment conducive to studying. A recent study, adopting more complex and sensitive statistical modelling (Southgate and Roscigno, 2009), using national datasets including 45,000 children and young people, addressed this issue using three measures of music participation – in school, outside school and parental involvement in the form of concert attendance. Associations between music and attainment persisted even when prior achievement was taken into account. The effects of social class on parental music involvement were strong and consistent. Southgate and Roscigno suggested that this was likely to be related to resource issues. As a mediator of educational outcomes, music involvement was significant for both mathematics and reading achievement. Although it generally increased attainment, gains were not distributed equally among all students – a white student advantage existed. This may have been related to the type of musical activity engaged in and the opportunities afforded the students for performance which may have contributed to enhanced self-esteem and increased motivation.

Overall, academic attainment depends on the development of literacy and numeracy skills which themselves are influenced by engagement with music. A further factor in how well children perform at school is motivation, which is closely linked to self-perceptions of ability, self-efficacy and aspirations (Hallam, 2005). If active engagement with music increases positive perceptions of self, this may transfer to other areas of study and increase motivation to persist in the light of initial failure. This may account for the impact of music on general attainment.

Creativity

Active engagement with music also has an impact on creativity. Singing and musical group play, twice weekly for three years, enhanced creativity, abstract thought and improvised puppet play in 3–4-year-old pre-school children (Kalmar, 1982), while first-grade pupils with 30 minutes of daily music instruction for a year exhibited significant increases in creativity and perceptual motor skills, compared with controls (Wolff, 1979). High school music students and those at university have been found to score higher on creativity; the longer the engagement with music, the greater the effects (Simpson, 1969; Hamann et al., 1990). The development of creative skills may depend on the type of musical engagement. This is supported by recent work by Koutsoupidou and Hargreaves (2009). They studied 6 year olds, comparing those who had opportunities for musical improvisation with those where music lessons were didactic. Performance on creative thinking tests was greater when the children had opportunities for improvisation. To enhance general creativity, music lessons themselves need to be based on creative activities.

Social and personal development

The impact of participation in music on social and personal development has received less attention than the impact on intellectual development, despite the fact that the positive effects on attainment may, in part, be mediated by an increase in self-esteem, social skills and enhanced relationships with adults (Broh, 2002). The Norwegian Research Council for Science and Humanities established a connection between having musical competence and high motivation, which led to a greater likelihood of success in school (Lillemyr, 1983). Whitwell (1977) drew similar conclusions and argued that creative participation in music improves self-image and self-awareness, and creates positive self-attitudes. Similar findings have been found with urban black middle school students (Marshall, 1978) and children of low economic status (Costa-Giomi, 1999). It would appear that success in music can enhance overall feelings of confidence and self-esteem, increasing motivation for study more generally.

Increasing the amount of time spent in class music lessons can have beneficial effects on personal and social skills. Research in Switzerland showed that increasing the amount of classroom music within the curriculum did not have a detrimental effect on language and reading skills, despite a reduction of time in these lessons (Spychiger et al., 1993; Zulauf, 1993). Benefits included an increase in social cohesion within the class, greater self-reliance, better social adjustment and more positive attitudes. These effects were particularly marked in low-ability, disaffected pupils. In the UK, Harland et al. (2000) showed that engagement with music increased awareness of others, social skills, well-being and transfer effects, with some students referring to the therapeutic nature of music – how it gave them confidence to perform in front of others, facilitated group work and enabled them to learn to express themselves.

The positive aspects of active engagement with music have been acknowledged by parents and teachers. In the USA, the perceived benefits of school band participation included accomplishment, appreciation, discipline, fun, and maturing relationships. Ninety-nine per cent of parents of non-band participants believed that band provided educational benefits not found in other classrooms. Band directors referred to discipline, teamwork, coordination, development of skills, accomplishment, self-confidence, sense of belonging, responsibility, self-expression, creativity, performance, improving self-esteem, social development and enjoyment (Brown, 1980). Similarly, in the UK, peripatetic instrumental teachers reported considerable benefits of learning to play an instrument, including the development of social skills, gaining a love and enjoyment of music, teamwork, developing a sense of achievement, confidence and self-discipline, and enhanced physical coordination (Hallam and Prince, 2000).

Extra-curricular activities are also beneficial. Rehearsing and performing in a school show has been found to facilitate the development of friendships with like-minded individuals and make a contribution to social life through a widespread awareness of the show by non-participants (Pitts, 2007). Such participation can increase pupils' confidence, social networks and sense of belonging, despite the time commitment which inevitably impinges on other activities. Involvement in group music activities can also help individuals learn to support each other, maintain commitment and bond together for group goals (Sward, 1989). Reflecting on previous and current group music-making activities, university music students report benefits in terms of pride in being an active contributor to a group outcome, developing a strong sense of belonging, gaining popularity, making friends with like-minded people, enhancement of social skills, and the development of a strong sense of self-esteem and satisfaction. Students also report enhanced personal skills contributing to the students' personal identity and encouraging the development of self-achievement, self-confidence and intrinsic motivation. A further study with non-music students who had previously participated in musical groups established similar benefits, but there was a greater preoccupation with the impact of group music making on the self and personal development. Students reported that active involvement in music helped them develop lifeskills such as discipline and concentration, and provided a relaxation outlet during demanding study periods (Kokotsaki and Hallam, 2007, in press).

Working in small groups without teacher supervision can support the development of teamworking skills. Good social relationships and the development of trust and respect are crucial to the successful functioning of small musical groups (Davidson and Good, 2002; Young and Colman, 1979). For long-term success, rehearsals have to be underpinned by strong social frameworks because interactions are typically characterised by conflict and compromise, related mainly to musical content and its coordination. In other words, participants learn to negotiate (Young and Colman, 1979; Murningham and Conlon, 1991; see also Chapter 14).

In adolescence, music makes a major contribution to the development of self-identity. Teenagers typically listen to a great deal of music – in the UK, almost three hours a day. They do this to pass time, alleviate boredom, relieve tension, and distract themselves from worries (North et al., 2000; Tolfree and Hallam, 2007). Music is seen as a source of support when young people are feeling troubled or lonely, acting as a mood regulator, helping to maintain a sense of belonging and community (Zillman and Gan, 1997). Music's affect on moods at this time can be profound. It is also used in relation to impression-management needs, enabling adolescents to portray their own peer groups more positively than other groups, thus sustaining positive self-evaluations (Tarrant et al., 2000).

In addition to developing personal and social skills, music has the capacity to increase emotional sensitivity. Resnicow *et al.* (2004) found that there was a relationship between the ability to recognise emotions in performances of classical piano music and measures of emotional intelligence which required individuals to identify, understand, reason with and manage emotions using hypothetical scenarios conveyed pictorially or in writing. The two were significantly correlated, which suggests that identification of emotion in music performance draws on some of the same skills that make up everyday emotional intelligence.

While it is clear from the research outlined above that music can have very positive effects on personal and social development, it must be remembered that the research has tended to focus on those currently participating in active music making, not taking account of those who have not found it an enjoyable and rewarding experience and who have dropped out. The quality of the teaching, the extent to which individuals experience success, whether engaging with a particular type of music can be integrated with existing self-perceptions, and whether, overall, it is a positive experience – these will all contribute to whether personal change is beneficial or not and subsequently whether it has an impact on motivation.

Music and physical skills

Music is often linked with movement, particularly dance. The easy availability of music has made it a common, supportive accompaniment to keep-fit activities – jogging, for instance. In children, performance accuracy and endurance have been found to be enhanced when rhythmically synchronised (Anshel and Marisi, 1978) and throwing, catching, jumping and leaping improved when children participated in a programme involving rhythm (Beisman, 1967). A ten-week music and movement programme also improved the quality of locomotor performance in 4–6 year olds (Derri *et al.*, 2001). In addition, learning to play an instrument improves fine motor skills (Schlaug *et al.*, 2005).

Music and health

There has recently been a surge of interest in the specific benefits of singing to health and well-being. Almost all of this research has been carried out with adults but there is no reason to suppose that these benefits would not also apply to children. Positive outcomes include:

- physical relaxation and release of physical tension
- emotional release and reduction of feelings of stress
- a sense of happiness, positive mood, joy and elation

- a sense of greater personal, emotional and physical well-being
- an increased sense of arousal and energy
- stimulation of cognitive capacities – attention, concentration, memory and learning
- an increased sense of self-confidence and self-esteem
- a sense of therapeutic benefit in relation to longstanding psychological and social problems
- a sense of exercising systems of the body through the physical exertion involved, especially the lungs
- a sense of disciplining the skeletal–muscular system through the adoption of good posture
- being engaged in a valued, meaningful worthwhile activity that gives a sense of purpose and motivation.

(Clift *et al.*, 2008; Stacey *et al.*, 2002)

Endnote

This overview provides a strong case for the wider benefits of active engagement with music from early childhood throughout the lifespan. Unfortunately, the easy availability of recorded music in our lives has led to a tendency for music to be taken for granted. At the same time as music is becoming a more integral part of everyday life, the place of music in formal education worldwide is constantly being questioned. Given the benefits of music for the individual, and for our functioning in groups and society more generally, it is important not only that music has a place within education systems but that what is on offer is available to all and is also of the highest quality.

References

Anshel, M. and Marisi, D. (1978) 'Effect of music and rhythm on physical performance'. *Research Quarterly*, 49, 109–13.

Anvari, S.H., Trainor, L.J., Woodside, J. and Levy, B.Z. (2002) 'Relations among musical skills, phonological processing, and early reading ability in preschool children'. *Journal of Experimental Child Psychology*, 83, 111–130.

Atterbury, B. (1985) 'Musical differences in learning-disabled and normal achieving readers, age eight and nine'. *Psychology of Music*, 13(2), 114–123.

Barwick, J., Valentine, E., West, R. and Wilding, J. (1989) 'Relations between reading and musical abilities'. *The British Journal of Educational Psychology*, 59, 253–257.

Beisman, G. (1967) 'Effect of rhythmic accompaniment upon learning of fundamental motor skills'. *Research Quarterly,* 38, 172–176.

Bilhartz, T.D., Bruhn, R.A. and Olson, J.E. (2000) 'The effect of early music training on child cognitive development'. *Journal of Applied Developmental Psychology,* 20, 615–636.

Broh, B.A. (2002) 'Linking extracurricular programming to academic achievement: Who benefits and why?' *Sociology of Education,* 75, 69–95.

Brown, J.D. (1980) *Identifying Problems Facing the School Band Movement.* Elkhart, IN: Gemeinhardt.

Butzlaff, R. (2000) 'Can music be used to teach reading?'. *Journal of Aesthetic Education,* 34, 167–178.

Catterall, J., Chapleau, R. and Iwanga, J. (1999) 'Involvement in the arts and human development: General involvement and intensive involvement in music and theatre arts. In *Champions of Change: The impact of the arts on learning.* Washington, DC: Arts Education Partnership.

Chan, A.S., Ho, Y.C. and Cheung, M.C. (1998) 'Music training improves verbal memory'. *Nature,* 396, 128.

Cheek, J.M. and Smith, L.R. (1999) 'Music training and mathematics achievement'. *Adolescence,* 34, 759–761.

Clift, S., Hancox, G., Staricoff, R. and Whitmore, C. (2008) *Singing and Health: A systematic mapping and review of non-clinical research.* Canterbury: Sidney de Haan Research Centre for Arts and Health, Canterbury Christ Church University.

Costa-Giomi, E. (1999) 'The effects of three years of piano instruction on children's cognitive development'. *Journal of Research in Music Education,* 47(5), 198–212.

Davidson, J.W. and Good, J.M.M. (2002) 'Social and musical co-ordination between members of a string quartet: An exploratory study'. *Psychology of Music,* 30, 186–201.

Derri, V., Tsapakidou, A., Zachopoulou, E. and Kioumourtzoglou, E. (2001) 'Effect of a music and movement programme on development of locomotor skills by children 4 to 6 years of age'. *European Journal of Physical Education,* 6, 16–25.

Douglas, S. and Willatts, P. (1994) 'The relationship between musical ability and literacy skill'. *Journal of Research in Reading,* 17, 99–107.

Flohr, J.W., Miller, D.C. and de Beus, R. (2000) 'EEG studies with young children'. *Music Educators Journal,* 87(2), 28–32.

Gaab, N., Gaser, C. and Zaehle, T. (2005) 'Neural correlates of rapid spectrotemporal processing in musicians and nonmusicians'. *Annals of the New York Academy of Sciences,* 1069, 82–88.

Gardiner, M.E., Fox, A., Knowles, F. and Jeffrey, D. (1996) 'Learning improved by arts training'. *Nature,* 381(6580), 284.

Geoghegan, N. and Mitchelmore, M. (1996) 'Possible effects of early childhood music on mathematical achievement'. *Journal for Australian Research in Early Childhood Education,* 1, 57–64.

Gromko, J. (2005) 'The effect of music instruction on phonemic awareness in beginning readers'. *Journal of College Reading and Learning,* 53(3), 199–209.

Haley, J.A. (2001) 'The relationship between instrumental music instruction and academic achievement in fourth grade students'. Doctoral Dissertation, Pace University. *Dissertation Abstracts International,* 62(09), 2969A.

Hallam, S. (2005) *Enhancing motivation and learning throughout the lifespan.* London: Institute of Education, University of London.

Hallam, S. and Prince, V. (2000) *Research into Instrumental Music Services.* London: Department for Education and Employment (DfEE).

Hamann, D., Bourassa, R. and Aderman, M. (1990) 'Creativity and the arts'. *Dialogue in Instrumental Music Education,* 14, 59–68.

–– (1991) 'Arts experiences and creativity scores of high school students'. *Contribution to Music Education,* 14, 35–47.

Harland, J., Kinder, K., Lord, P., Stott, A., Schagen, I. and Haynes, J. (2000) *Arts Education in Secondary Schools: Effects and effectiveness.* London: National Foundation for Educational Research (NFER)/The Arts Council of England, Royal Society for the Encouragement of the Arts, manufacture and commerce (RSA).

Hetland, L. (2000) 'Learning to make music enhances spatial reasoning'. *Journal of Aesthetic Education,* 34(3/4), Special Issue: 'The Arts and Academic Achievement: What the evidence shows' (Autumn/Winter), 179–238.

Ho, Y.C., Cheung, M.C. and Chan, A.S. (2003) 'Music training improves verbal but not visual memory: Cross-sectional and longitudinal explorations in children'. *Neuropsychology,* 17, 439–450.

Hurwitz, I., Wolff, P.H., Bortnick, B.D. and Kokas, K. (1975) 'Non-musical effects of the Kodaly music curriculum in primary grade children'. *Journal of Learning Disabilities,* 8, 45–52.

Kalmar, M. (1982) 'The effects of music education based on Kodaly's directives in nursery school children'. *Psychology of Music,* Special Issue, 63–68.

Kokotsaki, D. and Hallam, S. (2007) 'Higher Education music students' perceptions of the benefits of participative music making'. *Music Education Research,* 9(1), 93–109.

Kokotsaki, D. and Hallam, S. (in press) 'The perceived benefits of participative music making'. *Music Education Research.*

Koutsoupidou, T. and Hargreaves, D. (2009) 'An experimental study of the effects of improvisation on the development of children's creative thinking in music'. *Psychology of Music,* 37(3), 251–278.

Lillemyr, O.F. (1983) 'Achievement motivation as a factor in self-perception'. Paper presented at the Annual Meeting of the American Educational Research Association, April, Montreal.

Long, M. (2007) 'The effect of a music intervention on the temporal organisation of reading skills'. Unpublished PhD dissertation, Institute of Education, University of London.

Magne, C., Schon, D. and Besson, M. (2006) 'Musician children detect pitch violations in both music and language better than nonmusician children: Behavioural and electrophysiological approaches'. *Journal of Cognitive Neuroscience,* 18, 199–211.

Marshall, A.T. (1978) 'An analysis of music curricula and its relationship to the self-image of urban black middle school age children'. *Dissertation Abstracts International,* A 38, 6594A-5A.

Moreno, S. and Besson, M. (2006) 'Musical training and language-related brain electrical activity in children'. *Psychophysiology,* 43, 287–291.

Murningham, J.K. and Conlan, D.E. (1991) 'The dynamics of intense work groups: A study of British string quartets'. *Administrative Science Quarterly,* 36, 165–186.

Musacchia, G., Sams, M., Skoe, E. and Kraus, N. (2007) 'Musicians have enhanced subcortical auditory and audiovisual processing of speech and music'. *Proceedings of the National Academy of Sciences of the USA,* 104(40), 15894–15898.

Nicholson, D. (1972) 'Music as an aid to learning'. Doctoral dissertation, New York University. *Dissertation Abstracts International,* 33(01), 0352A.

North, A.C., Hargreaves, D.J. and O'Neill, S.A. (2000) 'The importance of music to adolescents'. *British Journal of Educational Psychology,* 70, 255–272.

Overy, K. (2003) 'Dyslexia and music: From timing deficits to musical intervention'. *Annals of the New York Academy of Science,* 999, 497–505.

Patel, A.D. and Iverson, J.R. (2007) 'The linguistic benefits of musical abilities'. *Trends in Cognitive Sciences,* 11, 369–372.

Patel, I. (2009) 'Music and the brain'. In S. Hallam, I. Cross and M. Thaut (eds) *The Oxford Handbook of Psychology of Music*. Oxford: Oxford University Press.

Peynircioglu, Z., Durgunoglu, A.Y. and Uney-Kusefoglu, B. (2002) 'Phonological awareness and musical aptitude'. *Journal of Research in Reading*, 25(1), 68–80.

Pitts, S.E. (2007) 'Anything goes: A case study of extra-curricular musical participation in an English secondary school'. *Music Education Research*, 9(1), 145–165.

Rafferty, K.N. (2003) 'Will a music and spatial–temporal math program enhance test scores? An analysis of second-grade students' mathematics performance on the Stanford–9 Test and the Capistrano Unified School District CORE level test'. Doctoral dissertation, University of Southern Carolina. *Dissertation Abstracts International*, 64(12), 4301A.

Rauscher, F.H. (2009) 'The impact of music instruction on other skills'. In S. Hallam, I. Cross and M. Thaut (eds) *The Oxford Handbook of Psychology of Music*. Oxford: Oxford University Press.

Rauscher, F.H., Shaw, G.L., Levine, L.J., Wright, E.L., Dennis, W.R. and Newcomb, R. (1997) 'Music training causes long-term enhancement of preschool children's spatial–temporal reasoning abilities'. *Neurological Research*, 19, 1–8.

Resnicow, J.E., Salovey, P. and Repp, B.H. (2004) 'Is recognition of emotion in music performance an aspect of emotional intelligence?' *Music Perception*, 22(1), 145–158.

Schellenberg, E.G. (2004) 'Music lessons enhance IQ'. *Psychological Science*, 15(8), 511–514.

Schlaug, G., Norton, A., Overy, K. and Winner, E. (2005) 'Effects of music training on the child's brain and cognitive development'. *Annals of the New York Academy of Science*, 1060, 219–230.

Simpson, D.J. (1969) 'The effect of selected musical studies on growth in general creative potential'. Doctoral dissertation, University of Southern California. *Dissertation Abstracts* 30, 502A–503A.

Southgate, D.E. and Roscigno, V.J. (2009) 'The impact of music on childhood and adolescent achievement'. *Social Science Quarterly*, 90(1), 4–21.

Spychiger, M., Patry, J., Lauper, G., Zimmerman, E. and Weber, E. (1993) 'Does more music teaching lead to a better social climate?' In R. Olechowski and G. Svik (eds), *Experimental Research in Teaching and Learning*. Bern: Peter Lang.

Stacey, R., Brittain, K. and Kerr, S. (2002) 'Singing for health: An exploration of the issues'. *Health Education*, 102(4), 156–162.

Sward, R. (1989) 'Band is a family'. *Today's Music Educator*, Winter, 26–27.

Tallal, P. and Gaab, N. (2006) 'Dynamic auditory processing, musical experience and language development'. *Trends in Neurosciences, 29*, 382–390.

Tarrant, M., North, A.C. and Hargreaves, D.J. (2000) 'English and American adolescents' reasons for listening to music'. *Psychology of Music*, 28, 166–173.

Thomson, M. (1990) 'Teaching the dyslexic child: Some evaluation studies'. In G. Hales (ed.), *Meeting Points in Dyslexia: Proceedings of the First International Conference of the British Dyslexia Association (Bath, 1989)* Reading: British Dyslexia Society.

Tolfree, E. and Hallam, S. (2007) 'Young people's uses of and responses to music in their everyday lives'. Paper presented at the British Psychological Society Psychology of Education Section Conference, Staffordshire University, 9-11 November 2007.

Trehub, S.E., Bull, D. and Thorpe, L.A. (1984) 'Infants' perception of melodies: The role of melodic contour'. *Child Development, 55*, 821–830.

Whitehead, B.J. (2001) 'The effect of music-intensive intervention on mathematics scores of middle and high school students'. Doctoral dissertation, Capella University. *Dissertation Abstracts International*, 62(08), 2710A.

Whitwell, D. (1977) *Music Learning through Performance.* Texas: Texas Music Educators Association.

Wolff, K. (1979) 'The non-musical outcomes of music education: A review of the literature'. *Bulletin of the Council for Research in Music Education, 55*, 1–27.

Young, V.M. and Coleman, A.M. (1979) 'Some psychological processes in string quartets'. *Psychology of Music*, 7, 12–16.

Zillman, D. and Gan, S. (1997) 'Musical taste in adolescence'. In D.J. Hargreaves and A.C. North (eds), *The Social Psychology of Music.* Oxford: Oxford University Press

Zulauf, M. (1993) 'Three-year experiment in extended music teaching in Switzerland: The different effects observed in a group of French-speaking pupils'. *Bulletin of the Council for Research in Music Education, 119*, Winter, 111–121.

Chapter 2

Contextualising music education in the UK

Pauline Adams, Hilary McQueen and Susan Hallam

Music is universal and found in all cultures. It is a human construct which, along with language, distinguishes us from other species. For sound to be defined as 'music' requires human beings to acknowledge it as such. What is acknowledged as music varies between cultures, groups and individuals. What may be music to the ears of one individual may not be to the ears of others. Music has a multiplicity of functions which operate at several levels – that of the individual, the social group and society in general. At the individual level it provides opportunities for emotional and physical expression, aesthetic enjoyment and entertainment and it can enhance communication. In groups and society it can act as a symbolic representation, it can support conformity to social norms, validate social institutions and religious rituals, and contribute to the continuity and stability of culture and the integration of society. The justifications for the inclusion of music in formal education reflect these functions, ranging from those stressing its intrinsic worth – art for art's sake – to those stressing its wider benefits. This chapter traces the development of music education in the UK and the influences on it.

The historical perspective

The role of music in education has been controversial since the inception of compulsory schooling in 1880, with an ongoing debate between those proposing a curriculum of highly structured activities and those advocating freer and more creative approaches. For instance, John Hullah, the first music inspector, appointed in 1872, introduced the Sol-Fa system. This was criticised as mechanistic and inappropriate, inhibiting the role of music as an art that fosters the language of the emotions. He also hoped that music teaching could contribute to an improved quality of life for the socially disadvantaged, an approach which was not shared by everyone, music being viewed by some as a non-academic and somewhat trivial activity (Cox, 1993), a perception that still prevails in some quarters today.

By the beginning of the twentieth century, music had begun to be established as a subject in its own right, at least in elementary education. Singing was important and a number of song books were published, including Stanford's (1906) *National Song Book*, reflecting the patriotic and nationalistic culture of Edwardian England (Cox, 1993). The child-centred movement began to make an impact on teaching methods in all areas of the infant (5–7) curriculum. Froebel was an influential figure in this movement, his philosophy founded on the principle of nurturing children through practical engagement with prescribed resources. In music, this included the playing of simple percussion instruments, giving children contact with sound itself and some manipulation skills in handling and playing an instrument. In 1912, Jacques Dalcroze came to London to demonstrate his method of Eurythmics, a series of graded exercises for children that encouraged them to react physically to rhythm, then to pitch and harmony. This method was subsequently promoted by those teachers interested in developing 'music and movement' as part of the elementary curriculum, and in 1934 the BBC Schools Broadcasting Service introduced and relayed its first *Music and Movement* series. The 1931 report of the Consultative Committee of the Board of Education, led by Sir William Henry Hadow, recommended that the primary curriculum 'be thought of in terms of activity and experience, rather than of knowledge to be acquired and facts to be stored' (Maclure, 1973: 189). This marked a new way forward, and themes of the report were reflected in developments in music. The popularity of percussion bands, the introduction of the Dolmetsch descant recorder into schools and the existence of the 'Pipers Guild' (encouraging children to make and play bamboo pipes) were all viewed as a means to engage children in practical music making. These activities signalled a departure from the limited singing curriculum of the past, although they provided little freedom for creative experimentation or improvisation.

At secondary level, the Secondary School Regulations of 1904 laid down what should be studied from ages 12 to16 and included reference to singing. Music was available for the School Certificate Examination although it did not 'count' on the certificate, which only included core subjects such as English and science. Better music provision was reported in girls' than boys' schools, suggesting music as a more feminine activity (so arguably less academic), although the key figures in composition and the inspectorate were men. There was a shift away from singing as the main medium for music towards instrumental playing, along with listening to recorded music (Cox, 1993).

The 1944 Education Act

The 1944 Education Act (HMSO, 1944) established primary, secondary and further education sectors and increased the school leaving age to 15, with a mention of raising it to 16 in the future (although that did not occur until 1972). Secondary provision was usually divided into grammar, secondary modern and technical schools, a tripartite system which divided pupils on aptitude and ability at 11 years of age, the curriculum varying between grammar and secondary modern schools, and within individual schools. The focus on exams in grammar schools led to the School Certificate, and later the General Certificate of Education (GCE), becoming a driver for lesson content in these schools. Theoretical and essay-type assessments led to a less practical approach to music teaching. In the classroom, aside from learning the basics of music theory, 'music appreciation' – through listening to recorded music – was usual practice. The usefulness of that as part of the curriculum was later questioned by Paynter, for instance, who argued that 'a recording has about the same amount of value as a photograph of a painting' (1982: 25). Practical music making was largely extra-curricular, requiring a combination of appropriate musical skills and sufficient motivation from the students to stay on after school or miss their lunch break. Not surprisingly, most students did not participate. Mainwaring (1941) had earlier described a tension between expectations and the reality of the classroom. While the Board of Education was encouraging appreciation of music, and school authorities expected musical performances, teachers were faced with students, many with no obvious musical skills, for only one or two lessons per week. Music lessons, in many schools, largely consisted of singing and learning to read musical notation. There was ongoing debate about what to include in the music curriculum, with concerns that it had developed for the minority of generally, middle- or upper-class learners (see Chapter 14).

The 1963 Newsom Report: *Half our Future*

1963 saw the publication of the Newsom Report: *Half our Future*. The criticism contained within it regarding the unsuitability of much of education for the majority of pupils prepared the way for comprehensive as opposed to selective education. The report was critical of music education:

> *If the scope of music in school is restricted to choral singing, difficulties and discouragement may arise at the stage when the boys' voices begin to change, though many schools have seized the opportunity to introduce fresh types of choral music congenial to adolescent male voices. Apart from singing, however, there is much else that can*

profitably be attempted: various forms of instrumental music, training in selective and critical listening with the aid of scores, a combined musical and scientific approach to the phenomena of sound, all can play their part in the scheme.

(The Newsom Report, 1963: 140)

Issues relating to the relatively small numbers of pupils taking music beyond the third year of secondary education were also raised. The Schools Council 1971 working paper *Music and the Young School Leaver: Problems and opportunities* also expressed concerns (see Chapter 14). For example, Small talked about the need to experience music above acquiring knowledge, and about the curriculum only suiting a few while 'boring the daylights out of the rest' (1975: 164). However, little changed in the classroom. Finding ways to engage young people with school music led to the further discussion of the content of the curriculum and consideration of the inclusion of popular music, which was advocated as offering an important contribution to the pedagogic, social and cultural aspects of education – encouraging social interaction, building on what young people already knew and making learning more student-centred. The inclusion of world music genres was also considered as a means to encourage exploration of different cultural values (Vulliamy and Lee, 1976).

Through the 1970s and 1980s a broad consensus developed about the nature of the music curriculum (see Chapter 14). Paynter's book, *Music in the Secondary School Curriculum* (1982), made a number of suggestions for improving the music offered in schools, with an emphasis on experiencing rather than passive learning. He suggested starting with a musical concept such as rhythm, using ostinati, non-Western music and jazz, while melodic work might include gamelan – all relying on aural rather than notational skills (graphic scores being the exception). A student-centred approach was encouraged, offering learning based on practical experience rather than theory (Hargreaves, 1986). As Paynter pointed out:

Too strong an instructional bias at the start, with the teacher doing most of the work, will not encourage pupils to take seriously opportunities for self-directed exploration when they are offered. . . . It is so easy to create the impression that the 'real' work is what the teacher directs and the experimental work is not serious music-making.

(Paynter, 1982: 53)

These views contributed to the development of the National Curriculum for Music (see also Chapter 14).

The 1967 Plowden Report

Primary education was reviewed in 1967 in the Plowden Report: *Children and their Primary Schools* (Central Advisory Council for Education, England, 1967). This recognised that curriculum development in music had advanced less than in other subjects, such as language and literacy or the visual arts. In those subjects a much freer approach had begun to be adopted, placing children's own experience and discovery at the heart of the learning process, whereas practical music-making developments, although a step in the right direction, had not allowed opportunities for pupil imagination and creativity. The influence of Carl Orff's 'Schulwerk', which had been adapted for British schools by Margaret Murray (1957), had had an impact in primary schools. The use of tuned percussion such as glockenspiels, xylophones and chime bars had enabled children to participate in melodic work, in addition to the rhythmic percussion work that used instruments such as drums and triangles. Such systems, including the Orff and Kodaly methods, had their critics, some viewing aspects of the methods as at odds with the freer Froebel approach and the recommendations of the Plowden Report. However, the use of tuned percussion instruments and ear-centred activity through vocal work did take away the dominance of the piano. The shift from performer-teacher who directed from the piano to the more child-centred approach had implications for all primary teachers, and the idea of the primary generalist teacher offering musical experiences to children was heavily promoted throughout the 1970s and 1980s (see Chapter 13).

Early instrumental provision

During the 1930s and 1940s Rural Music Schools were founded to support the revival of music in English country life, enabling teachers of music to reach villages in order to help and advise about music at a local level. The activities were mainly choral. A few Rural Music Schools remain, but many were integrated into wider local authority provision. Following the Second World War, the number of local education authority (LEA) music advisers increased and there was an increase of peripatetic teaching of instruments in schools (Pitts, 2000). The advisers played a significant part in influencing the future shape of music provision across the UK and in the development of instrumental teaching services which offered free individual or group tuition to pupils, the free loan of instruments and 'Music Centres' to accommodate additional instrumental teachers and the many emerging ensembles, including youth orchestras. Recognition of the importance of instrumental learning was reflected in the founding of the National Youth Orchestra in 1947.

Time for change: 1976

During the mid-1970s the oil crisis and industrial unrest led to economic constraint, and politicians began to look at reforms in public services such as health, welfare and education. In 1976, James Callaghan, the Labour Prime Minister, delivered a speech at Ruskin College which favoured a 'basic curriculum with universal standards' and which prepared pupils better for the workplace (Gordon *et al.*, 1991: 95). At around this time too there was criticism of the child-centred approach to education and of the secondary curriculum. In 1979, Margaret Thatcher led a Conservative government into power. Teachers, who had experienced autonomy and had gained a stake in curriculum development, now found themselves engulfed in a more accountable and prescriptive climate (Barber, 1996). The Education Reform Act (HMSO, 1988) established the core subjects of English, maths and science, and designated ten foundation subjects, one of which was music, as the National Curriculum. Bitter controversy ensued despite the fact that the National Curriculum Music Working Group, set up in 1990 to advise the National Curriculum Council (NCC), drew on the widely established understanding that music should comprise a practical curriculum, based on the interrelated activities of listening, composing and performing (Gammon, 1999; see also Chapter 14). The NCC played down the practical dimension of music and the result was that from January 1992 the music curriculum became a 'political football', being passed between those who supported the Working Group and those right-wing aesthetes such as Roger Scruton and Anthony O'Hear, who were firmly opposed to the Working Group's recommendations (Gammon, 1999). The fierceness of the debate was well documented in a large number of articles and letters published in the national press. In the end, the Working Group did realise some of its philosophical and pedagogical aspirations for the music curriculum.

Devolved government was created in the UK following referendums in Wales and Scotland in 1997. In 1998, the Scottish Parliament, the National Assembly for Wales and the Northern Ireland Assembly were established. The education system in Scotland had well-established differences in educational provision from the rest of the UK, while devolution led to Wales and Northern Ireland developing their own versions of the National Curriculum. Despite this, the overarching principles of the music curricula for the four countries were broadly similar. Box 2.1 summarises the key focus of the original National Curriculum for England as an example. Curricula across the whole of the UK have since been subject to revision.

> **Box 2.1 The Music National Curriculum for England**
>
> Music is described as 'a powerful, unique form of communication that can transform the way pupils feel, think and act'. Pupils learn to listen and to apply their knowledge and understanding as they develop performing skills – controlling sounds through singing and playing; composing skills – creating and developing musical ideas; and appraising skills – responding to music and reviewing their work.
>
> *This has now been superseded by revisions at Key Stages 1, 2 and 3. See Chapters 13 and 14.*

Local authority Music Services

Instrumental Music Services have not been unaffected by wider educational changes. During the 1980s, with ever-increasing centralisation, the decline of power within LEAs and swingeing funding cuts, Music Services found themselves in the position of not being able to retain the status for music that had been hard-won over a long period of time. Some Music Centres contracted out of the music teaching service, being partly funded by grant aid by some LEAs, while others disbanded their services in order to comply with government rate-capping and devolution of funding to schools. A key concern raised by the 1988 Education Bill was the proposed introduction of charges for 'extra' activities, which included individual music tuition. With the introduction of charges, instrumental tuition was available for pupils with parents who could afford it, rather than being offered to any pupils who demonstrated aptitude, ability and keen interest (see Chapter 17).

The inspection of music education

Changes were also introduced to the system of inspection. In 1837, the government had introduced two 'inspectors' of schools to monitor the effectiveness of the grants given to charities providing schools for poor children. After 1902, inspections were expanded to include state-funded secondary schools and were subsequently located in LEAs, with Her Majesty's Inspectorate focusing on reporting on education conditions across the country. In 1992, following the introduction of the National Curriculum, a reconstituted inspectorate, the Office for Standards in Education (Ofsted), took over the supervision of the inspection of each state-funded school. This changed the role of Her Majesty's Inspectorate from being an independent body advising and encouraging good practice to becoming the voice of government. In Northern Ireland, Scotland and Wales similar functions came to be undertaken by the Education and Training Inspectorate, Her Majesty's Inspectorate of Education, and her Majesty's Inspectorate for Education and Training in Wales. The inspection process, alongside publication of schools' performance on a range of indicators, has had a major impact on the way that schools operate, leading to a culture of 'performativity', with a focus on attainment and a reluctance to be innovative. Music teachers work within this culture with its inevitable impact on the way that music is taught.

Assessment

Assessment procedures have also changed over time. The GCE was introduced in the UK (with the exception of Scotland) in 1951, replacing the older School Certificate and Higher School Certificate. The examinations were graded into ordinary 'O levels' for 16 year olds and advanced 'A levels' for 18 year olds. From 1965 to 1987, the Certificate of Secondary Education (CSE) was introduced to provide a qualification available to all school children because many children at secondary modern schools had been leaving school with no qualifications. This dual system proved divisive, and in 1988 the General Certificate of Secondary Education (GCSE) was introduced to replace both O levels and CSE examinations. A levels were retained. In parallel to this, a range of vocational qualifications originating from the Business and Technology Education Council (BTEC) were developed. Music is represented in all of these qualifications, with recent developments taking greater account of technology and the performing arts (see Chapter 9) including the new Creative and Media Diploma for 14–19 year olds which teaches practical skills through a mixture of class work and hands-on experience.

A range of graded instrumental examinations has also been developed in the UK. These date back to 1852 when John Curwen instigated Certificates of Proficiency (Crocker, 1982). Curwen's view was that testing pupils was essential to learning. The Trinity College of Music in London examined theory, piano, organ and singing from 1877, in 2004 merging with Guildhall external examinations to form Trinity Guildhall (GSMD, 2007). The Associated Board was founded in 1889, combining examinations offered by the Royal Academy of Music and the Royal College of Music. Now it is known as the Associated Board of the Royal Schools of Music (ABRSM) and includes the Royal Northern College of Music and the Royal Scottish Academy of Music and Drama. Over time, graded examinations have developed to include a wide range of instruments and genres (see Chapters 9 and 15) including pop and rock music (Rockschool, 2010).

Many of the graded examinations are part of the National Qualifications Framework (NQF) and contribute to the points which individuals accrue in relation to university application.

Specialist Schools programme

A further policy development in England has been the Specialist Schools programme which encourages schools to specialise in specific areas of the curriculum to boost achievement. Currently, 88 per cent of state-funded secondary schools in England are specialist schools. They are allowed to select up to ten per cent of their intake on aptitude in their specialism, although many do not do this. Currently, there are 31 schools with music as a first specialism, ten have music as a combined specialism, and 16 have music as a second specialism. In addition, there are 490 schools with arts (performing, visual or media) as a first specialism, 52 have arts as a combined specialism, and 24 have arts as a second specialism. The extent to which these schools will have a long-term impact on attainment in music remains to be seen.

Preparing for a career in music

Historically, musicians developed their skills by learning from others with more highly developed expertise, within the family or through formal or informal apprenticeships. As early as 1350 there was a guild of musicians in London, and the master apprentice model established by the guilds underpins much instrumental teaching even today (see Chapters 6, 16 and 18). The Royal Academy of Music, established in 1822, was the first music conservatoire in the UK, followed by the Royal College of Music in 1873, the Royal Scottish Academy of Music in 1930, and the Welsh College of Music and Drama in 1970. There is currently no conservatoire of music and drama in Northern Ireland. Since their establishment the conservatoires have been the main route through which professional classical musicians receive their training, with conservatoires introducing new areas of study in response to changes in the music profession – for instance, jazz and musical theatre.

Prior to the establishment of the first conservatoire in the UK, universities offered degrees in music, the first in Cambridge in 1463 with Oxford following in 1499. Developments were later in the other parts of the UK, with music degrees offered in Edinburgh in 1893, the University of Wales in 1905, and Queens University Belfast in 1953. Like the conservatoires, degree programmes have adapted to meet current needs, with a greater emphasis on practical music making (see Chapter 16).

Further education

Further education (FE) colleges were established in the 1944 Education Act. They had a remit to provide vocational education and also opportunities for adults to engage in a range of cultural activities, which included those relating to music – although cuts in funding periodically reduced the budgets for such activities (see Chapter 10). Technological developments since the introduction of radio have provided FE with a crucial role to play in music education, the performing arts and music technology. Indeed, some colleges have chosen to specialise in 'popular' music (see Chapter 15).

Specialist music schools

The government in England also provides support for highly specialised schools through its Music and Dance Scheme. Before 1973, LEAs provided support for gifted children, under discretionary powers provided in the 1944 Education Act. Following the Gulbenkian Report (1978) on the training of musicians, five specialist music schools – Chetham's School of Music, Wells Cathedral School, the Purcell School, the Yehudi Menuhin School and St Mary's Music School (Edinburgh) – were allocated government-aided places. In 2002, the scheme was renamed the 'Music and Dance Scheme'. Since 2004, the scheme has broadened to include newly designated 'Centres for Advanced Training' that provide out-of-school-hours training and learning opportunities for many more talented children. These organisations or consortia include existing Saturday provision at junior departments of music conservatoires and new weekend schools, and after-school-hours and holiday courses for young musicians and dancers. They provide children with local access to the best available teaching and facilities, alongside strong links with the music and dance profession. They ensure that children who are talented and committed musicians and dancers have appropriate, tailor-made, specialist provision, even if they do not choose to attend specialist boarding schools.

Teacher education

The Training and Development Agency for Schools (TDA) is the national agency and recognised sector body responsible for the training and development of the school workforce. Currently, the main route for the training of teachers who wish to teach music in schools is through obtaining a Postgraduate Certificate in Education (PGCE), usually acquired through a one-year full-time course at a designated college or university. There are also a number of employment-based routes into teaching, where teachers train while working in schools. 'Teach First' is one such route which is designed to recruit highly qualified graduates to teach in difficult schools. Primary school teachers may take a Bachelor of Education (BEd) degree, as part of which they can specialise in music or they can complete a one-year PGCE course if they have already obtained a degree. Concerns have been expressed about the relatively little time that trainee primary teachers spend in learning to teach music. Most primary teachers lack confidence in teaching music, despite numerous initiatives over the years to offer them in-service training and a range of different types of support (see Chapters 11 and 13).

Technology

Since the 1940s access to recorded music has become easier, such that most people are now able to listen to music at any time. Technology has impacted on the development of instruments, the means of creating and notating music through computers, the making of music through a range of console games and the production, marketing and sale of music (see Chapter 8). In the future, technology is likely to have an increasing impact on learning in music (see Chapters 3, 4, 7, 14, 15 and 20).

Recent developments

The Music Manifesto

The Music Manifesto was launched in 2004 with the intention of bringing together interested parties who would sign up to its aims, which were to:

- provide every young person with first access to a range of music experiences
- provide more opportunities for young people to deepen and broaden their musical interests and skills
- identify and nurture the most talented musicians
- develop a world-class workforce in music education
- improve the support structures for young people making music.

The manifesto has 2000 signatories and its work continues through the Music Manifesto Partnership and Advocacy Group. Since its inception there has been considerable investment in music education in England by the government to support these aims.

Wider Opportunities programme

The Wider Opportunities programme provides whole-class instrumental tuition across schools within the primary sector, offering every child the opportunity to access tuition (see Chapters 6 and 17). The programme is accompanied by a major continuing professional development scheme, developed by the Open University and Trinity Guildhall. The training is free and open to anyone concerned with primary music education, including specialist teachers, class teachers, instrumental teachers, community musicians and learning support assistants.

Sing Up programme

The Sing Up programme aims to put singing back into the classroom and enable every primary school to be a singing school by 2011 (see Chapter 5). The programme comprises a national bank of resources for singing, a workforce development programme and a media and schools campaign highlighting the benefits of singing.

Musical Futures programme

The Musical Futures programme, funded by the Paul Hamlyn Foundation, explores innovative approaches to music education at Key Stage 3. It aims to promote music education through starting from the existing knowledge and interests of the students, enhancing motivation and encouraging independent learning (see Chapter 14).

Music Partnership projects

Music Partnership projects are one-year programmes funded by the Department for Children, Schools and Families (DCSF) which are designed to deliver high-quality music activity to young people. The partnerships must include a local authority and an organisation regularly funded by the Arts Council England. To date, two groups of projects have been funded (see Chapter 19).

Creative Partnerships

Creative Partnerships is the government's creative learning programme, designed to develop the skills of children and young people across England, raising their aspirations, achievements, skills and life chances. It is one of a number of programmes generated by the national organisation 'Creativity, Culture and Education' (CCE). An evaluation suggests that it has contributed to raising achievement (Sharp et al., 2007) (see also Chapter 7).

Find Your Talent

Find Your Talent is the scheme through which the government is delivering its commitment to provide comprehensive cultural opportunities over the next five years so that all children and young people in England can participate in at least five hours of high-quality culture a week, in and out of school. The pathfinder programme was launched in ten areas in 2008, and different methods of delivering the scheme are currently being explored.

Youth Music

Youth Music was founded in 1999 to support music-making opportunities for pupils, held mainly out of school hours and delivered by non-profit-making organisations. The organisation works across the 0–18 age range and attracts its funding from the Arts Council. It funds 23 Youth Music Action Zones, and provides training for music leaders (see Chapter 19). Its current priority areas are early years, singing, transition, young people at risk and workforce development (see Chapters 5, 12, 10, 19 and 20).

MusicLeader

MusicLeader is a Youth Music initiative which provides access to professional development for music leaders at all stages of their career. It aims to increase the quality, value and impact of music leadership, operating through regional networks providing one-to-one support and guidance, training and networking opportunities and an online resource (see Chapter 19).

In Harmony

Inspired by the success of the Venezuelan 'El Sistema' project, the DCSF has funded three 'In Harmony' projects in Liverpool, Norwich and Lambeth. The projects, which are primarily social and community programmes, aim to bring positive change to the lives of very young children in some of the most deprived areas of England. Children are taught to play instruments, play in orchestras and perform from an early age (see Chapter 20). A similar programme 'Sistema Scotland', run by a charitable trust, pre-dates the English programmes and aims to use music to foster confidence, teamwork, pride and aspiration in participants and the wider community.

Local authority music plans (LAMPs)

Since December 2008 all local authorities have been expected to audit and identify in their LAMPs details of the music provision in their area, including reference to the organisations regularly funded by the Arts Council England, the work of community musicians, Youth Music-funded activity and anyone who is involved in music education, in and out of school. The intention is that this information can be used to develop more coherent musical opportunities for young people (see Chapter 20).

Endnote

Music education in the UK in the twenty-first century is thriving. New initiatives have addressed many of the issues that have been problematic historically. This book considers its achievements, analyses the nature and quality of provision, and considers where there is still work to be done. Chapters 3–11 focus on issues that arise across all sectors: music for all, listening, singing, learning to play an instrument, creativity, the role of technology, assessment, learning through life and the initial and ongoing training of music teachers. Chapters 12–19 provide an overview of the different contexts of music education: early years, primary, secondary, further and higher education, Music Services, the music studio, and community music. The final chapter considers the ongoing challenges for music education and suggests ways in which they might be overcome.

Further reading

Cox, G. (1993) *A History of Music Education in England 1872–1928*. Aldershot: Scolar Press.

Cox, G. (2002) *Living Music in Schools 1923–1999: Studies in the history of music education in England.* Aldershot: Ashgate.

Pitts, S. (2000) *A Century of Change in Music Education: Historical perspectives on contemporary practice in British secondary school music.* Aldershot: Ashgate.

Useful links

The Advisory Centre for Education (ACE) www.ace-ed.org.uk

Department for Education (DfE) www.education.gov.uk

Department for Culture, Media and Sport www.culture.gov.uk

Federation of Music Services (FMS) www.thefms.org

KS2 Music CPD Programme www.ks2music.org.uk

Incorporated Society of Musicians (ISM) www.ism.org

London Schools Arts Service (LONSAS) www.lonsas.org.uk

Music Education Council (MEC) www.mec.org.uk

MusicLeader www.musicleader.net

National Association of Music Educators www.name.org.uk

Office for Standards in Education, Children's Services and Skills (Ofsted) www.ofsted.gov.uk

The Qualifications and Curriculum Development Agency (QCDA) www.qcda.gov.uk

Sing Up www.singup.org

Schools Music Association (SMA) www.schoolsmusic.org.uk

Teaching Music www.teachingmusic.org.uk

Training and Development Agency for schools www.tda.gov.uk

Youth Music www.musicispower.youthmusic.org.uk

References

Associated Board of the Royal Schools of Music (ABRSM). <http://www.artscea.com/english/abrsm.html> (accessed 18/02/2010).

Barber, M. (ed.) (1996) *The National Curriculum: A study in policy*. Staffordshire: Keele University Press.

Calouste Gulbenkian Foundation (1978) *Training Musicians: A report to the Calouste Gulbenkian Foundation on the training of professional musicians*. Tillicoultry: W.M. Bett.

Central Advisory Council for Education, England (1967) *Children and their Primary Schools. The Plowden Report*. London: DES/HMSO.

Cox, G. (1993) *A History of Music Education in England 1872–1928*. Aldershot: Scolar Press.

Crocker, R.J. (1982) 'Local external practical examinations in music, with special reference to the ABRSM'. Masters dissertation, Institute of Education, University of London.

Curwen, J.S. (1882) *Memorials of John Curwen*. London: J. Curwen & Sons. <http://www.archive.org/details/memorialsofjohncoocurwuoft> (accessed 18/02/2010).

Department for Education and Skills (DfES) (2004) *The Music Manifesto: More music for more people*. London: DfES.

Gammon, V. (1999) 'Cultural politics and the English National Curriculum for Music 1991–1992'. *Journal of Administration and History*, 31(2), 130–147.

Gordon, P., Aldrich, R. and Dean, D. (1991) *Education and Policy and Practice in England in the Twentieth Century*. Chippenham: Woburn Press.

Guildhall School of Music & Drama (GSMD) (2007) *Examinations Service*. <http://www.gsmd.ac.uk/school/introduction/examinations.html> (accessed 18/02/2010).

Hadow, W.H. (1931) *The Primary School: Report of the Consultative Committee*. London: HMSO.

Hargreaves, D.J. (1986) *The Developmental Psychology of Music*. Cambridge: Cambridge University Press.

Her Majesty's Stationery Office (HMSO) (1944) *Education Act*. London: HMSO.

–– (1988) *Education Act*. London: HMSO.

Maclure, S. (1973) *Educational Documents: England and Wales 1816 to the present day* (Fourth edition). London: Methuen.

Mainwaring, J. (1941) 'The meaning of musicianship: A problem in the teaching of music'. *British Journal of Educational Psychology,* 11(3), 205–214.

Murray, M. (1957) *Music for Children: Orff's Schulwork*. London: Schott & Co.

The Newsom Report (1963) *Half our Future*. London: HMSO.

Paynter, J. (1982) *Music in the Secondary School Curriculum*. Cambridge: Cambridge University Press.

Pitts, S. (2000) *A Century of Change in Music Education: Historical perspectives on contemporary practice in British secondary school music*. Aldershot: Ashgate.

Rockschool (2010) <http://rockschool.co.uk/rsl/index.aspx?pageID=178> (accessed 18/02/2010).

Schools Council (1971) *Music and the Young School Leaver: Problems and opportunities* (Working Paper 35). London: Evans & Methuen Educational.

Sharp, C., Pye, D., Blackmore, J., Brown, E., Eames, A., Easton, C., Filmer-Sankey, C., Tabary, A., Whitby, K., Wilson, R. and Benton, T. (2007) *National Evaluation of Creative Partnerships*. Slough: National Foundation for Educational Research (NFER).

Small, C. (1975) 'Towards a Philosophy Part 2: Metaphors and Madness'. *Music in Education,* July/August,163–164.

Stanford, C.V. (1906) *The National Song Book*. London: Boosey.

Vulliamy, G. and Lee, E. (1976) *Pop Music in Schools*. Cambridge: Cambridge University Press.

CURRENT ISSUES IN MUSIC EDUCATION

Chapter 3

Music for all

Graham Welch and Adam Ockelford

According to a recent House of Commons enquiry into special educational needs (House of Commons, 2006), around 18 per cent of all pupils in schools in England were categorised as having some sort of special educational need (SEN), amounting to 1.45 million children. Approximately 2.9 per cent (242,500 children) had a 'Statement' (see below) and 1 per cent (90,000) were being educated in the special schools sector (representing one-third of children with Statements). The latest guidance for parents (DCSF, 2009) concerning the definitions of, and provision for, SEN states that:

> Children with special educational needs all have learning difficulties or disabilities that make it harder for them to learn than most children of the same age. These children may need extra or different help from that given to other children of the same age.
>
> (DCSF, 2009: 6)

Within mainstream (non-special) schools, teachers will often create an 'Individual Education Plan' (IEP) for discussion with parents to make explicit the kinds of help that is being made available for the pupil with an identified special need. For a small minority of these, if a particular child does not make the expected progress, despite having an IEP, then customarily a more formal and detailed multi-professional assessment takes place, leading to a 'Statement of Special Educational Needs' that describes the outcomes of the assessment and the special help that is required. The majority (60+ per cent) of children with 'Statements' will continue to be educated in their mainstream school. Only a minority (approximately one-third) will be in special schools.

The types of SEN cover a very broad spectrum, including social, emotional and behavioural difficulties, autism spectrum disorder, sensory impairment, physical impairment, and learning disability. However, not all pupils with disabilities have SEN, in the sense that their disability affects their ability to learn. Key elements of the statutory framework that surrounds SEN include the *Special Educational Needs: Code of practice* (2001), and the Special

Educational Needs and Disability Act (SENDA) of 2001. This generated a legal requirement for disabled pupils to not be discriminated against and for equality of opportunity to be promoted for all pupils.

Special educational needs *in* music in mainstream settings

As far as music education (or any other school curriculum area) is concerned, therefore, the concept of 'special educational need in music' has to take account of these different and diverse groupings within the mainstream and special school populations. Within mainstream schools, for example, it may be that (at any one time) one-fifth of pupils will have a particular learning difficulty in music that requires some individual adjustment to the music curriculum for them. This kind of pedagogical differentiation is a normal expectation of the music teacher's professional role. Such children may have experienced little or no music education up to that point, or they may have had a music education that was inappropriate for the realisation of their underlying (species-wide) musical potential (Welch, 2005). Left unaddressed, this minority can develop negative self-images of their musical abilities that can be lifelong (see Knight, 2010). Nevertheless, empirical evidence suggests that, in an appropriately nurturing environment (Tafuri, 2009), all children in mainstream schools are capable of engaging purposefully in musical activity, and of musical development (see Stevens and Byron, 2009; Barrett, 2010).

Notwithstanding the new English primary curriculum's 'Understanding the arts' area of learning from 2011, and the important advocacy of the UK government alongside the impact of its music education programmes, such as 'Sing Up', 'MusicLeader' and 'In Harmony', the relatively short amounts of time devoted to music in the school week and, in some schools, its low status in comparison to the expectations for the established 'core' subjects of English, mathematics and science means that it is highly unlikely that the legal SEN conceptualisation would be applied in the mainstream music classroom to generate a music-focused IEP. In part, this weakness in the application of the SEN concept in mainstream school music also relates to limitations in teacher education. Many primary school teachers, for example, commonly report a 'lack of confidence' in the teaching of music that arises from their self-view of limitations in their own musical ability and music education (Stunell, 2006; Seddon and Biasutti, 2008). This issue of 'confidence' is likely to be nurtured by a bipolar view within wider society that people are either 'musical' or 'not musical' (see Ruddock and Leong, 2005). Furthermore, much of the research on music and special needs has focused on music therapy, not music education (Jellison, 2006a), leaving music educators with limited external sources of evidence on which to base their practice.

In secondary schools, there is likely to be limited opportunity for music teachers to have engaged significantly with the concept of 'SEN' as applied to music within their conventional one-year, full-time postgraduate preparation. They will have acquired knowledge of the legal framework – although this is reportedly 'too variable', (Ofsted, 2009a: 57) – but the limited research data available on adolescent musical development (in contrast to that available for younger children – see Hallam *et al.*, 2009, for example – or on adolescents and musical culture), combined with the demands of a postgraduate course that is two-thirds school-based, suggests that beginning secondary school music teachers will not necessarily have a clear idea of what counts as a 'special need' in music, other than by application of the National Curriculum for Music's 'level descriptors', although these do not contain details of the descriptors' evidence base (see http://www.standards.dfes.gov.uk/schemes2/secondary_music/teaching?view=get).

Given this context, it is not surprising, therefore, that the most recent Ofsted report on music expressed concern over 'inadequate provision' in some secondary schools and teachers' 'lack of understanding of musical progress' (2009b: 6/26). Ofsted also reports that the 'extremes in the quality of provision and teachers' lack of understanding about what "making musical progress" looks like were frequently the result of the isolation that many music teachers and subject leaders were experiencing' (Ofsted, 2009b: 5), a finding echoed in other research into early-career secondary music teachers in England and overseas (Welch *et al.*, 2010). Furthermore, these challenges are compounded by the relative lack of engagement with SEN in music within recent official documentation. The special Ofsted report on music (2009b) makes no reference to SEN, even though the Ofsted Chief Inspector's most recent report states that:

> too few trainees are well prepared to work with pupils with special educational needs and/or disabilities. They gain experience in the areas of specific concern to the schools in which they are working, but too few have experience of the full spectrum of special educational needs and/or disabilities. This leaves them ill-prepared to meet the needs of all such pupils.
>
> (Ofsted, 2009a: 103)

In summary, although we should expect that a minority of children in mainstream schools will need extra and different forms of assistance from the majority of their peers in order to access the music curriculum, this issue is rarely discussed in official or research literature (an exception being the work of Judith Jellison in the USA, see References for examples). Furthermore, although we can anticipate that teachers' craft knowledge will recognise differences in children's musical behaviours and development, the depth of such perceptions and their implications for pedagogical practice are likely to be subject to considerable variation.

Special educational needs *in* music, special educational needs *and* music: Evidence from special education

As mentioned in the introduction, a small proportion of the school population in England (90,000) are educated in special schools. In general, comparative studies of children and young people with and without disabilities suggests that there are similarities between such groups in their musical behaviours (for example, in singing, clapping, describing music, musical preferences). Where differences exist, 'anecdotal reports challenge the notion that students with disabilities have "special needs" in *all* dimensions of music behaviour' (Jellison, 2006b: 261). Furthermore, 'the capabilities of children with autism and Williams Syndrome may exceed those of children without disabilities' (Jellison 2006a: 239). However, until very recently, there has been no overall perspective on what might count as an appropriate music curriculum for pupils with complex needs in special schools – children with Severe Learning Difficulties (SLD) or Profound and Multiple Learning Difficulties (PMLD).

Ofsted's 1999 review of special education reported that in a third of the inspections of special schools, secure units and pupil referral units, insufficient music lessons were seen to provide secure judgements of pupils' progress, or that music was not taught. Where it was possible to make a judgement, progress was satisfactory or better in only just over half of schools. The implication of these figures was that only one-third of special schools were observed to have effective music education provision. Inspectors found that, across the curriculum, teachers' lack of subject knowledge reduced the overall quality of teaching in almost half of special schools, with insufficient subject-specific in-service training taking place. Moreover, there were often difficulties in recruiting staff with a background in music – especially in secondary and all-age special schools. At that time, almost half of schools were reported to have insufficient specialist accommodation for music, which limited the range of pupils' experiences and the standards that they could attain. These findings existed despite the entitlement of all pupils in England to music education as part of the National Curriculum for all children aged 5–14 years. Given this official concern about teaching provision, allied to the relative absence of evidence on which to agree appropriate music education principles and practice for children and young people with complex needs, a series of studies was subsequently undertaken to address this need.

The PROMISE research

It was evident that, if music provision for pupils with learning difficulties – and particularly those with complex needs – were to be improved, a necessary preliminary stage was to gather detailed and reliable information as to what was happening in schools. It was with this broad aim in mind that the PROMISE (Provision of Music in Special Education) research project was set up – a joint initiative between the Institute of Education, University of London and the Royal National Institute for the Blind (RNIB) (Welch *et al.*, 2001; Ockelford *et al.*, 2002). The research was designed as an exploratory study of three phases, using questionnaire sampling, school visits, and informal discussions with teachers and other professionals. A total of 53 schools participated. The evidence gathered from the project suggested that 'there is considerable variation in the quantity and quality of music education and music therapy available to pupils' (Welch et *al.*, 2001: 5). Possible compounding features of this variability were the wide range of disabilities being catered for within any one school and the fact that most of the participating schools encompassed a broad age range from early years to post-16.

Among the main findings from the PROMISE report were:

- Virtually all schools had a designated music coordinator, although over half of these had no qualification in music.
- Most children received music tuition from their own class teacher.
- Approximately one-third of schools reported that they provided music therapy on site, although only about 5 per cent of children were actually receiving music therapy at the time of the survey.
- Further professional development (FPD) in music education appeared to be ad hoc and depended mainly on local provision.
- The majority of schools based their schemes of work on the current version (at that time) of the National Curriculum for Music in England, but there was neither a common curriculum framework evident for children with complex needs, nor any advice in the formal documentation as to how the National Curriculum might be applied to these young people.
- Nevertheless, all head teachers were very positive about the benefits to their students engaging in music activities.
- All schools made extensive and often informal use of music and musical activities within the wider curriculum, although there was little or no obvious connection between this and the formal music curriculum.
- The majority of music coordinators stated that musical objectives appeared regularly on most SLD/PMLD children's IEPs.

- The resources for music varied across schools, with the widespread use of unpitched percussion instruments. This probably reflected the music curriculum being conceived within an Early Years' framework, as well as the lack of specialist music expertise within the teaching force.
- The technology used in schools for music largely comprised sound-reproduction equipment.
- The linkage between the schools' provision and that available from the wider music community was widespread, but varied.
- The majority of respondents did not distinguish between attainment and progress in music.
- However, music was a significant component in the daily lives of pupils with SLD and PMLD, whether at home, travelling to and from school, or in the classroom.

(Welch *et al.*, 2001: 5–8)

From the findings in the PROMISE report, it seemed that most of the head teachers thought that development *through* music is more widely recognised than development *in* music. The PROMISE survey suggested that children and young people participating in musical activities were helped in other areas of development through musical engagement, including the development of communication skills, concentration, attentive behaviour, and emotional regulation. The findings of the survey also revealed the lack of an agreed musical curriculum, the wide variation within pupil populations, and the lack of empirically based research data on SLD and PMLD children's musical behaviours and development.

To supplement and update the findings of the original PROMISE research, information was distilled subsequently from the music sections of 50 Ofsted reports on special schools that make provision for pupils with complex needs. These reports were carried out under Section 10 of the School Inspections Act 1996 in the period 2000–2005, and each related to a school in a different LEA region, selected at random from across England. The Ofsted reports indicated that insufficient evidence had been obtained in nine cases (18 per cent) to enable inspectors to make an overall judgement. In the remainder of the schools, music provision was deemed to be unsatisfactory in only one instance. Hence it can be inferred that 80 per cent of music education offered to pupils with SLD or PMLD was perceived to be satisfactory or better. Although the comparison is not an exact one, this appears to represent a considerable improvement upon the 1990s Ofsted position that underpinned the rationale for the PROMISE research. However, this positive improvement assumption should be treated with caution for two reasons. First, in only 40 per cent of the 2000–2005 reports was music provision said to have improved to a degree that the inspectors regarded as 'satisfactory' or better. Secondly, many of the observations that are cited in the reports – which are used as evidence to inform the overall judgements of teaching and learning that are made – are often so bland ('In lessons pupils have the opportunity to perform by singing or playing instruments'), lacking in any form of wider comparator ('PMLD pupils respond well to music'), or downright nonsensical ('pupils learnt rhythm, tempo, pitch and instruments') that the validity of the findings must be open to question. These concerns notwithstanding, other elements of the reports – those pertaining to resources, leadership and management, for example (that do not rely on specialist music-educational knowledge) – appear to be more securely based on credible evidence, and it is largely from these that inferences will be drawn in what follows.

The music curriculum

Almost all schools reported that they based their music lessons on the National Curriculum (for 5–14 year olds) across each age phase, including the early years group (for which the National Curriculum was not then intended). This was supplemented in most cases by schemes of work produced by the school itself. Of the schools with early years pupils, 40 per cent reported the use of baseline assessment – 'creative development'. Over half extended this to classes beyond the early years. Twenty per cent of schools reported using 'Equals' documents, which at the time included a creative development scheme of work. A few schools used schemes of work produced either by their own or another LEA. For post-16 students, two schools used the ASDAN creative development scheme and one school used the Certificate of Achievement: Music. When schools were asked about the usefulness of the National Curriculum for Music, approximately two-thirds were positive, but one-fifth were not. Surprisingly, the government's own 'P levels' for music (designed as preparatory to entry to the National Curriculum), introduced in 2001 by the then Qualifications and Curriculum Authority (QCA) (2001; revised in 2009) were not widely reported as being used.

In the view of music coordinators, the most successful activities in early years classrooms utilised action songs and involved the children playing simple instruments. Similar activities were mentioned at Key Stages 1 and 2 (ages 5–11), with the addition of other types of instrument, including some tuned percussion. Coordinators referred to the introduction of keyboards at Key Stages 3 and 4 (ages 12–16), with more references to composing and performing activities, as well as mention of 'popular' and 'world' music for listening. With regard to curriculum content, the following types of music were mentioned: pieces with a strong beat, pieces with repetition, chants, pieces with simple tunes, nursery rhymes, songs with names in, songs about animals, rounds, pop, jazz and non-Western styles. The musical techniques employed included performing, composing and improvising.

Resources

With regard to accommodation, just under half the schools reported having a discrete music room. Two-thirds had multisensory rooms (in which sound and music activities took place) or other areas containing musical equipment. Unpitched percussion instruments typically formed the staple of schools' music-making resources, although autoharps, guitars, 'whirlies', hand-chimes and 'pentatonic percussion' were also mentioned. Over half the schools had a piano, with 12 having more than one, and a number of schools mentioned the use of keyboards in class music lessons with secondary-age pupils. Only one school reported having no keyboard of any type.

The main forms of music technology used across the school day were what are best described as 'domestic' sound-reproduction systems – namely CD and tape players. Most classrooms had some means of playing recorded music, though five schools stated that they had no stereo system at all. The quality of sound reproduction available, however, was likely to be variable if extrapolated from the detail of the earlier PROMISE findings. Schools' collections of CDs and audio cassettes typically reflected a broad range of musical styles, including 'world', popular and classical music, tracks specifically intended for multisensory work and children's tapes (such as nursery rhymes and 'educational' music recordings). In addition, although the majority of schools (80 per cent) had some form of ultrasonic beam technology (such as 'Soundbeam' and 'MIDIcreator'), only a small proportion (11 per cent) used this on a regular basis each week, perhaps indicating that staff were unsure of how best to use such technology. Some schools stated that they used electromechanical switches to enable pupils to turn music on or off. Some used karaoke machines, particularly with older students.

Within the PROMISE research data, a notable feature of the schools visited by the research team was the range of sound-making toys, which typically played nursery rhymes or made animal noises, although none was mentioned in the questionnaire returns, even in the detailed sound audits that were submitted. In terms of the resources that teachers used for curriculum planning and delivery, the most popular were children's songbooks – including music written specifically for pupils with special needs (such as Nordoff Robbins music therapy songbooks) and those produced with the mainstream in mind. Local authority provision of instrumental teaching varied, as it did in mainstream schools. One school had free instrumental lessons, while another required a £10 contribution per pupil.

Music in the wider curriculum

Head teachers in the PROMISE survey were asked what they considered the value of music in the wider curriculum to be. Their views may be summarised as follows:

- *Language and communication development:* 'improved eye contact'; 'increased vocalisation'; 'developing expressive and receptive language'; 'singing along with signing using British Sign Language (BSL)'.
- *Behavioural, emotional and social development:* 'showing pleasure during musical activities'; 'for reflection times'; 'encourages facial expressions'; 'gives pupils a means to make choices'; 'inclusion and participation'; 'learning to mix through shared musical activity'; 'waiting your turn, sharing, being quiet, noisy'; 'building and demonstrating confidence to play an instrument to an audience'; 'prestige of playing drum kit, using a microphone, full-sized synthesizer, bass guitar'; 'builds self-esteem'; 'awareness of style and culture through listening to music'.
- *Sensory and cognitive development:* 'improved attention'; 'Soundbeam has made a great difference to concentration and understanding of cause and effect'; 'learning the starts and ends of activities through using a song'; 'music gives structure and routine to an activity'; 'learning discrimination, sequencing, closure and completion'; 'developing numeracy'.
- *Physical development:* 'encourages intentional movement'; 'head control'; 'hand function'; 'increased looking, reaching, grasping'; 'increased movement, more controlled movement'; 'learning motor skills, body awareness, laterality, coordination'; 'balance'; 'Soundbeam has made a great difference to mobility'.

Similarly, teachers were asked what they considered the educational benefits of these special musical activities to be. Their many comments included the belief that such events:

- provided pupils with the opportunity to hear *live* music of a high quality, which was perceived to have a particularly strong effect on pupils with the most severe complex needs
- fostered pupils' musicality, including listening skills and rhythmic abilities
- nurtured their development in *extra*-musical domains, such as language, socialisation and movement
- offered them new, stimulating, multisensory experiences and promoted multicultural awareness
- above all, they brought pupils enjoyment and gave them a sense of excitement.

Both the PROMISE research and the subsequent accounts by Ofsted suggest that the use of music as a medium for the delivery of a wider curriculum – as an agent to enhance learning throughout the school day – is valued and widespread in special schools with pupils who have complex needs. However, there are no indications that music is systematically conceptualised in this role, nor that education *through* music is coherently linked to education *in* music (although there is bound to be an overlap). Yet common sense suggests that, for pupils whose perception of the world is likely to be fragmented and confusing, a joined-up approach could only benefit learning and development.

The assessment of development *in* music in a special education context

A common challenge reported within Ofsted music inspection reports of the past decade or so, across all school education sectors, is a weakness in the ways that musical attainment and progress are perceived and reported, particularly in relation to the more creative aspects of music learning (Ofsted, 1999, 2009a; Welch, 2001). A major contextual feature of music education during this period is that there has been a general trend since the 1980s towards an 'outcomes-based' curriculum design, with the pedagogical 'process' subsumed into specified learning goals. Musical learning is conceived as a product of action (such as 'performing', 'listening', 'composing', 'improvising'), even though various iterations of official curricula for music make no specific reference to research evidence to justify or illuminate this stance.

Consequently, it is perhaps unsurprising that music teachers in mainstream and in special education have had to rely on an eclectic mix of personal biography (including their own craft knowledge), available resources, and interpretations of official curricula expectations to inform their judgements about musical attainment and progress. While there is research evidence available of musical development in childhood and adolescence in the absence of disability (e.g. McPherson, 2006), this is rarely available in a comprehensive and/or practice-focused format, and until recently was almost non-existent in any form in relation to children with complex needs.

Sounds of Intent

The published outcomes of the PROMISE research were distributed to every special school in England and promoted at a national conference in London. Subsequently, the research team held regular meetings with a small panel of teachers from the special education sector, to launch the 'Sounds of Intent' project. Many of the teachers had attended the national conference and, consequently, had expressed a wish to be involved in investigating more fully the significance of music in the lives of children and young people with complex needs.

The data from the PROMISE survey suggested that significant non-musical benefits had been noted by teachers and parents as one of the outcomes of their children's participation in musical activity (Ockelford, 2008). These included reports of heightened interpersonal communication skills, more focused, attentive behaviour, and increased emotional and social development. Nevertheless, in terms of education *in* music (as opposed to education *through* music), although head teachers were generally extremely positive about the potential and actual benefits of their pupils engaging in music activities, until the advent of the P levels for music, there was no formal music curriculum for special schools. An analysis of this document by Ockelford *et al.* (2002) revealed serious weaknesses in the performance descriptions that were set out. A major difficulty was that these were not rooted in music-developmental research of children with complex needs, since none existed in the field, a problem that had been acknowledged by the QCA themselves in subsequent discussions with the research team. Both QCA and Ofsted indicated that they would welcome input into a reformulation of what might be expected for the complex needs population. Consequently, the evidence-based difficulties that the P levels represented stimulated an ongoing process of charting an alternative and empirically based route for the musical development for children with SEN in special school contexts, particularly those with complex needs.

The initial approach was to invite the teachers on the 'Sounds of Intent' panel to bring in video examples of individual children engaging with music (following appropriate ethical permissions). The group discussed these case study examples in detail in order to build a consensus of the musical behaviours being observed. Whenever possible, teachers were asked to gather several examples of the same child over a period of time. Then a variety of different conceptual structures were explored in order to identity clusters of like behaviours among the observations, to see if these could be structured into some form of hierarchical, developmental sequence with an appropriate linguistic tag line. The emergent draft 'Sounds of Intent' framework comprised three main areas of musical engagement, embracing 'reactive', 'proactive' and 'interactive' musical behaviours. Progressing from simple to complex, these drew on a combination of the case study evidence and published research of the musical behaviour and development of children and young people, including perception and cognition of music (see Ockelford, 2006).

Subsequently, the Esmée Fairbairn Foundation provided funding from 2005 to 2007 for two years of extended fieldwork. Five special schools participated, generating 630 music class observations of 68 pupils aged from 4 to 19 years. When the data for the children with the most profound needs were analysed, relatively few participants had their musical behaviours rated at the most basic level of the draft framework. In contrast, the vast majority of behaviours (82 per cent) were identified as having some sense of personal agency, such as 'makes sound in response to an external stimulus' or 'makes sounds intentionally' (see Welch *et al.*, 2009 for more details). Although very small numbers of behaviours were classified at the most advanced level, a distinct minority of behaviours (approximately 8 per cent) were classified as having distinctive musical features, such as the production of simple patterns through repetition. When the data for children with less severe needs were considered, more advanced musical behaviours tended to be evidenced (that is, in relation to the middle-to-outer levels specified in Figure 3.1).

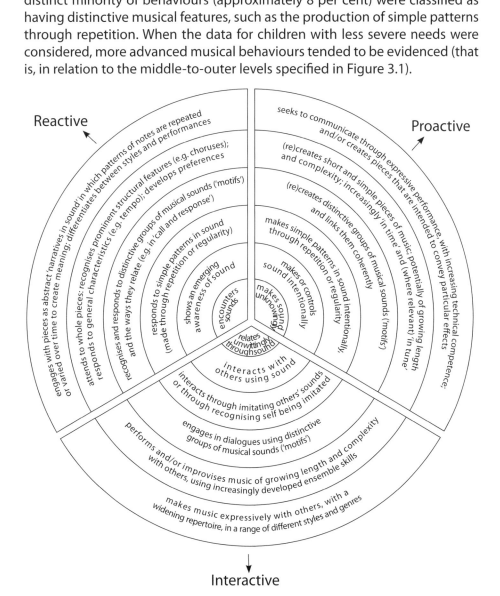

Figure 3.1: The 'Sounds of Intent' framework for the mapping of musical behaviours in children and young people with complex needs

Most recently, this research has been extended in two directions. First, longitudinal case study data have been gathered over one calendar year of a small number of young people with complex needs in an inner London special school (Cheng *et al.*, 2009). Analysing hundreds of classroom observations using the 'Sounds of Intent' framework reveals a shifting distribution in musical behaviours towards the more complex, indicating the presence of musical development across all three domains (see case study example in Figure 3.2). This development was in a context where the individuals were immersed in a rich musical environment provided by an experienced, sensitive and empathic music teacher supported by a group of classroom assistants.

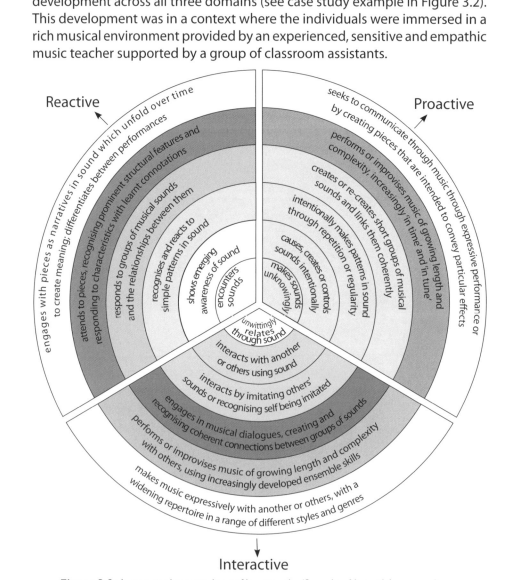

Figure 3.2: A case study example profile using the 'Sounds of Intent' framework, demonstrating patterns of development over time for one young person with complex needs, with darker shading indicating greater numbers and weighting of observations (Cheng *et al.*, 2009)

Secondly, since 2009, additional funding from the Esmée Fairbairn Foundation is enabling a further period of extended fieldwork to create a 'Sounds of Intent' website to support musical behaviour assessment profiling and development by anyone with internet access (teacher and parent/carer). This will be an interactive resource on which many examples of children's musical behaviours will be available for reference, fulfilling three main functions:

1. It will enable those working musically with children and young people with complex needs (SLD or PMLD) – teachers (music specialists and non-specialists), therapists and carers – to assess their pupils' levels of musical development accurately and consistently. It will also be available to help parents in supporting the musical development of their children.

2. It will enable practitioners to record pupils' individual attainment and progress as individual profiles – both quantitatively and qualitatively (with the option of attaching audio and video files of the children in action) – and enable comparisons to be drawn between individuals and groups (for example, to evaluate the effectiveness of different interventions).

3. It will provide ready access to curriculum materials, including specially composed music, to promote musical and wider learning and development.

The new interactive website will foster greater insight into musical behaviour in the presence of special needs and is intended to create a community of practice concerning music education in the special school sector, both nationally and internationally.

Implications for practice

The primary function of music educators is to nurture and develop each individual's inherent musicality (Welch, 2005: 117). The 'Sounds of Intent' research shows that even the most profound disabilities need not prevent musical engagement at some level, while pupils with visual impairment or autism (or both) are statistically many thousands of times more likely than those in the 'typical' population to possess exceptional musical abilities, such as absolute pitch (Ockelford and Matawa, 2009). As the move to inclusion continues to strengthen in the UK and internationally (see Jellison, 2010; UNESCO, 2009), the issue for teachers – and, beyond them, teacher-educators and policymakers – is how to ensure appropriate levels of differentiation within classes that are likely to embrace ever-wider spectrums of special ability and need. Access and quality of education should be inseparable.

Yet if true inclusion of *all* learners is possible in any curriculum area, surely it is in the domain of music. As we have seen from the 'Sounds of Intent' research, musical engagement can occur reactively, proactively or interactively. Hence participation in musical activity does not necessarily require the production of sound. Equally, the capacity to engage in advanced musical dialogues does not require language (Ockelford, in press); so, by its very nature, music circumvents one of the major barriers to participation in mainstream classes by non-verbal children.

The challenge, then, to the concept of 'music for all' lies not in pupils and students themselves, but in the capacity of the education system to deliver it, in mainstream as well as in special school classrooms. Reacting in an ad hoc way to individual special needs as and when they are encountered is no longer good enough (whether these are special needs *in* music, or special needs *and* music); The Special Educational Needs and Disability Act places an *anticipatory* duty on all service providers to make provision for those with exceptional requirements. We need to address organisational and attitudinal barriers to musical inclusion, such as in the case where there are negative attitudes from peers and adults towards children who are 'different', including 'different' musically. We need to review the nature of the input to initial teacher education courses of issues around disability, SEN and music; and to ensure that all teachers have access to the necessary advice, support and CPD to enable them to support all pupils who enter the door of the music room. To be human is to be musical, and to be offered the opportunities for musical engagement is every child's right.

Further reading

Jellison, J.A. (2010) *Including Everyone: Music for today's schools*. Austin, TX: Learning and Behavior Resources.

Ockelford, A. (2008) *Music for Children and Young People with Complex Needs*. Oxford: Oxford University Press.

References

Barrett, M. (ed.). (2010) *A Cultural Psychology for Music Education*. Oxford: Oxford University Press.

Cheng, E., Ockelford, A. and Welch, G.F. (2009) 'Researching and developing music provision in Special Schools in England for children and young people with complex needs'. *Australian Journal of Music Education*, (2), 27–48.

Department for Children, Schools and Families (DCSF) (2009) *Special Educational Needs: A guide for parents and carers.* Nottingham: DCSF.

Department for Education and Skills (DfES) (2001) *Special Educational Needs: Code of practice.* London: DfES.

Hallam, S., Cross, I. and Thaut, M. (2009) *The Oxford Handbook of Music Psychology.* Oxford: Oxford University Press.

House of Commons (2006) *Special Educational Needs* (Education and Skills Committee). London: Stationery Office.

Jellison, J.A. (2006a) 'What research tells us about music and the needs of children in special education'. Paper presented at Beijing International Forum on Music Education, 15-17 May.

–– (2006b) 'Including everyone'. In G. McPherson (ed.) *The Child as Musician.* New York: Oxford University Press.

–– (2010) *Including Everyone: Music for today's schools.* Austin, TX: Learning and Behavior Resources.

Knight, S. (2010) 'A study of adult non-singers in Newfoundland'. Unpublished PhD thesis, Institute of Education, University of London.

McPherson, G. (2006) *The Child as Musician.* New York: Oxford University Press.

Ockelford, A. (2006) 'Using a music-theoretical approach to interrogate musical development and social interaction'. In N. Lerner and J. Strauss (eds), *Sounding Off: Theorising disability in music.* New York: Routledge.

–– (2008) *Music for Children and Young People with Complex Needs.* Oxford: Oxford University Press.

–– (in press) 'Songs without words: Exploring how music can serve as a proxy language in social interaction with autistic children who have little speech, and the potential impact on their wellbeing'. In R. Macdonald, G. Kreutz and L. Mitchell (eds) *Music, Health and Wellbeing.* Oxford: Oxford University Press.

Ockelford, A. and Matawa, C. (2009) *Focus on Music 2: Exploring the musicality of children and young people with retinopathy of maturity.* London: University of London Institute of Education.

Ockelford, A., Welch, G.F. and Zimmermann, S.-A. (2002) 'Music education for pupils with severe or profound and multiple difficulties: Current provision and future need'. *British Journal of Special Education*, 29(4), 178–182.

Office for Standards in Education (Ofsted) (1999) *Special Education 1994–1998: A review of special schools, secure units and pupil referral units in England.* London: Stationery Office.

–– (2009a) *The Annual Report of Her Majesty's Chief Inspector of Education, Children's Services and Skills, 2008/09*. London: Stationery Office.

–– (2009b) *Making More of Music*. London: Ofsted.

Qualifications and Curriculum Authority (QCA) (2001) *Planning, teaching and assessment for pupils with learning difficulties*. London: QCA.

Ruddock, E. and Leong, S. (2005) '"I am unmusical!": The verdict of self-judgement'. *International Journal of Music Education*, 23(1), 9–22.

Seddon, F. and Biasutti, M. (2008) 'Non-specialist trainee primary school teachers' confidence in teaching music in the classroom'. *Music Education Research*, 10(3), 403–421.

Stevens, C. and Byron, T. (2009) 'Universals in music processing'. In S. Hallam, I. Cross and M. Thaut (eds), *Oxford Handbook of Music Psychology*. Oxford: Oxford University Press.

Stunell, G. (2006) 'The policy context of music in English primary schools: How politics didn't help music'. *Research Studies in Music Education*, 26, 2–21.

Tafuri, J. (2009) *Infant Musicality*. Farnham: Ashgate.

United Nations Educational, Scientific and Cultural Organization (UNESCO) (2009) *Policy Guidelines on Inclusion in Education*. Paris: UNESCO. <http://unesdoc.unesco.org/images/0017/001778/177849e.pdf>(accessed 21/02/2010).

Welch, G.F. (2001) 'UK'. In D. Hargreaves and A. North (eds), *Musical Development and Learning: The international perspective*. London: Continuum.

–– (2005) 'We *are* musical'. *International Journal of Music Education,* 23(2), 117–120.

Welch, G.F., Ockelford, A. and Zimmermann, S.-A. (2001) *Provision of Music in Special Education (PROMISE)*. London: Royal National Institute for the Blind (RNIB)/Institute of Education, University of London.

Welch, G.F., Ockelford, A., Carter, F.-C., Zimmermann, S.-A. and Himonides, E. (2009) '"Sounds of Intent": Mapping musical behaviour and development in children and young people with complex needs'. *Psychology of Music*, 37(3), 348–370.

Welch, G.F., Purves, R., Hargreaves, D. and Marshall, N. (2010) 'Early career challenges in secondary school music teaching'. *British Educational Research Journal*. First published on 26 March 2010 (iFirst).

Chapter 4

Listening

Susan Hallam

Listening is central to all musical activity. Whenever we engage with music, whether as performers, composers or audience, we are listening. As we listen to music we also appraise and respond to it.

Humans are born equipped with the necessary neural and physical structures to perceive and respond to music. The human auditory system is functional 3–4 months before birth. Near-term foetuses reliably react to external sounds, and infants show recognition responses to music that they have heard in the womb. Infants have a predisposition for processing rhythm and by the age of 2 their spontaneous songs show evidence of a beat and rhythmic subdivisions. By the age of 5 they have quite sophisticated rhythmic skills and can reproduce steady beats and subdivisions of them. By the age of 7 there is little difference between children's rhythmic processing and that of adult non-musicians (Drake, 1993). Infants also have the same capacity to process pitch as adults. As early as 6 months they easily notice differences in melodies, although they are not born with knowledge of the tonal system of their culture (e.g. Trehub and Trainer, 1990). This, like language, is learned. The speed with which knowledge of the tonal system is acquired depends on the extent of exposure to music, although, generally, by the age of 5, children can organise songs around stable tonal keys (Lamont and Cross, 1994) and can recognise familiar tunes across many different types of transformations. Overall, infants and young children are sophisticated listeners to music and remember what they have listened to (Trehub *et al.*, 1997).

Responses to music

Human beings, as a species, respond to music in a variety of different ways: physiologically, through movement, intellectually, aesthetically, and emotionally. Historically, in education, there has been a focus on aesthetic and intellectual responses (Hallam, 2010a). However, recently there has been an acknowledgement of the wider impact of music. For instance, the programme of study for Key Stage 3 in England (QCA, 2007) states that 'Music is a unique form of communication that can change the way pupils feel, think and act. Music brings together intellect and feeling and enables personal expression, reflection and emotional development.' Similarly, at primary level, the recent review of the curriculum (DCSF, 2009) recognised the importance of moving in response to stimuli, and exploring how the arts can evoke and express feelings. This recognition is long overdue as there is considerable evidence that music has a very powerful effect on the emotions (see Gabrielsson, 2010 for a review) and that young learners respond to this. When those in secondary education have been encouraged to appraise music not only analytically but also using figurative language including similes, analogies and metaphors (O'Brien, 1992) and references to emotion (Bula, 1987) they consistently score higher on attitudinal and conceptual understanding, the exception being when there are strong initial attitudinal reactions to the music. It seems that taking account of a wide range of responses to music has considerable educational benefits.

Listening in everyday life

Since the advent of recording techniques it has been possible for music to be played at any time, in any place, easily and cheaply. This has led to a proliferation of music in our lives. Increasingly, in everyday life music is used to mediate moods and emotional reactions and provide individuals with support as they undertake a variety of relatively uninteresting activities – for instance, housework, travel, physical exercise (see Sloboda *et al.*, 2009; Hallam and MacDonald, 2009). Young people use music in ways very similar to those of adults (Tolfree, 2005) often employing it as an accompaniment to studying (Kotsopoulou, 1997). Even quite young children demonstrate multiple musical understandings: intellectual (acknowledging musical elements, dynamics, musical structure, instruments, deriving an overall conception of the music); through lyrics; through association with events linked to music; through images generated by music; and through their emotional responses (Hallam, 2009). Music also helps young people overcome powerful emotions (Behne, 1997).

Listening to music in everyday life enables the development of sophisticated listening skills which differ little, in many respects, from those of professional musicians. Those with no formal musical training can recognise melodies as well as trained musicians (Dowling, 1978), although they find some tasks more difficult – for instance, interval recognition (Cuddy and Cohen, 1976), and the identification of important thematic material (Aiello *et al.*, 1990). Remembering atonal music is difficult for musicians and non-musicians (Dowling, 1991) and all make mistakes when identifying quarter tones which do not fit within the Western tonal system with which they are familiar (Dowling, 1992). Musicians are no better at understanding large musical structures than non-musicians (Poulin *et al.*, 2001) and the perceptions of the two groups barely differ in relation to different kinds of cadence and chord progression (Tillman *et al.*, 2000). In some cases the listening and learning skills of non-musicians are greater than those of trained musicians. Mito (2004) asked young people to memorise the same Japanese pop song, by ear, over four 10-minute practice sessions and reproduce it after each session. Those without formal music training, particularly those who performed regularly at karaoke sessions, memorised the song better than those who had received formal training, the latter reporting particular difficulties in learning without notation to support the process. Overall, listeners with no musical training are musical experts – although they may find it difficult to describe in words what they hear (Flowers, 1983). The role of education, therefore, is not to enhance listening skills per se, but to increase knowledge about what is heard and enhance understanding and the ability to articulate that understanding in spoken language.

Listening and hearing

Commonly, a distinction is made between listening and hearing. Hearing is seen as essentially passive, a form of reception, which occurs without conscious attention and is part of the constant process of monitoring the environment. Listening requires conscious cognitive activity and concentration, and involves focusing on particular elements in the music. Both hearing and listening provide valuable means through which different kinds of learning can occur. Repetitively hearing particular pieces of music enables aural representations to be developed, a crucial element of enculturation. Music educators sometimes underestimate the importance of the incidental learning that can occur from just hearing music, believing that only active listening to music – consciously undertaken, where some form of cognitive evaluation takes place – is of value. Frequently hearing music enables it to become internalised so that we know and remember it. This facilitates the development of audiation (Gordon, 1993), the ability to internally hear and comprehend music for which the sound is no longer or may never have been physically present. This includes the ability to internally hear and understand notated music without actually playing it. This is a highly advanced skill and some professional musicians only partially acquire it. Audiation is important in both improvisation and composition.

Listening for understanding

Listening is key to developing musical understanding. Repeated listening to a piece of music changes a listener's perceptions, leading to a greater understanding of the structure of the music and how themes within it are related (Pollard-Gott, 1983). There seems to be intuitive recognition of this. A recent study exploring how individuals believe that musical understanding is acquired showed that 63 per cent of a sample of adults and children believed that musical understanding developed through listening. This increased to 75 per cent in the professional musicians in the sample, 74 per cent of whom also acknowledged the importance of active music making in developing understanding (Hallam, 2009).

Listening skills are fundamental to all musical activities. The revised programme of study at KS3 (in England) states:

> Performance, composing and listening are inter-related. Pupils should be encouraged to develop listening skills through performance and composition activities. Knowledge, skills and understanding in each of these areas should be developed interactively though practical music-making.
>
> (QCA, 2007: 180)

In addition, pupils should be able to 'listen with discrimination and internalise and recall sounds' and 'identify the expressive use of musical elements, devices, tonalities and structures.' They should study 'a range of live and recorded music from different times and cultures, including a range of classical and popular traditions and current trends in music that reflect cultural diversity and a global dimension'.

At primary level, in England, the recent curriculum review (DCSF, 2009) also stresses the importance of children being given access to a range of music of different genres from different cultures. This is particularly important as there is some evidence that very young children are more 'open-eared' and tolerant of music which is unfamiliar and unconventional than older children (Gembris and Schellenberg, 2003; Kopiez and Lehmann, 2008). This tolerance may be, in part, because they have become less familiar with other genres.

Listening, familiarity and musical preferences

The more familiar we are with a piece of music, the more we like and value it, although over-familiarity may lead to boredom or even dislike (North and Hargreaves, 1997). The speed with which familiarity leads to boredom seems to be related to the complexity of the music – the degree of variability or uncertainty. The relationship between complexity and liking can be described by an inverted U-shaped curve. A moderate level of complexity elicits the maximum liking for the music. The effect of exposure to music, repetition, training, or practice is to lower the perceived complexity. These changes seem to develop cyclically, occurring in a spiral as music is listened to more than once (Bamberger, 1991). The logical corollary of this is that musical preferences can be changed through prolonged exposure. Indeed, this can be the case. For instance, Shehan (1987) engaged sixth-grade students over a period of five weeks in studying southeast Asian music in its cultural context and found a marked change in liking. However, other factors can also contribute to musical preferences. Musical taste is not acquired in a vacuum. It is an integral part of the lifestyle of the individual, reflecting their identity and their cultural, historical, societal, familial and peer group background. Current negative attitudes towards 'classical' music may be more related to these factors than the music itself. Where 'classical' music is presented in contexts outside the concert hall – for instance, in advertisements, TV programmes, film, or sporting contexts – it is not only accepted but becomes part of popular culture. This, in part, may be because it has been allowed to become familiar.

The extent to which a piece of music is liked depends on a hierarchical set of factors (LeBlanc, 1980). These are set out in Figure 4.1. At the lowest level in the hierarchy is the nature of the music itself and the listening situation including the physical properties of the music, its level of complexity, its meaning for the individual and the quality of the performance. The listening situation includes the media through which it is presented, and who is present, members of the listener's peer group, members of his or her family or authority figures, for instance, the teacher. Beyond this initial level a range of factors act as filters. Firstly, there are physiological and psychological factors, for example, ease of hearing, the level of attention being paid to the listening process and the current mood of the listener. Any of these may preclude careful listening. Continuing the filtering process are the elements that the individual brings to the listening process including their level of auditory sensitivity in relation to music, their level of musical training, their personality (in particular whether they are generally receptive to new experiences), their gender, ethnic group, socioeconomic status and maturity. These all affect the way the process of listening is undertaken, what is attended to and how the listener processes the music. Having passed through these filters the music is processed. This may occur at a holistic level or the listener may take note of the detail, paying attention to instrumentation, structure, the style, and so on. The listener then judges whether there is sufficient information to establish a preference. It may be that more information is required in which case the music may be listened to again or listening may continue more carefully. The individual will then be in a position to make a preference judgement. This illustrates clearly that there are a range of factors involved in developing preferences for particular kinds of music and that they interact in complex ways.

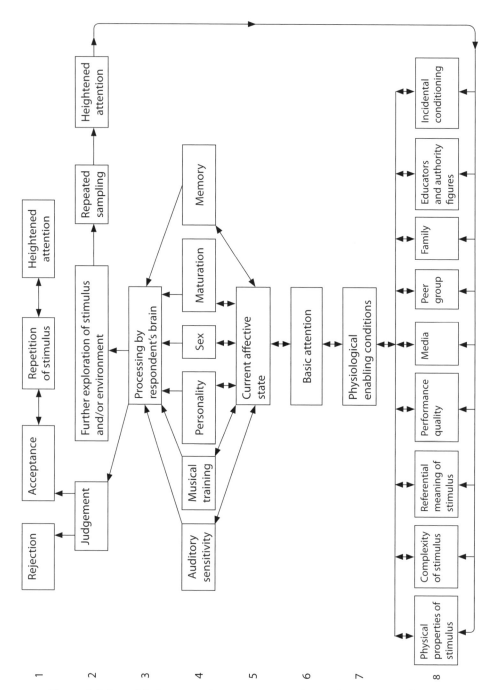

Figure 4.1: A model of sources of variation in musical taste (LeBlanc, 1980, © Music Educators National Conference)

Appraisal and evaluation

Appraisal and evaluation are central activities in music making. The musician, whether professional, amateur, expert or novice, constantly appraises his or her work and that of colleagues. This guides future planning and activity. The process of appraising involves listening and making comparisons (implicit or explicit) with already acquired internal representations of music. These may be specific, of the same piece of music; generalised to particular types or styles of music; or generalised relating to particular features of performance, e.g. intonation, tone quality. The principle of comparison is central. Without comparison with some already held conception appraisal cannot occur. The process of appraisal can take place on a number of different levels, including description and comparison, or evaluation within the broader musical context. Even quite young children are able to articulate ideas about their listening, and as they get older they are able to predict, compare, evaluate, express preferences, reflect, recognise and make judgements about music (Bundra, 1993). Musically trained children demonstrate similar skills to adults, including classifying, elaborating, comparing, predicting and evaluating (Richardson 1996, 1998) suggesting that the ability to think critically while listening to music is related to experience with music rather than age. Appraising also involves learners making judgements about their liking of particular pieces of music. These judgements can be made independently of whether the individual has any understanding of the music, although being able to justify preferences has educational value (Swanwick, 1994).

Promoting listening skills

As we have seen, as a species, humans have systems for processing music which are in place prior to birth and which develop to full capacity very early, providing that there is appropriate environmental input. Most children who are exposed to music will, without any training, develop quite sophisticated listening skills. These can be enhanced through practical music making, and exposure to a wide variety of different musical styles and genres (see Chapter 12).

Learning to play or sing by ear

One way to enhance listening skills is to require learners to learn to play or sing by ear. A number of music educators, historically, have advocated such an approach, including John Curwen, Kodaly and Jacques-Dalcroze, while some instrumental teaching methods have been devised which have as their basis learning through listening – the Suzuki method, for instance. Historically, much music education in the UK involved learning to sing through rote learning by ear, and at primary level this practice is still not uncommon. Playing by ear has tended to be neglected in instrumental tuition, except where skills of improvisation are taught, and in some cases it has been actively discouraged. However, many musicians working in the field of popular music cannot read music and rely totally on their aural skills to enable them to perform, some having developed their aural skills to an incredible extent (Macek, 1987). The skills of musical savants, who can memorise and perform lengthy pieces of music by ear, suggest that human beings have neural structures which facilitate links between remembered aural templates and relevant motor programmes so that what has been remembered can be turned into sound (Sloboda *et al.*, 1985). These skills can be developed if the environment is conducive and the individual has sufficient commitment.

Recent interest in informal learning (see Green, 2001) illustrates clearly the extent to which learning by ear can be a powerful means of developing musical skills. Green distinguishes between 'purposive' and 'attentive' listening, the former being listening in order to copy music, the latter being listening to a piece of music in order to answer questions on it. She also refers to what she calls 'distracted listening' – listening to music in the background. She describes how popular musicians frequently teach themselves, relying on purposive and attentive listening so that they can imitate the music of others. Such an aural approach is adopted in many different cultures where music is not notated but passed from generation to generation through reliance on aural memory (see Hallam, 2010b).

Listening while actively making music

Any music-making activity encourages the development of critical listening skills. Whether working with groups or individuals, teachers typically encourage listening through focusing on particular elements which need to be improved – for instance, intonation, rhythm, phrasing, articulation, musicality. There may be even greater benefits to listening through independent small group work where learners have to constantly evaluate their work and that of others in the group to improve it. This has been demonstrated in the 'Musical Futures' approach (see Chapter 14) and in research on group work in higher education (Kokotsaki and Hallam, 2007). Through music making, teachers can also encourage learners to engage with a wide variety of different types of music. Exposure to different genres, for instance, through formal instrumental tuition leads to familiarisation and subsequent liking of a wider range of music than might otherwise be the case (Kotsopoulou, 2001).

Listening to live and recorded music

Live performance not only provides listening opportunities but provides learners with authentic musical experiences which enrich their learning more generally. A particular advantage of live music is that the movements of the performer can be seen. These are important in communicating musical meaning (Davidson, 1993). In schools, there are opportunities for learners to perform to each other regularly within the classroom and in concerts of various types. Schools can also organise performances by visiting artists and attendance at public concerts, the benefits of which, in terms of learning, can be much enhanced by related instruction before and after the event (Shehan, 1986).

There are limits to the extent to which live access to a wide range of music can be made available to all. Recorded music provides opportunities for listeners to learn about and appreciate a much wider range of genres and styles of music than would be possible if there was a reliance on live music alone. It provides educators with the opportunity to familiarise learners with music to which they would not normally be exposed, giving them the opportunity to develop understanding and liking. Savan (1999), in her work with children with emotional and behavioural difficulties, found that some of those exposed regularly over long periods of time to the music of Mozart while they were studying science came to enjoy it and continued to listen to it at home after the research was over. Educators need to find ways to make unfamiliar music familiar. Opportunities for playing music while children are engaged in other activities frequently present themselves, particularly in the early years, and may be preferable to formal 'listening' opportunities for developing wider musical preferences. Music can be used as a stimulus for art, writing and a range of other creative activities in addition to being played in assemblies, during lunch times and at other social occasions. Introducing into the classroom music that may be perceived as 'shocking' can also stimulate listening and subsequent discussion, while making links with other arts can reinforce understanding of particular periods and schools of thought – for instance, the use of impressionist paintings to illustrate musical impressionism (Haack, 1982).

Few adults engage in listening to music as a sole activity. Music usually accompanies other activities even if these are not immediately obvious – for instance, thinking or reminiscing. In music lessons students are likely to be more focused if they listen purposefully, whether this is to get ideas for a composition of their own, to copy the music, to write prose or draw reflecting their understanding of the music, or to identify particular musical features. Encouraging students to listen to music while following a part or score will also begin to develop the process of audiation (being able to hear music from the written page) and enable the development of internal aural representations of phrasing in different musical styles, as musicians do not play written notation literally (Gabrielsson, 1988).

The instructions given to learners when they are asked to listen to recorded music may be important in determining what they learn. Heddon (1988) suggested that it is helpful to focus student attention directly on the musical elements that they are comfortable with and capable of discussing, while Zalonowski (1986), exploring different ways of instructing listening groups, found that no approach was consistently most effective. Instructions to encourage free-form mental imagery led to the greatest enjoyment, while thinking of a story was most relevant to understanding programme music.

Box 4.1 Listening task 1

The room was set up with five large tables. As the students came into the room they were given an envelope which set them a task. They were asked to listen to the song 'Eternal Flame' and to place the cards containing graphic notation of the melody into the correct order. They were engaged and challenged by this activity. They were then provided with the learning objectives and taught the five key terms for the lesson: solo, a cappella, unison, imitation, and call and response. These were explained and demonstrated by the teacher. The students then listened to music from a range of styles and cultures and identified which of the five key terms was being demonstrated. The teacher then directed some vocal warm-ups, focusing on diction and breathing, and sang the song 'Eternal Flame'. The students were then asked questions about how to improve their singing and what they noticed about the structure of the song. They were asked to suggest ways in which they could use the five key terms and apply them to performance of the song. They then tried some of these out. The lesson concluded with a recap of the new vocabulary and asking the students to reflect on what they had learned. The students were clear about what they had learned and why. They were highly engaged and motivated by the task. The teacher gave much positive feedback, knew the students well and offered an appropriate level of challenge and support, and chose materials that would appeal to a wide range of learners.

(derived from Green, 2009)

Box 4.2 Listening task 2

The teacher used the *Batman* theme from the 1989 film. The teacher posed questions such as 'How does this piece of music create the mood of a camera drifting through the gloomy alleyways of the city of Gotham?' The teacher divided the class into groups of about six students and gave each group about 20 statements, for instance:

- The music was composed by Danny Elfman in 1989 for the film *Batman*.
- The music starts with a single line, and the texture builds up gradually, creating a creeping effect.
- The music starts slowly and quietly.
- The opening is based on a five-note motif that is heard throughout the film played in different ways.
- Glockenspiels (metallic-sounding instruments) are used to create a spooky effect.
- A repeating pattern of notes moving down in pitch (descending) on the glockenspiels creates tension.
- The music was composed to accompany the *Batman* film.
- There are sustained (long-held) chords.

The students listened to the music and then placed the cards on a grid designed to focus their decision making. The grid had a box at the centre where they were to place the statements that they felt were most important in relation to the question, with less important statements around those and then, on the outside, the statements that were irrelevant. They were asked to agree where each statement should be placed in response to the teacher's question. Some of the cards used language that students were not familiar with. The activity encouraged them to discuss and find out the meanings of new vocabulary within this context. Once the groups had completed the task they were asked to write their own sentence to answer the question, drawing upon their discussions. The students were encouraged to understand that there were no right or wrong answers and that the purpose of the activity was to improve appraisal and thinking skills, musical understanding and the use of musical vocabulary.

(derived from Green, 2009)

Movement and music

Music with movement provides ways of encouraging listening, particularly in young children, and develops rhythmic skills. The natural extension of this is dancing which requires acute listening to enable accurate time keeping and is a popular activity among teenagers. School musical theatre productions also provide opportunities for linking music with movement.

Box 4.3 Music, imagination and movement for young children

A range of activities are possible to support young children in listening to recorded music. While music is playing (different genres and types of music should be played over time) children can be asked to:

- suggest the mood of the music and think about how it has made them feel
- draw a picture of what they think the music means
- make up a story relating to the music
- think about and perform actions which represent the music.

These activities can be followed up by small group or whole-class activities where responses are shared. This can lead to increased understanding, not only of music but also a range of other topics.

Endnote

When facilitating listening activities, educators need to acknowledge the power of music to influence mood and emotions (Hallam, 2010a). Too often the study of music is seen as an intellectual pursuit with little reference to what it may mean to young people. In the latest stages of primary education, children begin to use music in similar ways to adults, to express their feelings and change moods. These emotional responses to music can be used as a way of encouraging exploration of structure, instrumentation, timbre and so on. Engaging rather than ignoring the emotional power of music can assist learners in developing listening and appraisal skills and may also enhance the learning experience.

Further reading

Green, S. (2009) 'Improving motivation for music at Key Stage 3'. In D. Bray (ed.), *Creating a Musical School*. Oxford: Oxford University Press.

References

Aiello, R., Tanaka, J. and Winborne, W. (1990) 'Listening to Mozart: Perceptual differences among musicians'. *Journal of Music Theory Pedagogy,* 4(2), 269–293.

Bamberger, J. (1991) *The Mind Behind the Musical Ear: How children develop musical intelligence.* Cambridge, MA: Harvard University Press.

Behne, K.E. (1997) 'The development of "Musikerleben" in adolescence: How and why young people listen to music'. In I. Deliege and J.A. Sloboda (eds), *Perception and Cognition of Music.* Hove: Psychology Press.

Bula, K. (1987) 'The participation of the verbal factor in perception of musical compositions'. *Bulletin of the Council for Research in Music Education,* 91, 15–18.

Bundra, J. (1993) 'A study of music listening processes through the verbal reports of school-aged children'. *Dissertation Abstracts International,* UMI No. 9415701.

Cuddy, L.L. and Cohen, A.J. (1976) 'Recognition of transposed melodic sequences'. *Quarterly of Experimental Psychology*, 28, 255–270.

Davidson, J.W. (1993) 'Visual perception of performance manner in the movement of solo musicians'. *Psychology of Music,* 21(2), 103–113.

Department for Children, Schools and Families (DCSF) (2009) *Independent Review of the Primary Curriculum: Final report.* London: DCSF.

Dowling, W.J. (1978) 'Scale and contour: Two components of a theory for memory for melodies'. *Psychological Review*, 85, 341–354.

— (1991) 'Tonal strength and melody recognition after long and short delays'. *Perception and Psychophysics*, 50, 305–313.

— (1992) 'Perceptual grouping, attention and expectancy in listening to music'. In J. Sundberg (ed.), *Gluing Tones: Grouping in music composition, performance and listening.* Stockholm: Royal Swedish Academy.

Drake, C. (1993) 'Reproduction of musical rhythms by children, adult musicians, and adult nonmusicians'. *Perception and Psychophysics*, 53, 25–33.

Flowers, P.J. (1983) 'The effect of instruction in vocabulary and listening on nonmusicians' descriptions of changes in music'. *Journal of Research in Music Education,* 31, 179–190.

Gabrielsson, A. (1988) 'Timing in music performance and its relations to music experience'. In J.A. Sloboda (ed.), *Generative Processes in Music: The psychology of performance, improvisation and composition.* Oxford: Oxford University Press.

— (2010) 'Strong experiences with music'. In P.N. Julsin and J.A. Sloboda (eds), *Handbook of Music and Emotion: Theory, research, applications.* Oxford: Oxford University Press.

Gembris, H. and Schellenberg, G. (2003) 'Musical preferences of elementary school children'. In R. Kopiez, A.C. Lehmann, I. Wolther and C. Wolf (eds), *Proceedings of the Triennial Conference of the European Society for the Cognitive Sciences of Music (ESCOM)*. Hanover, 8–13 September.

Gordon, E.E. (1993) *Learning Sequences in Music: Skills, contents, and patterns – a music learning theory*. Chicago: GIA Publications.

Green, L. (2001) *How Popular Musicians Learn: A way ahead for music education*. London: Ashgate.

Green, S. (2009) 'Improving motivation for music at Key Stage 3'. In D. Bray (ed.), *Creating a Musical School*. Oxford: Oxford University Press.

Haack, P.A. (1970) 'A study involving the visual arts in the development of musical concepts'. *Journal of Research in Music Education*, 18, 392–398.

–– (1982) 'A study of high school music participants' stylistic preferences and identification abilities in music and the visual arts'. *Journal of Research in Music Education,* 30, 213–220.

Hallam, S. (2009) 'In what ways do we understand music?' Keynote presentation at the XVII Australian Society of Music Education Annual Conference, Launceston, Tasmania, July.

–– (2010a) 'Music education: the role of affect'. In P.N. Juslin and J.A. Sloboda (eds), *Handbook of Music and Emotion: Theory, research, applications.* Oxford: Oxford University Press.

–– (2010b) 'Cultural perceptions of musicality and musical expertise'. In M. Barrett (ed.), *A Cultural Psychology for Music Psychology.* Oxford: Oxford University Press.

Hallam, S. and MacDonald, R. (2009) 'The effects of music in educational and care settings'. In S. Hallam, I. Cross and M. Thaut (eds), *Oxford Handbook of Music Psychology*. Oxford: Oxford University Press.

Heddon, S.K. (1988) 'Music listening in grades six through nine'. *Update*, 7, 17–18.

Kokotsaki, D. and Hallam, S. (2007) 'Higher Education music students' perceptions of the benefits of participative music making'. *Music Education Research,* 9(1), 93–109.

Kopiez, R. and Lehmann, M. (2008) 'The 'open-earedness' hypothesis and the development of age-related aesthetic reactions to music in elementary school children'. *British Journal of Music Education*, 25, 121–138.

Kotsopoulou, A. (1997) 'Music in students' lives'. Unpublished MA dissertation, University of London.

-- (2001) 'A cross-cultural study of the use and perceived effects of background music in studying'. Unpublished PhD thesis, University of London.

Kotsopoulou, A. and Hallam, S. (2010) 'The perceived impact of playing music while studying: age and cultural differences'. *Educational Studies,* 36.

Lamont, A. and Cross, I. (1994) 'Children's cognitive representations of musical pitch'. *Music Perception*, 12(1), 27–55.

LeBlanc, A. (1980) 'Outline of a proposed model of sources of variation in musical taste'. *Bulletin of the Council for Research in Music Education,* 61, 29–34.

Macek, K. (1987) 'The photographic ear'. *Piano Quarterly*, 35(137), 46–48.

Mito, H. (2004) 'Role of daily musical activity in acquisition of musical skill'. In J. Tafuri (ed.) *Research for Music Education.* The 20th Seminar of the International Society for Music Education (ISME) Research Commission, Las Palmas, Spain. Salt Lake City, UT: ISME.

North, A.C. and Hargreaves, D.J. (1997) 'Experimental aesthetics and everyday music listening'. In D.J. Hargreaves and A.C. North (eds), *The Social Psychology of Music.* Oxford: Oxford University Press.

North, A.C., Hargreaves, D.J. and O'Neill, S.A. (2000) 'The importance of music to adolescents'. *British Journal of Educational Psychology*, 70, 255–272.

O'Brien, W. (1992) 'The effects of figurative language in music education instruction'. *Contributions to Music Education,* 19, 20–31.

Pollard-Gott, L. (1983) 'Emergence of thematic concepts in repeated listening to music'. *Cognitive Psychology*, 15, 66–94.

Poulin, B., Bigand, E., Dowling, W.J. *et al.* (2001) 'Do musical experts take advantage of global musical coherence in a recognition test?' Paper presented at Conference of the Society of Music Perception and Cognition, Queens University, Kingston, Ontario, August.

Qualifications and Curriculum Authority (QCA) (2007) National Curriculum 2007. London: QCA.

Richardson, C.P. (1996) 'A theoretical model of the connoisseur's musical thought'. *Bulletin of the Council for Research in Music Education,* 128, 15–24.

-- (1998) 'The roles of the critical thinker in the music classroom'. *Studies in Music from the University of Western Ontario*, 17, 107–120.

Savan, A. (1999) 'The effect of background music on learning'. *Psychology of Music*, 27(2), 138–146.

Shehan, P.K. (1986) 'Music instruction for live performance'. *Bulletin of the Council for Research in Music Education*, 88, 51–57.

–– (1987) 'Stretching the potential of music: Can it help reduce prejudices?' *Update*, 5, 17–20.

Sloboda, J.A., Hermelin, B. and O'Connor, N. (1985) 'An exceptional musical memory'. *Musical Perception*, 3, 155–170.

Sloboda, J., Lamont, A. and Greasley, A. (2009) 'Choosing to hear music: motivation, process, and effect'. In S. Hallam, I. Cross and M. Thayer (eds), *Oxford Handbook of Music Psychology*. Oxford: Oxford University Press.

Swanwick, K. (1994) *Musical Knowledge: Intuition, analysis and music education*. London: Routledge.

Tillman, B., Bharucha, J.J. and Bigand, E. (2000) 'Implicit learning of tonality: A self-organising approach'. *Psychological Review*, 107(4), 885–913.

Tolfree, E. (2005) 'An investigation into children's uses of and responses to music in their everyday lives'. Unpublished MA dissertation, Institute of Education, University of London.

Trehub, S.E. and Trainor, L.J. (1990) 'Rules for listening in infancy'. In J. Enns (ed.), *The Development of Attention: Research and theory*. Amsterdam: Elsevier.

Trehub, S.E., Schellenberg, E.G. and Hill, D. (1997) 'The origins of music perception and cognition: A developmental perspective'. In I. Deliege and J. Sloboda (eds), *Perception and Cognition of Music*. Hove: Psychology Press.

Zalonowski, A.H. (1986) 'The effects of listening instructions and cognitive style on music appreciation'. *Journal of Research in Music Education*, 33, 43–53.

Zillman, D. and Gan, S. (1997) 'Musical taste in adolescence'. In D.J. Hargreaves and A.C. North (eds), *The Social Psychology of Music*. Oxford: Oxford University Press.

Chapter 5

The role of singing

Jo Saunders, Maria Varvarigou and Graham Welch

Unlike many human attainments where a high degree of excellence must be reached before rewards can be received, singing offers rewards for everyone who attempts it.

(Mann, 1836, cited in Kincheloe,1985)

'I can't sing. As a singist I am not a success. I am saddest when I sing. So are those who hear me. They are sadder even than I am.'

('Artemus Ward's Lecture', *Oxford Dictionary of Quotations*, 1953)

Singing is a human activity whose value and purpose is observed in cultures throughout the world. Yet there is also a common paradox evidenced. Despite singing being a characteristic behaviour of the human condition, particularly within group settings, its development is subject to belief systems. Singing is often perceived as something that you either can or cannot do, often giving rise to formal negative labels, such as 'tone idiot' (*Onchi* in Japanese) (Welch, 1979). Many adult narratives about their childhood experiences in music provide evidence of this paradox, of being surrounded by singing, but not necessarily part of it.

Box 5.1 Musical self-concept and singing

Then in Grade 6 age 11+ . . . I stood up to sing it and she told me to sit down, that I couldn't sing. Well, I was devastated. . . . I'm sure I wanted to cry. Of course you came home, it was no good telling your parents at the time that something like this had happened to you. . . . And she was such a powerful person in the community. . . . It stayed with me for so long. It was so degrading at the time. Even in high school, if there was anything to do with music, I hated music. . . . I didn't learn it. I couldn't learn it, as I thought. . . . I'm sure that [incident] affected it, in a lot of ways . . . maybe she just didn't have the knowledge and it didn't come to her – 'I am doing something that's going to affect this child for most of her life.' That's probably the way it was.

(Knight, 2010: 105)

As can be seen from Box 5.1, another facet of the paradox is that research suggests that singing behaviours are subject to developmental processes in which individual potential is shaped (nurtured and/or hindered) by learning experiences within the culture (Welch, in press; Knight, 2010). Although singing is commonplace, it is also marked by cultural diversity, with development related to opportunity (e.g. Mang, 2007), the patterns of stress and intonation of the indigenous language (Azechi, 2008) and also the dominant characteristics of the local musical soundscapes (Welch *et al.*, 1997; Welch, 2006).

In many parts of the world, the ability to sing is seen as a mark of an individual's underlying musicality (see Sloboda *et al.*, 2005). Consequently, those individuals whose singing development has been hindered in some way are often labelled (including self-labelled) in some 'absolutist' sense under a bipolar categorisation of 'can'/'cannot' sing, with variations in their ascribed musical identity as a 'non-singer', 'tone-deaf', or 'tone-dumb' being found in virtually all cultures. Yet, as mentioned above, contrary evidence from developmental and neurological studies continues to emerge that singing and musical behaviours are context-bound and susceptible to improvement with appropriate experience which can be informal as well as formal (see Welch, 2006 for review). Furthermore, the recent wealth of studies into the neurosciences and music (see Avanzini *et al.*, 2005) continue to amass evidence of the multi-sited representation of musical behaviours in various regions of the brain, including singing (Kleber *et al.*, 2007).

An historical perspective

During the Middle Ages, song schools were founded throughout Europe for the dissemination of Roman church psalms and hymns, which were an important medium for worship (Plummeridge, 2001). Song schools were established in England, in Canterbury and York, where rigorous choral and liturgical training were central components of the curriculum. The Trivium and Quadrivium, originally developed by Alcuin (735–804) of York, put psalms and chants at the centre of the curriculum for monastic and song schools. With the increased power of the church and monasteries until the twelfth century, liturgical singing was a dominant part of the 'curriculum' for these children. The dissolution of the monasteries between 1536 and 1540 led to the closure of many schools and institutions associated with monasteries and chantries (Smith and Young, 2001). However, Henry VIII and his successors supported cathedral and collegiate choral foundations, sustaining a musical tradition that continues to the present day.

During the seventeenth and eighteenth centuries, singing and instrumental competence was, especially for the young girls of middle-class families, a desirable social skill and was viewed by parents as 'an asset to their daughters' matrimonial stock' (Cox, 2007) rather than as the 'meaningful or gainful substance of that success' (Banfield and Russell, 2001). For the working class, English folk songs that passed from generation to generation provided some form of musical literacy. For example, there has been a long tradition of musical performance among Northumbrian Pipers, in which tunes have been passed on or exchanged in manuscripts or printed form, as well as by aural memory across generations (Banfield and Russell, 2001).

During the nineteenth century, the need for school singing was stressed by church leaders in Britain as a way of improving congregational participation at worship. Also, in 1833, John Turner, published his *Manual of Instruction in Vocal Music,* in order to encourage the study of music and the engagement in music-making activities as a 'healthy leisure pursuit' for the working class, 'which could provide much needed alternatives to the vicious indulgences of the day' (Plummeridge, 2001: 619).

Choral singing outside the church has also been a popular activity in British society since the eighteenth century. For example, Handel's works, such as the *Messiah*, are believed to have encouraged participation by amateur singers in oratorios, which until then were mainly performed by professionals, and many societies came into being (Smith and Young, 2001). Such bodies promoted the development of musical literacy and the appreciation of choral music per se, especially among the middle class. The increasing availability of vocal scores for amateur singers, at a low cost, published by Alfred Novello (in England) and Breitkopf & Härtel (in Germany) also contributed to a remarkable growth in secular choral societies (Smith and Young, 2001). By 1900, a large number of choral societies and festivals, especially in the northern industrial towns and the cathedral cities in England, used the oratorio tradition as a form of mass cultural expression. Choral singing helped thousands of working men and women develop music sight-reading skills, which were pioneered by Sarah Glover, John Hullah and John Curwen in various Sol-Fa systems (Cox, 1996). Singing was viewed by Hullah as 'a potent force for good because it encouraged a relation to the whole and a subjection of individual interest to society' (Cox, 1996: 32).

Singing in schools

Free and compulsory education was established in 1870 in order to introduce literacy and numeracy to the working classes (Galton *et al.*, 1980), although the 'curriculum' requirements were formally restricted to reading, writing and arithmetic. Financial support for these 'day schools' was subject to 'payment by results', an element of which depended on pupils being able to 'sight sing' (Cox, 1993). Sight singing was also taught in schools to improve congregational singing in church (Rainbow, 1996). By the beginning of the twentieth century, music education for the majority was confined largely to the singing of folk songs and hymns, alongside choral singing for a minority. Singing was believed to promote 'positive moral qualities: patience, temperance, power of attention, presence of mind, self-denial, obedience and punctuality' (Hullah, 1854: 15, cited in Cox, 1993: 30). There was a perceived danger that singing in school would become a 'moral commissary, with the subject being incorporated less for its own merits, than as a means to an end'.

However, by 1907 the value of a music education (as opposed to a singing education) was increasingly recognised in the broadening of the secondary school curriculum, and music formed part of the School Certificate Examinations established in 1917 (see Chapters 2 and 14). As a result of a concerted effort from the then Inspector for Music, Arthur Somervell, and a growing belief about the potential of a *music* education, the subject title evolved from 'singing' to 'music' (Cox, 1993). A collection of 'national' songs was published for use in schools which aimed to describe the perceived positive characteristics of the English 'nature', including that of patriotism, self-reliance and good fellowship. The *National Song Book* was published in 1906 and became so widely used that by 1917 'it could be boasted that there was hardly a school in the country that did not possess a copy' (Cox, 2010).

Nevertheless, as evidence of the mixed progress of singing in schools, an inspection report based on London elementary schools (Board of Education, 1913) highlighted four main areas of concern: (1) the vocal quality used in song singing was inferior to that used during exercises; (2) insufficient thought was given to a graduated course of instruction; (3) there was an over-reliance on the Tonic Sol-Fa system; and (4) a need to focus on national and folk songs to improve the repertoire.

With a broadening in understanding of music education came a shift away from the dominance of vocal activity which was to mark a relative decline of singing in schools for subsequent decades. For example, during the 1920s, many teachers had embraced the use of the gramophone in class, enabling pupils to listen and 'appreciate' recorded music. Central to this advance was the belief that musical experiences should not be restricted to what the children could themselves perform (Moutrie, 1976). With the first Schools Radio broadcast made by BBC in 1924 and the invention of the reel-to-reel tape player in the 1930s, there were an increasing number of resources with which both specialist and non-specialist teachers could enrich the musical education of their pupils. The advocacy of the instrument-maker Arnold Dolmetsch was pivotal in the revival of the recorder. Later advancements in manufacturing processes enabled the subsequent mass production of the plastic recorder. This simple wind instrument was widely accepted as a classroom instrument. The Hadow Report (Board of Education, 1931) outlined a primary curriculum emphasising activity and experience for the pupil rather than a restatement of facts. Value was now attributed to music as part of a broader curriculum. It was suggested that teachers of music and singing should be able to read staff notation and play the piano, again, still appealing to the specialist interests of individual members of the teaching profession. One resource that appealed directly to the generalist primary teacher was *Time and Tune*, a long-running radio series first created by the BBC Schools Music Department in 1951. Alongside the broadcast programme were illustrated booklets (including notation) that enabled teachers to support and extend learning, with recordings of the programme that provided examples of the songs, accompaniments and suggestions for further work. This model of educational resource was to reappear as a fundamental support for primary school teachers faced with the requirements of the National Curriculum in the latter part of the twentieth century (see Chapters 2 and 13). Despite the suggestions of the Hadow Report (1931), this expanded range of musical resources meant that it was no longer a necessity that the teacher of music in a primary setting be a formally trained musician.

During the 1960s, as an outcome of the earlier work of Carl Orff, new pitched percussion instruments were introduced to the classroom. Xylophones and glockenspiels were manufactured and used in many primary settings, although the adoption of Orff's programme was partial at best – scant regard being paid to the continued need to develop aural and singing skills (Rainbow, 1996). The widespread adoption of instruments and recordings within the classroom mirrored the skills and training of the music teachers, themselves pianists or instrumentalists rather than singers (Rainbow, 1996).

In a review of primary education in England (HMI, 1978) singing was still firmly linked to the daily act of worship. In addition, the continued use of radio programmes was widespread and made a significant contribution to the music curriculum for those teachers who lacked confidence in their own vocal abilities, but recognised the importance of singing opportunities. It was noted, however, that the quality of pupil achievement inevitably 'reflected the teacher's competence as a musician' (HMI, 1978).

Music education in primary schools had travelled a very long way since the introduction of sight singing in the elementary schools of the 1870s. Resources and approaches to the teaching of music had flourished, although some had later withered. Plowden's assertion that 'at the heart of the educational process lies the child' (CACE, 1967) was replaced by 'the school curriculum is at the heart of education' (DES, 1981, cited in Gillard, 2004). What was clear was that there had been a gradual erosion of the centrality of singing within the primary classroom. Pupils who had rarely sung at school became teachers who rarely sang with their classes. The lived reality that only musicians taught music allowed self-identified 'non-musicians' (in the sense of non-specialist) to continue not to teach music to their own classes (Hennessy, 1995).

The Education Reform Act of 1988 stipulated the implementation of a uniform music curriculum for England and Wales (Stunell, 2006) (see Chapter 2). For singing, there was an expectation that the majority of pupils reaching the end of Year 6 (aged 11) would achieve Level 4. In practical terms, this would mean that the pupil would already be able to 'use their voices in different ways such as speaking, singing and chanting' (Level 1), 'sing with a sense of the shape of the melody' (Level 2), and 'sing in tune with expression' (Level 3) (DfEE/QCA, 1999).

Box 5.2 Singing resources

Publishers such as Oxford University Press and A&C Black responded to the renewed demand for resources, generated by the National Curriculum, by commissioning guides to singing and music making in and beyond the classroom context. One series of booklets called *Music Express* was published by A&C Black from 2002, with the *Singing Express* series following late in 2009. *Music Express* was widely adopted as a key text for primary school music across England. It was designed to cater not only for the music specialist teacher, but also the non-specialist, enabling all teachers to lead singing and music making in the classroom. The content of each booklet was explicitly linked to the National Curriculum for Music, both in content and design. Both the structure and the signposting used reflected the terminology and appearance of National Curriculum documents with which teachers had become increasingly accustomed. These publications provided teachers with additional schemes of work, individual lesson plans, and prompts for assessment and evaluation opportunities. Resources to support learning included recordings of the material and accompaniments, song sheets for photocopying and additional links for further learning. The *Voiceworks* series, published by Oxford University Press from early 2000 onwards, focused predominately on the use of the voice and singing, both within the classroom context and beyond. The materials included a wide repertoire from around the world, reflecting the stated aim of the National Curriculum to introduce pupils to an ever-widening breadth of available musics. Suggestions for warm-up activities and rehearsals techniques were included, as were recordings and scores for simple accompaniments. Subsequent publications extended both the age range and the repertoire available, continuing to make explicit links between the material presented and the National Curriculum requirements.

More widely, the popular media have recently been dominated (both as part of national campaigns and by public demand) by talent shows and competitions in which singing ability is rated and celebrated, including *Choir of the Year* (BBC), *X Factor* (ITV), *Britain's Got Talent* (ITV) and more recently, *Pop*

Star to Opera Star (ITV). Others have focused on the personal and social impact of singing, such as *The Choir: Boys Don't Sing* (BBC) and *The Choir: Unsung Town* (BBC). To date, a large number of these initiatives, programmes and sources of supplementary funding have focused on music outside the classroom context or music outside the school context.

New initiatives for singing

Recent political will has led to a flourishing of interest and funding for music initiatives aimed at young people in order to promote the intrinsic value of participation in the arts. Among these, the Music Manifesto was launched in July 2004 in order to 'provide greater opportunities for our children and young people to develop their creative potential through music' (DfES, 2005) (see Chapter 2). Singing was described as offering 'a universal route into participative music making for every child' and should therefore be made 'a central element of the universal music offer' (DfES, 2006: 8). As part of the 'new music education offer' the Music Manifesto suggested 'steps to a singing nation', in which a framework was introduced that would both stimulate and support singing in schools. Suggestions included teams of area 'singing leaders', who through modelling good practice would provide guidance and inspiration to teachers and professionals working with children. 'Singing clusters' would be created, both among primary or secondary schools (facilitating horizontal peer learning and social interaction) as well as between primary and secondary schools (facilitating vertical peer learning and providing opportunities for older pupils to lead singing activities). In addition, there was a need for an interactive website offering resources and advice about all things singing.

Local initiatives to encourage singing in primary settings included the 'Singing School Project' in Manchester. The aim of the scheme was to revive the tradition of singing in the classroom by providing free songbooks and CDs to the schools involved. Each year-group had about 100 songs on their CDs. Those children at the participant schools who achieved high levels of singing competency were able to join an area choir and access further voice training by professionals.

In addition, an area of renewed interest in singing activity across primary schools included the Chorister Outreach Programme, in which staff and choristers from cathedrals around England undertook visits to local primary schools to work with pupils and teachers. Workshops and rehearsals were undertaken during the school day in which pupils were introduced to a wide repertoire of songs. In most settings, this would lead to a joint concert at the cathedral, providing a prestigious venue and the opportunity for pupils and parents to celebrate singing in a community context.

In the summer of 2007, the suggested elements of the framework came together in the form of 'Sing Up', the Music Manifesto national singing programme. Focusing specifically on singing in primary schools, Sing Up offered an alternative and comprehensive attempt to re-ignite interest in singing. Selected schools became 'Singing playgrounds' schools. Expert adult singers would attend the school regularly and work with pupils in both classroom and playground contexts. 'Song leaders' were selected from among the pupil body, taught new material and given the responsibility of both passing on these songs and enabling other pupils to play singing games during playtimes. 'Singing stops' akin to bus stops were created in playgrounds so that pupils who wanted to sing could meet with other like-minded individuals. A magazine offering resources and guidance was distributed to every primary school, three times a year, closely linked to the Sing Up website. Teachers could search, download and bookmark relevant songs from an extensive 'song bank' for use in the classroom, as well as guidance on suitable vocal warm-up or extension activities. Materials could be searched according to topic (in order to feed into thematic lesson plans or to support learning in subjects other than music) or level of difficulty. Perhaps more importantly for the teaching staff involved, extensive training was available that gave practical advice and demonstration of the use of voice in the classroom.

In the autumn of 2007, the Institute of Education, University of London was appointed to undertake an evaluation of the national singing programme. Over the first two years of the Sing Up programme, 155 primary schools from across 26 different English administrative counties were visited. Researchers assessed the individual singing behaviour and development of 8,162 children (including 637 children more than once), mainly aged 7+ to 10+ years (Years 3–6) as well as gathering questionnaire data that related to children's attitudes to singing. During the second year, the data collection included an additional focus on the possible wider benefits of singing with pupil responses relating to their sense of self and social inclusion.

Previous research (Welch, 2006), as well as the Sing Up data, indicated that children's singing competency normally improves with age. When those children who had experience of Sing Up were compared with those who had not, evidence of a beneficial impact is found. Those with experience of Sing Up were found to demonstrate significantly greater gains in their singing development skills (see Figure 5.1) (Welch et al., under review).

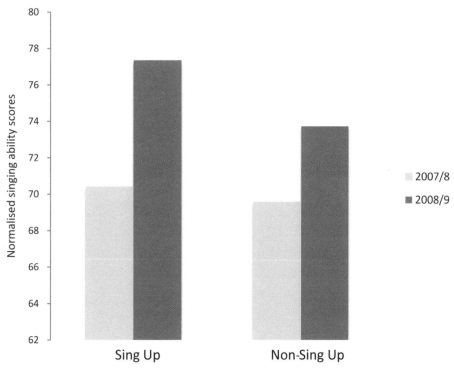

Figure 5.1: Average changes in assessed children's singing development over time (2007/8–2008/9). Children's singing behaviours were similar at the initial assessment but, one year later, those with experience of Sing Up had improved significantly more

These improvements were found irrespective of social background and ethnicity. There were examples of Sing Up linked improvements for boys as well as girls.

Box 5.3 Children's attitudes to singing

Attitudinal data from the participants' questionnaire responses suggested that girls tended to have a more positive attitude towards singing than boys. Younger children were likely to be more positive about singing than their older peers. This paradox – that as the child ages, they become more competent at singing, but report to like it less – can be related to the changes in the musical identity of the individual. Singing in a school context may, for many children, become a less attractive activity, as the influence of peer and popular music culture become more dominant in their concept of musical self. However, the data revealed that in settings where (a) children experienced singing activities provided by positive and expert role models (whether child and/or adult) and (b) also experienced a rich musical repertoire with opportunities for collective performance, then older children (both boys and girls) were much more likely to develop and sustain positive attitudes towards singing, as well as remaining engaged and motivated.

Children who were the most competent singers were also found to have a more positive view of themselves – not only as singers – but in general, linked to a stronger sense of social inclusion (see Figure 5.2) (Welch *et al.*, under review).

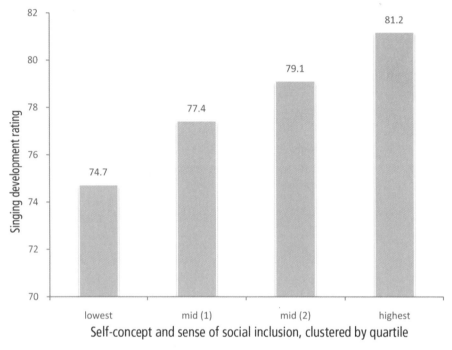

Figure 5.2: Chart illustrating the relationship between children's assessed singing development (where 100 = very competent) and their reported attitudes towards themselves (self-concept) and their sense of social inclusion

This research is ongoing, but the evidence so far would seem to indicate that the Sing Up portfolio of activities has been able to effect a significant improvement in children's singing and their attitudes towards singing as an activity.

Ways forward

Multidisciplinary research evidence suggests that a wide range of benefits accrue from participation in singing activities. These benefits are physical, psychological, social, musical and educational.

- The *physical* benefits include improved cardio-physiological fitness due to the aerobic nature of singing (e.g. Price and Gosling, 2003) and positive influences on emotional response and the immune system (Kreutz *et al.*, 2004), such as from modulation of the 'stress hormone' cortisol (Trehub, 2001).

- *Psychological* impacts include singing as a key form of intra- and inter-personal communication (Welch, 2005), associated with emotional bonding in infants (DeCasper and Fifer, 1980) and improvements in singers' mood states (Unwin *et al.*, 2002).
- *Social* benefits are often related to the psychological, particularly in choral settings, where participants report feeling more positive, alert and spiritually uplifted (Durrant and Himonides, 1998) and a strong sense of community (Bailey and Davidson, 2005).
- *Musical* and *educational* benefits arise because singing is a whole-brain activity that includes manipulation of musical parameters, such as pitch, rhythm, phrasing, loudness (Freudenhammer and Kreutz, 2009) and text (Welch, 2005). Learning and rehearsing the lyrics of songs in written format, for example, can have a beneficial impact on reading (Biggs *et al.*, 2008). Other educational benefits arise in relation to the topics of songs, promoting an increased social, cultural and historical awareness of the world.

These physical, mental and social benefits of singing (e.g. Kenny and Faunce, 2004) are particularly recognised by those charitable organisations, such as the Alzheimer's Society and Heart Research UK, whose work is focused on supporting older and/or health-threatened citizens.

It is important, therefore, that the educational system ensures that music graduates who are singers have followed a broadly based educational programme that embraces knowledge of the wider benefits of singing. This will provide them with additional skills and understanding that underpin their future effectiveness in a portfolio career of performance, teaching and other community activities (Welch and Papageorgi, 2008). Music graduates should also be expected to become relatively expert in more than one musical genre. The majority of specialist music teachers have a classical music background, but the kinds of music that they need in school (and the musics of their pupils) are much more diverse (Welch *et al.*, 2010). Undergraduate music courses should embrace this diversity as part of the preparation for the portfolio career that is common to the music profession.

For those musicians and music teachers who already have a grounding in singing, as well as those teachers new to this activity, there continues to be a need to advance their understanding of effective singing and choral pedagogy. For example, in the UK, choral education continues to be very uneven in its provision (Varvarigou, 2009) – unlike in the USA with its tradition of choral conducting degrees (DMAs) – resulting in scarce opportunities for extended study into how to foster collective singing development in others. Sing Up has proposed a set of seven principles for effective vocal leadership and these should continue to be interrogated to ensure that best practice is disseminated widely.

As far as children are concerned, since 2007, a groundwork has been established by the Sing Up programme to ensure that all those of primary age have high-quality singing experiences each week. Although 85 per cent of primary schools in England are now accessing the programme in some way, for many this is still only a beginning in their journey to consolidate singing into the lives of all their children. Sing Up is due to finish in March 2011 and, with over 17,000 mainstream state primary schools to reach as well as music provision outside school, its impact continues to need consolidation, not least because several recent studies have continued to emphasise that many primary school teachers lack confidence in their abilities to lead music education (in general), as well as singing and choral activities in particular (e.g. Stunell, 2006; Varvarigou, 2009).

Singing also needs to be supported in the musical lives of adolescents. While they are likely to spend many hours each week engaging with their own music outside school, the provision of singing in secondary schools continues to be variable in quality and 'an area of relative weakness' (Ofsted 2009: 22). Consequently, it would seem sensible for the concept of a 'national singing programme' to be extended systematically to secondary school pupils, as well as into the early years (following the positive Italian data – see Tafuri, 2009). Such provision should also include professional development opportunities for new and established secondary school teachers to engage more formally and collectively with the diverse singing cultures of their pupils. Too often there is a sense of professional isolation in the work of secondary music teachers (Ofsted, 2009; Welch et al., 2010), which is why there should be an emphasis on their collective development in leading singing. This provision will promote a deeper sense of shared professional identity and of professional inclusion, echoing the intrinsic social benefits that arise when people have the opportunity to sing as a group.

The recognition of the importance of singing has changed fundamentally for the better in recent years, not least because of the Sing Up initiative, the advocacy activities of many professional groups, and new multidisciplinary and interdisciplinary research. Recognition is also because of the word-of-mouth and media accounts of those who frequently daily experience the widespread benefits that singing can bring, such as in schools, homes, community settings, hospitals, daycare centres, prisons and workplaces. The evidence base is extensive. Hopefully, we will never again revert to a time when singing is for the few rather than the many.

Further reading

Welch, G.F. (2006) 'Singing and vocal development'. In G. McPherson (ed.), *The Child as Musician*. New York: Oxford University Press.

Welch, G.F., Himonides, E., Saunders, J., Papageorgi, I., Vraka, M., Preti, C. and Stephens, C. (2009) *Researching the Second Year of the National Singing Programme In England: An ongoing impact evaluation of children's singing behaviour and identity.* Institute of Education, University of London.

References

Avanzini, G., Koelsch, S., Lopez, L. and Majno, M. (2005) *The Neurosciences and Music II* (Vol. 1060). New York: Annals of the New York Academy of Sciences.

Azechi, N. (2008) 'Young children's rhythmic behaviour in singing: The influence of mother tongue on their development'. In S.D. Lipcomb, R. Ashley, R.O. Gjerdingen and P. Webster (eds), *Proceedings of the International Conference on Music Perception and Cognition 10* (CD-ROM). Society for Music Perception and Cognition.

Bailey, B.A. and Davidson, J. (2005) 'Effects of group singing and performance for marginalised and middle-class singers'. *Psychology of Music,* 33(3), 269–303.

Banfield, S. and Russell, I. (2001) 'England'. In S. Sadie (ed.), *The New Grove Dictionary of Music and Musicians.* London: Macmillan.

Biggs, M.C., Homan, S.P., Dedrick, R., Minick, V. and Rasinksi, T. (2008) 'Using an interactive singing software program: A comparative study of struggling middle school readers'. *Reading Psychology,* 29(3), 195–213.

Board of Education (1913) *Report on the Teaching of Singing in the London Elementary Schools.* London: HMSO.

Board of Education Consultative Committee and Hadow, W.H. (1931) *Report of the Consultative Committee on the Primary School.* London: HMSO.

Central Advisory Council for Education (CACE) (1967) *Children and Their Primary Schools: Report of the Central Advisory Council for England.* London: HMSO.

Cox, G. (1993) 'From Hullah to Somervell: The influence of HMI on music education in English schools, 1872–1928'. *Journal of Educational Administration and History,* 25(1),16–32.

–– (1996) 'A history of music education in England 1872–1928: A reflexive account of historical research'. *Research Studies in Music Education,* 6, 27–37.

–– (2007) 'The teaching and learning of music in the setting of family, church, and school: Some historical perspectives'. In L. Bresler (ed.), *International Handbook of Research in Arts Education.* New York: Springer.

–– (2010) 'Britain: Towards "a long overdue renaissance"'. In G. Cox and R. Stevens (eds), *The Origins and Foundations of Music Education*. New York: Continuum Press.

DeCasper, A.J. and Fifer, W. (1980) 'Of human bonding: Newborns prefer their mother's voices'. *Science,* 208, 1174–1176.

Department for Education and Employment (DfEE)/Qualifications and Curriculum Authority (QCA) (1999) *The National Curriculum for England: Music Key Stages 1–3*. HMSO/QCA.

Department for Education and Skills (DfES) (2005) 'Smith and Lammy welcome Music Manifesto's progress'. *Press Notice 2005/0088* (29 July). Online. <http://www.dcsf.gov.uk/pns/DisplayPN.cgi?pn_id=2005_0088> (accessed 08/04/2010).

Department for Education and Skills (DfES) (2006) *Making Every Child's Music Matter: Music Manifesto Report No 2*. London: DfES.

Durrant, C. and Himonides, E. (1998) 'What makes people sing together? Socio-psychological and cross-cultural perspectives on the choral phenomenon'. *International Journal of Music Education*, 32, 61–70.

Freudenhammer, W. and Kreutz, G. (2009) 'Development of vocal performance in 5th grade children: A longitudinal study of choral class singing'. *Proceedings,* 7th Triennial Conference of European Society for the Cognitive Sciences of Music (ESCOM) Jyväskylä, Finland, August.

Galton, M., Simon, B., Croll, P. and ORACLE (Project) (1980) *Inside the Primary Classroom*. London: Routledge & Kegan Paul.

Gillard, D. (2004) *The Plowden Report*. The Encyclopedia of Informal Education. <http://www.infed.org/schooling/plowden_report.htm> (accessed 11/02/2010).

Hennessy, S. (1995) *Music 7–11: Developing primary teaching skills*. London: Routledge.

Her Majesty's Inspectorate (HMI) (1978) *Primary Education in England: A survey by HM Inspectors of Schools*. London: HMSO.

Kenny, D.T. and Faunce, G. (2004) 'The impact of group singing on mood, coping and perceived pain in chronic pain patients attending a multidisciplinary pain clinic'. *Journal of Music Therapy*, XLI(3), 241–258.

Kincheloe, J.L. (1985) 'The use of music to engender emotion and control behaviour in church, politics and school'. *The Creative Child and Adult Quarterly*, 10(3), 187–196.

Kleber, B., Birbaumer, N., Veit, R., Trevorrow, T. and Lotze, M. (2007) 'Overt and imagined singing of an Italian aria'. *Neuroimage*, 36(3), 889-900.

Knight, S. (2010) 'A study of adult non-singers in Newfoundland'. Unpublished PhD thesis, Institute of Education, University of London.

Knowles, E. (ed.) (2009) *Oxford Dictionary of Quotations*. Oxford: Oxford University Press.

Kreutz, G., Bongard S., Rohrmann S., Hodapp, V. and Grebe, D. (2004) 'Effects of choir singing or listening on secretory immunoglobulin A, cortisol and emotional state.' *Journal of Behavioral Medicine*, 27, 623–635.

Mang, E. (2007) 'Effects of musical experience on singing achievement'. *Bulletin of the Council for Research in Music Education,* 174, 75–92.

Moutrie, J. (1976) 'The appreciation movement in Britain: MacPherson, Read and Scholes'. In K. Simpson (ed.), *Some Great Musical Educators: A collection of essays.* Borough Green: Novello.

Office for Standards in Education (Ofsted) (2009) *Making More of Music.* London: Ofsted.

Plummeridge, C. (2001) 'Music in schools'. In S. Sadie and J. Tyrrell (eds), *The New Grove Dictionary of Music and Musicians*. London: Macmillan.

Price, K. and Gosling, C. (2003) *The Effects of Vocal Function Exercises on the Lung Function of Trained Female Singers: A pilot investigation.* Melbourne: School of Health Sciences, Victoria University.

Rainbow, B. (1996) 'Onward from Butler: School music 1945–1985'. In G. Spruce (ed.), *Teaching Music*. London: Routledge.

Sloboda, J.A., Wise, K.J. and Peretz, I. (2005) 'Quantifying tone deafness in the general population'. *Annals of the New York Academy of Sciences,* 1060, 255–261.

Smith, J.G. and Young, P.M. (2001) 'Chorus'. In S. Sadie and J. Tyrrell (eds), *The New Grove Dictionary of Music and Musicians*. London: Macmillan.

Stunell, G. (2006) 'The policy context of music in English primary schools: How politics didn't help music'. *Research Studies in Music Education*, 26, 2–21.

Tarfuri, J. (2009) *Infant Musicality*. Farnham, UK: Ashgate.

Trehub, S.E. (2001) 'Musical predispositions in infancy'. In R.J. Zatorre and I. Peretz (eds), *The Biological Foundations of Music* (Vol. 930). New York: Annals of the New York Academy of Sciences.

Unwin, M.M., Kenny, D.T. and Davis, P.J. (2002) 'The effects of group singing on mood'. *Psychology of Music,* 30, 175–185.

Varvarigou, M. (2009) 'Modelling effective choral conducting education through an exploration of example teaching and learning in England'. Unpublished PhD thesis, Institute of Education, University of London.

Welch, G.F. (1979) 'Poor pitch singing: A review of the literature'. *Psychology of Music*, 7(1), 50–58.

–– (2005) 'Singing as communication'. In D. Miell, R. MacDonald and D. Hargreaves (eds), *Musical Communication*. New York: Oxford University Press.

–– (2006) 'Singing and vocal development'. In G. McPherson (ed.), *The Child as Musician*. New York: Oxford University Press.

–– (in press) 'Culture and gender in a cathedral music context: An activity theory exploration'. In M. Barrett (ed.), *A Cultural Psychology of Music Education*. New York: Oxford University Press.

Welch, G.F. and Papageorgi, I. (2008) *Investigating Musical Performance* (Briefing 61). London: Teaching and Learning Research Programme.

Welch, G.F., Sergeant, D.C. and White, P. (1996) 'The singing competencies of five-year-old developing singers'. *Bulletin for the Council for Research in Music Education*, 127, 155–162.

Welch, G.F., Sergeant, D.C. and White, P. (1997) 'Age, sex and vocal task as factors in singing "in-tune" during the first years of schooling'. *Bulletin of the Council for Research in Music Education*, 133, 153–160.

Welch, G.F., Purves, R., Hargreaves, D. and Marshall, N. (2010) 'Early career challenges in secondary school music teaching'. *British Educational Research Journal*. First published on 26 March 2010 (iFirst).

Welch, G.F., Himonides, E., Saunders, J., Papageorgi, I., Vraka, M., Preti, C. and Stephens, C. (under review) 'The impact of a national programme "Sing Up" on children's singing behaviour, development, attitudes to singing, self-concept and sense of social inclusion: An interim report'. *Psychology of Music*.

Chapter 6

Learning to play an instrument

Susan Hallam and Andrea Creech

Background

People have been playing musical instruments for centuries, with the earliest recorded examples being cave paintings from 33,000 BC showing flutes being played (Conard *et al.*, 2009). We can only speculate as to whether those playing were self-taught, had informal instruction from family or other musicians in wider communities of practice, or engaged in more formal tuition. In the more recent past we know that all of these approaches have been adopted although, for those learning Western classical instruments, tuition has typically been one-to-one and framed within a master–apprenticeship model (see Gaunt and Creech, 2011). The technological changes that have taken place since the latter part of the twentieth century have led to an explosion in the availability of recorded music, more and more access to world musics, and extensive media coverage of popular music – all of which has had an impact on the instruments and music that learners wish to engage with and on the ways in which they wish to learn. Opportunities to actively participate in music making have increased, and more children now learn to play an instrument than ever before. A 2005 YouGov survey, undertaken by the Music Industries Association of a representative sample of 2,000 people in the UK, found that 22 per cent currently played an instrument, while 85 per cent had learned to play an instrument as a young person and, of those no longer playing, 73 per cent regretted giving up playing (also see Chapters 17 and 18). Most of those learning to play an instrument during childhood will not go on to be engaged with music professionally. Educators need to adapt to these changing circumstances, redefine the aims of tuition and what are considered to be successful learning outcomes and develop more flexible approaches to pedagogy appropriate for particular genres, instruments, the aspirations of learners, and the opportunities available for long-term participation in making music.

The development of musical expertise

Whatever instrument is played, to attain even moderate levels of expertise requires practice (individual or group) and commitment (Ericsson, 2006). This enables complex motor and cognitive skills to become automated so that players can concentrate their attention on other elements of performance, for instance, communicating musical intentions to an audience, listening to other members of the group, following a conductor. There are generally considered to be three stages in such skill learning (Fitts and Posner, 1967). In the cognitive – verbal – motor – stage, learning is largely under conscious, cognitive control. The learner has to understand what is required to undertake the task and carries it out while consciously providing self-instruction. Teachers can support this by ensuring that students understand what is required of them and by providing learners with opportunities to develop a mental template of what they are aiming to achieve. This may be aural (knowing the sound), visual (knowing what a movement looks like) or kinaesthetic (knowing what a movement feels like). The teacher can act as a verbal prompter, providing a simultaneous scaffold for the learner gradually phasing out the prompts as the learner becomes proficient. In the associative stage, the learner begins to put together a sequence of responses which become more fluent over time. Errors are detected and eliminated. Feedback from the sounds produced and from the teacher play an important role in this process. In the autonomous stage, the skill becomes automated, is carried out without conscious effort, and continues to develop each time it is used, becoming more fluent and quicker. As one set of skills becomes increasingly automated, others are developing at earlier stages (Fitts and Posner, 1967). As learners develop these skills they also develop knowledge-based mental representations of what they are trying to learn so that they can check for errors, select possible future strategies and monitor progress. They also acquire more effective practising strategies – identifying difficult technical sections, rehearsing slowly, and placing a greater focus on interpretation (Jorgensen and Hallam, 2009). Changes also occur in the way that learning is conceptualised, with a move away from a focus on playing correctly to understanding the interpretative and constructive nature of playing music (see Hallam and Bautista, 2011).

An important element in the acquisition of musical expertise is the development of meta-cognitive (learning to learn) skills. Executive meta-cognitive strategies are concerned with the planning, monitoring and evaluation of learning and are crucial to all aspects of practising. They include knowledge of personal strengths and weaknesses, the nature of the task to be completed, possible strategies, the nature of the learning outcome and how to maintain motivation. Beginners, novices and experts vary in their knowledge and deployment of different practising and self-regulating strategies. There are also individual differences among musicians and novices at the same level of expertise (see Jorgensen and Hallam, 2009; Hallam and Bautista, 2011). Learning how to maintain high levels of motivation is crucial in developing expertise. Those who are most successful in motivating themselves balance formal or required practice tasks and informal, creative or motivating activities such as playing a favourite piece, improvising or playing in groups with others (McPherson and McCormick, 1999).

In the early stages of playing an instrument, learners are exploring possibilities and need to have encouraging, relatively uncritical support from teachers. If they decide to make an ongoing commitment to music they will look to teachers to act as role models and to provide constructive feedback on how they can improve (Sosniak, 1985; Manturzewska, 1990). Why some learners continue to play when others give up depends on a wide range of external factors (see Chapter 18) and also on the extent to which music satisfies internal motives and provides personal fulfilment. Musical activity can satisfy desires for achievement, curiosity and self-actualisation, and meet emotional needs, providing opportunities for positive social responses to performance, some degree of exhibitionism and the exploration of aggressive drives through the development of motor skills (see Hallam, 2009 for a review).

Selection to learn to play an instrument

In the early and mid-twentieth century, there was an assumption that individuals were endowed with different levels of 'musical ability' that were genetically based, relatively immutable and unchanging. A range of musical ability tests based on aural skills were developed to be administered to groups of students of different ages to assist teachers in the selection of pupils to access limited opportunities to play instruments, although some teachers preferred to use ability to sing as their assessment measure, while parents' ability to pay for lessons can also determine access (for a review see McPherson and Hallam, 2009). The concept of musical ability has been severely criticised in recent years and it has now been acknowledged that every child has the potential to develop musical skills. We know that musical ability tests assess what has been learned already and may therefore discriminate against those who have experienced an impoverished musical environment prior to testing. The diverse and complex skills involved in musical endstates (aural, cognitive, technical, musicianship, performance, learning and life skills) – and how the relationships between them and different combinations are required for any particular musical task or branch of the music profession – have now been recognised. If resources are limited and selection procedures are needed to allocate those resources, interest in music and motivation to engage with it are likely to be better determinants of success than traditional tests of musical ability. Initiatives in England and Scotland (see Chapter 17) which give every child the chance to learn to play an instrument for a limited period of time provide ample opportunities for children, their families and teachers to assess the extent to which they have a real commitment to and interest in music.

Choice of instrument

Choice of instrument is affected by many complex and interacting factors including convenience, availability, gender, parents' views, influence of the school or other providers, friends, interests, and enthusiasms (for a review see Gaunt and Hallam, 2009). The main reason for wanting to play an instrument is a personal desire to do so, although social influences are important for girls, school factors for boys. There continue to be gender differences in instrument preference, girls preferring small high-pitched orchestral instruments, boys large low-pitched instruments and, recently, drums, guitars and those dependent on other forms of technology (Green, 1997). These differences have resisted current trends where gendered roles are less well defined, although girls are less inhibited about selecting a masculine instrument (Hallam *et al.*, 2008). These stereotypical preferences can be manipulated, indicating that they are learned (Bruce and Kemp, 1993). The issue for teachers is whether they believe that it matters that the playing of some instruments is dominated by one gender.

The role of the family in learning

Sustained parental support is an important factor in the attainment of high levels of musical expertise. Having musical parents or a musical home environment influences participation in music and musical development. The parents of high achievers tend to be more involved in initial practice, attend lessons with their children and receive feedback from the teacher (Davidson *et al.*, 1996). Practical help in taking pupils to concerts and providing financial support is critical. Few children appear to be totally self-motivated to practise and the parents of those achieving at a high level tend to support practice, by encouragement, monitoring the length of time spent practising, or supervision. This sometimes leads to family friction, particularly in adolescence where the child wishes to exert their independence, and can lead to the child giving up playing (Sloboda and Davidson, 1996). Although there are examples of successful individuals who lacked parental support, in such cases aspects of the wider environment compensated, accompanied by intense personal determination (MacKinnon, 1965). For teachers, promoting positive relationships with parents is clearly important in supporting learning. Providing opportunities for children to perform in public is an extremely effective way of engaging parents, who frequently are unaware of the extent of the accomplishments of their children.

Goals and aims of learning to play an instrument

The goals and aims of learning to play an instrument are rarely made explicit by teachers or learners but are crucial in determining what is learned. While there are no 'correct' aims it is important that teachers and learners share similar aims if progress is to be made. Most who learn to play an instrument will not pursue careers in music. They may become active amateur music makers, express their love of music through listening, or if their musical experiences have been particularly negative turn to other recreational activities. The recognition that everyone should have the opportunity to learn to play an instrument presents particular challenges relating to the aims of tuition. While expecting high standards and making learning enjoyable are not mutually exclusive there is a need to ensure that a balance is maintained. Overall, most teachers perceive that there are a wide range of benefits of learning to play an instrument beyond pursuing a career in music. These include:

- enhanced social skills
- love of music
- teamworking
- a sense of achievement
- increased confidence and self-discipline
- opportunities for relaxation
- enhanced concentration, physical coordination, and cognitive, listening, creative and organisational skills
- giving enjoyment to others.

(Hallam and Prince, 2000)

The aims of instrumental tuition need to be formulated in ways that take these factors into account. One way forward is to formulate aims in terms of the wide variety of skills which can be acquired through active engagement with music. Box 6.1 provides an outline of the kinds of skills which might be included. This could serve as a resource for teachers in establishing what they can offer to learners and could also be used to negotiate a curriculum with individual students.

Box 6.1 Skills which can be acquired in learning to play an instrument

Aural skills, supporting the development of:
- rhythmic accuracy and a sense of pulse
- good intonation
- the facility to know how music will sound without having to play it
- playing by ear
- improvisational skills.

Cognitive skills, supporting the development of:
- reading music
- transposition
- understanding keys
- understanding harmony
- understanding the structure of the music
- the memorisation of music
- composing
- understanding different musical styles and their cultural and historic contexts.

Technical skills, supporting the development of:
- instrument-specific skills
- technical agility
- articulation
- dynamic control
- good intonation
- expressive tone quality.

Musicianship skills, supporting the development of:
- expressive playing
- sound projection
- control
- conveying musical meaning.

Performance skills, supporting the development of:
- communication with an audience
- communication with other performers
- being able to coordinate a group
- presentation to an audience.

Creative skills, supporting the development of:
- interpretation
- improvisation
- composition.

Evaluative skills, supporting the development of:
- listening with understanding
- being able to describe and discuss music
- being able to make comparisons between different types of music and performances
- critical assessment of personal performance, improvisation and compositions
- being able to use technology to provide feedback (recording, video)
- monitoring progress.

Self-regulatory skills, supporting the development of:
- managing the process of learning
- managing practice
- enhancing concentration
- enhancing motivation
- preparing for performance.

Perhaps the most important set of skills which need to be developed are those which enable learners to become independent and autonomous. Equipped with these skills learners can continue their engagement with music long after they cease to have tuition. What are these key skills? Learners need to develop meta-cognitive and self-regulatory skills, be able to identify goals, work towards them and ensure that the learning environment is conducive to meeting their goals, and have and be able to apply a range of critical and self-evaluative techniques. They need to recognise the importance of listening extensively to all kinds of music, comparing and critically evaluating it and its performance and seek out and act upon feedback from others in relation to their own playing. They need to understand the importance of practice and have developed effective strategies for undertaking it. We might expect that they would also take advantage of opportunities for playing, improvising, composing and performing with others. For this they would need social, planning, and organisational skills.

Where tuition is on a one-to-one basis, decisions about repertoire and genre can be negotiated with the learner. Where groups of children are learning, it is the responsibility of the teacher to establish an overarching framework, providing some choices within it to maintain motivation. In some situations the framework will be prescribed by an organisation – but where it is not, and the teacher has the opportunity to determine the nature of the curriculum, factors which might be taken into account include:

- the musical culture of the local community
- the long-term prospects for learners to engage in music making in that community

- the likelihood of support for the musical activity in families
- available resources and sustainability in the longer term
- the teacher's personal musical and pedagogic skills and efficacy in relation to the particular musical activity.

It is particularly important to consider issues relating to the long-term sustainability of the activity and the opportunities for ongoing engagement.

Creative activities in instrumental tuition

Until relatively recently, instrumental tuition tended to focus on the learning of repertoire, with creativity largely being limited to the development of interpretation. Being able to play by ear and improvise is now becoming more accepted as a legitimate element of instrumental tuition across a range of instruments. Improvisation relies on the prior automation of a range of skills which the performer can then draw on to develop unique musical contributions. However, initially, memorising short fragments can generate acceptable improvisations even in rule-governed genres like jazz, although they may be somewhat mechanical.

The development of high-level aural skills is central to learning to improvise. For the expert improviser, knowing how a melody will sound before it is played is key. In reaching this expert level the learner develops through a series of stages:

- exploration through play
- process-oriented improvisation – musical doodling without any overall coherence
- product-oriented improvisation where some musical techniques are adopted into the playing
- a more fluid improvisation where there is more control over the technical aspects of performance
- more structured improvisation
- the development of a personal style where the improvisation is fluent and the appropriate musical style is adopted.

(Kratus, 1996)

This level of expertise takes considerable time to develop and for most instrumentalists relies on frequent opportunities to play in improvising groups, although there are notable exceptions – organists, for instance.

While learning to improvise as part of instrumental tuition is valuable in its own right, the skills acquired also provide students with clearer comprehension of music performed with notation (Azzara, 2002) and more highly developed aural and sight-reading skills (Wilson, 1971). There also seem to be personal and social benefits to group improvisation. Students who reported anxiety regarding solo performances found that playing in group improvisations and making rhythmic embellishments of familiar tunes helped alleviate their concerns and gave them greater opportunities for self-expression (Leavell, 1997).

Musical literacy

Closely related to the debate about the inclusion of improvisation in the instrumental curriculum is that relating to teaching the reading of musical notation. Many cultures have devised systems to encode and notate their music for the purpose of ensuring that the music can continue to be played by future generations – the more complex the music, the greater the necessity for notation. Cultures where music is based within aural traditions rely on musicians playing by ear and passing on knowledge to the next generation through shared experiences. In the twenty-first century, both cultures exist alongside each other. Whether reading notation is taught to students or they learn by ear needs to be an informed decision, based on the musical genre within which they are engaged and their future likely needs. Both sets of skills will be useful to most learners and there is no reason why they cannot be taught in parallel. Difficulties can arise when a learner has been taught exclusively in one mode and then needs to develop the other.

No methods have been demonstrated to consistently assist learners in reading music, although possibilities include tonal pattern instruction, the use of mnemonic devices, tape-recorded aural models or computer software, changes to notation systems, the use of body movements, singing, practising with accompaniments, emphasising the vertical aspects of the score with pianists, engaging students in creative activities such as composing, performing and listening, experiencing music-reading activities before formal explanations and placing song texts higher or lower in conjunction with higher and lower melodic pitches. There is currently no evidence to indicate that any of these methods is any more effective than any other (Hodges, 1992). Once students have acquired some skill, sight-reading and fluency can be improved by making music with others where momentum has to be maintained – for instance, by accompanying someone or playing in a group (Banton, 1995; Kornicke, 1995; Lehmann and Ericsson, 1996).

Technique and musicianship

Instrumental teachers are frequently berated for spending too much time focused on issues of technique and accuracy at the expense of musicianship. Observations of lessons tend to support this (Thompson, 1984; see also

Chapter 18). However, there are good reasons for this focus. If music is played inaccurately, with a lack of articulation, poor intonation, and an unattractive tone it will be evaluated negatively by listeners, whoever they are. It is only when these technical skills are sufficiently secure that interpretation becomes paramount in the evaluative process. In developing these skills instrumental teachers provide very high levels of detailed formative feedback of the kind that teachers in other subjects are currently being exhorted to deliver (Kennell, 1992). It is ironic that instrumental teachers have been criticised for this, although there may be some justification for the criticism if learners are not praised for what they have achieved and feedback is destructive or consistently negative. Teachers are increasingly developing ways of teaching technique musically to enhance pupils' enjoyment and motivation – for instance, teaching and playing scales with 'jazzy' rhythms, asking groups of students to play scales in thirds or contrary motion, getting students to compose 'studies' which rehearse particular techniques.

What kind of instrumental tuition is needed?

Historically, individuals have learnt to play instruments in a variety of ways. Some have been self-taught, modelling their practice on recordings or deriving guidance from self-help tutors. Some have learnt through joining a community of practice where their instrumental tuition has been part of a wider musical experience – for instance, the brass band or jazz traditions. Some have engaged in informal learning through combinations of trial and error, repetition, reading, listening, and emulating, and watching and taking advice from other players (Green, 2001; Cope, 2002). Some have received formal tuition individually, or in small or large groups. There are now emerging opportunities to learn instruments using a variety of computer software, through the web, or other interactive technology.

There is no 'best' way to learn to play a musical instrument. Human beings are pre-programmed to learn. It is a natural process, and musical skills can be acquired in a variety of ways. The particular method selected needs to be appropriate for the particular context and the desired aims. It needs to be 'fit for purpose'. Combinations of methods may be the most effective. Table 6.1 sets out the advantages and disadvantages of various approaches. Where learning is within a formal teaching context the teacher can adopt didactic methods of transmitting knowledge or more facilitative methods which support discovery learning. Teacher practices tend to be related to their beliefs about learning, although the elements of the context within which they are working exert very powerful influences – for instance, school, college, university, the genre, the instrument, the curriculum, the assessment system (Hallam and Ireson, 1999). In music, which requires the acquisition of a wide range of different skills, teachers need to be to able adapt their teaching strategies to meet current needs. They also need to develop good relationships with learners, be enthusiastic, offer inspiration and provide feedback which is constructive rather than destructive.

Table 6.1 Advantages and disadvantages of different learning contexts

	Advantages	Disadvantages
Self-tuition through experimentation or tutor books	• Inexpensive • Learning is independent of time and location • The pace of learning is set by the individual • Engenders independent learning	• Lack of expert feedback and guidance • Requires high levels of self-motivation and self-regulation • Lack of musical interaction with others
Self-tuition through technology	• Learning is independent of time and location • The pace of learning is set by the individual • Some systems allow learners to interact with others • Students may find using technology natural and motivating	• Depending on the program, may not include feedback • Possible lack of musical interaction with others • Requires high levels of self-motivation and self-regulation • More suited to some instruments than others
Informal peer learning	• Encourages listening skills • Fosters teamwork and other transferable skills • Fosters independence • Can promote creativity • Supportive environment	• Lack of immediate access to expert feedback and guidance • Unsupportive peers • Destructive criticism
Workshop sessions/ master classes	• Can be motivating, inspirational and creative • Can provide advice on technical and musical issues	• Lack of continuity • Limited opportunities for long-term developments • Can undermine previous learning
Consultation or top-up lessons	• Cost- and time-effective • Provides a fresh eye • Supports autonomous learning	• Could undermine previous learning • Could identify problems with no ongoing support

Learning through a community of practice	• Provides an immediate authentic musical experience • Expert advice immediately available	• Learning of technique is determined by the group repertoire • Limited opportunities for creative work
Advanced student mentoring	• Provides supervision for practice • Ensures practice is focused • Supports the learner • Consolidates skills for the mentor	• Could inhibit learning of self-regulatory and meta-cognitive skills • Could encourage the development of dependency
One-to-one tuition	• Individual can progress at their own speed • Allows focus on the needs of the individual • Detailed feedback and guidance provided at the individual level	• Resource intensive • Students and teachers can be isolated
Small group tuition with students of same standard and instrument	• Effective use of time • Students learn from and support each other • Opportunities for group and individuals to receive feedback and guidance	• Not always possible to identify individual difficulties
Small group tuition with students of different instruments	• Provides ensemble opportunities	• Time not used effectively if teacher listens to each instrument separately • Lack of repertoire and tutor books
Large group tuition of same instruments	• Effective use of time and resources	• Feedback and guidance to individuals is difficult
Large group tuition of ensembles	• Provides immediate musical experience	• Progress may be slow, as teacher needs to explain and teach technical demands of each instrument separately

Box 6.2 Example of whole-class teaching from the Wider Opportunities programme: A string class in Sutton

All of Year 4 in a primary school in Sutton is learning the violin, viola or cello. Their classroom teacher is learning alongside the children, gaining a first-hand insight into the complexity and rewards of learning a musical instrument. The lessons are led by a team including a violin/viola specialist, a cello specialist and a musicianship teacher. These teachers demonstrate an enthusiasm and love for making music that is evidently infectious among the learners, who all appear to be highly motivated and engaged. The class has two 40-minute lessons each week. Instruments are provided but pupils do not take them home between lessons. Bows are tightened and rosined and violins, violas and cellos tuned by the teachers before the class arrive in the hall. The lesson is well organised and moves along at a fast pace, involving rhythm activities away from the instruments, motor control games relating to instrumental technique and playing by ear as well as from notation (read from an overhead projector). Questionnaires about their experience in this Wider Opportunities pilot were completed by Year 4. The responses indicate that the programme provided pupils with a highly enjoyable and motivating introduction to string instruments. Ninety-two per cent of the pupils said they enjoyed learning an instrument and that they were happy they had this opportunity at school. Seventy-seven per cent of pupils would have liked to be able to practise, and 76 per cent wanted their parents to hear them play. The responses suggested that there could be a substantial number of pupils who would wish to carry on learning.

(Creech, in preparation)

Box 6.3 Example of instrumental teacher support for classroom work at secondary level

Lathom High School developed their own version of Musical Futures (see Chapter 14), inspired by the Whole Curriculum Approach. Pupils have taster sessions on different instruments, form bands and develop their own versions of songs with support from visiting musicians. The head of music secured support from Lancashire Music Service. This involved the school paying for one peripatetic instrumental teacher and the Music Service funding another peripatetic music teacher for each class, as well as some extra instruments. After piloting it was felt by staff and pupils that Year 8s responded best to the activity, so the programme has continued primarily with Year 8. The pupils have become more motivated. This is attributed to the level of ownership that they have over their learning. Teaching has changed, and pupils are now trusted to work alone. There has been a major impact on the music department, with increased activity during break and lunch times, with queues of pupils wanting to use practice rooms and instruments. Many more pupils perform in assemblies – usually pupils who have not previously played an instrument. This has led to other staff commenting on the performance of pupils that they had not realised had musical skills.

(Musical Futures, 2009)

Box 6.4 Widening participation: An observation report of a whole-class clarinet lesson

Opening

The group entered the room, placed their instruments at the side and formed a circle (standing). Each teacher then sang 'Hello Year 5' to the class which the pupils copied back (the melody shape varied between each teacher).

Warm-up

'Eights': The pupils performed a physical routine (gradually reducing the number of times each pattern was repeated from eight down to one), first with counting out loud and then by internalising the pulse.

Song: 'John Kanaka' (new last week)

The teacher briefly revised last week's discussion about the type of song – a sea shanty. Pupils performed a short vocal warm-up which drew attention to breathing and clear diction. Pupils enjoyed the song and the added actions supported pulse work. Effective questioning was used to encourage pupils to listen to words describing the structure of the song. The teacher checked that the whole class was on task by asking them all to show on their fingers the number of times the words 'John Kanaka' were sung. 'Discuss with your partner' also worked well.

Teacher demonstration was clear and 'off we go' was always sung by the teacher at pitch, in preparation for the class to pitch accurately. As the pupils were asked to repeat, clear guidelines were given for improvement and progress was made. Reference was made to how the song was to be used the following week.

Song: 'Harry Potter' round ('Frère Jacques' tune)

The teacher sang the song to the class, with excellent modelling. All were asked to sing and encouraged to show the pitch shape with their hands. The quality of singing improved when the teacher asked the class to sing more quietly. Demonstrations from the teacher supported the learning, e.g. the ostinato 'Harry Potter – where's he gone?' was sung expressively, and attention was drawn to the phrasing. Pupils sang as a two- and three-part round, with the ostinato making a fourth part. The class teacher was involved in leading one of the singing lines. The pitch fluctuated when four parts were involved and a challenge was set to improve this with more practice over the coming weeks.

Music Service workshop for Wider Opportunities pupils

The teacher highlighted those in the class who had attended the Music Service workshop the previous week, and pupils were asked to share their experience with the class.

Instruments

The class took their instruments and put the clarinets together. The class teacher was very involved in supporting pupils.

Warm-up: Call and response

Pupils copied accurately and the other two teachers modelled fingering. There was constant reference through demonstration and questioning to posture and tonguing (cheeks not puffed out). On the last call, pupils were asked to recognise the tune (the last line of Harry Potter) and asked to notice that the pitch went up rather than down, necessary because the pupils' class had not learnt the lower note yet on the clarinet.

'Harry Potter' round

The notation was displayed on the wall and pupils were asked to point to the notation and find the melody they had just played. Different sections were looked at. This built on the previous week's work where they had used a series of flash cards to order the melodic line. Pupils were asked to decide which part was the most difficult, and why. Pupils were asked to sing notes and put the correct fingering on the instrument while singing. The teacher often invited pupils without their hands up to answer questions. Mistakes were recognised by the teacher and used constructively to facilitate learning. Individual praise was used effectively.

Russian folk tune

The other two teachers performed the piece. The sensitive accompaniment on the piano set the musical context. Effective questioning was used to describe the expressive quality of the music and the structure of the piece. The notation was displayed and the new note – dotted minim 'stroll' – explored. During the next demonstration all pupils were asked to try to finger correctly on their instrument while listening to the performance. All played the piece and, with careful step-by-step guidance, improved the quality of reading and the quality of the sound.

Listening extract: Tchaikovsky's Symphony no. 4

Active listening was encouraged and the pupils were asked to pick out the 'Russian folk tune' whenever it featured in the extract. There was a brief discussion about the instruments used and the mood and character of the piece.

Homework set

Pupils were asked to look at the 'Russian folk tune' for next time, and reference was made to their *Pupil Practice Book*.

(Derived from observation of a class in Barking & Dagenham)

To what extent do instrumental teachers need to be specialists?

An ongoing issue in instrumental teaching concerns the extent to which instrumental teachers need to be specialists, and how far their skills can be transferred to teaching other instruments. It is not uncommon for instrumental teachers to play or teach more than one instrument. Violinists may also teach the viola, cellists may teach the double bass. In some cultures a teacher may teach children to play a range of instruments that they may not be able to play themselves. Is this likely to be detrimental to the attainment and progress of learners? This is a contentious issue. While there are benefits to teachers being able to demonstrate in lessons, the evidence suggests that teachers model musical behaviour relatively infrequently (Rosenthal, 1984) and models can be provided through videos and recordings which students can use at home to support their learning. While in an ideal world teachers might only teach the instruments that they are able to play to a high standard, there may be circumstances where it is preferable to enable pupils to access a wider range of instruments than would be possible if this was the case.

Assessment issues

The effects of assessment on learning are powerful (see Chapter 9). In music, public performance and graded examinations can enhance motivation. However, there have been criticisms of the nature of the graded examination syllabuses, their relative lack of change since their inception and the way that they have determined, over many years, much of the instrumental music curriculum. While current graded examination systems have considerable value in motivating students it is difficult to see how they can be utilised with the very large groups of pupils currently being offered opportunities to play an instrument. New assessment systems may need to be devised.

Endnote

The processes underpinning the learning of a musical instrument are universal and apply across all cultures. All require time, effort and commitment, although the extent to which these are needed depends on the nature of the music itself and the particular cultural traditions which pertain in relation to its creation and performance. As more people have opportunities to learn to play an instrument, educators need to consider what the aims of tuition should be. Most learners will not go on to pursue careers in music, but if they experience enjoyable and stimulating musical experiences they may continue to actively participate in music making throughout their lives. The aims of instrumental (and vocal) teaching should therefore be to make musical experiences enjoyable while continuing to provide challenge and intellectual stimulation. Focusing on supporting learners to be able to learn independently – so that they can adapt easily and rapidly to new musical environments and draw on the skills they have learned to satisfy current and future needs – may be the way forward.

Further reading

Creech, A. (2009) 'The role of the family in supporting learning'. In S. Hallam, I. Cross and M. Thaut (eds), *The Oxford Handbook of Music Psychology*. Oxford: Oxford University Press.

Hallam, S. (2006) *Music Psychology in Education*. London: Institute of Education, University of London.

References

Azzara, C.D. (2002) 'Improvisation'. In R. Colwell and C. Richardson (eds), *The New Handbook of Research on Music Teaching and Learning*. Oxford: Oxford University Press.

Banton, L. (1995) 'The role of visual and auditory feedback during the sightreading of music'. *Psychology of Music*, 23(1), 3–16.

Bruce, R. and Kemp, A. (1993) 'Sex stereotyping in children's preferences for musical instruments'. *British Journal of Music Education*, 10, 213–217.

Conard, N.J., Malina, N. and Munzel, S.C. (2009) 'New flutes document the earliest musical tradition in south western Germany'. *Nature*, 460, 737–740.

Cope, P. (2002) 'Informal learning of musical instruments: The importance of social context'. *Music Education Research*, 4(1), 93–104.

Creech, A. (2009) 'The role of the family in supporting learning'. In S. Hallam, I. Cross and M. Thaut (eds), *The Oxford Handbook of Music Psychology*. Oxford: Oxford University Press.

–– (in preparation) *Pupil Motivation and Engagement in Learning a String Instrument: A wider opportunities strings pilot*. London: Institute of Education.

Davidson, J.W., Howe, M.J.A., Moore, D.G. and Sloboda, J.A. (1996) 'The role of family influences in the development of musical ability'. *British Journal of Developmental Psychology*, 14, 399–412.

Ericsson, K.A. (2006) 'The influence of experience and deliberate practice on the development of superior expert performance'. In K.A. Ericsson, N. Charness, P.J. Feltovich and R.R. Hoffan (eds), *The Cambridge Handbook of Expertise and Expert Performance*. Cambridge: Cambridge University Press.

Fitts, P.M. and Posner, M.I. (1967) *Human Performance*. Belmont, CA: Brooks Cole.

Gaunt, H. and Creech, A. (2011) 'The changing face of individual instrumental tuition: value, purpose and potential'. In G. McPherson and G. Welch (eds), *Oxford Handbook of Music Education*. Oxford: Oxford University Press.

Gaunt, H. and Hallam, S. (2009) 'Individuality in the learning of musical skills'. In S. Hallam, I. Cross and M. Thaut (eds), *Oxford Handbook of Music Psychology*. Oxford: Oxford University Press.

Green, L. (1997) *Music, Gender and Education*. New York: Cambridge University Press.

–– (2001) *How Popular Musicians Learn: A way ahead for music education*. London: Ashgate.

Hallam, S. (2009) 'Motivation to learn'. In S. Hallam, I. Cross and M. Thaut (eds), *Handbook of Psychology of Music*. Oxford: Oxford University Press.

Hallam, S. and Bautista, A. (2011) 'Processes of instrumental learning'. In G. McPherson and G. Welch (eds) *The Oxford Handbook of Music Education*. Oxford: Oxford University Press.

Hallam, S. and Ireson, J. (1999) 'Pedagogy in the secondary school'. In P. Mortimore (ed.) *Pedagogy and its Impact on Learning*. London: Sage.

Hallam, S. and Prince, V. (2000) *Research into Instrumental Music Services: Final report*. London: Department for Education and Employment.

Hallam, S., Rogers, L. and Creech, A. (2005) *Survey of Local Authority Music Services 2005 (Research Report 700)*. London: Department for Education and Skills.

Hallam, S., Rogers, L. and Creech, A. (2008) 'Gender differences in musical instrument choice'. *International Journal of Music Education,* 26(1), 7–19.

Hodges, D.A. (1992) 'The acquisition of music reading skills'. In R. Colwell (ed.), *Handbook of Research on Music Teaching and Learning.* New York: Schirmer Books.

Jorgensen, H. and Hallam, S. (2009) 'Practising'. In S. Hallam, I. Cross and M. Thaut (eds), *Oxford Handbook of Music Psychology.* Oxford: Oxford University Press.

Kennell, R. (1992) 'Toward a theory of applied music instruction'. *The Quarterly Journal of Music Teaching and Learning*, III(2), 5–16.

Kornicke, L.E. (1995) 'An exploratory study of individual difference variables in piano sight-reading achievement'. *Quarterly Journal of Music Teaching and Learning*, 6, 56–79.

Kratus, J. (1996) 'A developmental approach to teaching music improvisation'. *International Journal of Music Education*, 26, 3–13.

Leavell, B. (1997) 'Making the change: Middle school band students' perspectives on the learning of musical-technical skills in jazz performance'. Doctoral dissertation, University of North Texas. *Dissertation Abstracts International*, 57(7), 2931A.

Lehmann, A.C. and Ericsson, K.A. (1996) 'Structure and acquisition of expert accompanying and sight-reading performance'. *Psychomusicology,* 15, 1–29.

MacKinnon, D.W. (1965) 'Personality and the realization of creative talent'. *American Psychologist*, 20, 273–281.

Manturzewska, M. (1990) 'A biographical study of the life-span development of professional musicians'. *Psychology of Music,* 18(2), 112–139.

McPherson, G. and Hallam, S. (2009) 'Musical potential'. In S. Hallam, I. Cross and M. Thaut (eds), *Oxford Handbook of Music Psychology.* Oxford: Oxford University Press.

McPherson, G.E. and McCormick, J. (1999) 'Motivational and self-regulated learning components of musical practice'. *Bulletin of the Council for Research in Music Education*, 141, 98–102.

Musical Futures (2009) Online. <http://www.musicalfutures.org> (accessed 27/12/2010).

Rosenthal, R.K. (1984) 'The relative effects of guided model, model only, guide only, and practice only treatments on the accuracy of advanced instrumentalists' musical performance'. *Journal of Research in Music Education*, 32, 265–273.

Sloboda, J.A. and Davidson, J. (1996) 'The young performing musician'. In I. Deliege and J.A. Sloboda (eds), *Musical Beginnings: Origins and development of musical competence.* Oxford: Oxford University Press.

Sloboda, J.A., Davidson, J.W., Howe, M.J.A. and Moore, D.G. (1996) 'The role of practice in the development of performing musicians'. *British Journal of Psychology*, 87, 287–309.

Sosniak, L.A. (1985) 'Learning to be a concert pianist: Developing talent in young people'. In B.S. Bloom (ed.), *Developing Talent in Young People.* New York: Ballantine.

Thompson, W.F. (1984) 'The use of rules for expression in the performance of melodies'. *Psychology of Music,* 17(1), 63–82.

Wilson, J. (1971) 'The effects of group improvisation on the musical growth of selected high school instrumentalists'. Doctoral dissertation, New York University. *Dissertation Abstracts International*, 31(7), 3589A.

YouGov Survey (2005) October. <http://www.mia.org.uk> (accessed 30/01 /2010).

Chapter 7

Creativity

Susan Hallam and Lynne Rogers

Innovation is a crucial element of modern economies. New ideas are constantly needed to generate new products and address the problems faced by increasingly globalised and technological societies. In the twenty-first century a workforce is required which has creative skills and is able to use initiative independently while also being able to work in teams. Education systems are faced with the challenge of equipping individuals with skills that will enable them to fulfil their potential in a world where change is rapid and relentless. Music education can play a crucial role in enabling young people to develop independent and teamworking skills and enhance their creativity through composing and improvising.

Globalisation has had an impact on the way that we think about composition and improvisation. In many cultures, particularly where music is not notated, music making is a social activity, the role of the individual as a composer is of less importance, and the division between improvisation and composition is blurred – as indeed it was in much early Western music and continues to be in jazz. A wide range of activities involve improvisational elements. Young children improvise songs, while free improvisation can be used as a means of communication in music therapy or to develop self-esteem and a range of skills in those with special educational needs or mental health problems. The common element in all improvisations is that creative decisions take place within the real time of the performance. Composers nowadays are able to explore a much wider range of sounds in their compositions, and technology has made composition at a very high level possible for those who do not have highly developed technical skills on an instrument. This has opened up the possibility of composition for all and made possible a revolution in the music classroom (see Chapter 8).

The introduction of composition and improvisation into the UK school curriculum

The UK has been a world leader in promoting creative music making in schools. Initiatives were developed during the 1970s as a result of dissatisfaction with music education in secondary schools, where the curriculum was largely dependent on singing and musical history (DES, 1956/69) and with the publication of the Plowden Report *Children and their Primary Schools* (DES, 1967) which proposed a more child-focused education. During the early 1960s a number of young teacher-composers had begun to challenge traditional teaching methods, and the publication of their ideas generated interest in composition within education. *New Sounds in Class: A practical approach to the understanding and performing of contemporary music in schools* (Self, 1967) included a collection of graphic scores to be performed by classroom percussion ensembles. Dennis (1970) invited pupils to compose using electronic distortion techniques, drawing parallels with the music of Stockhausen, Berio and Cage. *The Composer in the Classroom* (Schafer, 1965) initiated debate about the nature of music; while *Sound and Silence* (Paynter and Aston, 1970) offered practical models for teachers as to how to introduce practical music making into the classroom. Some primary school teachers embraced these ideas enthusiastically. For instance, Pape (1970) provided an account of whole-class improvisation sessions with her infant classes inspired by pictures and poems, and generally at primary level there was an increase in improvisation and composition, although this was mainly a whole-class activity, with teachers being reluctant to facilitate small-group work (DES, 1967). At secondary level the initiatives created much controversy. In schools where a fulfilling music education was already being offered teachers saw no reason to change (Pitts, 2000). Even teachers committed to the initiatives reported that when initial exploration was over there were insufficient opportunities for progression, and in many schools there were practical constraints relating to the length of lessons and appropriate accommodation. Despite these initial difficulties the ideas took hold and, over time, a curriculum which included composition in addition to performance and more traditional studies emerged (see, for instance, Swanwick, 1979). The role of composition in the curriculum was confirmed in the requirements for the GCSE in Music and the development of the National Curriculum in Music (1992).

Composition and improvisation

Composition is usually viewed as requiring the highest levels of creativity, in part, perhaps, because of its greater permanence in comparison with improvisation and the development of interpretation. In the education of young people, however, the distinction between composition and improvisation is frequently blurred. The early stages of children's composing can be conceptualised as free improvisation. Very young children can improvise and do so spontaneously, usually in the form of songs (see Azzara, 2002 for a review). Given instruments, pre-school children tend to improvise exploring tone, timbre, and rhythmic patterns with a steady beat. Older children use a greater variety of rhythm patterns. Not surprisingly, the improvisations made by children reflect the musical culture within which they have been brought up and the musical experience of their teacher.

Interestingly, the processes of composing seem remarkably similar for children, young people and professional composers (Folkestad, 2004). The process consists of interactions between the participant's musical experiences and competences, their cultural environment, the available tools and instruments, and the instructions that they are given. Externally imposed constraints, the professional composer's commission and the instructions given to learners by the teacher provide the framework. Composing without such a framework is very difficult, although too much detail limits creativity. An overarching framework is not only helpful but necessary.

Unsurprisingly, creative skills change in focus as children gain in experience. Swanwick and Tillman (1986) developed a descriptive spiral outlining such changes. It considers mastery, imitation, imaginative play and metacognition and eight areas of development: sensory, manipulative, personal expressiveness, vernacular, speculative, idiomatic, symbolic and systematic. These are set out in Box 7.1. There are also common elements to each creative act, and early formulations suggested four main stages (see Table 7.1) (Wallas, 1926; Ross, 1980). Recent conceptualisations have built on these ideas.

Box 7.1 Eight areas of development (Swanwick and Tillman, 1986)

Sensory

Up to age 3, children are responsive to sound, particularly timbre. They are fascinated by dynamic levels, and they experiment. The elements of music are disorganised, unpredictable and the focus is the exploration of sound.

Manipulative

At age 4–5, children are acquiring an interest in the techniques involved in handling instruments. They organise pulse better and use techniques such as glissandi, trills, tremolo. The compositions tend to be long and rambling with repetitions before they move on to the next possibility.

Personal expressiveness

Between ages 4 and 6, elements of personal expressiveness appear, initially in song. There is evidence of exploitation of changes of speed and volume. There are signs of elementary phrases but little structural control. Compositions are spontaneous and uncoordinated musical ideas, emanating directly from feelings.

Vernacular

Between ages 5 and 8, compositions are characterised by melodic and rhythmic figures that are able to be repeated. Pieces tend to be short and musically conventional, consisting of 2-, 4- or 8-bar phrases. There is evidence of metric organisation. This is the first phase of conventional music making. Compositions tend to be predictable, demonstrating that they have absorbed ideas from elsewhere. Sometimes melodies are copied.

Speculative

Between ages 9 and 11, the deliberate repetition of patterns makes way for imaginative diversions. Surprises occur. There is less control of pulse and phrase. There is evidence of experimentation and a desire to explore structural possibilities.

Idiomatic

The structural surprises become more integrated. Contrast and variation occur on the basis of emulated models. Answering phrases, statement and response, variation by elaboration, and contrasting sections appear. Sometimes there appears to be a need to conform to external models. Technical, expressive and structural control is firmer.

Symbolic

Once students reach the age of 15, there is evidence of a strong personal identification with particular pieces of music, musicians, pieces, phrases, harmonic progressions and a growing consciousness of music's affective power. There is a tendency to reflect on the experience of composition and communicate about it to others – that is, the operation of metacognitive processes.

Systematic

At this level the individual's skills are highly developed. They are able to reflect on and be discursive about music and their experiences in intellectual terms.

Table 7.1 Four stages of creativity

Stage	Wallas (1926)	Ross (1980)
1	Preparation: gathering of relevant information	Initiating: beginning of the creative impulse, tactile explorations, doodling, playing, chance and accidents
2	Incubation: time to mull over the problem	Acquainting: becoming conversant with sound, practice, invention, further tactile motoric experience, playing around with ideas
3	Illumination: derivation of a solution	Controlling: mastery of basic skills and techniques to manipulate the medium, manipulating, constraints and limitations
4	Verification: formalisation and adaptation of the solution	Structuring: gathering into a comprehensible whole, relatedness, rescanning, reviewing, building blocks

In music there is a long tradition of considering creativity in terms of the individual. For instance, we refer to the genius of particular composers as if creativity is a facet of them as individuals. While composers differ in their individual characteristics they do have some common experiences, including: the opportunity to become involved in music; commitment; extensive knowledge of music; and extensive experience of working in the musical domain. Those acknowledged as among the greatest also began composing when they were very young, made their first contributions to the repertoire at a very young age and continued to be prolific in their writing throughout their lives (Simonton, 1997). Other characteristics and experiences attributed to creative individuals are broad and varied and it has been increasingly recognised that it is the interaction between the individual and the environment which ultimately shapes creativity.

Studies of groups of children who have demonstrated high levels of creativity in their composing suggest that they tend to be focused on the end product rather than the process (Daignault, 1997), with their ideas for the final composition tending to emerge early on (Hickey, 1995). A range of 'enabling skills' have also been identified, including musical expertise, conceptual understanding and aesthetic sensitivity, which in turn are influenced by enabling conditions (motivation, subconscious imagery, personality and environment) (Webster, 1988, 1991). Highly creative groups also tend to generate more musical ideas, and experiment and repeat them more than other children.

Creative Partnerships

The Creative Partnerships programme was set up in 2002 by the government to explore alternative cross-curricular methods of delivering creative learning for pupils and teachers, particularly in primary schools. Creative Partnerships seek to achieve this by providing safe, creative, spaces for cross-curricular exploration. Practitioners (school artists) are placed in schools to deliver creative projects and work alongside 'creative agents' who in turn work closely with school staff to examine schools' *in situ* learning structures and to identify continuing professional development opportunities for staff who wish to extend and explore their creative skills. Based on needs assessment and interviews with staff and students, the creative agent engages practitioners who meet school needs and with whom they can work on developing projects that can effect systematic change in the creative learning management of the school. Box 7.2 provides an example of a partnership working in a special school and Box 7.3 an example of a creative music project in a primary school.

Box 7.2 Example of partnership working in a special school

The Vale is a pioneering and innovative day special school, catering for children with physical disabilities and associated special educational needs. Staff worked with their partner artists (storytellers from Wizard Stories and a 'creative agent') to transform the swimming pool area, helped by the pupils. This created a 'sensory environment' – incorporating music, movement and light – to support unique storytelling sessions. Together, the adults and pupils developed a sea-based story called 'We are going on a Treasure Hunt', linking the curriculum areas of light and identity. The story saw pupils directing other pupils to battle sea creatures and dive to reclaim the king and queen's treasure. The story was devised with input from the speech therapist to encourage repetition in supporting language development, and the swimming instructor to encourage movement. The project supported the school's wider plan to explore a sensory-based curriculum. The project enhanced cross-phase links and provided opportunities for staff with different roles to communicate with a joint purpose – for example, the swimming instructor working with the information and communication technology (ICT) technician. The project enabled time for more adventurous activities at a crucial time when the school was at an early stage of curriculum change.

(Creative Partnerships London North, 2008)

Box 7.3 Example of a creative project in a primary school

The Making Waves project at Gallions Mount Primary School was delivered by Trinity College of Music through 'Raising the Roof', Trinity's music education programme for schools in Greenwich and Lewisham. The project aimed to 'enthuse, inform and encourage children and adults alike in developing confidence in composition, to support structuring and shaping original work for sharing and performing'. The whole school took part, using an overarching theme of 'water'. Five Trinity music leaders went into the school in order to structure the work appropriately for different classes. There were three in-service education and training (INSET) sessions, eight planning meetings with teachers, 50 workshops sessions and 16 performances took place – to other classes and teachers in the school. While the school engages in a lot of singing and some instrumental work, support was needed in delivering the music National Curriculum because none of the teachers was a music expert. In particular, staff needed support with organising music in open-plan classrooms and knowing how to manage composition. The central theme of water was convenient and unifying because of the possibilities it represented throughout the curriculum, e.g. in science, geography, measures. Each class worked with a musician to create and perform an original piece of music, based on the central theme. Younger pupils worked with stories they knew, creating a musical accompaniment to the telling of the story or writing poems that, with the help of the music leader, were set to music. At nursery level, the learning was in terms of the music curriculum and more widely in terms of social skills and giving pupils confidence with communication. Teachers observed that some pupils found it easier to sing something than to say it, and described one pupil who found it difficult to express himself because he could not sequence words properly – but who could do so when singing.

(Adapted from Creative Partnerships, 2010a)

Combined arts

From time to time there have been proposals for developing combined arts programmes in schools. For instance, the Arts 5–16 project (NCC Arts in School Project, 1990a, 1990b) aimed to find a coherent framework for arts teaching throughout compulsory schooling, recommending that pupils should be allowed to specialise in 'areas where their interests were sharpest, spending their final years of compulsory schooling pursuing one or two arts in depth with the support of combined arts courses'. The new National Curriculum for primary schools in England, for implementation from September 2011, puts forward 'areas of learning' rather than separate subjects. Music is subsumed in the area 'Understanding the arts' together with art and design, dance and drama. The model has been positioned as advocating direct subject teaching, complemented by serious and challenging cross-curricular studies. However, although reassurances have been given that this will not lead to a diminution of the place of individual subjects in the curriculum there are considerable risks that this will occur, particularly in the case of music where some schools without a music specialist already experience difficulties in delivering the music National Curriculum. The new 14–19 Creative and Media Diploma (see Chapter 15) also requires that students demonstrate understanding of two or more disciplines and by necessity is challenging teachers in schools and colleges to work across the arts.

Technological developments

As will be seen in Chapter 8, research into the use of music technology is a growing area, the main areas of investigation being the ways in which participants use technology to create music compositions, the effects of prior formal instrumental music tuition on the strategies used in the composition process, and the extent to which these responses can be called 'creative' (Mellor, 2008). Some argue that music technology enables individuals to explore, create and manipulate sounds through a variety of processes which in turn stimulate further ideas. Technology can enable ideas to be realised when motor skills lag behind ideas (Ley, 2004).

Music technology also has the potential to break down the barriers between composer, performer and listener, providing extensive opportunities for non-musicians to undertake creative musical activities (Crow, 2006) (see also Chapter 8). Crow describes how children can develop creative skills utilising DJ-ing techniques. He points out that DJ remix software allows the user to control and alter the music in a number of different ways, including adding spatial effects, removing frequencies, manipulating tempos and adding voiceovers and vocals, while loop-based sequencers make use of readymade and repeatable sound slices (loops) and typically allow the user to choose the loops from large instrumental and stylistic catalogues and assemble them by dragging and dropping them on to a grid. The loops can be repeated, layered, triggered, and enhanced with a range of effects and processes. Some software offers sound-creation facilities and the opportunity to record and mix musical performances. Essentially this software enables the creation of original compositions. Choices made involve learners in decisions about rhythmic structures, instrumental and vocal timbres, the roles and functions of instruments, the expressive nature of sound and its placement, repetition and dynamic contrast, form and texture.

Clearly there is potential here for teachers to support students enthusiastic about the use of technology to develop creative skills. There are also challenges for educators using this technology. For example, how do students gain access to support when using complex tools in creative work? What is the nature of the problems that they encounter (King and Vickers, 2007)? How do teachers adapt their approach to teaching composition when seeking to integrate the use of technology in music, given that some have concerns about teaching composing and improvising effectively (MacDonald and Miell, 2000)? Perhaps because of the challenges, music technology continues to be underused in schools (Ofsted, 2009).

Increasingly, youth services and organisations are using music and sound technology to good effect. Often aimed at young people who may be disengaged from education, training or employment, projects implemented range from those which provide space for young people to practise and perform, to those which enable them, through music, to explore such themes as identity or sub-cultures or to develop their technical skills of mixing, recording and producing. In many instances, the young people at whom such projects are directed have not fared well in mainstream education and the informal nature of youth work suits their needs (Ofsted, 2009).

World musics

Globalisation has created extensive opportunities for the development of skills in world musics and schools can now draw on the skills of community musicians to introduce them (see also Chapter 19). Many have done so. These offer further opportunities for creative music making. Local authority Music Services have also contributed significantly to broadening music provision, with specific initiatives in England, Scotland and Wales having a focus on increasing the breadth of provision (see Chapter 17), including African ensembles, Asian instrumental groups, gamelan ensembles, guitar groups, jazz/big band groups, steel pan ensembles, samba and pop/rock groups, in addition to ensembles reflecting classical Western music, e.g. orchestras, string ensembles and brass groups (Hallam *et al.*, 2005). Boxes 7.4, 7.5 and 7.6 provide examples of the development of world musics in education.

Box 7.4 'Big Beat' – pupils and teachers in a rural primary school making exciting music using African drums

One Music Service serving several Local Authorities provided schools with a project aimed at developing pupils' and teachers' skills in rhythm. 'Big Beat' is a global rhythm and drumming project for pupils in Year 5 involving three 2-hour workshops for pupils, two workshops for teachers, and a half-day

---

festival when participating schools perform together in a final concert. The project is led by a specialist percussion teacher with much expertise and experience in music from different cultures. During their second workshop session in the hall, pupils began by reinforcing skills developed in the previous session. Pupils showed well-developed skills in listening when performing rhythmic patterns, action songs and coordinated dance movements. They responded quickly to a range of prompts and cues from the specialist teacher. At one point in the workshop, pupils created complex rhythmic patterns using sticks and drums based on words, calls and rhythmic patterns to describe a range of African animals. In the final part of the session, pupils played authentic African drums in an exciting and well-controlled group performance which included opportunities for improvisation.

(Estyn, 2006)

Box 7.5 'Welcoming the World' – exploring the cultural landscapes of where young people live

In July 2008, over 450 school pupils from the five London 'Olympic boroughs' joined forces at the Hangar in Woolwich, to celebrate their involvement in 'Welcoming the World', an education project (organised by Creative Partnerships London East and South and London 2012) exploring the cultural landscapes of where young people live. 'Welcoming the World' was designed to encourage young photo-journalists, film-makers and music-makers from schools across the five boroughs to document their local areas to showcase to the rest of the world. It was an important first step towards empowering young people to understand their local and regional community and to reach out to young people internationally – sharing their values and thoughts and starting an invaluable dialogue. The project began in February, and had two elements: 'My World' – a photography and music project – and 'Our World'– a film and music project. The schools worked with leading experts in film, photography and music. This pilot education project was an important early strand of the 'London 2012 Education Programme' which is about inspiring young people to join in, capturing their imaginations, helping them realise their potential in whatever context that may be.

(Creative Partnerships, 2010b)

> **Box 7.6 A music programme serving young offenders institutions in Leicester and Henley-on-Thames**
>
> The Good Vibrations gamelan project is a music programme for young offenders between the ages of 15 and 25. The gamelan music ensemble lends itself well to encouraging group interaction and the development of social skills. The aim of the project was to help prisoners to acquire the social skills to help them find employment after their release from prison, since research shows that if you can get and keep a job when you get out of prison you are less likely to reoffend. Unlike most prisoner education schemes, Good Vibrations is run in an 'out of classroom' manner, making it more accessible to young offenders who find the classroom environment too stressful. The project was integrated into the prison's own educational and rehabilitation activities. Sessions were coordinated with the prison educational staff. The programme had record attendance levels, with stories of difficult inmates taking to the gamelan classes and in some cases becoming central to the project. One Henley-on-Thames participant on suicide watch was particularly violent at the start of the project. As classes continued he settled down and displayed excellent concentration skills. He later commented: 'The music makes me relax. I enjoyed being in the team. The highlight was the play-through at the end because I had learnt something and I felt good doing it.' Many participants, including staff, benefited from a new cultural experience, and many may not have otherwise experienced such diversity.
>
> (Youth Music, 2008)

Devising creative tasks

Creative tasks must be purposeful and facilitate progression if they are to be musically and educationally worthwhile. While open-ended tasks might seem optimal for creativity, having some constraints seems essential. The task for the teacher is to provide a framework which is appropriate to the intended outcome and for particular groups of students. Students may vary in their preferences. Burnard (1995) found that prescriptive directions were preferred by adolescent students who had advanced practical and theoretical backgrounds, but a relatively free task where directions indicated merely to write for the voice were preferred by students who had strong interpersonal interest, desire for individuality in expression and independent working styles. The stimulus provided for creative work depends on the age and interests of those participating. Intrinsic motivation is central to creativity, so tasks must be enjoyable, students must feel that they have ownership and control of them and they must be set at a level which is challenging but not too difficult. Very young children can participate effectively in creative musical activities and should be encouraged to do so. This can be at the level of the whole class or in small groups.

If students are to work creatively within particular musical genres, they need to acquire considerable knowledge of them. This knowledge can be acquired through listening, imitation and analysis and by participating in making music with others more expert than themselves. Whatever specific strategies are adopted, developing high levels of expertise takes time and effort. Similar processes are required whatever the genre – extensive aural immersion, semi-structured experimentation and, particularly important, active participation in the genre (Berliner, 1994). The informal learning undertaken by 'garage bands' follows this pattern (Jaffurs, 2004; Green, 2002).

Group work

There are many advantages in group creative composition, including:

- collective involvement and decision making
- support for the less confident
- opportunities for playing and practising together
- exchange of ideas
- opportunities for the less skilled to learn from the more experienced
- increased opportunities for experimentation
- more choice of instrumentation
- shared opportunities for the rejecting and selecting of ideas.

Allocation of pupils to groups can be made on the basis of the nature of the task, although children working on a collaborative composition with someone nominated as their best friend produced compositions rated as superior to those of children working with someone who was only an acquaintance. The communication – both verbal and musical – between best friends was characterised as being of a type more conducive to good quality collaboration (MacDonald et al., 2002; Miell and MacDonald, 2000).

Music in and out of school

Several authors have highlighted the divides that exist between classroom music, individual instrumental lessons and various community activities, and have called for greater integration (Everitt, 1997; MacDonald et al., 2002). Certainly, when learners are developing creative musical skills they benefit from becoming members of communities of practice. Jazz musicians report the importance of developing keen listening skills through interacting musically with others – enabling them to learn to improvise, and through anticipating and responding to each other's musical ideas (Monson, 1992). Encouraging students to engage with musical groups, in and out of school, in the area of creative expertise that they wish to develop is therefore of huge benefit. The task for the teacher is to facilitate the integration of skills which may be developed outside the classroom into creative activities within it.

Notating compositions

A particular dilemma in music education is the extent to which musical literacy is seen as essential. While there has been research on the way that children notate their compositions, it has largely focused on how their notation illuminates their intentions rather than the extent to which it contributes to their creativity, although there is evidence that abstract symbolic notational strategies are more effective than representational/pictorial notational strategies in retrieving musical meaning over time (Barrett, 2003). Children familiar with and competent users of conventional music notation also attend to and construct rhythmic patterns in different ways to those for whom such notation is an unknown. Mastery of conventional notation shapes and reflects musical perception and conception (Bamberger, 1991). Whether learners should be encouraged to formally notate compositions depends on the practices adopted within the relevant musical community to which they aspire to belong.

Need for technical skills

Early initiatives in developing musical creativity in the classroom experienced difficulties because the experimental resources used produced music which lacked credibility with older students, who wanted to create music which was authentic. This required technical instrumental skills which many did not have. Many young people still do not have these skills. The Musical Futures approach and the Wider Opportunities scheme are addressing this issue through giving pupils the opportunity to develop instrumental skills in the classroom (see Chapters 14 and 17). Certainly, musically trained students have more confidence in composition tasks and are able to develop the skills of their partners when composing in pairs (MacDonald and Miell, 2000; Seddon and O'Neill, 2006). If we wish to develop creative skills in music in a meaningful way we have to equip students with the means of doing this. This may mean enabling them to develop instrumental skills or promoting the utilisation of the wide range of computer programs now available which support composition.

Teacher confidence and skills

At primary level, generalist teachers lack confidence in teaching music unless they have considerable experience of playing a musical instrument. Many have particular concerns about teaching composition and, despite the National Curriculum, music is sometimes neglected in the curriculum (Hallam and Creech, 2008; Hallam et al., 2009). At secondary school the majority of music teachers have been trained in the classical performance tradition which may make them reluctant to engage their pupils in creative activities in genres with which they are unfamiliar or which they may even dislike. Teachers' backgrounds are a significant factor in their own work, with the intention to embrace new ideas often undermined by existing beliefs and expectations. Music educators sometimes have concerns about teaching composing and improvising effectively (MacDonald and Miell, 2000). Perhaps because of this, creative tasks may be underused in music education despite the fact that there is clear value in encouraging creativity from the earliest years. The development of creative skills reinforces other musical skills, including listening and understanding and, particularly where children work in groups, can enhance children's personal and social development.

Classroom management

Creative music making offers considerable challenges for classroom management. While whole-class creativity may be no more challenging to organise than other musical performance activities, small-group work presents particular problems. Teachers have to monitor the work of groups by visiting them in turn. This provides opportunities for the disaffected to misbehave and can be stressful for the teacher. In addition, pupils who require specific help may have to wait for a considerable time for the teacher to visit their group. Where there are insufficient rooms for small-group work this lack of discipline will be exposed to a wide audience in the school. This can also be stressful for teachers (see Chapter 14).

Resources

If musical creativity is to be supported through small-group work, accommodation needs to be appropriate – sufficiently large for instruments to be used, with sound proofing, and easily accessible so the teacher can visit each group in turn. Such facilities are not always provided in secondary schools and are rarely available in primary schools. A range of instruments and technological equipment needs to be available and maintained in good working order. Teachers may need technical support to ensure that instruments meet safety regulations, are properly tuned, and that they and other equipment (computers, software, recording equipment) are prepared in readiness for each class. Providing pupils with meaningful opportunities to develop creative skills is not a cheap option.

Endnote

Having a creative workforce is important for sustaining economic growth at a time when technology is rapidly and continuously changing the way that we live and work. Music education not only develops musical creativity but also contributes to the development of creative skills more generally (see Chapter 1). Young people are innovative and need opportunities to create and perform music which is authentic and has credibility with their peers. To do this they either need to acquire instrumental music skills or to make use of music technology. To support them, teachers may need to acquire a range of new skills. Opportunities need to be made available for them to do this.

Further reading

Burnard, P. (2007) 'Reframing creativity and technology: Promoting pedagogic change in music education'. *Journal of Music, Technology and Education,* 1(1), 37–55.

Qualifications and Curriculum Authority (QCA) (2000) *The Arts, Creativity and Cultural Education: An international perspective*. London: QCA.

References

Azzara, C.D. (2002) 'Improvisation'. In R. Colwell and C. Richardson (eds), *The New Handbook of Research on Music Teaching and Learning*. Oxford: Oxford University Press.

Bamberger, J. (1991) *The Mind Behind the Musical Ear: How children develop musical intelligence*. Cambridge, MA: Harvard University Press.

Barrett, M.S. (2003) 'Invented notations and mediated memory: A case-study of two children's use of invented notations'. *Bulletin of the Council for Research in Music Education*, 153/154, 55–62.

Berliner, P. (1994) *Thinking in Jazz: The infinite art of improvisation*. Chicago: University of Chicago Press.

Burnard, P. (1995) 'Task design and experience in composition'. *Research Studies in Music Education*, 5(2), 32–46.

Creative Partnerships London North (2008) *Making Waves*. Online. <http://www.creative-partnerships.com/area-delivery-organisations/anewdirection/resources/making-waves,61,ART.html> (accessed 04/01/2010) Arts Council England.

Creative Partnerships (2010a) Online. <http://www.creative-partnerships.com/data/files/cross-curricular-creative-projects-98.pdf> (accessed 01/01/2010).

Creative Partnerships (2010b) Online. <http://www.creative-partnerships.com/area-delivery-organisations/anewdirection/projects/welcoming-the-world,48,PRO.html> (accessed 04/01/2010).

Crow, B. (2006) 'Musical creativity and the new technology'. *Music Education Research*, 8(1), 121–130.

Daignault, L. (1997) 'Children's creative musical thinking within the context of a computer-supported improvisational approach to composition'. *Dissertation Abstracts International,* 57(11), 4681A.

Dennis, B. (1970) *Experimental Music in Schools: Towards a new world of sound.* London: Oxford University Press.

Department for Education and Science (DES) (1956/69) *Music in Schools* (Pamphlet No. 27). London: HMSO.

–– (1967) *Children and their Primary Schools: A report of the Central Advisory Council for Education* (England) (The Plowden Report). London: HMSO.

Estyn (2006) *An Evaluation of the Use Made by Local Authorities and Schools of Resources Made Available by the Music Development Fund in Wales.* Cardiff: HMSO.

Everitt, A. (1997) *Joining In: An investigation into participatory music.* London: Calouste Gulbenkian Foundation.

Folkstad, G. (2004) 'A meta-analytic approach to qualitative studies in music education: a new model applied to creativity and composition'. In J. Tafuri (ed.), *Research for Music Education*: The 20th Seminar of the International Society for Music Education (ISME) Research Commission, Las Palmas, Spain.

Green. L. (2002) *How Popular Musicians Learn.* Aldershot: Ashgate.

Hallam, S. and Creech, A. (2008) *EMI Music Sound Foundation: Evaluation of the impact of additional training in the delivery of music at Key Stage 1.* London: Institute of Education, University of London.

Hallam, S., Rogers, L. and Creech, A. (2005) *Survey of Local Authority Music Services 2005 (Research Report 700).* London: Department for Education and Skills.

Hallam, S., Burnard, P., Robertson, A., Saleh, C., Davies, V., Rogers, L. and Kokatsaki, D. (2009) 'Trainee primary school teachers' perceptions of their effectiveness in teaching music'. *Music Education Research*, 11(2), 121–140.

Hickey, M. (1995) 'Qualitative and quantitative relationships between children's creative musical thinking processes and products'. Unpublished doctoral dissertation, Northwestern University, Evanston, IL.

Jaffurs, S.E. (2004) 'The impact of informal music learning practices in the classroom, or how I learned to teach from a garage band'. *International Journal of Music Education*, 22(1), 189–200.

King, A. and Vickers, P. (2007) Problem solving with learning technology in the music studio. *Journal of Music, Technology and Education*, 1(1), 57–67.

Ley, B. (2004) 'Using music technology'. In A. Paterson and B. Ley (eds), *Ideas In – Music Out: Using technology in music education*, Matlock: National Association of Music Educators, 2–3.

MacDonald, R.A.R. and Miell, D. (2000) 'Creativity and music education: The impact of social variables'. *International Journal of Music Education,* 36, 58–68.

Macdonald, R.A.R., Miell, D. and Mitchell, L. (2002) 'An investigation of children's musical collaborations: The effect of friendship and age'. *Psychology of Music*, 30, 148–163.

Mellor, L. (2008) 'Creativity, originality, identity: Investigating computer-based composition in the secondary school'. *Music Education Research*, 10(4), 451–472.

Miell, D. and MacDonald, R.A.R. (2000) 'Children's creative collaborations: The importance of friendship when working together on musical composition'. *Social Development,* 9(3), 348–369.

Monson, I. (1992) *Saying Something: Jazz improvisation and interaction*. Chicago: University of Chicago Press.

National Curriculum Council (NCC) Arts in School Project (1990a) *The Arts 5–16: A curriculum framework*. London: Oliver & Boyd.

—— (1990b) *The Arts 5–16: Practice and innovation*. London: Oliver & Boyd.

Office for Standards in Education (Ofsted) (2009) *Making More of Music: An evaluation of music in schools 2005–08*. London: Ofsted.

Pape, M. (1970) *Growing Up with Music*. London: Oxford University Press.

Paynter, J. and Aston, P. (1970) *Sound and Silence: Classroom projects in creative music*. Cambridge: Cambridge University Press.

Pitts, S. (2000) *A Century of Change in Music Education: Historical perspectives on contemporary practice in British secondary school music.* Aldershot: Ashgate.

Ross, M. (1980) *The Arts and Personal Growth.* London: Pergamon Press.

Schafer, R.M. (1965) *The Composer in the Classroom.* Toronto: BMI Canada.

Seddon, F.A. and O'Neill, S. (2006) 'How does formal instrumental music tuition impact on self- and teacher evaluations of adolescents' computer-based compositions?' *Psychology of Music,* 34(1), 27–45.

Self, G. (1967) *New Sounds in Class: A practical approach to the understanding and performing of contemporary music in schools.* London: Universal Press.

Simonton, D.K. (1997) 'Products, persons and periods'. In D.J. Hargreaves and A.C. North (eds), *The Social Psychology of Music.* Oxford: Oxford University Press.

Swanwick, K. (1979) *A Basis for Music Education.* Slough: National Foundation for Educational Research (NFER).

Swanwick, K. and Tillman, J. (1986) 'The sequence of musical development: A study of children's composition'. *British Journal of Music Education,* 3(3), 305–339.

Wallas, G. (1926) *The Art of Thought.* London: Watts.

Webster, P.R. (1988) 'New perspectives on music aptitude and achievement'. *Psychomusicology,* 7(2), 177–194.

–– (1991) 'Creativity as creative thinking'. In D. Hamann (ed.), *Creativity in the Classroom: The best of MEJ.* Reston, VA: Music Educators National Conference.

Youth Music (2008) Online. <http://www.youthmusic.org.uk/About_us/case_studies_research/case_studies/Good_vibrations_gamelan_in_prison.html> (accessed 04/01/2010).

Chapter 8

The role of technology

Evangelos Himonides and Ross Purves

We all use technology to a certain extent, whatever our background, qualifications, expertise, attitudes towards 'technology', everyday commitments, philosophical stance on 'technology', tastes, needs, practices and beliefs. From pre-birth, technology has been part of our lives, whether for ultrasound screening, a foetal heart rate monitor, a hanging mobile that emits sounds over the cot, toys, remote controls, or any of the other diverse array of objects or devices that allow us to manipulate aspects of the world around us.

As educators, students and lifelong learners we are required to distil, assess, adopt, rethink, apply and communicate knowledge continually, using a plethora of interwoven channels, modalities and media. Technology – any form of technology – enables us to do so. 'Music technology' is a term that is broadly used and freely interpreted but is, paradoxically, loosely defined. For example, music technology can be seen as something that is strongly connected to sound engineering, acoustics, electronic music and the digital world; but it can also be witnessed in mainstream school practice and in the home as a personal computer-based platform for supporting music composition and, to a lesser extent, music performance. Throughout this chapter the terms 'technology', 'information technology' (IT) and 'information and communication technology' (ICT) can be used interchangeably. After all, concepts such as 'information' and 'communication' cannot exist in a vacuum, especially within our broader field of education. Furthermore, this chapter advocates the use of the term 'music technology' as a broad concept that can help us to:

- become better musicians
- understand music and/or the wider impact that music has on our lives and ongoing development
- record, capture, experience, study, create, compose, document, analyse and archive sound and music
- enhance the teaching and learning experience in the music classroom
- enhance our lives through experiencing music in new ways

- facilitate the communication of *our* musics (performances or compositions)
- provide wider access to other people's musics (individuals' as well as other cultures' in general)
- provide access to music for people with special needs and requirements
- monitor and assess our teaching practices in the music classroom
- monitor and assess our students' development and learning experiences
- research, scrutinise, assess and evaluate current educational theories (and their application to practice) and allow the development of new theories, practice and policy for music education.

Background

The National Curriculum (NC) for England advocates the use of ICT across school subjects and ages. As an overarching compass, ICT is prescribed as an agent for information retrieval, distillation and synthesis, as an aid for the development of ideas, refinement and enhancement of pupils' work, as a platform for the exchange of information and, finally, as a means for reviewing, modifying, evaluating and also critically reflecting upon one's work (DfEE/ QCA, 1999: 34). In line with the somewhat ambiguous interpretation of ICT there appears to be limited further official information on how to celebrate, adopt and apply the NC's noble views regarding ICT, especially within music education – perhaps being one of the reasons why music technology is reported by Ofsted in its latest report as being 'underused' in the music classroom (Ofsted, 2009: 6).

Although references to creating, manipulating and refining sounds using ICT exist, the development of IT skills is asserted, somewhat oddly, as a 'halo effect' (or, at least, a positive outcome) of music education – that is, through 'using a range of ICT to compose and perform music' (DfEE/QCA, 1999: 8). Not much conceptual support is offered with regard to using technology in order to become 'better' *in* music (to become better musicians), nor also 'better' *with* music (music being a conduit for the enhancement of extra-musical experiences and the development of other-than-musical skills). This is despite other government publications suggesting that there is an explicit ICT need in music. In 2004, for example, according to the UK government's 'Music Manifesto' (see Chapter 2):

> *By 2003, only 2 per cent of teachers in primary school made substantial use of ICT in music. This rose to 11 per cent in special schools and 24 per cent in secondary schools. In primary schools, more use is made of ICT in religious education than in music. Again, only 5 per cent of*

primary teachers reported that ICT had a substantial positive effect compared with 15 per cent of teachers in special schools and 30 per cent of secondary teachers. Pupils use ICT in music more at Key Stage 2 in primary school than at Key Stage 3 in secondary school.

(DfES, 2005a: 60)

It is interesting to note that, rather unsurprisingly, focus is put on the 'use' of ICT (whatever that 'use' might be). It is argued within the same report that lack of equipment and lack of resources are the most significant factors that limit the effective use of technology in schools. Although a lack of teacher training and choice of software platforms were presented as 'additional concerns', these were not seen as significant.

At the time of publication (2005a), the Music Manifesto group also reported on the formation of a DfES-funded National Music Management Group, set up by the National Association of Music Educators (NAME) and Schools Music Association that was planned to work in association with the British Educational Communications and Technology Agency (Becta) in order to embed ICT more in the music curriculum. This initiative resulted in a number of outcomes, mainly useful 'hands-on' information regarding ICT in music for teachers in Key Stages 2 and 3 (upper primary and lower secondary school). Things became much more focused, though, with the advent of the second Music Manifesto report (DfES, 2006). This report marked the beginning of a new attitude towards using technology with music in education. A clear shift was evidenced – from treating technology as a 'black box' (or even panacea) towards reasoning about technology as a polymorphic concept. The second Music Manifesto report emphasised the following technology-related points:

- Teachers' professional development in using new technology is essential and it is crucial for schools to support this.
- In line with the DfES e-strategy *Harnessing Technology: Transforming learning and children's services* (2005b), the report highlighted the enormous impacts that new and emerging technologies were having on music and argued that these needed to be embraced, both by teachers and by learners.
- Besides the need for accessing a wide-ranging supply of musical instruments in schools, there was also a need for sufficient and renewable music resources, including ICT equipment and software.
- New digital technology developments had introduced novel ways for music making, often removing barriers between different musical styles and genres.
- Such new digital technologies were seen also to increase pupils' autonomy in their engagement with music 'with profound implications across the music and education sectors in terms of what they provide, and where and how they do so'.

- Levels of knowledge, expertise and access to technology were argued to be discrepant across schools.
- The existence was acknowledged of educators and leaders who were either uneasy incorporating technology in their teaching, or could not even see how music technology might be applicable to their work.
- It was highlighted that pupils' technological expertise might often be greater than that of their teachers. This could potentially discourage teachers from using technology in their classroom for fear of losing face (although it could be argued that such pupil-based knowledge is a considerable asset to the teacher).

One outcome of this new attitude concerning technology's potential role in music education is that it breeds a new conceptual enquiry: How should we assess the effectiveness of any given technology in the music classroom? Numerous journal articles in the field of music education focus on 'using' a popular piece of notation or sequencing software tool in a particular classroom context and report on analyses of observational data. Similarly, professional web-based resources offer advice and technical tips on how to 'use' specific software packages. However, few offer critical evaluations of *how* the suggested tools had been used; nor discussed *why* they had been used, nor conferred *what* educational principles the authors had been celebrating. The music ICT discussion has been further augmented by a plethora of parallel focuses to that of 'conventional' music education practice, such as creativity, development, identity, the learning experience, the psychology of the learner, assessment, furthering professional development, disengagement, leadership and communication.

A framework for consideration of the possible effectiveness of music technology in the music classroom is provided by the more generic standpoint of the UK government's Teaching and Learning Research Programme (TLRP http://www.tlrp.org) and its ten holistic principles of effective teaching and learning, discussed below.

Ten holistic principles of effective teaching and learning

TLRP invested over £37m in nine generic phases of funding from its inception in 1999 to 2009. A review of common findings across more than 80 initiatives suggests that there are ten holistic (generic) principles of effective teaching and learning emerging within the school system (TLRP, 2009).

Such principles can be applied in the evaluation of the effectiveness of 'a' technology, in order to take account of how the dynamic teacher–pupil–parent model/relationship may benefit from it and how learning and teaching might be supported. The ten holistic principles are presented below as reference points which one might consider as salient when interrogating any form of technology, and include illustrative examples of recent and current externally funded music technology research and postgraduate case studies.

1. Equipping learners for life in its broadest sense

> *Learning should aim to help individuals and groups to build the intellectual, personal and social resources that will enable them to participate as active citizens, contribute to economic development and to flourish as individuals in a diverse and changing society. This may mean expanding conceptions of worthwhile learning outcomes and taking seriously issues of equity and social justice for all.*
>
> (TLRP, 2006: 6)

'Development is more than academic attainment and includes group as well as individual development' (TLRP, 2009). How could a technology assist an individual's as well as the group's development outside the narrow scope of academic attainment? What are our (as educators) planned learning outcomes for a session that have been enriched with technology and might these accord with our own and our students' diversity, social status and parity? One current example of this is to be found in a European Community-funded, multidisciplinary and transnational research project (2008–2011) that is investigating the application of new music technology to support social inclusion in various European settings. While intended for all children, the Usability of Music for the Social Inclusion of Children (UMSIC) project aims particularly to support, through music and technology, those children who are at increased risk of being marginalised, such as children who are newly immigrant in a host community or otherwise in danger of marginalisation (e.g. children with moderate learning difficulties and threatened by low attainment). The project is designed to address the social inclusion of children by the use of modern, mobile technology to draw on children's intrinsic motivation for play, exploration and musical activities, and thereby, implicitly, on their human existential need to experience the feeling of belonging to a wider social community. The child-centred software and interface (which can be used on a mobile phone or PC) enables young children to listen, compose, improvise, sing along, gather musical examples from home and swap music files with friends (see http://www.umsic.org/).

2. Engaging with valued forms of knowledge

> *Teaching and learning should engage learners with the big ideas, key processes, models of discourse and narratives of subjects so that*

they understand what constitutes quality and standards in particular domains. Teachers need to posses both good understanding of the subjects that they teach and also of the best ways to teach these subjects.

(TLRP, 2006: 7)

The TLRP team presents this principle as an argument that supports the change in the teacher's role from transmitter of information to facilitator of opportunities for children to formulate their own understanding of new concepts. It is, therefore, useful to consider how a technology can facilitate this process, and also to enable students and teachers to share valid information and support subject-specific discourse. One major technology resource for teachers and their pupils which enables users to engage with music as a form of knowledge and also as an art form is ABRSM's 'SoundJunction' (see also Box 8.1). This web-based resource is designed to enable the user to explore music, to discover 'how music works', to provide examples of many different cultural expressions in music from across the world and to promote musical creation (see http://www.soundjunction.org/default.aspa). It is an example of how technology enables an individual or group to access and experience a much wider world of music, spanning time and place, as well as diverse musical genres and styles outside the immediate community – an example of a 'glocal' (think globally, act locally) music learning opportunity.

3. Recognising the importance of prior learning and experience

Teaching and learning should take account of what the learner knows already in order to plan their next steps. This includes building on prior attainment, but also taking into account the personal and cultural experiences of different groups of learners. (Learners often need time and teachers need time to diagnose learning difficulties and to help others to improve.)

(TLRP, 2006: 7)

According to the findings of the various research strands that the TLRP oversaw, 'few people these days think that children arrive at schools as "empty vessels" [or tabulae rasae – empty slates] to be filled with knowledge' (TLRP, 2007: 15). It is, therefore, essential for us to employ technological means that will celebrate pupils' individual needs, strengths, weaknesses as well as their backgrounds and provide context-sensitive and user-adaptive tools that will enhance their learning experiences, as well as challenge and extend their existing knowledge. Both of the examples mentioned above, UMSIC and SoundJunction, are designed on the premise that music learning requires a content-rich experience that is, to a significant extent, under the control of the learner. The challenge is in uncovering what the learner brings to the task, not least because much learning may be other than conscious and not readily accessible to discussion. One way that technology can help is by both enabling the learner to act on the musical material, while also capturing these actions to build a profile (a data log) which can be accessed subsequently for analysis by the teacher to ensure that future activity is appropriately framed to promote development (see next principle). An example of the diversity between different learner/user groups can be seen in Box 8.1.

Box 8.1 An evaluation of SoundJunction: Participant diversity

The overall impression from this research-based evaluation is that the different participant user groups have diverse approaches to SoundJunction.

Figure 8.1 Screenshot of SoundJunction

Experienced secondary school teachers of music (especially those who are heads of department and who have a regular role in the development of intending and newly qualified teachers) have established ways of working in the classroom related to the perceived needs of different pupil groups and individuals. Their responses within this research suggest that they see SoundJunction as an extended resource, possibly as a 'warehouse' (a concept from Kenny and Gellrich's 2002 study of the knowledge base that experienced performers bring to the art of improvisation). This resource is there to be used to extend and supplement their existing approaches, resources and tools. They do not (yet) necessarily see SoundJunction as a way of changing pupil (and perhaps their own) thinking in and about music. Nevertheless, we believe that the technology resource has this potential.

In contrast, **pupils** of both focus ages within the research (Key Stage 3 and Sixth Form) demonstrated generally a much more open engagement with SoundJunction. Given the wide range and depth of information that the site offers, it should be possible for their thinking in and about music to be extended significantly. Whether this will happen purely by informal exploration (in school and/or at home), however, is not clear.

It would be better, therefore, if the ABRSM continued to offer more explicit guidance about these two forms of musical engagement, namely that SoundJunction offers extensive information about music and that this can be used by users (teachers and their pupils) to extend their thinking in music and the fashioning of new (for the individual) musical products.

4. Requiring the teacher to scaffold learning

> *Teachers should provide activities and structures of intellectual, social and emotional support to help learners to move forward in their learning so that when these supports are removed the learning is secure.*
>
> (TLRP, 2006: 7)

Technology could enable educators to assess when a particular intervention would be more appropriate, thus helping them to engage in their pupils' development more effectively. As reported by the TLRP (2007: 15), 'ICT in the classroom will not help learning on its own' and students might end up ill-informed or confused about how certain rules apply if left to their own devices in front of a computer for extended periods of time. This matter was also discussed within the research evaluation of the ABRSM's SoundJunction. This particular technology does offer the tools for the educator to build 'learning trails' (see Box 8.2), depending on the subject matter, thus enabling the student to stay 'on course' without the risk of being lost in a vast information repository.

Box 8.2 An evaluation of SoundJunction: Scaffolding learning

SoundJunction can be used by teachers in order to scaffold learning (*pace* Bruner, 1996). Similarly, the 'learning trails' technology that SoundJunction provides is a praiseworthy fusion of browsing 'cookie crumble' technology with site-mapping functionality. This is a very powerful feature of SoundJunction that needs to be both advertised widely and continually enriched with additional 'trails'. SoundJunction can be used as a dynamic – and systematic – virtual learning tool, instead of a relatively stagnant one and amorphous anthology of useful learning materials. In the TLRP's 'Decalogue' for effective teaching and learning, they report: 'Scaffolding is about teachers recognising when they should intervene to help the child move on to a higher level of understanding.' The TLRP's 'Learning with ICT in Pre-school Settings' study (TLRP, 2007: 15) found that young children's encounters with computers and other technology were enhanced when practitioners stepped in to guide them.

One particular and major strength of the SoundJunction package is the `learning trails' option. These 'journeys', as well as any 'cognitive walk-throughs' elsewhere on the site, should be highlighted, advertised and presented as a centre-point of the site and not just as one of the options. Future pathways could enable more context- and user-sensitive learning trails via the suggested user-adaptable interface that draws on both data mining and qualitative/statistical analyses of paradigmatic use.

5. Needing assessment to be congruent with learning

Assessment should be designed and implemented with the goal of achieving maximum validity both in terms of learning outcomes and learning processes. It should help to advance learning as well as determine whether learning has occurred.

(TLRP, 2006: 7)

According to the TLRP (2007: 15), the outcomes of their 'Learning How to Learn' study, suggest that 'the ultimate goal of assessment for learning is to promote learning autonomy so that pupils can reflect on where they are and where they need to go, and then act in such a way as to get there'. Although the aims of 'assessment' appear to be apparent, the TLRP reports that there was a general agreement between teachers that 'the assessment system in England militates against good learning', sometimes forcing teachers to 'end up teaching to test'. Furthermore, examples like the Sounds of Intent project (see Chapter 3) demonstrate that contexts exist (e.g. special needs education and pupils with severe or profound and multiple learning difficulties) where an innovative technology can be essential in monitoring, assessing, documenting and enhancing children's development.

6. Promoting the active engagement of the learner

A chief goal of teaching and learning should be the promotion of learner's independence and autonomy. This involves acquiring a repertoire of learning strategies and practices, developing learning dispositions, and having the will and confidence to become agents in their own learning.

(TLRP, 2006: 7)

Technology can play an active role in the dynamic of the student–teacher learning relationship, including supporting both the student's personal understanding and the teacher's 'target understanding'. An example of these two, potentially conflicting, notions is offered from the VOXed research project (see Boxes 8.3 and 8.4). See also Welch *et al.* (2005) and Howard *et al.* (2007).

Box 8.3 VOXed: The application of multimedia technology and the challenges faced by teacher and student

There are at least two major challenges that face the teacher of singing when attempting to foster the development of their students. First, the linguistic metaphors for vocal behaviours that are employed (by either teacher or student or both) may be misunderstood and, secondly, the ongoing temporal nature of the teaching process relies on multiple successive translations of student singing behaviour and spoken commentary. The student's current knowledge, understanding and skill levels are embedded in their singing behaviours and reflected in the nature of the performance strategy, effort and engagement that they bring to the lesson. A key task is for the student's 'personal understanding' to be matched against the 'target understanding' presented by the teacher (Entwistle and Smith, 2002), who, in turn, draws on their individual expert subject knowledge, as well as their attitudes and beliefs about the teaching and learning process. In such a pedagogical context, the application of multimedia technology allows any particular moment of the student's singing behaviour to be captured and 'frozen' in time. This facilitates the possibility of a better relative match between a teacher's target understanding (their specific teaching aim at that moment) and the personal understanding of an individual student. This relationship is evidenced in the participants' comments that the feedback technology provided a stable external and shared focus on which to base their interactions.

Box 8.4 VOXed: Practice-related issues and new technologies in the singing classroom

There is an extensive research literature on effective instrumental (including vocal) practice (Hallam, 1997; Barry and Hallam, 2002) that embraces the earlier concepts of 'deliberate practice' (Ericsson *et al.*, 1993) and 'formal practice' (Sloboda *et al.*, 1996). The literature indicates that optimal practice conditions include opportunities to: (1) develop appropriate auditory schemata that focus on elements of the music (phrases, sections) as well as the whole; and (2) experience models of desired behaviour. In the case of the VOXed technology, for example, the 'modelled' behaviour can equally be from the student (as displayed on the laptop computer screen) as from the teacher. It is also likely that practice will be more systematic and motivated in the presence of 'Knowledge of Results'.

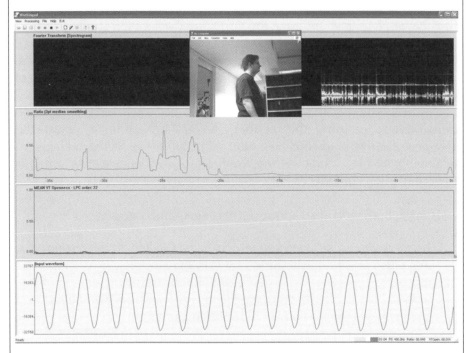

Figure 8.2: Screenshot of VOXed

At least two other aspects of the research literature on practice relate to the use of the VOXed multimedia technology in the singing studio, namely students' likely practice histories and teachers' instructional style. With regard to the former, a study at the Oslo conservatorium of music (Jørgensen, 2000) revealed that 40 per cent of new students over three successive years reported that their former teachers had put 'very little' or 'no' emphasis on practice behaviour. This is in contrast to the findings of a USA-based study (Barry and McArthur, 1994) in which the majority of teachers reported that they 'always' or 'almost always' discussed the importance of practice and specific practice techniques with their students. In such a context of possible contradictory perceptions, the introduction of a robust multisensory feedback system of singer behaviour should ensure that imagery, commentary and singing are more likely to be integrated so that the student understands how best to achieve the requisite 'target' behaviour. With regard to the teachers' instructional style, notwithstanding the evidence that it is normal for there to be a lot of teacher talk in instrumental teaching, there is also evidence that the teacher's style – what they actually do during the lesson (such as demonstrating a particular technique or having the student try a particular approach) – can be more important than what is said (Barry and Hallam, 2002). If this is the case, then having real-time auditory and visual feedback of the student singer's behaviour (and feedback that can be replayed back at any point) should also ensure a greater cohesiveness between teacher talk, instructional style and student singing behaviour. This was evidenced in transcripts of teacher–student dialogue from the VOXed recordings (Howard *et al.*, 2007).

Subsequently, the participant teachers and their students reported clear benefits in using the feedback technology within a lesson and also over a series of lessons and were very supportive of the principle of technology use in a studio setting. Confirmatory evidence was recorded in the observations of other members of the research team.

7. Fostering both individual and social processes and outcomes

Learners should be encouraged and helped to build relationships and communication with others for learning purposes, to assist the mutual construction of knowledge and enhance the achievements of individuals and groups. Consulting learners about their learning and giving them a voice is both an expectation and a right.

(TLRP, 2006: 6)

TLRP rejoices over the social character of learning. There are numerous examples to demonstrate that technology can play an instrumental part in enhancing the social aspects of learning. It can provide the means for an extra-classroom social experience that would otherwise be impossible to have. It can record social interaction, document social interaction discourse and facilitate networking and group/peer support. There are, of course, possible threats in using modern social networking technologies in the classroom and/or at home (see Adams and McCrindle, 2008). Besides the concerns regarding security, equality and dignity, the teacher has to provide an overall structure (see also above, regarding 'scaffolding') for pupils' group (and other networking) activities. This can ensure that a general focus is in place and that the learning group will be able to interact meaningfully and more effectively. Evidently, social interaction and group collaboration does not only benefit students. Computer-mediated forums, discussion boards, blogs, podcasting resources, information repositories, electronic libraries and general networking websites can be valuable for the teachers who are themselves lifelong learners.

8. Recognising the significance of informal learning

Informal learning, such as learning out of school, should be recognised as being at least as significant as formal learning and should be valued and used in formal processes.

(TLRP, 2006: 6)

The research evidence base supports that learning occurs both inside and outside school. It is, therefore, important for the educator to welcome knowledge and expertise that pupils might bring into the classroom from other contexts (e.g. home/family, peers, community) and seek to bridge the commonalities, but also the diversities, that this might entail. This TLRP principle should not be perceived as conflicting with previously reported principles (related to scaffolding and assessment), but as a celebration of the multimodality of the learning process. The Musical Futures-funded research project (Green and Walmsley, 2006) has provided valuable insights regarding the application of informal learning practices in the music classroom (see Chapter 14). Many of Green's examples (2008) involve the use of technology in the classroom and show how technology aids the various informal learning experiences. This is further supported by Savage (2003, 2005) and Folkestad (2006), who highlight that formal and informal learning should be perceived as a continuum and not as two discrete (and maybe conflicting) concepts.

9. Depending on teacher learning

The need for teachers to learn continuously in order to develop their knowledge and skill, and adapt and develop their roles, especially through classroom enquiry, should be recognised and supported.

(TLRP, 2006: 6)

The TLRP claim that this theme appeared consistently throughout the span of the research enquiry. Continuous professional development is also raised in both Music Manifesto reports (see above), although mainly as a possible concern regarding why teachers might feel discouraged to employ ICT in their classroom. It is important, therefore, for teachers to appreciate that both their own development and their students' development are inevitably ongoing and that the advent of new technologies can only be seen as positively challenging and stimulating. Teachers can learn a new technology in tandem with their students, offering their experiences in being critical reflectors/assessors of the learning process, without necessarily being heuristic experts of the new tools.

Box 8.5 provides examples of teachers' personal reflections relating to music technology education and celebrating the 'lifelong learner' role.

Box 8.5 Teachers as lifelong learners: two personal reflections

I've done the online survey, but I just wanted to send a personal note of appreciation to say how much I enjoyed the Music Technology module, and the way it was delivered. I have got so much out of it: I've discovered software I didn't know about, become much more creative and knowledgeable with the software that I was using already, learned loads about approaches to using IT in education. It's provoked some really useful deep thinking and evaluation. The way that the module was run and delivered, and your own role as a tutor has been a great way to learn by example. With most modules you're kind of glad when they're over – but this one I'm going to miss, now it's finished!

(J, June 2009)

What can I say? . . . I will always remember what you said about nobody teaching you Microsoft Word for 'Creative Writing', so why teach people how to use Sibelius or Finale for creative music composition? I don't feel that I have to learn how to become a 'button pusher' any more, I know that I can read 'the manual' for that (or 'press F1') (the usual Microsoft Windows-based shortcut to the 'Help' menu) . . . after all, that Chinese proverb was right – Better teach someone how to fish . . .

(B, May 2007)

---

10. Demanding consistent policy frameworks with support for teaching and learning as their primary focus

> *Institutional and system-led policies need to recognise the fundamental importance of teaching and learning and be designed to create effective learning environments for all learners.*
>
> (TLRP, 2006: 6)

It is rather self-evident that, as educators, our effectiveness may be constrained in part by the schools' (micro) and the state's (macro) policies and educational guidelines and associated support. Initiatives such as the TLRP and the Music Manifesto demonstrate that the public sector is very positive in enhancing education in general and music education. Active participation of educators in such initiatives is, therefore, advisable. New technology can play an instrumental role in this by enabling users and policymakers to monitor the application of existing policy, record practice that is based on existing policy and evaluate the effectiveness of such practice. It is also useful for: engaging in online discussion with other practitioners regarding existing policy (e.g.

online discussion groups) and sharing/communicating arguments in support of change; experiencing foreign policy examples virtually and reflecting upon novel (or different) ideas; accessing published research and critical evaluation of existing policies; and networking and publicly voicing individual and group beliefs. One of the ongoing challenges for policymakers (rehearsed in several places in this volume) is to identify, understand and act on whether or not different policies are interrelated or joined-up. Technology is such a case in official music policy documents which rarely devote explicit space to the details of music technology practice (although this is more evidenced by Ofsted, 2009).

Several common themes emerge from this overview of recent research into music technology in the music classroom:

- Although it is vital to have the resources to incorporate ICT in the classroom, this does not mean that successful learning is guaranteed simply by ownership of ICT resources.
- Emphasis needs to be given to the *effective* use of any technology or technological means in the classroom (or any other learning context).
- A sound approach in evaluating the effectiveness of using technology in music and music education is the inspection of such technologies through the prism of the TLRP's ten holistic principles of effective teaching and learning.
- Music technology is a much broader concept than we might have been personally accustomed to, and does not necessarily translate to the composition of music or manipulation of sound using popular software applications.
- The use of technology needs to be made explicit within the music curriculum and not lost as some conceptual 'theme' that is buried within official documents. For example, the word 'technology' appears twice in the QCA's latest 2007 Programme of Study for Key Stage 3 Music and 'ICT' (as a separate concept) once. However, technology offers the teacher and the learner a means for researching, monitoring, recording, enabling, celebrating and promoting musical participation and development, as well as emotional engagement through music and sound.
- The music education plateau is constantly evolving as new generations of teachers come to practice. The stereotypical music educator's (or music specialist's) profile becomes blurred. This is supported by national statistics from A level qualifications and undergraduate degrees as well as testimonials from the teacher training sector (see also Chapter 11).

Humanity has always been musical and will always be musical. Humanity has always been learning and will continue to learn. Technology can only celebrate, facilitate, enhance, advance, enrich, further and augment this, if used meaningfully. We are all musical, we are all learners and we are all technology users.

Further reading

Brown, A.R. (2007) *Computers in Music Education: Amplifying musicality*. New York: Routledge.

Buckingham, D. (2005) *Schooling the Digital Generation: Popular culture, the new media and the future of education*. London: Institute of Education, University of London.

Savage, J. (2007) 'Reconstructing music education through ICT'. *Research in Education,* 78, 65–77.

References

Adams, A. and McCrindle, R.J. (2008) *Pandora's Box: Social and professional issues of the Information Age*. Chichester: John Wiley.

Barry, N.H. and Hallam, S. (2002) 'Practice'. In R. Parncutt and G. McPherson (eds), *The Science and Psychology of Music Performance*. New York: Oxford University Press.

Barry, N.H. and McArthur, V. (1994) 'Teaching practice strategies in the music studio: a survey of applied music teachers'. *Psychology of Music*, 22(1), 44–55.

Bruner, J. (1996) *The Culture of Education*. Cambridge, MA: Harvard University Press.

Department for Education and Employment (DfEE)/Qualifications and Curriculum Authority (QCA) (1999) *Music*. London: DfEE/QCA.

Department for Education and Skills (DfES) (2002a) *Pupils' and Teachers' Perceptions of ICT in the Home, School and Community*. London: DfES.

–– (2002b) *Transforming the Way We Learn*. London: DfES.

–– (2005a) *Music Manifesto Report No. 1*. London: HMSO.

–– (2005b) *Harnessing Technology: Transforming learning and children's services*. London: DfES.

–– (2006) *Music Manifesto Report No. 2*. London: HMSO.

Entwistle, N. and Smith, C. (2002) 'Personal understanding and target understanding: Mapping influences on the outcomes of learning'. *British Journal of Educational Psychology*, 72, 321–342.

Ericsson, K.A., Krampe, R.T. and Tesch-Römer, C. (1993) 'The role of deliberate practice in the acquisition of expert performance'. *Psychological Review*, 100, 363–406.

Folkestad, G. (2006) 'Formal and informal learning situations or practices vs formal and informal ways of learning'. *British Journal of Music Education,* 23(2), 135–145.

Green, L. (2008) *Music, Informal Learning and the School: A new classroom pedagogy.* London: Ashgate.

Green, L. and Walmsley, A. (2006) 'KS3: Musical Futures'. *Classroom Music,* 2(3), 19–25.

Hallam, S. (1997) 'What do we know about practising? Towards a model synthesizing the research literature'. In H. Jørgensen and A.C. Lehmann (eds), *Does Practice Make Perfect? Current theory and research on instrumental music practice.* Oslo: Norges Musikkhøgskole.

Himonides, E., Laurence, K., Purves, R. and Welch, G.F. (2008) *SoundJunction: A research-based evaluation.* London: Institute of Education, University of London.

Hodges, R. (2001) 'Using ICT in music teaching'. In C. Philpott and C. Plummeridge (eds), *Issues in Music Teaching.* London: RoutledgeFalmer.

Howard, D., Brereton, J., Welch, G.F., Himonides, E., DeCosta, M., Williams, J. and Howard, A. (2007) 'Are real-time displays of benefit in the singing studio? An exploratory study'. *Journal of Voice*, 21(1), 20–34.

Jørgensen, H. (2000) 'Student learning in higher instrumental education: Who is responsible?'. *British Journal of Music Education*, 17(1), 67–77.

Kenny, B. and Gellrich, M. (2002) 'Improvisation'. In R. Parncutt and G. McPherson (eds), *The Science and Psychology of Music Performance.* New York: Oxford University Press.

Moggridge, B. (2006) *Designing Interactions.* Cambridge, MA: MIT Press.

Moore, A. (ed.) (2006) *Schooling, Society and Curriculum.* London: Routledge.

Murray, A. (2004) 'Lessons from my past'. In A. Paterson and B. Ley (eds), *Ideas In – Music Out: Using technology in music education.* Matlock: The National Association of Music Educators.

Office for Standards in Education (Ofsted) (2009) *Making More of Music.* London: Ofsted.

Philpott, C. (ed.) (2000) *Learning to Teach Music in the Secondary School: A companion to school experience*. London: RoutledgeFalmer.

Philpott, C. and Plummeridge, C. (eds) (2001) *Issues in Music Teaching*. London: RoutledgeFalmer.

Savage, J. (2003) 'Informal approaches to the development of young people's composition skills'. *Music Education Research*, 5(1), 81–85.

–– (2005) 'Working towards a theory for music technologies in the classroom: How pupils engage with and organise sounds with new technologies'. *British Journal of Music Education*, 22(2), 167–180.

Sloboda, J.A., Davidson, J.W., Howe, M.J.A. and Moore, D.G. (1996) 'The role of practice in the development of performing musicians', *British Journal of Psychology*, 87, 287–309.

Teaching and Learning Research Programme (TLRP) (2006) *Improving Teaching and Learning in Schools*. London: TLRP.

–– (2007) *Principles into Practice: A teacher's guide to research evidence on teaching and learning*. London: TLRP.

–– (2009) Online. <http://www.tlrp.org> (accessed 10/03/2010).

Welch, G.F. and Preti, C. (2007) *Soundabout: A research evaluation*. London: Institute of Education, University of London.

Welch, G.F., Howard, D., Himonides, E. and Brereton, J. (2005) 'Real-time feedback in the singing studio: an innovatory action-research project using new voice technology', *Music Education Research*, 7(2), 225–249.

Chapter 9

Issues of assessment and performance

Ioulia Papageorgi and Susan Hallam

Assessment has a very powerful effect on learning. This is illustrated only too well by the way that teachers tend to focus on preparing children for national tests in schools and the way that graded instrumental examinations, since their inception, have determined much of what is taught in instrumental lessons. This effect is so powerful that Elton and Laurillard (1979) suggested that if educators want to change teaching and learning they should change the assessment system. Any learning outcome which is not assessed is unlikely to be given priority by either learners or teachers. To optimise the impact of assessment, the aims of learning, the processes adopted and the assessment procedures should be aligned (Biggs, 1996). In music the most appropriate way of achieving this is to ensure that assessment procedures are authentic and have real-life relevance. This might take many forms.

Assessment is commonly recognised to be either summative or formative. Summative assessment of learning evaluates what has been learned by a particular point in time and is usually graded in some way. Formative assessment is when feedback from learning activities is used to inform future learning and teaching (Black and Wiliam, 1998). Summative assessment can be used formatively, for instance, when comments on a submitted composition or performance are discussed to set future goals.

Formative, self- and peer assessment

Much music tuition has at its heart formative assessment, with instrumental teachers and music group leaders, in particular, spending the majority of their time highlighting how performance or composition can be improved through commenting, instructing, asking questions and making gestures. These strategies assist the teacher in identifying the student's level of understanding while also shaping learning behaviour (Kennell, 2002) (see also Chapter 6). Learners also receive aural feedback from the sounds that they make when they are playing or singing, enabling them to judge their progress – whether it be in interpreting their own compositions or improvisations or those of others. The way that humans internalise and remember musical sounds without conscious awareness – and the immediacy of the aural feedback that the learner receives when making music – enable comparisons to be made between what learners are aiming to do and what they are actually doing. This requires that they learn to listen critically (see Chapter 4).

Formative assessment needs to be provided in such a way that it enables learners to be able to work independently and develop critical skills so that they can objectively reflect on and evaluate their work, identifying areas for improvement, while also recognising their achievements. The development of these skills depends on the assistance of teachers, other more experienced individuals, or peers. Teacher modelling of evaluative and learning processes is important in this respect. Where students are undertaking written work teachers typically comment on it when it is complete, whereas in the case of practical work teachers and others can give feedback during the process.

Fautley (2004) provided an analysis of four case studies illustrating how teachers can provide formative feedback as part of the musical composition process. Two teachers adopted what appeared to be a 'laissez-faire' approach, not interfering in the composing process immediately, preferring to address issues in the post-composing plenary session or in the structure of the next composing task. This meant that pupils were able to work in a relatively uninterrupted fashion. Other teachers adopted a 'stop and question' approach, leading or challenging students in their thinking or practice. Analysis of when teacher intervention occurred was based on nine stages:

1. Initial confirmatory (pupils discuss the task)
2. Generation (ideas are produced)
3. Exploration (ideas are explored and potentialities investigated)
4. Organisation (ideas are explored and ordered)
5. Work in progress performance (formally requested by the teacher, undertaken informally by the group)
6. Revision
7. Transformation/modification
8. Extension and development
9. Final performance.

The majority of teacher interventions were related to the organisation phase, where concerns focused on pupils meeting the requirements of the task as set, followed by the generation phase and the requirement for a performance of work in progress. Comments did not focus on musicality or aesthetic concerns, perhaps because teachers are aware of the complex issues arising from assessing creative work. These will be considered later.

Despite the evidence of critical formative assessment in instrumental lessons, Ofsted (2009) suggests that such procedures are not embedded in secondary class music lessons. Audio recording tends to be used at the end of a unit of work and does not facilitate development, although there are exceptions. For instance, one school used recording as a natural part of lessons and filed work in the school's music database, so that it could be used to monitor progress and direct improvement. This resource also supported teachers in understanding standards and expectations. Other good practice identified by Ofsted included developing assessment criteria with students so that they could judge the extent of their progress and ultimately their level of success. Some schools have provided students with checklists against National Curriculum levels so that they can self-assess their level and progress. An example of a possible format for the English National Curriculum levels is provided in Box 9.1.

Box 9.1 A possible format for students to self-evaluate their progress			
Level 4 Pupils identify and explore the relationship between sounds and how music reflects different intentions	**No**	**Not sure**	**Yes**
Can you use sound to create a piece of music which sounds as you intended?			
Can you play and hold your part in a group?			
Can you read simple musical notation?			
Can you play simple tunes by ear?			
Do you know how your part fits with other players?			
Do you know what a good performance sounds like?			
Do you know how to structure your musical ideas?			
Can you improvise melodies and rhythms when playing in a group?			
Can you evaluate your performance?			
Do you know how to improve your work?			
Do you know how to help others improve their work?			
Do you know how to describe different pieces of music in words using musical terms?			
Do you know how to compare different pieces of music?			
Do you know how to evaluate different pieces of music?			

Level 5 Pupils identify and explore musical devices and how music reflects time and place	No	Not sure	Yes
Can you play sections of music from memory?			
Can you play sections of music using notation?			
Can you use different types of notation?			
Do you know when to take the lead in a group?			
Do you know when to play a solo in a group?			
Do you know when to provide rhythmic support to others in the group?			
Can you improvise rhythms and melodies within a clear structure?			
Can you compose music for different occasions?			
Do you know how to improve your own work?			
Do you know how to help others improve their work?			
Can you identify musical structures and specific musical devices?			
Can you recognise different types and genres of music and music from different cultures?			
Can you explain and compare different elements in music?			
Can you describe why music is composed and performed for different occasions or audiences?			

Level 6 Pupils identify and explore the different processes and contexts of selected musical genres and styles	No	Not sure	Yes
Can you play expressively?			
Can you adjust your playing so that your part fits sensitively within a group?			
Can you improvise and compose in different styles and genres?			
Can you use chords and other harmonies?			
Can you use a range of different rhythms?			
Can you use different notations?			
Can you plan, revise and improve your work?			

Can you help others plan, revise and improve their work?			
Can you develop your musical ideas to achieve the effects that you want?			
Can you recognise different styles and genres of music?			
Do you understand the traditions of the music that you compose, play and listen to?			
Can you compare, analyse and evaluate different pieces of music?			
Are you able to discuss how music relates to where and when it is created and performed?			

Level 7 Pupils discriminate and explore musical conventions in, and influences on, selected genres, styles and traditions	**No**	**Not sure**	**Yes**
Can you perform in a range of different styles, genres and traditions?			
Can you make an important contribution to your group and support the work of others?			
Can you compose something which is original in a particular style?			
Can you generate, develop, abandon or adapt ideas when you are composing or performing?			
Can you recognise and tell the difference between different styles, genres and traditions of music?			
Can you evaluate and criticise a range of music?			
Can you explain and talk about how musical conventions are used?			
Can you demonstrate your understanding of how music is linked to its context?			

Level 8 Pupils discriminate and exploit the characteristics and expressive potential of selected musical resources	**No**	**Not sure**	**Yes**
Can you perform, improvise and compose extended pieces of music in a range of different styles, genres and traditions?			

When composing, improvising and performing do you take account of direction and shape in relation to rhythm, melody and overall form?			
Do you take account of musical expression when composing, improvising and performing?			
Can you play by ear and from a range of different notations?			
Can you differentiate between a wide range of genres, styles and traditions, discuss their characteristics and historical and geographical backgrounds and critically evaluate them?			
Can you critically evaluate pieces of music challenging musical conventions?			

Peer assessment, whether formal or informal is increasingly being recognised as having a crucial role to play in the development of self-evaluation skills. Even young children are able to assess the compositions of their peers, although their assessments do not consistently match those of their teachers (Hickey, 2001). Peer assessment occurs informally in group work, whether the task involves creating renditions of existing music or composing new pieces (see Chapter 14). In higher education, students are increasingly involved in the summative assessment of their peers where typically they are issued with guidelines and agreed criteria. These might relate to the extent to which performance is convincing, technically assured, informed by a sense of style, communicates the music in a way that demonstrates understanding, and displays individuality (Hunter and Ross, 1996). The evidence from a range of informal learning contexts has demonstrated the effectiveness of group working, not only in developing independent learning and self-assessment, but also in promoting a range of transferable skills (see Green, 2002; Kokotsaki and Hallam, 2007; and Chapter 14).

The development of self-evaluative skills can be supported by the use of recordings. Video feedback has the advantage of being direct, combining visual and auditory senses and bypassing the interpersonal communication process between teacher and learner which can sometimes be biased (Baker-Jordan, 1999). Using recordings is particularly important as perceptions derived while actually performing can be distorted by a range of external and self-image factors (Gordon, 2006). A survey investigating the effectiveness of video recording found that almost half of the students reported that seeing the video helped them identify their errors more clearly than at the time of performance. They indicated that it was easier to pinpoint areas of difficulty and address them. It also enabled them to take an audience perspective, although in some cases it increased anxiety levels (Daniel, 2001). The increase in recording technology – in mobile phones, for instance – has made the recording process easily accessible to young people and many now seem to be using it as a normal part of practice (Hallam, 2010). There is clearly the potential for much greater use of such technology in music teaching.

Issues in summative assessment in the arts

There has long been debate as to whether there is any value in undertaking formal assessment of contemporary creative endeavours, or indeed, whether it is possible to provide objective evaluation, a perspective legitimised by the frequent disagreements among professional music critics. Assessment of composition, improvisation and performance is subjective and depends on the assessor's personal preferences and their level of expertise (Hickey, 2001). Composition is normally assessed through its performance, which creates the problem of differentiating between the performance and the composition, while assessing performance is problematic because there is the need to distinguish between the music (the composer's intentions, as indicated in the score) and the performer's use of expression in order to evaluate technical and interpretative abilities (Thompson, 2009). Overall, the assessment of performance is not reliable (e.g. Wrigley, 2005; Wapnick et al., 2004). Judges do not give the same grades when they are presented with the same performance twice (without being informed) (Fiske, 1978), and there is high variability even when they are assessing performance on the same instrument using the same assessment protocol (Ciorba and Smith, 2009).

Preconceptions affect assessment. When presented with two identical performances, labelled so that one was perceived to be by a student and the other by a professional musician, students tended to assign lower ratings to the student performance (Duerksen, 1972). Other reported biases include variation in the performer's physical attractiveness, gender and race (Elliott, 1995; Davidson and Coimbra, 2001). During performance, the performer's facial expression, body movement, gestures and physical image influence judgements (Davidson and Correia, 2002; Kokotsaki et al., 2001; Thompson et al., 2005). In preparing learners for assessment all of these factors need to be taken into account as they influence the aesthetic and perceptual experience of listeners (Thompson, 2009). There may also be effects of order of performance. In a highly prestigious international violin and piano competition, performers appearing on the last day of the event were more likely to be highly ranked (Flores and Ginsburgh, 1996). Such effects may occur in other contexts.

Having more experienced assessors does not necessarily increase the consistency of assessment. For instance, Elliot (1987) investigated the perceptions and judgements of performance made by three professional musicians and six young performers. Comments made by the judges were categorised into five groups: context, technique, expressive features, structural features and value judgements. Assessments of individual performances showed considerable variation, although some performances commanded more consensus than others, but in the area of technical skills where one might have expected to find the most agreement there was a large measure of disagreement even between the three professional judges. Overall, this demonstrates the complexities of assessing performance and indicates how individual listeners may attend to and give different weight to diverse elements.

Similar differences have emerged in relation to composition. Evaluations of 10-year-old children's music compositions showed that there was most agreement between those involved in teaching music, followed by the children (seventh and second grade) with the least agreement between professional composers (Hickey, 2000). The more specialist the assessors of composition, the more specific structural characteristics of the music they seem to take into account (Seddon and O'Neill, 2001).

There are also issues relating to the genre in which assessment takes place, as each has its own stylistic conventions. Expertise in one area of music does not necessarily transfer to others, so it may be difficult for a classically trained examiner to assess jazz. Similarly, assessing improvisation needs to be based on different criteria to other types of performance.

Current practices in summative assessment

In spite of the problems in assessing musical improvisation, composition and performance, in our current educational system there is a need for summative assessment, not least, to provide verification of attainment for accessing further educational opportunities.

One approach to dealing with some of the difficulties outlined above has been a proposal to adopt a system of negotiated assessment, which is based on a series of interviews between teachers and pupils where they agree on the evaluation (Pupil Assessment Conversations with Teachers – PACT). Ross and Mitchell (1993) argue that summative assessment of a child's art work invades their self-expression and that adopting such conversations ameliorates this and also supports the development of self-assessment. Unfortunately, while representing an ideal, such a system would be very time-consuming to implement and is unlikely to provide sufficient credibility to be accepted as accredited evidence of specific levels of attainment.

There have been many attempts to develop objective systems which assess holistically or through grading specific elements. For instance, detailed criteria might be established for phrasing, balance, articulation, rubato and dynamic range, and assessors could be required to comment or give a mark for each element (Thompson, 2009; Boyle, 1992). Similarly, checklists have been developed to assess improvisation skills, including elements such as first impression, originality, imaginativeness, instrumental fluency, musical syntax, general impression and final appraisal (Hassler and Feil, 1986; McPherson, 1993). If improvisation or performance is undertaken within a group then a decision has to be taken as to whether it is group performance, individual performance or a combination which will be assessed, and care has to be taken to ensure that the process adopted is fair to all of the participants.

At university level, where the stakes are high, multidimensional assessment rubrics have been developed to assess instrumental and vocal performance. For instance, in one university, the rubric measured student achievement across all instruments and voice. The dimensions of assessment (musical elements, command of instrument, presentation) were derived by a panel of performance experts, who also outlined the various levels of achievement within each dimension, from basic to advanced. Scores were given for each scale dimension, written comments were provided and a final grade given (Ciorba and Smith, 2009).

While much effort has been spent on developing detailed assessment criteria, open techniques which take a holistic approach can be as – or more – reliable, than criterion-defined scales (Webster and Hickey, 1995). Video recording can also contribute to ensuring that assessment is fair, making it possible for additional assessors to be recruited where there are doubts about (or challenges to) the outcomes. While these issues have been discussed in relation to practical work many apply equally to written work, particularly where there are not easily identifiable correct answers – for instance, in essays, reports, portfolios.

Formal summative assessment systems in the UK

In England, children have been among the most assessed in the world. During the 1990s a range of monitoring systems was developed which culminated in children in compulsory education undergoing assessment of some kind at ages 5, 7, 11, 14 and 16, with further assessment at 17 and 18 if they remained in full-time education. In music, much of this assessment has been undertaken by the teacher. While this might appear to be less forbidding, at secondary level teachers are under pressure to ensure that student progress is demonstrated and are often required by the school's senior management team to undertake assessment frequently (Fautley and Savage, 2008). More formal assessment in music in schools has been through GCSE, GCE A level and BTEC examinations, while for those learning to play instruments there are graded examinations (see Chapter 10). Other, more recent, qualifications include the Young People's Art Award, the Creative and Media Diploma for 14–

19 year olds and creative apprenticeships for 16–24 year olds. The system in Scotland is different, with Standard Grades (equivalent to GCSEs) studied over two years in years S3 and S4 and students then moving on to Intermediate, Highers and Advanced Highers.

Assessment of musical activities carried out by teachers inevitably depends on their level of expertise. At primary level, where many teachers lack even moderate levels of musical expertise (see Chapter 13), it is not surprising that they have difficulty in carrying out assessments (Hallam *et al.*, 2005). Ofsted (2009) reported that of the 47 primary schools where assessment was evaluated in detail, ten were judged as good or outstanding and 16 were judged as inadequate. In addition, teachers rarely used the simple definitions of progress in the National Curriculum to help provide a focus for lessons. Even at Key Stage 3, assessment was only good or outstanding in about one-third of schools and was inadequate in about one-quarter. Ofsted reported that it remained one of the weakest areas of teaching and that there was an inadequate understanding of the National Curriculum levels and issues of progression (Ofsted, 2009).

Beyond Key Stage 3, relatively few pupils take music (see Chapters 10 and 14). Despite the low take-up, attainment at GCSE is above average when compared to all GCSE subjects. In 2008, some 29 per cent of candidates obtained A*/A grades and over 73 per cent of candidates achieved a grade C or above in music, although attainment in the listening component was less than in the performing and composing components. In 2008, slightly more boys took GCSE music than girls, but girls continued to gain higher grades (Ofsted, 2009). Overall standards at A level Music in 2008 were below the national average (9 per cent below average for A–C grades in 2008), although attainment at AS level was broadly in line with the national average. More boys are entered for the music technology course (five times as many as girls), reflecting their general interest in music technology, although broadly similar numbers of boys and girls are entered for the general music course. In Scotland, the different pattern of examinations makes comparisons difficult. In 2008, 37 per cent of students were awarded an A grade in Higher Music and 44 per cent in Advanced Higher Music, and overall 92 per cent passed the latter examination.

There is a wide range of BTEC courses which tend to focus on the performing arts, music practice and musical technology. All have a very practical focus. For example, the Level 2 First Certificates and Diplomas in Music are designed to introduce learners to working in the sector or prepare them for further study. Learners can choose from a wide variety of options including DJ technology, rehearsal techniques, and working as a musical ensemble. Equivalent to three A levels, the BTEC National Diploma in Music Technology is a two-year course which includes 18 units of study relating to developing skills for working in the music industries. Units focus on the development of a wide range of skills – for instance, sound-recording techniques, creating and marketing a music product, planning a music recording, music sequencing, and computer music systems, as well as those typically included in A level programmes, such as composition, listening, theory and harmony. There is limited evidence about attainment and standards in these courses.

The 14–19 diplomas are designed to complement GCSE and A levels and have been developed in partnership with employers to equip students with the skills required for specific careers. The Creative and Media Diploma considers four main areas of the creative process: creativity in context; thinking and working creatively; principles, processes and practice; and creative businesses and enterprise. The diploma can be taken at foundation, higher and advanced levels. It is assessed through a 'creative portfolio' which represents a collected body of work documenting the creative process as well as the outcome, providing evidence of expertise in a range of skills and creative problem solving, and a collection of work over time that demonstrates the personal and professional development of the learner. Relatively small numbers of students have so far completed diplomas, so it is not possible to draw any conclusions about their effectiveness.

Systems of graded instrumental, vocal and theory examinations were developed in the UK at the end of the nineteenth century to provide teachers and their students with a means of assessing progress. In 2008, over a quarter of a million children were entered for the Associated Board of the Royal Schools of Music (ABRSM) practical examinations, with over 40,000 taking theory examinations. Examinations are taken when the learner is ready and provide an assessment of their level of expertise (through the grade taken) and quality (through the mark given). Such examination systems promote motivation, enable comparisons to be made, provide a structure for learning, enable individuals to compete against their previous examination performance, and can provide some assessment of the effectiveness of teachers. There has been some criticism of the relative lack of change in syllabuses since the inception of the examinations in the late nineteenth century (Salaman, 1994), although the range of instruments and genres included has expanded considerably in recent years, and different examination boards offer different syllabuses. Rockschool, for instance, offers examinations in guitar, bass, drums, popular piano and vocals. Although students are motivated to increase their levels of practice prior to impending examinations (Hallam 2008), they also find graded examinations the most anxiety-provoking performance context because there is a concrete outcome, a mark (Hallam, 1997). Teachers sometimes find themselves under pressure from parents and pupils to rigidly follow examination syllabuses, inhibiting what they teach and how they teach it.

Performance anxiety

Performance increases motivation to practise and if successful has a positive impact on self-esteem and confidence, but there is huge variability in the extent to which learners find it rewarding. For some it is an exhilarating and joyful experience (Howe and Sloboda, 1991), while for others any pleasure which may be derived from it is minimal because of stage fright. Such performance anxiety is multidimensional (Papageorgi *et al.*, 2007), operating over different time scales: in the long-term lead up to performance, immediately before, and during it. Arousal levels may change depending on the interaction between:

- the performer's susceptibility to experiencing anxiety (which may include individual characteristics such as gender, age, trait anxiety, self-esteem, self-concept and self-efficacy)
- the performer's task efficacy (the process of preparation, the learning approach, motivation to learn, task difficulty and value attached to it, and anxiety-coping strategies)
- the characteristics of the specific environment where the individual is expected to perform (which can be influenced by audience presence, perceived degree of exposure and venue characteristics).

Performance anxiety is an issue for a significant proportion of musicians – novices and experts – and at all ages (see Papageorgi, 2007, 2008; Papageorgi *et al.*, 2010). Although musical performance anxiety is one of the most debilitating and frequently reported negative influences on musicians' development, when it is controlled it can facilitate optimal arousal as it assists in preparing the body for the demands of the forthcoming task, increasing motivation and improving concentration (Papageorgi, 2007). There is therefore a need to differentiate between maladaptive (debilitating) and adaptive (facilitating) forms of musical performance anxiety. The perception of physiological changes which accompany performance anxiety (increase in heart rate and respiration, tension in all bodily muscles, 'butterflies' in the stomach, dry mouth, sweaty palms, cold hands, tremors, frequent urinary need) can increase fear in performers, particularly if they do not understand what is happening to them. This can further exacerbate anxieties. Physiological responses to anxiety are also accompanied by behavioural indicators and effects on cognition. Behavioural indicators include tremors, trembling and shaky hands, quivering voice, difficulty in moving naturally, moistening lips and errors in performance, while the effects of anxiety on cognition can result in loss of concentration and attention, heightened distractibility, memory failure, distorted thinking and misreading of the musical score (Steptoe, 2001).

The key elements to overcoming the maladaptive effects of performance anxiety include appropriate preparation (technical and psychological) and the development of appropriate coping strategies – for instance, maintaining a positive attitude to the performance, reducing its perceived level of importance, and focusing on communication of the music to the audience. The development of a positive self-concept in music and the promotion of effective strategies for coping with performance anxiety in students need to be addressed by music teachers. Box 9.2 provides an example of how teachers can support students in overcoming stage fright.

Box 9.2 Supporting learners who experience stage fright

1. Assess the extent to which performance anxiety might be a problem, either through discussion or using a scale – for instance, the Adolescent Musicians' Performance Anxiety Scale (AMPAS; Papageorgi, 2007).

2. Offer support – discuss the nature of performance anxiety, how it can affect people, help put the performance in perspective, try to alleviate negative emotions.

3. Plan – ensure students have prepared the music well, provide opportunities for informal performances, encourage a focus on musical communication, support them in gaining opportunities to practise in the venue, arrange the order of pieces so that they begin with a less demanding piece.

4. Relieve the stress of performance – suggest that the students take some time off from practising to do things they like (e.g. see friends and family, watch a movie, read a book).

5. Help students visualise post-performance goals and rewards. This can be useful in maintaining motivation and perseverance.

Implications for education

Successful learning depends on having appropriate feedback. In the early stages of any musical engagement, the feedback provided by the sounds themselves may need to be augmented by teacher or other feedback until learners develop aural templates, against which they can judge their own performance. As a wide range of templates are developed, learners become more able to evaluate their own performance. This process can be enhanced through encouraging peer assessment, using video recordings to provide learners with an audience perspective on their work, and teachers modelling processes and providing aural models which can be emulated, discussed and critiqued. The value of this cannot be overstated. Learners need to develop independent, evaluative skills if they are going to be able to successfully continue engagement with music when they cease to be involved in formal education.

The issues relating to summative assessment in the arts are longstanding and there are no simple solutions. There will always be controversy as to whether holistic or itemised assessment procedures are better. The outcomes in terms of marks may be little different but having clear criteria which are easy to understand may assist learners in evaluating and improving their work. There is also a role for technology in ensuring equity and reliability. Assessment itself determines much teaching and learning. To enhance motivation it needs to be authentic and have real-life relevance. Overall, in the UK, examination bodies appear to be responding to these issues.

Developing performing skills is crucial for most musicians. There are many opportunities for performance in a range of widely differing informal and formal settings. Teachers can draw on these to provide opportunities best suited to the needs of particular groups of learners. A minority of learners experience debilitating stage fright. For those wishing to pursue careers in music this presents a serious problem, and higher education institutions have a responsibility to support such students in developing coping strategies for managing their difficulties.

Further reading

Fautley, M. and Savage, J. (2008) *Assessment for Learning and Teaching in Secondary Schools*. Exeter: Learning Matters.

Harris, D. and Paterson, A. (eds) (2002) *How Are You Doing? Learning and assessment in music*. Matlock: National Association of Music Educators.

Papageorgi, I. (2008) 'Investigating musical performance: Performance anxiety across musical genres'. *Teaching and Learning Research Briefing (No. 57)*.

Useful link

National Database of Accredited Qualifications www.accreditedqualifications. org.uk/qualification/

References

Baker-Jordan, M. (1999) 'What are the pedagogical and practical advantages of "three or more" teaching?' In *Pedagogy Saturday III*. Cincinnati, OH: Music Teachers National Association.

Biggs, J.B. (1996) 'Enhancing teaching through constructive alignment'. *Higher Education*, 32, 1–18.

Black, P. and Wiliam, D. (1998) 'Inside the black box: Raising standards through classroom assessment'. *Phi Delta Kappan,* 80(2), 139–149.

Boyle, J. (1992) 'Evaluation of music ability'. In R. Colwell (ed.), *Handbook of Research on Music Teaching and Learning*. New York: Schirmer.

Ciorba, C.R. and Smith, N.Y. (2009) 'Measurement of instrumental and vocal undergraduate performance juries using a multidimensional assessment rubric'. *Journal of Research in Music Education*, 57(1), 5–15.

Daniel, R. (2001) 'Self-assessment in performance'. *British Journal of Music Education*, 18(3), 215–226.

Davidson, J.W. and Coimbra, D.C.C. (2001) 'Investigating performance evaluation by assessors of singers in a music college setting'. *Musicae Scientiae*, 5(1), 33–53.

Davidson, J.W. and Correia, J.S. (2002) 'Body movement'. In R. Parncutt and G.E. McPherson (eds), *The Science and Psychology of Music Performance*. New York: Oxford University Press.

Duerksen, G.L. (1972) 'Some effects of expectation on evaluation of recorded musical performance'. *Journal of Research in Music Education*, 20, 268–272.

Elliott, C.A. (1995) 'Race and gender as factors in judgements of musical performance'. *Bulletin of the Council for Research in Music Education*, 127, 50–55.

Elliott, D. (1987) 'Assessing musical performance'. *British Journal of Music Education*, 4(2), 157–184.

Elton, L.B.R. and Laurillard, D. (1979) 'Trends in student learning'. *Studies in Higher Education*, 4, 87–102.

Fautley, M. (2004) 'Teacher intervention strategies in the composing processes of lower secondary school students'. *International Journal of Music Education,* 22(3), 201–218.

Fautley, M. and Savage, J. (2008) *Assessment of Composing at KS3 and KS4 in English Secondary Schools.* Birmingham: Birmingham City University.

Fiske, H.E. (1978) *The Effect of a Training Procedure in Music Performance Evaluation on Judge Reliability*. Brantford, Ontario: Ontario Educational Research Council Report.

Flores, R.G. and Ginsburgh, V.A. (1996) 'The Queen Elisabeth musical competition: How fair is the final ranking?'. *The Statistician*, 45(1), 97–104.

Gabrielsson, A. (1999) 'The performance of music'. In D. Deutsch (ed.), *The Psychology of Music*. San Diego: Academic Press.

Gordon, S. (2006) *Mastering the Art of Performance: A primer for musicians*. New York: Oxford University Press.

Green, L. (2002) *How Popular Musicians Learn: A way ahead for music education*. Aldershot: Ashgate.

Hallam, S. (1997) 'Approaches to instrumental music practice of experts and novices: Implications for education'. In H. Jorgensen and A. Lehman (eds), *Does Practice Make Perfect? Current theory and research on instrumental music practice* (NMH-publikasjoner 1997:1). Oslo: Norges musikkhgskole.

–– (2008) 'Do examinations change students' practising habits?' Paper presented at the conference of the International Society for Music Education, Bologna, 14–16 July.

–– (2010) 'The development of practising strategies in young people'. Paper presented at the 11th International Conference on Music Perception and Cognition, University of Washington School of Music (Seattle), 23–27 August.

Hallam, S., Rogers, L., Creech, A. and Preti, C. (2005) *Evaluation of a Voices Foundation Primer in Primary Schools*. London: Department for Education and Skills.

Hassler, M. and Feil, A. (1986) 'A study of the relationship of composition improvisation to selected personality variables'. *Bulletin of the Council for Research in Music Education,* 87, 26–34.

Hickey, M. (2000) 'The use of consensual assessment in the evaluation of children's music composition'. In C. Woods, G. Luck, R. Brochard, F. Seddon and J. Sloboda (eds), *Proceedings from the Sixth International Conference on Music Perception and Cognition,* Keele, August.

–– (2001) 'An application of Amabile's consensual assessment technique for rating the creativity of children's musical compositions'. *Journal of Research in Music Education,* 49, 234–244.

Howe, M. and Sloboda, J. (1991) 'Young musicians' accounts of significant influences in their early lives: 2. Teachers, practising and performing'. *British Journal of Music Education,* 8(1), 53–63.

Hunter, D. and Russ, M. (1996) 'Peer assessment in performance studies'. *British Journal of Music Education,* 13(1), 67–78.

Kennell, R. (2002) 'Systematic research in studio instruction in music'. In R. Colwell, and C. Richardson (eds), *The New Handbook of Research on Music Teaching and Learning*. Oxford: Oxford University Press.

Kokotsaki, D. and Hallam, S. (2007) 'Higher education music students' perceptions of the benefits of participative music making'. *Music Education Research,* 9(1), 93–109.

Kokotsaki, D., Davidson, J. and Coimbra, D. (2001) 'Investigating the assessment of singers in a music college setting: The students' perspective'. *Research Studies in Music Education,* 16, 15–32.

McPherson, G. (1993) 'Evaluating improvisational ability of high school instrumentalists'. *Bulletin of the Council for Research in Music Education,* 119, 11–20.

Office for Standards in Education (Ofsted) (2009) *Making More of Music: An evaluation of music in schools 2005/2008.* London: HMSO.

Papageorgi, I. (2007) 'Understanding performance anxiety in the adolescent musician'. Unpublished PhD thesis. Institute of Education, University of London.

–– (2008) 'Investigating musical performance: Performance anxiety across musical genres'. *Teaching and Learning Research Briefing (No. 57).*

Papageorgi, I., Hallam, S. and Welch, G.F. (2007) 'A conceptual framework for understanding musical performance anxiety'. *Research Studies in Music Education,* 28(1), 83–107.

Papageorgi, I., Creech, A., Haddon, E., Morton, F., De Bezenac, C., Himonides, E., Potter, J., Duffy, C., Whyton, T. and Welch, G. (2010) 'Investigating musical performance: Perceptions and prediction of expertise in advanced musical learners'. *Psychology of Music,* 38(1), 31–66.

Priest, T. (2006) 'Self-evaluation, creativity and musical achievement'. *Psychology of Music,* 34(1), 47–61.

Ross, M. and Mitchell, S. (1993) 'Assessing achievement in the arts'. *British Journal of Aesthetics,* 33(2), 99–112.

Salaman, W. (1994) 'The role of graded examinations in music'. *British Journal of Music Education,* 11(3), 209–211.

Seddon, F.A. and O'Neill, S.A. (2001) 'An evaluation study of computer-based compositions by children with or without prior experience of formal instrumental tuition'. *Psychology of Music,* 29(1), 4–19.

Steptoe, A. (2001) 'Negative emotions in music making: The problem of performance anxiety'. In P.N. Juslin and J.A. Sloboda (eds), *Music and Emotion: Theory and research.* Oxford: Oxford University Press.

Thompson, W.F. (2009) *Music, Thought, and Feeling: Understanding the psychology of music.* New York: Oxford University Press.

Thompson, W.F., Graham, P. and Russo, F.A. (2005) 'Seeing music performance: Visual influences on perception and experience'. *Semiotica*, 156(1–4), 177–201.

Wapnick, J., Ryan, C., Lacaille, N. and Darrow, A. (2004) 'Effects of selected variables on musicians' ratings of high-level piano performances'. *International Journal of Music Education*, 22(1), 7–20.

Webster, P.R. and Hickey, M. (1995) 'Rating scales and their use in assessing children's composition'. *The Quarterly Journal of Music Teaching and Learning*, 6(4), 28–44.

Wrigley, W. J. (2005) 'Improving music performance assessment'. Unpublished PhD thesis, Griffith University, Queensland, Australia.

Chapter 10

Learning through life

Hilary McQueen and Maria Varvarigou

Musical learning can occur throughout life, with much of it being beyond the compulsory 5–16 period of education. It also occurs beyond formal boundaries (Green, 2002). The term 'lifelong learning' might seem to be a truism, to the extent that adding the word 'lifelong' to 'learning' is unnecessary, because learning does not stop the moment a person completes a period of education or training. In spite of the apparent inevitability of learning throughout life, by experience or by intention, 'lifelong learning' has become associated with a more structured and accountable provision than was previously the case. Hence the government report *Higher Education in the Learning Society*, also known as the 'Dearing Report', stated that 'over the next 20 years, the United Kingdom must create a society committed to learning throughout life'(Dearing, 1997: 8). That which had once been advocated as desirable shifted towards a necessity. As Hodgson suggests, the notion of lifelong learning became a kind of anchor for securing a means to deal with 'a changing, frightening and unknown technological, economic, social, and political environment' (2000: 4). Yet lifelong learning is not a new term. For example, Yeaxlee referred to it in his book, *Lifelong Education* (1929). While Hodgson (2000) describes lifelong learning as a 'slippery and multifaceted' term, it has been defined as 'a cradle-to-grave, learner-centred concept and process, including compulsory education'(Lifelong Learning Foundation webpage).

The importance of continuing to engage in learning has been recognised by the government as more than an economic necessity. A White Paper *The Learning Revolution* was published by the Department for Innovation Universities and Skills (DIUS, 2009a), in which there is reference to the widespread engagement of adults in lifelong learning, although it could be said to be more of an expansion than a revolution.

The boom in book clubs, online research and blogging, together with the continuing popularity of museums, public lectures and adult education classes, all demonstrate that people in this country have a passion for learning. They may not call it education, but this informal adult learning makes a huge contribution to the well-being of the nation. It is a revolution this Government is proud to foster and encourage.

(DIUS, 2009b: 1)

Longworth (2003) distinguishes between different types of learning. Studying for qualifications, either in or closely allied to recognised educational institutions, may be called 'formal' learning. Musical examples include graded music exams, GCSE and BTEC exams, degrees, diplomas, and so forth. Those activities that are engaged with for the purpose of learning without an associated qualification might be termed 'non-formal', such as community choirs, music appreciation courses and learning an instrument for enjoyment. Finally, he refers to learning that occurs unintentionally as 'informal'. For example, listening to music on the radio, CDs or via the internet might result in informal learning. There is also 'lifewide learning' (Longworth, 2003: 45), which can incorporate formal, informal and non-formal because it refers to learning that takes place simultaneously in a person's life, rather than to learning through their lifespan. In this chapter, any learning that does not lead to a qualification will be referred to as 'non-formal', and incidental learning as 'informal'.

Formal lifelong learning opportunities in music

There are many opportunities to gain qualifications in music, and the majority of these are open to people of all ages, providing that the cost of lessons and exam fees can be covered where necessary (see also Chapter 9 on assessment). Technology has had a major impact on formal learning. Indeed, the possibility of broadcasting information via the media gave rise to a formal lifelong learning opportunity, the Open University (OU), originally destined to be called the University of the Air (OU, 2009a) when it was established in the early 1960s. Adult learners enrolled in increasing numbers and by 1980 the OU had 70,000 students (OU, 2009a). It now has almost three times that number (OU, 2009b). The desire, or perhaps social expectation, to gain higher level qualifications is also evident from the total number – over two million – enrolled on higher education courses in all institutions in the UK (HESA, 2009a). Of those, approximately 22,000 are enrolled on full- or part-time music courses (HESA, 2009b), roughly two-thirds of whom are male. Almost 36,000 were enrolled on Access to Higher Education courses in 2008 (Access to Higher Education, 2009) as a route into higher education. Although Access courses do not include music, there is a dedicated Access to Music (2009) business that has been running since 1992 to provide popular music training.

Non-formal learning opportunities in music

It is difficult (if not impossible) to ascertain how many adults are involved in non-formal learning. A recent government White Paper, *The Learning Revolution* (DIUS, 2009a), includes some statistical data, such as 53% of adults engaging in sporting activities. The paper taps into the existing learning activities and opportunities, promoting them as a means to weather the economic recession. Four initiatives are outlined: an informal (that is, non-formal) Adult Learning pledge; a Festival of Learning; an Open Space Movement and a Transformation Fund (DIUS, 2009a: 6–7). The pledge refers to signing up to promote participation in adult learning; the Festival of Learning was planned for October 2009 to celebrate existing, and encourage further, participation in non-formal learning; Open Space refers to the idea that more places that could house learning activities offer facilities for free or for a low fee to help more learning groups to form; and a £20 million fund was promised for innovative projects that help overcome barriers to learning. It is worth noting that 'learning festivals' already take place in several countries and have done since the late 1990s, many offering a range of activities, including music. Some are aimed at young people, some at families. Stockton-on-Tees, for example, has run a family learning festival since 1998 with themes of skills, health, music and numeracy (Longworth, 2003: 92). An annual Adult Learners' Week has been held annually in May at various sites around the UK since 1992 (Government Skills, 2008) and is now an international event. Music features in many of the programmes offered. For example, in 2009 Merthyr Tydfil held workshops in African drumming and singing.

Yeaxlee mentions the instigation of Music Competition Festivals in England around the 1900s, which 'opened out wide prospects of revived community music as a recreational and cultural factor in the life of the people, especially in rural areas' (1929: 103). While similar activities continue to provide learning opportunities, changes in technology have allowed access to a wealth of information and experiences. Music, both recorded and in score or tab form, can be downloaded from the internet. Some music festivals, orchestral and choral performances, and music videos are broadcast on television channels, including via dedicated music channels such as MTV, which began in 1981. Radio channels similarly offer a variety of listening experiences to suit most musical tastes.

Live Music Now (LMN, 2010a) is an organisation dedicated to providing opportunities for potentially excluded groups to benefit from musical experiences. The four areas of their work are special needs, well-being (generally for older people), the justice system and early years. A range of workshops are on offer and these aim to foster self-esteem, creativity, and social and cognitive skills. The intention is to offer sustained opportunities where possible so that there are greater benefits to participants.

Opportunities for non-formal learning abound. Musically, these include choirs, orchestras, bands, ensembles, instrumental tuition, and programmes intended for various social groups – older learners, for example. There is a plethora of diverse opportunities across the country. 'British Choirs on the Net' (http://www.choirs.org.uk/) lists choirs by county – 167 in Yorkshire alone, for instance. Around the UK there are choirs for jazz, gospel, women, men, early music, mixed repertoire, and so on. No doubt other groups exist beyond those listed. The Sage in Gateshead (see The Sage, 2010) offers a range of musical learning opportunities, such as choirs and instrumental groups for adults over the age of 50 ('Silver Programme') as well as training for young community music leaders. Another initiative is Rock Choir which claims to be 'the largest and most popular contemporary choir in the UK' (Rock Choir, 2010), offering an alternative to more traditional choirs. The Workers' Education Association (WEA) continues to offer courses. For example, the North West Region advertises learning 'lines' such as the Music Line or the Engineering Line, a learning journey with five 'stops' offering a mixture of class-based activities and field trips (WEA, 2007). There are also many other UK regional opportunities for instrumental workshops and groups, including steel pans, African drumming, ukuleles, Taiko drumming and, as part of poetry workshops, rapping. Some of these are run as businesses, such as Drumming Up Business (see DUB in References below), which offers workshops for teambuilding, stress relief or enjoyment. Other music opportunities are funded through charity, such as Totally Talented in Birkenhead for anyone aged 10–100 (see Totally Talented).

Several education programmes have been established in the UK, such as Richmix (2008) in East London, the Shetland Music initiative in Scotland (see Shetland-Music), YMCA courses all over the country and various summer schools – Sing for Pleasure, for instance – or independent music camps (Pitts, 2004, 2005) with the aim of providing opportunities for adults to engage in and explore creative music making, music technology and the music business, through cross-arts events and activities. There are also several music rehabilitation programmes for women and men of all ages. The Irene Taylor Trust 'Music in Prisons' is one such organisation that has offered arts and rehabilitation opportunities since 1995 (see Irene Taylor Trust).

Who participates in music activities, and why?

In the UK, Hillman (2002) sketched out the profile of the adults participating in a year-long community arts project (Call That Singing?) in Glasgow. The findings from the survey showed that: (1) all respondents were over the age of 60; (2) the majority were women; (3) the majority left full-time education aged 14 or 15; (4) the majority participated in at least one other weekly leisure activity; and (5) all respondents had enjoyed some form of singing/musical interest before joining.

Similar findings were revealed by Bowles (1991) who undertook a study in Austin, Texas. The study showed that prospective participants in adult music education were more likely to: (1) be aged between 25 and 55; (2) live in the city; (3) be female; (4) have higher-than-average incomes; (5) hold at least a first degree; (6) have had some type of music lesson when they were younger; (7) participate in a performance group, most likely a choir; (8) have some basic music knowledge and skills, which derived from engagement with music in school; (9) have informal music experiences (a surprisingly high proportion); (10) be musically self-motivated and have some degree of confidence in their own knowledge and skills; and (11) choose a course closely related to their musical experiences. A later report on the characteristics of the amateur adult singer (Bell, 2004), also from the USA, described a very similar profile to the two above-mentioned studies. Particular emphasis was placed on the fact that adult community choir singers exhibited a high level of commitment to choral singing. On the whole, studies from Canada (Cohen *et al.*, 2002), the USA (Darrough and Boswell, 1992) and the UK (Bungay and Skingley, 2008) suggest that during retirement, except in cases of poor health, elderly persons tend to maintain consistency in their activities.

A continuity theory of ageing suggests that successful ageing entails the continuation of activities from earlier in life (Cohen *et al.*, 2002). Several studies also suggest that adult participation is an extension of engagement with active music making in childhood, either in the home or at school. The pattern of engagement seems to change over the life course, diminishing in the middle years and increasing in retirement. There are many reasons for adults' participation in music. Some of the most salient, which are also supported by the literature on musical engagement in adulthood and later life, are:

1. Personal motivations, such as self-expression, a need for achievement, enjoyment and self-confidence (Taylor and Hallam, 2008; Hallam, 2006) and the use of leisure time (Laukka, 2007; Agahi and Parker, 2005).
2. Musical motivations, such as love of music, performing for oneself and others (Taylor and Hallam, 2008; Cohen *et al.*, 2006), learning more about music (Boswell, 1992).
3. Social motivations, such as meeting new people and being with friends (Hays, 2005; Hillman, 2002) and having a sense of belonging (Laukka, 2007; Hallam, 2006; Hays, 2005).
4. Psychological motivations, such as pleasure, mood regulation and relaxation (Laukka, 2007).

5. Spirituality, a term often used by music participants with an intention to express a 'sense of timelessness'.

(Hays and Minichiello, 2005)

Benefits from learning music through life

Research has indicated that engaging in music activities has a range of benefits which contribute to overall well-being as well as to social cohesion. There has been recognition that learning is a valuable human process, and that the more we learn, the richer we become as human beings (Jarvis, 2009). Wolf asserts that adults are attracted to educational experiences in later life for a variety of reasons, such as 'meaning-making, employment, inclusion, self-efficacy, spiritual development, leisure and travel, the desire for intellectual maintenance, care-giving, health and wellness' (2009: 50). There is also developmental and neurological research advancing the appropriateness and the benefits of continued learning (Cabenza, 2002; Cabenza *et al.*, 2002). In addition, research indicates social, psychological, emotional and physical benefits from participation in learning interactions for all adults across the life span.

Hillman (2002) found that the 'Call That Singing' project (CTS) attracted participants from different backgrounds, and this was believed to be breaking down cultural barriers and contributing to the cultural infrastructure of the city of Glasgow. The benefits from participation were, first, some respondents suggested that they felt they had improved in breathing and walking. Moreover, singing had helped to counter depression, grief and concerns with physical health, particularly for those who were widowed. Improvements in social life and self-confidence were also identified by the respondents (see Box 10.1). Furthermore, improvement in singing and general understanding of music and self-confidence seemed to contribute to more visits to arts and cultural events. On the whole, the study suggested that participatory singing 'is combating the potentially negative effects of ageing, along with the debilitating effects of bereavement, widowhood, declining health and isolation' (Hillman, 2002: 170).

Box 10.1 'Call That Singing?' – Examples of responses from participants

'I was alone and withdrawn. I had isolated myself. Through my involvement with CTS my self-esteem has improved. I love singing. I am surrounded by like-minded people and have learnt to live in the present.'

(widow)

'I was married and part of a couple for 40 years and that habit is hard to break, but thank goodness for CTS where I am never alone on choir nights and now my little choir entertains people less fortunate than ourselves.'

(widow)

'CTS is a kind of therapy for most people who attend, especially people on their own, to meet friends and other people. '

(married woman)

'CTS gives so many people happiness and friendship and more musical knowledge than they would have had.'

(married woman)
(Hillman, 2002: 166–167)

Music activities for prison inmates have also indicated important benefits. The Irene Taylor Trust's Music in Prisons programme is believed to help participants 'raise their life aspirations, enabling them to play a positive role in their communities' (www.musicinprisons.org.uk). Similarly, an evaluation of the Music in Prisons project (Cox and Gelsthorpe, 2008) indicated that it offered opportunities for inmates to engage in skills training and gave them the confidence to participate in other educational programmes. The report adds that:

> the men's experiences of the project, particularly their feelings of encouragement to try things without judgement and to work together on a venture, clearly facilitated the development of their individual competences and self-esteem. The individual competencies that the men gained through the project may have implications, not only for behaviour in prison in the short term, but perhaps also for foundational aspects of selfhood and human capital (the capacity to cooperate, relate to others, negotiate and share, for example).

(Cox and Gelsthorpe, 2008: 2)

Those participating in opportunities provided by Live Music Now (LMN) have also gained socially (see Box 10.2).

Box 10.2 Live Music Now – 'Meaningful moments' for older people

In partnership with Nightingale, a care home in London, LMN carried out a sustained programme of interactive music workshops in a special dementia unit, under professional observation. In ten monthly sessions, working with the same two specially trained LMN musicians, patients engaged with the music and communicated with others.

> John, a quiet, disengaged man, showed no real awareness of the other people living in the dementia community around him . . . [he] spent much of his days roaming the corridors of the home. . . . On his third visit [to the workshop], instead of sitting down, he approached Paval, one of the musicians who was seated at the piano, shook his hand and said 'on personalised Beethoven, how are you today?' It was the first time that staff had seen him independently engage in any activity, and so began John's participation in the workshops that were to follow.
>
> (LMN, 2010b)

The Music for Life Project (Hallam *et al.*, 2009) based at the Institute of Education, University of London, is currently undertaking an exploration of the positive effects of older (50+) people's participation in music activities, as well as investigating possible barriers to participation. Funded by the New Dynamics of Ageing Programme, a cross-council research initiative, the research includes a survey and interviews with those taking part in and facilitating a range of activities offered by three case study sites: the Silver Programme at The Sage, Gateshead (see Box 10.3); Westminster Adult Education Service; and the Connect Programme at the Guildhall School of Music & Drama.

Box 10.3 The Silver Programme at the Sage – Examples of responses from participants

'I have enjoyed listening to all types of music through my adult life and we always played music at home together. However, it was not until my mid-fifties that I decided I would like to learn to sing. At primary school I have been told that I could not sing and so had never attempted to do so. After taking singing lessons for 18 months I joined a choir and can honestly say that it added a new dimension to my life. I could never call myself a singer but I love singing and I know the joy I feel spills over to all areas of my life. The Sage community music programme is a great idea.'

(woman aged 68)

'The extension of adult education into musical activities for the elderly is a wonderful thing and has shown a lot of people what they can do – albeit, possibly a little late for some – and has to be encouraged and promoted for the benefit of society as a whole.'

(man aged 79)

'For people like me who live alone, either widowed, single or divorced, whose children have flown the nest, outside activities are a very important, if not essential, part of life. They give us a chance to meet people, make new friends, socialise as well as learning new skills which give us a sense of achievement.'

(woman aged 62)

(Hallam *et al.*, 2009)

The Sidney De Haan Research Centre for Arts and Health (2009) at Canterbury Christ Church University is also involved in ongoing research into involvement in music activities and related benefits for well-being and health. Activities, including singing and drumming that are aimed at mental health service users and adults with physical difficulties, are being evaluated.

The possible benefits of adult participation in music, in a professional or amateur capacity, are many and varied. Choral singing seems to have positive emotional, social, psychological and creative outcomes (Clift *et al.*, 2008a, 2008b). (See Chapter 5 for details on collective singing.) Participation in musical ensembles provides adults with an opportunity to socialise and make new friends. Boswell (1992: 39) suggests that 'performing in an ensemble is an ideal vehicle for fostering the vital interchange among generations, fulfilling our human potential throughout the life cycle'. Hallam (2006) emphasises that engaging with music has a range of positive personal and social outcomes that do not seem to diminish with age. Research carried out at Brixton Prison similarly found the following benefits from engaging in the Good Vibrations gamelan project:

- greater levels of engagement and an increased openness to wider learning
- improved listening and communication skills
- improved social skills and increased social interaction
- improved relationships with prison staff
- decreased levels of self-reported anger and a greater sense of calmness.

(Wilson *et al.*, 2008: 32)

Box 10.4 Positive outcomes from music projects in prisons

Cox and Gelsthorpe (2008) found positive outcomes from five-day projects in eight prisons. These included self-confidence, self-efficacy, autonomy and relationships.

Autonomy

A number of men who participated in the music project described various ways in which it instilled a sense of autonomy in them. There were two main dimensions of this feeling: one, the sense by the men that the project made them feel 'human', and two, the sense of self-confidence that they gained. The project leaders also structured the project in a way that enhanced individuals' sense of autonomy by endowing participants with choices, acknowledging their feelings, and giving them opportunities for self-direction. . . . By allowing participants to choose which instruments they played, participate

> *actively in the creation and direction of songs, and teasing out people's resourcefulness, the project also became a kind of safe testing ground for people less accustomed to expressing their autonomy.*
>
> (Cox and Gelsthorpe, 2008: 17)

There seem to be direct health benefits for music participants. Studies on choral performance with adult singers, both amateur (Kreutz *et al.*, 2004) and professional (Beck *et al.*, 2000), have found that choral performance increases secretory immunoglobulin A (sIgA) and reduces cortisol levels before and after singing. As sIgA is part of the immune system, which offers 'frontline' defence in mucosal membranes against infection, these findings imply health benefits for singers. Moreover, there seem to be lower mortality rates in those who attend cultural events, read books or periodicals, make music, or sing in a choir (Agahi and Parker, 2005; Byrgen *et al.*, 1996, 2009). Studies in the USA by Cohen (2009) and Cohen *et al.* (2006) have reported a significant reduction in doctor visits, medication use and loneliness when comparing people participating in music programmes with those participating in other leisure activities, such as crafts. Music participation also contributes to the expression of identity for many adults (Hillman, 2002; Laukka, 2007; Taylor and Hallam, 2008) and to a sense of purpose, motivation, empowerment and control (Clift *et al.*, 2008b; Hays, 2005; Sixsmith and Gibson, 2007).

Potential challenges to participating in music activities

According to Feinstein *et al.* (2008: 8), a third of adults leave school without basic qualifications and five million people in the UK are 'functionally illiterate'. Furthermore, those in the population who lack such skills are less likely to engage in adult learning opportunities, thereby increasing the gap between those who may benefit from lifelong learning and those who do not. Research has been referred to earlier in this chapter that suggests participating in music activities is more likely if adults have been engaged with music earlier in life. Therefore one challenge is how to encourage those relatively new to taking part in music, as well as those who have fewer skills, to engage in the opportunities that exist. In addition, the importance of outreach work to engage the more socially isolated members of the community is supported by Cacioppo *et al.*'s (2009) research into the increased withdrawal from society of those suffering from loneliness. Another challenge is providing opportunities that will engage older learners. The Silver Programme in Gateshead (see The Sage, 2010) offers a very diverse programme, but not all areas of the UK have the resources for this kind of provision.

Funding learning opportunities is a constant challenge that providers face. The government rhetoric that promotes opportunities for adult learners already referred to (White Paper: *The Learning Revolution*) can appear to conflict with the reality of funding provision. The overall UK public spending on education in 2009 was £80 billion, compared with £97 million when Yeaxlee was writing in the 1920s (Cantrill, 2009). However, of the total budget, approximately £5 billion is spent on adult education (DCSF, 2009). It is difficult to ascertain from the Treasury's breakdown how much of that is for non-formal learning opportunities rather than formal ones. In 1998 the government set up the Adult and Community Learning Fund (ACLF), which passed to the Learning and Skills Council (LSC) in 2004. Educational provision for the compulsory sector is now managed by the Department for Children, Schools and Families (DCSF) and by the new Skills Funding Agency (SFA) as part of the Department for Innovation, Universities and Skills (DIUS) rather than the LSC. A greater emphasis on 14–19 education and the funding of courses that lead to qualifications has been queried by the National Institute of Adult Continuing Education (NIACE, 2008) in their response to the government White Paper (*Raising Expectations*), which outlined proposals for educational delivery (DCSF/DIUS, 2008). NIACE comments: 'the paper's proposals present a serious risk to both the breadth and depth of publicly funded learning opportunities for adults in England' (NIACE, 2008: 1). Similar concerns are expressed by Help the Aged in their response to *The Learning Revolution* document (DIUS, 2009a): 'Money remains an important barrier to learning' (Help the Aged, 2008: 12). It is evident that many projects depend on charity and goodwill, unlikely to guarantee sustainable provision either in the short or long term. Indeed, the £20 million Transformation Fund pledged in the government's 'Learning Revolution' White Paper is more about 'setting up' than 'carrying on'. For music projects, this is a major challenge. The cost of tutors, venues and resources such as instruments can be prohibitive because they are continuous. Although the Transformation Fund might offer a one-off opportunity to 'address the barriers to learning some adults currently face' (DCSF/DIUS 2008: 6), its sustainability is questionable. This is important because there is evidence that what older learners want is long-term provision. The running costs might be offset by contributions from learners, but they often prefer to pay a small fee on the day rather than the equivalent of a course fee for the sessions to come (Hallam *et al.*, 2009).

Future research in music making with adult learners and the implications for practice

Historically, music educators and researchers have concentrated on the teaching and learning of music in childhood. However, systematic learning is nowadays widely recognised as a lifelong endeavour, and demographic data suggest that there is a growing population of older adults (Wolf, 2009) who warrant further research attention. Current UK government education policy gives limited opportunities for self-expression and personal enrichment through music to older learners (Taylor and Hallam, 2008). One of the keys to increased opportunities for adults and senior adults is group instruction. Group instruction provides an important opportunity for socialisation and makes the cost of participation more affordable. Hence, music leaders and music educators should be given opportunities for training and preparation before they work with this population so that music activities are led in a way that is appropriate for an older age group (Darrough and Boswell, 1992; Myers, 1992; Taylor and Hallam, 2008).

There has been relatively little research investigating the benefits and challenges for participants and facilitators of non-formal music activities for adults, although its importance has been acknowledged:

> Dius [sic – Department for Innovation, Universities and Skills] should make it a priority to commission some robust research to demonstrate to the Treasury the benefits of informal adult learning in order to increase the safeguarded budget.
>
> (Help the Aged, 2008: 10)

Further areas for research might relate to the unequal spread of opportunities, with some areas such as Gateshead and some parts of London being well provided for, and the impact that might have on potential participators. It is also becoming apparent that accessing information can pose a difficulty, likely to depend on the mobility and social network of individuals. One suggestion is that there should be a more centralised source of information with a clearer strategy for disseminating information for those with limited access to libraries and computers. In addition, it may well be that outreach work is essential for some older people to access the benefits of social activities, not least given recent findings on the negative effects of loneliness on maintaining social ties and the conclusion that 'aggressively targeting the people in the periphery to help repair the social networks' (Cacioppo et al., 2009: 989) is required.

Further reading

Hallam, S. (2005) *Enhancing motivation and learning throughout the lifespan*. London: Institute of Education, University of London.

Hodgson, A. (ed.) (2000) *Policies, Politics and the Future of Lifelong Learning*. London: Kogan Page.

References

Access to Higher Education (2009) *Key Statistics*. Online. <http://www.accesstohe.ac.uk/partners/statistics/2009/AccessKeyStats09.pdf> (accessed 30/01/2010).

Access to Music (2009) Online. <http://www.accesstomusic.co.uk/about/profile/> (accessed 30/01/2010).

Agahi, N. and Parker, M. (2005) 'Are today's older people more active than their predecessors? Participation in leisure-time activities in Sweden in 1992 and 2002'. *Ageing and Society*, 25, 925–941.

Beck, R.J., Cesario, T.C., Yousefi, A. and Enamoto, H. (2000) 'Choral singing, performance perception, and immune system changes in salivary immunoglobulin A and cortisol'. *Music Perception,* 18(1), 87–106.

Bell, C. (2004) 'Update of community choirs and singing in the United States'. *International Journal of Research in Choral Singing*, 2(1), 39–50.

Boswell, J. (1992) 'Human potential and lifelong learning'. *Music Educators Journal*, 79(4), 38–40.

Bowles, C.L. (1991) 'Self-expressed adult music education interests and music experiences'. *Journal of Research in Music Education*, 39(3), 191–205.

British Choirs on the Net. Online. <http://www.choirs.org.uk/england.htm> (accessed 30/01/2010).

Bungay, H. and Skingley, A. (2008) *The Silver Song Club Project: A formative evaluation*. Canterbury: Canterbury Christ Church University.

Byrgen, L.O., Johansson, S.-E., Konlaan, B.B., Grjibovski, A.M., Wilkinson, A.V. and Sjostrom, M. (2009) 'Attending cultural events and cancer mortality: A Swedish cohort study'. *Arts and Health*, 1(1), 64–73.

Byrgen, L.O., Konlaan, B.B. and Johansson, W.E. (1996) 'Attendance at cultural events, reading books or periodicals, and making music or singing in a choir as determined for survival: Swedish interview survey of living conditions'. *British Medical Journal*, 313, 1577–1580.

Cabenza, R. (2002) 'Hemisphere asymmetry reduction in older adults: The HAROLD model'. *Psychology and Ageing*, 17(1), 85–100.

Cabenza, R., Anderson, N.D., Locantore, J.K. and McIntosh, A.R. (2002) 'Aging carefully: Compensatory brain activity in high-performing older adults'. *NeuroImage*, 17(3), 1394–1402.

Cacciopo, J.T., Fowler, J.H. and Christakis, N.A. (2009) 'Alone in the crowd: The structure and spread of loneliness in a large social network'. *Journal of Personality and Social Psychology*, 97(6), 977–991.

Cantrill, C. (2009) *UK Public Spending*. Online. <http://www.ukpublicspending.co.uk/> (accessed 30/01/2010).

Clift, S., Hancox, G., Staricoff, R. and Whitmore, C. (2008a) *Singing and Health: A systematic mapping and review of non-clinical research*. Canterbury: Canterbury Christ Church University.

–– (2008b) *Singing and Health: Summary of a systematic mapping and review of non-clinical research* (978-1-899253-30-2). Canterbury: Canterbury Christ Church University.

Cohen, A., Bailey, B. and Nilsson, T. (2002) 'The importance of music to seniors'. *Psychomusicology*, 18, 89–102.

Cohen, G. (2009) 'New theories and research findings on the positive influence of music and the art on health with ageing'. *Arts and Health*, 1(1), 48–62.

Cohen, G.D., Perlstein, S., Chapline, J., Kelly, J., Firth, K.M. and Simmens, S. (2006) 'The Impact of professionally conducted cultural programmes on the physical health, mental health and social functioning of older adults'. *The Gerontologist*, 46(6), 726–734.

Cox, A. and Gelsthorpe, L. (2008) *Beats and Bars – Music in Prisons: An evaluation*. London: The Irene Taylor Trust.

Darrough, G.P. and Boswell, J. (1992) 'Older adult participants in music: A review of related literature'. *Bulletin of the Council for Research in Music Education*, 111, 25–34.

Dearing, R. (1997) *Higher Education in the Learning Society*. Report of the National Committee of Inquiry into Higher Education. London: HMSO.

Department for Children, Schools and Families (DCSF) (2009) *Supplementary Budgetary Information 2008–09*. Online. <http://www.hm–treasury.gov.uk/d/sbi0809_dcsf.pdf > (accessed 20/01/2010).

Department for Children, Schools and Families (DCSF)/Department for Innovation, Universities and Skills (DIUS) (2008) *Raising Expectations: Enabling the system to deliver*. Online. <http://www.dius.gov.uk/~/media/publications/R/Raising_Expectations> (accessed 20/01/2010).

Department for Innovation, Universities and Skills (DIUS) (2009a) *The Learning Revolution*. Online. <http://www.dius.gov.uk/skills/engaging_learners/informal_adult_learning/~/media/publications/L/learning_revolution> (accessed 20/01/2010).

–– (2009b) *The Learning Revolution: Executive Summary*. Online. <http://www.dius.gov.uk/skills/engaging_learners/informal_adult_learning/~/media/publications/L/learning_revolution_exec_summary> (accessed 18/02/2010).

DUB – Drumming Up Business. Online. <http://www.drummingupbusiness. org/> (accessed 01/02/2010).

Feinstein, L., Vorhaus, J. and Sabates, R. (2008) 'Foresight Mental Capital and Wellbeing Project'. In *Learning through Life: Future challenges*. London: Government Office for Science.

Government Skills (2008) Online: <http://www.government-skills.gov.uk/ news/190508-adult-learners-week.asp> (accessed 01/02/2010).

Green, L. (2002) *How Popular Musicians Learn: A way ahead for music education*. Aldershot: Ashgate.

Hallam, S. (2006) *Music Psychology in Education*. London: Institute of Education, University of London.

Hallam, S., Creech, A., Pincas, A. and Gaunt, H. (2009) *Promoting Social Engagement and Well-Being in Older People through Community-Supported Participation in Musical Activities*. Institute of Education, University of London, (Funded by the ESRC/New Dynamics of Ageing, grant reference RES-356-25-0015).

Hays, T. (2005) 'Well-being in later life through music'. *Australasian Journal of Ageing*, 24(1), 28–32.

Hays, T. and Minichiello, V. (2005) 'The contribution of music to quality of life in older people: An Australian qualitative study'. *Ageing and Society*, 25, 261–278.

Help the Aged (2008) *Informal Adult Learning: Shaping the way ahead – consultation response*. Online. <http://www.helptheaged.org.uk/NR/rdonlyres /96BF871F–1CC3–4D9A–9314–17E5B8DF6C56/0/Informal_Adult_Learning_ response.pdf> (accessed 20/01/2010).

Higher Education Statistics Agency (HESA) (2009a) Online. <http://www. hesa.ac.uk/index.php/content/category/1/1/161/> (accessed 20/01/2010).

–– (2009b) Online. <http://www.hesa.ac.uk/index.php?option=com_ datatables&Itemid=121&task=show_category&catdex=3> (accessed 20/01/2010).

Hillman, S. (2002) 'Participatory singing for older people: A perception of benefit'. *Health Education*, 102(4), 163–171.

Hodgson, A. (ed.) (2000) *Policies, Politics and the Future of Lifelong Learning*. London: Kogan Page.

Irene Taylor Trust. Online. <http://www.musicinprisons.org.uk> (accessed 18/02/ 2010).

Jarvis, P. (2009) 'Introduction'. In P. Jarvis (ed.), *The Routledge International Handbook of Lifelong Learning*. London: Routledge.

Kreutz, G., Bongard, S., Rohrmann, S., Grebe, D., Bastian, H.G. and Hodapp, V. (2004) 'Effects of choir singing or listening on secretory immunoglobulin A, cortisol and emotional state'. *Journal of Behavioural Medicine*, 27(6), 623–635.

Laukka, P. (2007) 'Uses of music and psychological wellbeing among the elderly'. *Journal of Happiness Studies*, 8(2), 215–241.

Lifelong Learning Foundation. Online. <http://www.lifelonglearnresearch.co.uk> (accessed 06/12/2009).

Live Music Now (LMN) (2010a) Online. <http://www.livemusicnow.org.uk> (accessed 20/01/2010).

–– (2010b) Online. <http://www.livemusicnow.org.uk/how_do_they_benefit /item/63607/date/2009–08–19/title/case_history_older_people_39_ meaningful_moments_39.htm> (accessed 18/02/2010).

Longworth, N. (2003) *Lifelong Learning in Action: Transforming education in the 21st century*. London: Kogan Page.

Myers, D.E. (1992) 'Teaching learners of all ages'. *Music Educators Journal*, 79(4), 23–26.

National Institute of Adult Continuing Education (NIACE) (2008) *Raising Expectations: Enabling the system to deliver. A response to the White Paper* (Cm 7348) *from the National Institute of Adult Continuing Education*. Online. <http://www.niace.org.uk/sites/default/files/raising-expectations.pdf> (accessed 12/12/2009).

Open University (OU) (2009a) Online. <http://www.open.ac.uk/about/ou/p3.shtml> (accessed 20/12/2009).

–– (2009b) Online. <http://www.studentastic.co.uk/TheOpenUniversity.html> (accessed 20/12/2009).

Pitts, S. (2004) 'Lessons in learning: Learning, teaching and motivation at a music summer school'. *Music Education Research*, 6(1), 81–95.

–– (2005) *Valuing Musical Participation*. Aldershot: Ashgate.

Qualifications and Curriculum Development Agency (QCDA) (2009) *The National Qualifications Framework*. Online. <http://www.qcda.gov.uk/library Assets/media/qca-06-2298-nqf-web.pdf> (accessed 20/12/2009).

Richmix (2008) Online. <http://www.richmix.org.uk> (accessed 18/02/2010).

Rock Choir (2010) Online. <http://www.rockchoir.com/> (accessed 18/02/2010).

Shetland-Music. Online. <http://www.shetland-music.com> (accessed 18/02/2010).

Sidney De Haan Research Centre for Arts and Health (2009) Online. <http://www.canterbury.ac.uk/centres/sidney-de-haan-research/research-projects.asp> (accessed 20/12/2009).

Sixsmith, A. and Gibson, G. (2007) 'Music and the wellbeing of people with dementia'. *Ageing and Society,* 27(1), 127–145.

Taylor, A. and Hallam, S. (2008) 'Understanding what it means for older students to learn basic musical skills on a keyboard instrument'. *Music Education Research,* 10(2), 285–306.

The Sage (2010) Online. <http://www.thesagegateshead.org/l_and_p/joinin/silverprogramme.aspx> (accessed 18/02/2010).

Totally Talented. Online. <http://www.totallytalented.co.uk/> (accessed 01/02/2010).

Workers' Education Association (WEA) (2007) Online. <http://www.nw.wea.org.uk/tiki-index.php?page= Just+the+Ticket> (accessed 18/02/2010).

Wilson, D., Caulfield, L. and Atherton, S. (2008) 'Good vibrations: The long-term impact of a prison-based music project', *Prison Service Journal*, 182, 27–32.

Wolf, M.A. (2009) 'Older adulthood'. In P. Jarvis (ed.), *The Routledge International Handbook of Lifelong Learning*. London: Routledge.

Yeaxlee, B.A. (1929) *Lifelong Education: A sketch of the range and significance of the adult education movement*. London: Cassell.

Chapter 11

The initial and ongoing education of music teachers

Colin Durrant and Kate Laurence

Education or training? These are two of the terms used to denote the preparation of students embarking on a career in the teaching profession. While it remains a 'profession', we prefer generally and for the purposes of this chapter, to use the word 'education', because teaching should ideally promote and encourage thinking, reasoning and rationalising in preference to unquestioning obedience. We train dogs and horses to obey; whereas, hopefully, we educate humans to think for themselves. So, that is our preference, but during the chapter there will be references to the term 'training', as this is the term used, for example, by government agencies, at least at the time of writing in 2010. The choice of terminology itself lends a tacit qualitative inference to the perceptions of the preparation of teachers and the profession as a whole by the various agencies involved.

Initial teacher education and routes into teaching

Initial teacher education (ITE) has undergone significant change since 1992, with the move towards schools taking on more significant responsibility in conjunction with higher education providers. In tandem, the setting up of the Teacher Training Agency and now the Training and Development Agency (TDA) has shifted the agenda in teacher education on to a more political level. The TDA is, after all, a government agency that distributes and manages the provision, effectively stipulates the curriculum of teacher education, maintains a guiding hand over ITE and funds the whole enterprise. This paradigm shift was in response to an evident distrust of universities being able to design and adequately provide suitable courses for the education of teachers. In order to supply the profession, especially over the economic boom years of the 1990s and up to 2008, in addition to the normal college and university undergraduate and postgraduate programmes, new routes into teaching have been established and trialled.

The multiplicity of available training routes into the music teaching profession could be seen an increasing advantage, allowing potential teachers the opportunity to select programmes most suited to their particular needs and situations. The TDA's online 'Ways Into Teaching' statement claims that there are now 'options to suit everyone – no matter what your qualifications, experience, preferences or personal circumstances' (TDA, 2009a). Approximately 85 per cent of teacher education in England and Wales is offered by mainstream Initial Teacher Training providers (TDA, 2009b) and includes the traditional university-based routes such as the Postgraduate or Professional Graduate Certificate of Education (PGCE). Employment-based routes, such as the Graduate Teacher Programme (GTP) and the Teach First scheme, account for the remaining training provision. The Postgraduate Diploma of Education (PGDE) operates as the equivalent university-based route into teaching in Scotland. Significant in all these routes is the concept of 'partnership' between schools and higher education.

According to Ofsted (2007), the success of increasingly popular employment-based schemes is that they are particularly good at recruiting shortage-subject candidates into secondary teaching. Music has been identified as one of these shortage subjects for some time in England and Wales. Programmes such as these are believed to be beneficial because they draw applications from those with a wealth of skills and relevant experience. In addition, student-teachers (we will use this nomenclature in preference to 'trainees') are able to immerse themselves in the professional life of the school. The TDA (2009a) suggests that the GTP is a 'good option for those who might want to change career to teaching but continue earning while you train'. In addition, and borne out of the business community's desire to effect social change, independent charities such as Teach First have emerged as alternative employment-based routes. Since 2002, Teach First's mission has been to 'address educational disadvantage by transforming exceptional graduates into effective, inspirational teachers and leaders in all fields' (Teach First, 2009). Teach First's intention is for the best graduates, who would not normally consider a teaching career, to be placed in challenging schools for at least two years.

However, each of the routes present some issues:

- The GTP has been found to be problematic in secondary phase training in terms of teachers' abilities in 'applying their subject knowledge to teaching and devising strategies to support and assess pupils' learning' (Ofsted, 2007). Though schools can be seen to have greater responsibility and autonomy for training teachers on employment-based programmes, there may be issues if school-based training does not rigorously embed or underpin the practice of teaching in educational theory. Interestingly, the Scottish General Teaching Council operates independently from the rest of the UK and does not accept employment-based routes as a way into teaching, suggesting a possible mistrust of their validity.

- The Teach First scheme has largely favourable support (Ofsted, 2008) yet it could be viewed as a short-term solution for teacher recruitment, its altruistic mission unhelpful in dispelling the view that high-quality graduates are synonymous with long-term, exceptional teaching.
- More traditional routes, such as the PGCE, have recently undergone masters' level remodelling as part of a move to create a postgraduate profession. Though this has helped to strengthen links between educational theory and practice, the nine-month course remains a short induction into teaching. There are also implications for those trainees who might be deemed to be competent practitioners yet have difficulties with work at postgraduate level.

Musicians and initial teacher education

There are additional challenges to consider for musicians. The increase in personality and identity research of musicians and teachers (Kemp, 1996; Dolloff, 1999; Cox, 2002; Hargreaves *et al.*, 2007) illuminates musicians' socially constructed view of themselves as 'musicians who teach'. High-quality music graduates may wish to retain their work and identity as musicians by pursuing several employment pathways and may decide to continue teaching alongside a professional performance career path. The demands of full-time teaching and ITE courses are therefore unsuitable, and schemes such as Teach First, for example, may be too inflexible an option for high-quality music graduates who wish to continue with other professional work.

There remains considerable scope for ITE routes to respond to the individual needs of musicians wishing to pursue qualified teacher status (QTS). How, for example, could a musician who has a wealth of experience of working in schools, providing workshops and other valuable musical activities for children, gain accreditation for their experience and skills when they do not have the required qualification profile to enter the traditional model of ITE?

Boxes 11.1 and 11.2 show two examples that are typical of the increasingly common applications and enquiries to the primary and secondary PGCE-course teams at the Institute of Education, London.

Box 11.1 Application for a part-time route into teaching

An experienced sound engineer and session musician with experience working in the music industry for some years. She has a wealth of experience to offer as a musician but does not have appropriate qualifications, for example a degree in music. She is an exceptional musician in her field. She would also like to continue with part-time freelance work as this is important to her and would therefore like to pursue a part-time route into teaching.

Box 11.2 A music graduate finding a route into primary music teaching

A very able music graduate who is employed as an unqualified classroom music specialist in a number of primary schools, particularly focusing on the wider opportunities programme. He also has experience teaching individual instrumental lessons in the primary phase. He would like to gain QTS and continue to work with primary schools but is reluctant to teach and train in all areas of the primary curriculum. In order to avoid this, he applies for the secondary music PGCE course even though he does not intend to teach in this phase.

In response to the first example, there is good news for ITE as a number of models have emerged which address this person's needs. PGCE courses in London, Birmingham and the North West, for example, now provide part-time and flexible training routes and distance-learning modules, which encourage students to maintain and develop their independence and skills as musicians at the same time as they embark on their journey towards QTS. Some of these courses work alongside conservatoires and undergraduate programmes as effective ways to secure and develop highly skilled musicians in classroom and instrumental teaching. Other routes allow musicians who do not hold a music degree the opportunity to combine this qualification with QTS. But these courses are still few and, understandably, schools are still to be persuaded of the benefits of offering flexible and part-time placement experiences for these musicians.

The second example for the primary phase training is problematic. The need for good-quality music teaching in primary education continues to present challenges (Hallam *et al.*, 2009; Hennessy, 2000; Ofsted, 2007). Those who wish only to focus on their subject tend to make applications to secondary PGCE music courses in order to gain QTS, even though they intend to teach in primary schools. This particular provision of ITE is therefore not the most suitable for their needs.

Ofsted and the TDA are not yet persuaded that schools make the most of trainees' existing experience and skills. In addition, ITE providers would perhaps make more of Accredited Prior Learning and Skills in order to create suitable, flexible training programmes which appeal to musicians at different stages in their lives and which would better fulfil the TDA's 'Ways Into Teaching' online statement (2009a). Consequently, there is further need to personalise music teacher education programmes in order to attract the very best applicants to the profession.

Subject expertise

The number of degree programmes appearing since 1992 in areas such as popular music, jazz, world musics, screen music, multimedia applications of music, music business and music industry management can be seen as ways to reflect and engage with wider issues of music as cultural practice. As such, the range of degree courses now on offer is considerably broader than previously (QAA, 2002: 3).

ITE programmes draw students from a wealth of university first degree qualifications that offer both academic and more practical ways of gaining a music degree. Undergraduate courses are offered in specialist or joint areas such as 'Music Production for Film and Television' (Leeds College of Music), 'Physics with Studies in Musical Performance' (Royal College of Music in conjunction with Imperial College), as well as an increasing number of discrete music technology and popular music courses. Ethnomusicology specialist courses offer practical experience of learning non-Western instruments. School music will inevitably benefit from a department that can offer a variety of musical experiences provided by specialists within their field and where curriculum teaching has been broadened to reflect the interests of all pupils.

There are still challenges for ITE, however, as students who have come from undergraduate music courses that are very specialist in nature are not necessarily equipped to meet the breadth and demands of the National Curriculum or the examination specifications (Gammon, 2003; Ofsted, 2007). This becomes problematic for typically small secondary school music departments where only one or two teachers are employed to deliver a broad range of opportunities (see Chapter 14). The *Making More of Music* evaluation of music in schools identifies problems with the development of subject expertise, acknowledging that initial teacher education 'ensures subject expertise through entry requirements and provides support through developing pedagogy' (Ofsted, 2009: 49) yet suggests there are weaknesses as subject focus and expertise are mostly developed in response to the schools in which the trainees are placed and do not go beyond the practice which they observe in these departments. In addressing the possible need for greater breadth of subject knowledge and skill, we are aware that specialism may be compromised. Whether this trend towards a 'smorgasbord' of music is at the expense of providing a depth of musical experience for pupils is, nevertheless, open to debate.

Greater rigour in the auditing of subject expertise has been raised as being needed both within PGCE and within employment-based courses. However, auditing subject expertise through self-evaluation may mean that student-teachers and their school-based mentors do not always identify broader areas for development. Teacher education should not just be about auditing skills or reflecting on actions, without fundamentally making headway in identifying and developing those key skills that are really needed in school music teachers and that may not have been provided or developed in undergraduate programmes.

Until 2008, those entering ITE courses and identified as needing subject knowledge and skills development could be advised by the providers to attend TDA-funded subject-enhancement short courses. These were offered in order to 'improve recruitment to ITE courses, particularly priority subjects, by broadening the pool of individuals eligible to begin training' (TDA, 2008). Since then, changes in priorities at the TDA regarding subject enhancement mean that the subject-knowledge booster courses for music are no longer funded. What are the implications of such a move?

Subject knowledge and skills development continue to resonate in primary school discourse since musical expertise has been perceived to be the currency of a select few (Hallam *et al.*, 2009; Rogers *et al.*, 2008; Hennessy, 2000; Ofsted, 2007). Ofsted (2007) identified 'shortcomings' in the subject knowledge of primary music student-teachers as part of the employment-based route inspection and a recent study further illuminates the self-efficacy and perceptions of infant and primary education student-teachers in teaching music (Hallam *et al.*, 2009). One-year ITE courses are therefore limited in offering robust opportunities to develop a primary music specialism for all student-teachers, and even those who have chosen to take music as an option on their course of study have limited time to pursue this. Though a recent training day given by EMI Music Sound Foundation was found to be beneficial in addressing primary music teachers' confidence and their ability to teach music (Hallam, 2009; see Chapter 13), calls for further and significant investment into primary phase music training remains fundamental to teachers' long-term subject expertise development.

Continuing professional development of music teachers

It is interesting to note that, at the time of writing (late 2009), the political polemic regarding the professional development of teachers in England has gathered momentum, with government, through the auspices of the TDA, seeking to control the agenda both with the introduction of masters' level credits during postgraduate training and with the slow emergence of the Masters' degree in Teaching and Learning (MTL). The TDA (2009d) recognises continuing professional development (CPD) as consisting of 'reflective activity designed to improve an individual's attributes, knowledge, understanding and skills. It supports individual needs and improves professional practice.' It recognises that such development can be sourced from (1) within the school; (2) through cross-school and virtual networks; and (3) external expertise, such as local authorities and universities. While the recognition of professional development as a valuable entity in teaching and the encouragement of more sustained and structured courses in preference to one-off, quick-fix courses is to be welcomed, the swing from a more subject-determined model of professional development to a more generic one must be questioned. Indeed, the TDA has 'in collaboration with partner organisations' identified national priorities for teachers' continuing professional development for the academic years 2007–2010. These are grouped in three areas: (1) pedagogy (covering behaviour management, subject knowledge and supporting curriculum change); (2) personalisation (covering equality and diversity and special educational needs and disability); (3) people (covering working with other professionals and school leadership).

A wide range of professional development courses for teachers is offered by universities, local authorities, music colleges and independent organisations, such as the Associated Board of the Royal Schools of Music: a quick 'Google' will reveal almost bespoke events and courses – from training in the Kodaly method to enhancing musical leadership or developing skills in technology.

Purposes of professional development

Clearly the main thrust of professional development is to remain reflexive and abreast of current thinking and changes that occur in music teaching and learning. As in the case of other professions, particularly the medical profession, models of practice change according to research and government policy (notably in our case within the primary school curriculum) and, in some instances, in defiance of academic research findings. Burn-out in teachers, as with air traffic controllers, is noted as a relatively common phenomenon (Kelly, 1999; Madsen and Hancock, 2002) and the role that professional development courses and programmes play in renewing and revitalising teachers can potentially be key to the promotion of the human dynamic and dimension in teaching and learning. The professional development needs of teachers have naturally changed and varied according to the stage of career (Conway, 2008) and, whereas over the recent decades advances in technology and attitudes to world music – often outside the immediate comfort zone of teachers – have necessitated in-service courses in these areas, most effective in-service training involves problem-solving, skill-based and knowledge-based activities to update and refine classroom practice.

We are not only concerned with school classroom teachers – the peripatetic instrumental teacher must be included in the discourse on initial and continuing professional development. Baker (2005) discusses Music Service teachers' notions of pedagogical competence and occupational prospects as they approach mid-career. In this research, respondents were drawn from a comprehensive life history study of 28 local authority employees. Data were collected and analysed between October 2002 and March 2004 and the findings suggest a critical phase professionally between the ages of 36 and 42. At this stage teachers often reach a professional apex, plateau or crisis in the light of high pedagogical efficacy and career limitations. It culminates in a transformation of self-identity. Owing to respondents' unease about this period in their professional lives, the whole career structure of Music Service peripatetic teachers comes under scrutiny in Baker's study.

One of the key issues concerning professional development is the ability to discern what is needed. Teachers themselves may well be able to identify a particular need or a lack of skill and knowledge in a certain area, but there is always a possibility that 'you don't know what you don't know' (a somewhat Rumsfeldian concept). Continuing professional development, however, can raise awareness and begin to address such needs, as demonstrated in Durrant and Varvarigou (2008). At the newly qualified induction stage, teachers are more likely to grasp opportunities to continue their development, whereas mid-career, the pressures of perhaps a senior management or head of department role in the school might make choosing to embark on extensive further study more challenging. In which case – why bother?

Within our own context of an award-bearing professional development programme in music education, the pattern of change in recent years has been to note the move towards a wider age range of teachers embarking on the programme from both home and international contexts. Many teachers have traditionally regarded an MA as being a mid-career development, having gained experience in the classroom before taking the plunge. More recently, the moves towards creating a more fluid sequence between initial teaching education and continuing professional development has meant that younger, less experienced teachers are sitting alongside those who may well hold senior school positions. However, the needs of these two distinct groups are perceived as being different. The approaches to study between these two identified groups are also noticeably different, with some assuming a 'tick-box' mentality – 'which bit do I have to read for this essay?' – as opposed to a broader, more 'thinking outside the box' approach. However, this is merely perception and needs to be validated by more structured and robust research. Examples of student profiles are provided in Boxes 11.3–11.5.

Box 11.3 A newly qualified teacher

A student who has just completed her PGCE, specialising in music in the secondary phase. As she has gained 60 masters' credits during her PGCE year, she feels an obligation to continue her studies towards a full MA award, and realises that this is a sensible move professionally.

Box 11.4 A mid-career 'home' student

An experienced Head of Music at a London secondary school who is mid-career and undecided about whether to pursue a move towards senior management in the school system or remain in the music area. He anticipates that doing an MA will open doors and potentially create more options for him for the future. He also feels that there is an expectation that masters' level study is a key element in a teacher profile and that he does not want to feel left behind by younger, more newly qualified teachers.

Box 11.5 An international student

A student from Singapore who has enrolled on a award-bearing postgraduate professional development programme in order to be able to contribute more fully in her capacity as an official in the Singapore Ministry of Education Music Department. Her fees and salary are paid for by the Ministry, and she expects on return to make key decisions that will impact upon extra-core curricular activities, particularly with regard to the Singapore Youth Music Festival.

Programmes and courses

In England, professional development programmes in Music Education at masters' level are offered (at the time of writing) at a number of institutions, including the Institute of Education, University of London, and Newcastle, Kingston, Reading, Roehampton and Edge Hill universities, where it appears either as a discrete programme or as a pathway within an 'Education' structure. These are often curriculum-focused or discipline-focused (e.g. 'Psychology of Music') with the specific intention of attracting teachers in the local area on a part-time basis and, in some cases, full-time students from overseas.

Bauer *et al.* (2003) carried out a study to determine if one-week music technology workshops can be an effective means for the professional development of music teachers in using technology with their classes. The results indicated that three indicators of effectiveness – teacher knowledge, teacher comfort and frequency of teacher use – could be significantly improved in such settings. However, the researchers noted that although the level of competence and use of technology was significant immediately following the workshop, this level had dropped off at the end of the year, though not to the pre-workshop levels. This brings into question, of course, the length of courses to optimise their effectiveness. How much less effective would three-day, two-day or even one-day workshops be? How much more effective would a four-week course become? Naturally, release for teachers to attend lengthy courses outside the school impact upon school finances. But, to use the contemporary jargon: How can the impact be quantified?

Dolloff (1996) carried out research on the professional development of choral music educators in a region of Canada within a three-year project and identified three important features of the experience: (1) the participants were involved in a long-term commitment (three years) to professional development; (2) a master teacher was used to model instruction; and (3) the teachers were able to try out – with their own students – the techniques they'd discussed and seen modelled. This would suggest that longer courses have more significant and sustaining impact than shorter ones, though the consequent economic implications again have to be acknowledged. Similarly, Durrant and Varvarigou (2008) reported on the reflective procedures of students on a 'Choral Conducting, Leadership and Communication' module that takes place from January to June each year at the Institute of Education, University of London. Here students have time, following practice-based seminars, to look (in between teaching sessions) at videos of their own and other students' conducting, uploaded on to the virtual learning environment, 'Blackboard'. They could then reflect upon and review their own and others' conducting in relation to various issues that have been addressed in seminars. Examples of students' reflections on their progress in relation to gesture can be found in Durrant (2009) and include:

Small changes in conductors' gestures can evoke large difference in singing by groups, but why does this happen? How?

After viewing the video of me conducting, I have come to realise how the slightest movements made by a conductor can have a major effect on the outcome of the vocal quality from the choir.

The development of such skills as these impact on practice, but not only that, they enable the teacher to consider the issues that can make a difference and make choices accordingly. The realisation is almost more powerful and effective than the practice itself and can create a feeling of confidence and esteem that has additional and immeasurable value for the teacher. Again, longer more sustained courses have their benefits.

As part of his reflection-in-action research of his studies on an award-bearing programme, Garner (2009) used the Schönian (1983, 1987) model to evaluate the impact of this particular professional development on his work as an experienced Head of Music in a challenging secondary school in north London. He realised that:

> reflections 'in-action' or otherwise have never failed to quickly reveal that my continuous need for personal and professional development, including self-reflection, seem inexorably driven by the numerous changes and inadequacies of state educational provision and its unerring systemic and operational failures. Further reflection on the teaching profession reveals substantive and far-reaching differences between the disquieting omnipresence of teaching as opposed to that of the other caring professions.
>
> (Garner, 2009: 9)

This was not a 'how-to-teach more effectively in the classroom' style of professional development. He goes on to comment more specifically on the impact of individual modules on his teaching and thinking – yes, thinking. Referring to one particular module, Garner writes:

> The depth of the philosophical discourse occasionally and uncomfortably unearthed the very foundations on which both experienced and novice practitioners had, up until that moment based their musical pedagogy. Conversely the module had the tacit ability to reveal many misconceptions, unconscious prejudices and little thought through preferences.
>
> (Garner, 2009: 27)

And later:

> The module certainly informed my practice, but as Marx (1845) pointed out earlier with regard to the real effectiveness of philosophical discourse, the point is 'to change it'.
>
> (Garner, 2009: 30)

Philosophical discourse is not something that appears very often within the normal curriculum structure of ITE or CPD courses.

Organisations and associations

The worth of any professional development experience is dependent on the impact it has on teachers, and ultimately on those teachers' students (Bauer, 2007). Some professional music associations in the UK, such as the National Association of Music Educators (NAME, 2009) or associations for more specific interest – for example, the Association of British Choral Directors (ABCD) – hold conferences that may offer teachers some kind of professional renewal – a 'fix-it' for the coming year. In the UK, however, there is no bona fide umbrella organization equivalent to the Music Educators National Conference in the USA (MENC, 2009), where all teachers and student-teachers belong, regionally and within particular 'chapters' or interest groups, and thus have major impact on the general lives of music teachers. This association has an active membership of 75,000, with an additional 60,000 'honour' students and supporters. In contrast, even accepting the population difference between the two countries, the UK's NAME has a membership of 1,875 – a significantly lower proportion of music teachers. The culture of belonging to professional organisations does not appear to be as prevalent here as in the USA and is, therefore, not perceived as being a conduit for personal professional development in any significant way.

Ways forward for music and teacher education: Partnership, innovation and quality

In any situation, it is the networking among similar professionals that is a significant strength of professional development programmes and individual shorter courses. Indeed, Conway's (2008) findings support past research in that teachers perceived informal interactions with other music teachers as the most powerful form of professional development. Music teachers often work in small departments, sometimes in isolation from other musicians and even other teachers and need support and validation of their work through contact with others who are in similar situations. Rather than just concentrating on gaining knowledge of the latest curriculum or pedagogical enterprise, opportunities for music teachers to network, reflect, discuss, argue, learn, think, challenge and generally professionally develop should be paramount in order to maintain a healthy and motivated music teaching profession.

Partnership between initial teacher education programmes and schools involves a relationship that must go beyond merely a 'placement' experience for student teachers. This is a concept that could be further explored and creatively developed. Professional development is now key for all elements of teacher education partnerships and is moving towards a review and rethink of how best to support music teachers and their mentors.

For example, traditional one-day training session models for mentors may be viewed as outmoded, short-term and often ineffective, as research cited above has shown. Effective mentoring goes beyond pragmatic approaches to teaching and learning or using the professional standards as competency performance assessment. Another rethink of initial music teacher education might make more use of 'hubs' where successful primary schools, secondary phase music departments and further education colleges can offer collaborative placement models, which present specialist and cross-phase training activity and eliminate more isolated school experience models. Collaborative partnerships with professional arts organisations might be offered as a holistic approach to CPD and ITE. Collectively, they may play a significant part in the development process of music teachers, including improved integration and transition across phases, development of cross-curricular work, and sharing and support for subject expertise. Furthermore, and as part of the development of successful partnerships, it is important that ITE and CPD music programmes do not become a mirror or response to school or political agendas.

Personalisation is integral to successful teacher education reform, and music education programmes need to be reflexive to the needs of those wishing to pursue a music teaching career alongside other employment, or as a way to be inclusive of those whose personal circumstances do not allow them to access current provision. A music graduate with existing experience in educational settings may be viewed as having a reliable and current knowledge base for teaching. Music education programmes ideally will recognise the value of accreditation and recognition of prior skills and experiences, which may well then require a more imaginative approach to quality assurance procedures. This in turn would enable a really personalised, inspired and creative approach to the initial and continuing professional development of music teachers, responsive to the needs of teachers and those they teach.

References

Baker, D. (2005) 'Peripatetic music teachers approaching mid-career: A cause for concern?'. *British Journal of Music Education*, 22(2), 141–153.

Bauer, W. (2007) 'Research on professional development for experienced music teachers'. *Journal of Music Teacher Education*, 17, 12.

Bauer, W., Reese, S. and McAllister, P. (2003) 'Transforming music teaching via technology: The role of professional development'. *Journal of Research in Music Education*, 51(4) 289–301.

Conway, C. (2008) 'Experienced music teacher perceptions of professional development throughout their careers'. *Bulletin of the Council for Research in Music Education*, 176, 7–18.

Cox, G. (2002) *Living Music in Schools 1923–1999*. Aldershot: Ashgate.

Dolloff, L.A. (1996) 'Expertise in choral music education: Implications for teacher education'. Doctoral dissertation, University of Toronto, 1994. *Dissertation Abstracts International*, 56(07), 2600.

–– (1999) 'Imagining ourselves as teachers: The development of teacher identity in music teacher education'. *Music Education Research,* 1(2), 191–208.

Durrant, C. (2009) 'Communicating and accentuating the aesthetic and expressive dimension in choral conducting'. *International Journal of Music Education*, 27, 326–341.

Durrant, C. and Varvarigou, M. (2008) 'Real time and virtual: Tracking the professional development and reflections of choral conductors'. *Reflecting Education,* 4(1), 72–80.

Gammon, V. (2003) 'The subject knowledge of secondary music PGCE applicants'. *British Journal of Music Education,* 20(1), 83–99.

Garner, N. (2009) 'The paradox and paradigms of "Reflection in Action": A critical reflection on the modular Masters in Music Education at the Institute of Education with particular reference to Schön and his critics'. Unpublished Masters dissertation, Institute of Education, University of London.

Hallam, S. (2009) Online. <http://www.epolitix.com/stakeholder-websites/press-releases/press-release-details/newsarticle/lack-of-training-hampers-infant-school-music///sites/institute-of-education-university-of-london/> (accessed 23/11/2009).

Hallam, S., Burnard, P., Robertson, A., Saleh C., Davies, V., Rogers, L. and Kokatsaki, D. (2009) 'Trainee primary-school teachers' perceptions of their effectiveness in teaching music'. *Music Education Research,* 11(2), 221–240.

Hargreaves, D., Purves, R., Welch, G. and Marshall, N. (2007) 'Developing identities and attitudes in musicians and classroom music teachers'. *The British Psychological Society,* 77, 665–682.

Hennessy, S. (2000) 'Overcoming the red-feeling: the development of confidence to teach music in primary school amongst student teachers'. *British Journal of Music Education,* 17(2), 183–196.

Kelly, J. (1999) 'What stress factors specific to music teaching are critical to "burnout" in secondary school classroom music teachers in Queensland?'.

In N. Jeaneret and K. Marsh (eds), *Opening the Umbrella: An encompassing view of music education*. Australian Society for Music Education, XII National Conference, University of Sydney.

Kemp, A. (1996) *The Musical Temperament*. Oxford: Oxford University Press.

Madsen, C. and Hancock, C. (2002) 'Support for music education: A case study of issues concerning teacher retention and attrition'. *Journal of Research in Music Education,* 50(1), 6–19.

Music Educators National Conference (MENC) (2009) Online. <http://www.menc.org/> (accessed 25/11/2009).

National Association of Music Educators (NAME) (2009) Online. <http://www.name2.org.uk/home/P1.php> (accessed 25/11/2009).

Office for Standards in Education (Ofsted) (2007) *An Employment-Based Route into Teaching 2003–06* (HMI 2664). London: Ofsted.

–– (2008) *Rising to the Challenge: A review of the Teach First initial teacher training programme*. London: Ofsted.

–– (2009) *Making More of Music: An evaluation of music in schools 2005–08*. London: Ofsted.

Quality Assurance Agency for Higher Education (QAA) (2002) Honours degree benchmark statement. Online. <http://www.qaa.ac.uk/academic infrastructure/benchmark/statements/Music08.pdf> (accessed 18/11/2009).

Rogers, L., Hallam, S., Creech, A. and Preti, C. (2008) 'Learning about what constitutes effective training from a pilot programme to improve music education in primary schools'. *Music Education Research,* 10(4) 485–497.

–– (1983) *The Reflective Practitioner: How professionals think in action*. New York: Basic Books.

–– (1987) *Educating the Reflective Practitioner: Towards a new design for teaching and learning in the professions*. San Francisco: Jossey-Bass.

Teach First (2009) Online. <http://www.teachfirst.org.uk> (accessed 19/11/2009).

Training and Development Agency for Schools (TDA) (2008) 'Summary of feedback on proposed changes to the funding of supplementary subject knowledge training for postgraduate ITT trainees'. Online. <http://www.tda.gov.uk/partners/funding/ittfunding/supplementary_subject_training.aspx> (accessed 01/06/2008).

–– (2009a) Online. <http://www.tda.gov.uk/Recruit/thetrainingprocess/typesofcourse.aspx> (accessed 19/11/2009).

–– (2009b) Online. <http://www.tda.gov.uk/partners/funding/allocations/allocations0809.aspx> (accessed 23/11/2009).

–– (2009c) Online. <http://www.tda.gov.uk/Recruit/thetrainingprocess/typesofcourse/employmentbased/gtp.aspx> (accessed 19/11/2009).

–– (2009d) Online. <http://www.tda.gov.uk/teachers/continuing professional development/what_is_cpd.aspx> (accessed 24/11/2009).

PART 3

CONTEXTS OF LEARNING

Chapter 12

Music in the early years

Andrea Creech and Jessica Ellison

Are all children musical?

Anybody with an interest in children's musical development will surely be excited and intrigued by research in this domain that has been carried out during the 1990s and first decade of the twenty-first century. Certainly, early years practice and music provision in the UK and elsewhere stands to benefit greatly from this rapidly expanding evidence base. Trehub (2006: 34) summarises robust evidence which portrays infants as 'musical connoisseurs' whose musical perception in some cases surpasses that of adults. Innovative experimental procedures which track infants' attentive listening times and reactions to changes in musical stimuli have revealed that during the first year of life infants demonstrate sensitivity to subtle changes in pitch, rhythm, dynamics and timbre. Furthermore, Trehub (2009: 229) reports research where mother–infant speech and song interactions have been transcribed, revealing that babies and their carers together create 'signature tunes' and 'signature performances' whereby distinctive and person-specific musical interactions are reliably reproduced on subsequent occasions.

During their pre-school years, children continue to demonstrate abundant evidence of universal musicality. For example, the informal play of 3- and 4-year-old kindergarten pupils was found to be permeated with performing, listening and creative musical activities (Shehan Campbell, 1998). Organised rhythmic and melodic patterns were in constant evidence, whether or not they were fully intended by the children as music. Music, Shehan Campbell concluded, was 'on their minds and in their bodies', appearing 'to be everywhere in the lives of children' (1998: 168).

This body of research negates any suggestion that musicality is the privilege of a talented few. Rather, the evidence strongly supports an alternative view that, just as with language, a normal distribution of musical proclivity may be found among the human population. In other words, the vast majority of us are musical, and from infancy we actively engage with music in our everyday lives. Notwithstanding this, a number of factors have been identified that could influence musical development, including prenatal experience, enculturation and environment. These will be discussed in the following sections.

Prenatal experience

Early musical development may be traced to prenatal influences. Indeed, Parncutt (2009: 219) suggests that 'perceptual, cognitive, motor and emotional abilities' are acquired during this time. The auditory system is developed in the last trimester of pregnancy, during which time foetuses respond to factors such as the mother's voice, pitch and loudness, as well as the types of music being played. These formative musical experiences may influence both auditory abilities and predispositions to types of sounds later in life. For example, infants evidently recognise music they have heard in the womb, demonstrating attentiveness, positive emotional responses and preferences for familiar melodies (Hallam, 2006). Furthermore, during infancy engagement in infant-directed singing, speech and movement builds on prenatal associations between sound, movement and emotion.

Enculturation

As Welch (2005: 251) states, 'musical behaviours do not appear in a vacuum. They are the product of a complex interaction between biological, developmental and environmental factors over time'. Enculturation, comprising the processes by which infants and young children acquire a complex understanding of music within their own specific culture, takes time and clearly depends on the nature and extent of musical exposure during the early years (Hallam, 2006). As noted above, before the age of 12 months infants have been found to discern subtle differences in music that are sometimes not noticed by adults (Trehub, 2006). Trehub suggests that this may be explained by an open-mindedness to music that in the very early months has not yet been significantly influenced by immersion in the musical structures, tonality and rhythms of one culture. Although there is some evidence that by the age of approximately 12 months babies exhibit culturally specific musical biases, these seem to remain flexible and fluid throughout the pre-school years. Indeed, Trehub suggests that pre-schoolers' inventive musical play may be partly accounted for by their relative freedom from cultural constraints that later become embedded. Whatever the rate of enculturation, a remarkable characteristic of pre-schoolers around the world is 'their unbridled enthusiasm for music, which is apparent in the spontaneity and inventiveness of their chants and songs' (Trehub, 2006: 43).

Environment

It may be difficult to establish the exact extent to which a predilection for musical activity may be attributable to nature or nurture. However, there can be no doubt that social and cultural environmental factors contribute to shaping musical interests and abilities. Musical knowledge is derived first within the family unit and then from ever-widening cultural circles, including neighbourhood communities, early years settings and, not least, the media.

The question of how the home environment in particular contributes to children's musical development has been the focus of much research, summarised by Creech (2009). Positive relationships between musical home environments and the musical responsiveness of children from these homes have been reported, and children's musical development has been found to be influenced by parental musical background. Socioeconomic background, parental goals, aspirations and values, and family interaction patterns have also been found to be significant influences.

Nurturing musicality

We now have access to powerful evidence that all children possess precocious listening skills, an excellent memory for music and an intense interest in expressive musical performance (Trehub, 2006). This evidence challenges a 'talent account' that expounds the idea that musical development is dependent on fixed genetic endowment. Instead, the idea that musical response may be found universally among the early years population is endorsed. By implication, early years educators, carers and parents have a responsibility to consider how best to support children's musical engagement.

There is some debate over how best musicality among young children may be nurtured. Some educators (e.g. Suzuki, 1977) have advocated intensive musical training from a young age, suggesting that this will lead to a higher degree of discrimination in pitch and fluency in technical musical skills. However, Trehub (2006) points to the lack of empirical evidence that formal, guided music instruction during the early years is a necessary precursor of musical attainment later on, and cautions against prescriptive approaches to music making that may threaten intuitive musical interactions. For Trehub the greatest challenge for early years music practitioners is to 'foster and sustain the joy of music and musical creativity that are so clearly evident in early years' (2006: 44).

A structured framework for early years music is put forth by DfES, who turn their attention to programmes that ensure 'effective progression and assessment in music through the early years and a smooth transition to the Key Stage 1 curriculum in primary schools' (DfES, 2006: 41). Indeed, a key recommendation is that:

> *music providers, working collectively through the emerging music education hubs, work with Children's Services directors, Children's Trusts and, more locally, with Sure Start children's centres, Early Excellence Centres, Children's Centres and nursery and primary schools to deliver a regular, structured and progressive programme of music making for all children in their early years.*

> (DfES, 2006: 42)

The concept of early years music work that comprises the acquisition of specific skills in preparation for work in later years is critiqued by Young (2003), who advocates opportunities for self-initiated play on musical instruments. Young's observations of 95 children in three nurseries engaging in self-initiated play revealed complex forms of musical organisation and sophisticated competencies underpinning the children's music making. This view of music as an embodied, integrated component of generic play contrasts with the more structured view of musical activity that is geared towards discrete musical outcomes considered to be appropriate in terms of musical progression routes and developmental trajectories.

The value of early musical exploration that is informal and self-initiated is illustrated by Mullen:

> *My two year old finds drums out of everyday objects. He creates sounds and laughs . . . music is a part of his inner self. He makes music by creating what he wants and by imitating what he wants and many of the sounds he produces are interesting and well beyond my adult imagination or capability.*

> (Mullen, 2002: 2)

These illustrative examples are not intended to suggest that a totally 'hands off' approach should be taken in early years musical activities. Rather, they demonstrate the enormous potential that exists for children to be enriched by expert musical guidance and facilitation that will allow them to become all that they may musically be. Many children will have their first sustained experience of semi-formal or formal musical participation within the context of an early years setting. Although there is rather sparse evidence relating to what effective early years music provision comprises, some examples of innovative practice and proposals for enhancing good practice are discussed below.

Opportunities in early years music: Research, policy and practice

The time is ripe for innovative music initiatives within UK early years settings. The first section of this chapter has summarised some compelling evidence that supports the view that all children are musical and that both structured and unstructured musical activities may play a vital role in quality early years provision. Alongside this growing evidence base concerned with music, general early years care and education has been the focus of much recent UK government policy (DCSF, 2009b). Funding has been allocated to raising standards and regulating provision within this sector. Researchers have highlighted the far-reaching positive outcomes associated with high-quality early provision, particularly initiatives that foster strong parent–practitioner partnerships (Evaneglou and Sylva, 2003). Coinciding with this increasing commitment and interest in the early years sector and evidence base relating to children's musical proclivity, the music profession itself is experiencing rapid change. Music professionals can now expect to develop 'portfolio careers', comprising a wide range of educational, community and performance activity (see Chapter 16). Part of this widening portfolio is partnership work with early years settings, offering opportunities to develop as early years music professionals. An example is the 'Early Years Music Leader Trainee and Apprenticeship' programme offered at The Sage, Gateshead (2009), where skilled musicians acquire the expertise required for working effectively in early years environments. Arguably, in the UK the conditions are thus in place for early years practitioners, music professionals, researchers and policymakers to work collaboratively in order that sustainable and pedagogically sound musical opportunities become embedded within early years provision.

Current context – policy

The early years sector in the UK has been the focus of rapid policy change, over recent years. Attention to improving care and education for children aged from birth to 5 has arisen partly in response to government pledges to alleviate child poverty, enhance health and raise educational aspirations and attainment among young people (see, for example, DfES, 2002, 2003; DCSF, 2009a). Roberts (2006) suggests that changes in early years policy and programme development will accelerate further under the government's 'Ten Year Childcare Strategy'. A key part of this development is the Early Years Foundation Stage framework (DCSF, 2009b) which in 2008 became statutory for all early years care and education providers in Ofsted-registered settings and which aims to 'help young children achieve the five Every Child Matters outcomes of staying safe, being healthy, enjoying and achieving, making a positive contribution, and achieving economic well-being' (DCSF, 2008: 7). Alongside a recognition that 'the quality of early years experiences is the most important factor bar none in determining a child's life chances' (the Childcare Bill, cited in Roberts, 2006: 17) an increasing number of mothers returning to work has led to greater demand for childcare for children aged birth to

3 (Young, 2008). Within this climate, a complex array of early years settings, including maintained schools, non-maintained schools, independent nursery schools and childcare registered by Ofsted on the Early Years Register, as well as a range of private specialist programmes, provide care and educational opportunities for young children.

The provision of music within early years settings is similarly diverse, including, for example, daily singing activities led by early childhood practitioners, private music classes developed from a variety of pedagogical approaches, commercial franchises, foundation music skills sessions led by peripatetic music specialists and projects led by community musicians (Young, 2008). While much of this work has been found to be innovative, imaginative and inspirational (Bond *et al.*, 2002), early years music professionals do not currently have available a robust training and qualifications framework that would ensure the consistent and high standards that are now demanded by the statutory framework for the Foundation Stage.

Values underpinning early years music provision

Many children experience organised musical activities within the context of early years education or care settings. Early years music provision is largely driven by two dominant values that may be summarised as: (1) the transferable skills discourse, and (2) the creativity discourse. The compelling research noted above that supports the view that all children are musical seems to have had surprisingly little impact in terms of privileging the value of music for musicality's sake.

Transferable skills

With respect to the transferable skills discourse, early years policy documents and practitioner guidance documents, as well as promotional material for specialist early years music programmes, sustain a dominant discourse promoting the conviction that musical activity is developmentally beneficial. In this vein, the Arts Council of England (2007: 21) positions music as an enjoyable activity for children that has the potential to enhance 'sharing and collaboration skills, as well as improvements to their physical, emotional and psychological well-being. . . . music making also develops motor skills and physical coordination. . . . [music] supports the development of parenting skills and relationships with their children.' Youth Music, the UK's largest children's music charity, has prioritised music making for all children aged up to 5, based on a conviction that regular contact with musicians has a positive impact on pre-schoolers' 'communication, language and mathematical skills, and on emotional, social, physical and cultural development' (DfES, 2006: 31). Much evidence supports the view that music supports the personal, social and emotional development of young children (Pound and Harrison, 2003; Hallam, 2006). Indeed, Pound and Harrison (2003) demonstrate how music has been found to support each of the six areas of learning identified in the *Curriculum Guidance for the Foundation Stage* (QCA, 2000). This emphasis on the transferable skills discourse is repeated in a recent government report (DfES, 2006: 41), where it is claimed that 'many [early years] teachers already understand how children's involvement in music stimulates their learning in other areas of the curriculum'.

Recent research offers compelling support for the claims that music has powerful transferable benefits across a range of domains and lends much weight to the transferable skills discourse. For example, a key study was reported by Southgate and Roscigno (2009) who carried out analyses on the Early Childhood Longitudinal Study (ECLS–K), a nationally representative dataset from the USA containing information from 20,000 kindergarten children. Three measures of involvement in music, including in-school, out-of-school and parent involvement in music (measured by attendance at concerts) were tested as predictors of standardised measures of achievement in reading and mathematics. The researchers found that 'music clearly matters for achievement in statistically meaningful ways' (Southgate and Roscigno, 2009: 17).

It has been argued that it would require further research, undertaken outside of white, middle-class, North American or northern European contexts to adequately investigate sustained cognitive benefits of music making (Young, 2005a). Notwithstanding this, there can be little doubt of the potential for participation in music to positively influence a number of areas of cognitive development, as well as personal and social development, physical development, health and well-being (see Hallam, 2009 for a comprehensive review). Thus, there are clearly strong arguments for embedding music within an holistic early years pedagogy.

Creativity

An alternative discourse that offers support for an emphasis on musical experience in early years settings is concerned with the potential for music to foster creativity. Increasingly, attention in the UK has turned to the role of creativity in young children's learning and this is reflected in educational policy documents (Duffy, 2003). Roberts (2006: 17) argues that creativity is a 'cornerstone for successful lifelong learning' and that it is during the earliest developmental years that creative behaviours need to be fostered. From this view, initiatives that place the development of creativity at the heart of early years practice are a 'necessity not a luxury' (2006: 27). Creative approaches to learning, it is claimed, are central to the five Every Child Matters outcomes and the six key areas of the Foundation Curriculum.

The potential for music to offer opportunities for self-expression, imaginative play and exploration, among very young children, has been highlighted in a report published by the Arts Council of England (2005). According to their report, music has a role in developing creativity in babies and young children through activities that involve singing, making sounds with the body, home-made and conventional instruments and found objects, as well as composing, recording and listening to music. Research supports this view. To illustrate, Kalmar (1982) reported that pre-school children who had participated in singing and musical group play twice weekly for three years scored higher than controls on motor development, had higher levels of abstraction and showed greater creativity generally, with enhanced creativity particularly evident in improvised puppet play.

A commitment to the idea that musical activities may encourage creative thinking has been reported among both early years and arts sector representatives (Clark *et al.*, 2003), evidenced by responses from 71 per cent of participants in a survey of arts in the early years, indicating that music was included in work with young children. It must be of concern, however, that by implication nearly one-third of children in UK early years settings may not be accessing musical experiences. Particularly in light of the powerful evidence that all children are born with natural musical inclinations (Trehub, 2006) it seems incumbent upon those with responsibility for early years settings to ensure that in all such contexts music plays a vital role.

Early years music provision in practice

Involvement of families and carers

As noted above, the role of the home environment in supporting optimal musical development has been found to be inestimable (McPherson and Davidson, 2006; Trehub, 2006; Young, 2008). This has been recognised in UK policy documents (for example, DfES, 2006), where the regular involvement of children's parents and carers in early years music environments is recognised and promoted. The interface between home-based musical experiences and those occurring within the context of early years settings is an area where more research is needed (Young, 2008). Young (2005a) points out that the partnerships with families and carers need not always be one-way – bringing the curriculum into the home. Rather, multi-ethnic children bring a colourful and diverse range of prior musical experiences to early years settings and recognition of this diversity supports home-setting continuity as well as contributing to a strong musical self-concept among young children. The two case study examples below both involve the participation of parents and carers. Box 12.1 demonstrates a structured use of music embedded in an early years intervention and Box 12.2 demonstrates a more informal model, taking account of the cultural diversity of participants.

Box 12.1 Peers Early Education Partnership

Music played a significant role in the 'Peers Early Education Partnership' (PEEP), a pre-school intervention that aimed to enhance the educational development of disadvantaged children through partnerships with parents and carers. Weekly sessions, conducted over 33 weeks per year when the children were aged 3–4 included circle time, where nursery support workers worked with parents and carers in sharing songs, rhymes and stories with the children. Every participating family received resources that included an audiotape and songbook. In their evaluation of the intervention, involving 70 children, Evangelou and Sylva (2003) reported benefits in the areas of literacy, numeracy and self-esteem, after one year and two years in the programme. Although this programme was not specifically aimed at fostering musical creativity, music was embedded in quality provision. A key message in the context of this chapter was that strong parental/ carer partnerships formed a cornerstone of effective practice in early years musical activities.

Box 12.2 Fathers Make Music

'Fathers Make Music' was a project funded by the Arts Council of England (2007) that aimed to use music as a vehicle for encouraging fathers to become more involved with their children's development and care. Eleven fathers and 15 children attended weekly sessions over the course of one year. The musician facilitators adapted the sessions to the musical preferences and experiences of the participants. The sessions therefore were found to capture the cultural diversity of the participants and to contribute to a strong sense of community. Some of the other reported outcomes were enhanced father–child interactions and the development of love for and knowledge of a diverse range of music. Again, a key message was that the musical experience for children and parents alike was optimal when parent– child–practitioner partnerships were exploited.

Multi-modal approaches

The Early Years Foundation Stage guidance for creative development (DCSF, 2009b) promotes an integrated approach to creative development, including the exploration of sound, movement and music. Young (2003: 47) elucidates this view, observing that creative musical play cannot be separated from its 'situation of making'. Young (2005a) reported her action research, involving six arts professionals working in 20 diverse early years settings with babies and pre-school children (see Box 12.3).

Box 12.3 Early Years Arts Project

Six professional artists, representing music, visual arts, textiles, dance and drama, were employed by the Birmingham Advisory and Support Service (Central England) in partnership with the early years directorship. An objective of this project was to identify environmental factors that contributed to children's participation and deep engagement in arts activities.

Their brief was to deliver a two-year 'arts in the early years' project in the context of 20 settings, which included daycare, a surgery waiting room, stay and plays, family hostels, and private and local authority nurseries. Half-day sessions were delivered in these settings, over many weeks. The artists worked collaboratively with early years practitioners, with generous time allowed for joint planning and reflection. The artists were most challenged in their work with the youngest children. In rising to these challenges, the arts workers, regardless of their discipline, favoured generic arts work which allowed the scope for playful creative dialogues that included gesture, movement and vocalisations. The findings from this study provided support for multi-modal arts work in early years settings, allowing scope for babies and young children to experience embodied, cross-modal artistic responses, with their senses operating as one unified system. Young (2005a: 298) reflects that to try to separate activity into discrete art forms too early may 'cause the children's activity to lose touch with an important source of creativity'.

Resources

Rawstrone (2009) encourages early years practitioners to make use of outdoor spaces where children might explore environmental sounds as well as instruments such as drums, beaters, chimes and pipes. Young (2005a) adds that early years settings tend to be cramped, advocating that outdoor spaces be used.

Early years environments should be equipped with resources that allow children to engage in enjoyable and imaginative musical activities – moving to rhythms, makings sounds with instruments, singing, chanting and listening to a variety of musical genres. Young (2003) highlights the importance of musical instruments available for self-initiated play. In contrast to a developmental model that positions early years free play on instruments as exploratory and preliminary, Young reports her observations of musical patterns evident in young children's free play, arguing for accessible, enabling resources that offer young children a degree of autonomy in relation to the nature of their music making.

Music in the background

In addition to a music corner equipped with instruments for imaginative musical free play, Young (2005b) advocates incorporating recorded music into early years environments. Young children are arguably open to diverse musical genres and early years settings can, Young advises, introduce children to music that is representative of cultural diversity.

However, the outcomes of background music within early years settings are under-researched. In particular, there is a paucity of research concerned with the impact of background music on the behaviour of pre-school children aged 3–5 years. This is despite considerable evidence that infants and toddlers seek and initiate musical interactions (Custodero, 2002; Trevarthen, 2001) which act as the medium through which emotions are calmed, aroused and regulated (Trevarthen and Malloch, 2002). Pre-school children have been found to be capable of identifying music as being sad, happy, exciting or angry (Dolgin and Adelson, 1990; Gentile, 1988; Kastner and Crowder, 1990) so we might expect that different types of music will affect their behaviour. Of the studies which have been undertaken, Reiber (1965) found that the activity levels of 5–6 year olds increased when either fast or slow music was played, compared with no increase in the absence of music. Godeli *et al.* (1996) conducted a between-groups experiment with 27 4–6 year olds, investigating the effect of exposure to rock and roll compared with children's vocal folk music. The children were observed for ten minutes before the playing of music, during its playing and afterwards. Godeli *et al.* found a strong effect for both types of music on children's social peer interactions. Background orchestra and acoustic piano music was found by Love and Burns (2007) to have a positive impact on 20 pre-school children's sustained play and collaborative play. However, little information was provided about the mood or tempo of the musical conditions in these studies. The relatively little research in this area and the inadequacy of its coverage of salient aspects of the nature of the music points to the need for research that investigates the influence of different types of background music on pre-school children's social and emotional behaviour, attending behaviour, and communication. Moreover, research is needed that will inform early years practitioners about the potential for background music to activate and contribute to sustained interest in creative musical endeavours among young children.

Collaboration

The value of creative collaborations involving musicians and early years practitioners has been highlighted, over recent years (see Box 12.4). Roberts (2006: 17) advocates such partnerships and suggests that 'processes be put into place for sharing of best practice'. Artists and early years practitioners have voiced their support for collaborative work, with its potential for both inspiration and challenge (Clark *et al.*, 2003). To this end, the DfES (2006: 7) recommended that 'funding be made available to allow musicians to work regularly with early years settings and to aid progression and training for early-years workers'.

Box 12.4 MusicStart

'MusicStart', a community music initiative that took place in homes and early years settings on the Isle of Wight during 2005–06, was illustrative of the value of collaborative working (Mackenzie and Clift, 2008). A team comprising a lead musician, assistant musician, trainee community musician, two outreach workers, a speech and language specialist and administrative support worked with families with children up to age 5, aiming to make music making part of everyday creative life. In addition, members of the team provided training for 115 early years practitioners, focusing on how music might be used in early years practice as a vehicle for promoting learning and development. Further training was offered for six 'music motivators', early years professionals whose role was to cascade the new ideas and support sustained good practice. The programme was found to be successful in that its practical system of support helped early years practitioners develop their self-concept as music makers. Overall, the programme left 'a legacy of greater awareness, greater enthusiasm and greater confidence – which should continue to sustain an understanding of the value of music and singing in the first crucial five years of children's lives' (Mackenzie and Clift, 2008: 239).

Young (2005a), who participated in a creative partnership within early years settings (Box 12.3), draws attention to the potential for collaborative artist-researcher-practitioner trios to engage in critical and constructive reflection on practice. Increasingly, this view of the reciprocal value of collaborative work has been put forth, highlighting the collective potential to enhance musical experiences for young children.

Professional development

The Early Years Foundation Stage Framework subscribes to the aspiration of the highest levels of care for children (Steel, 2009). Yet, despite isolated initiatives such as The Sage, Gateshead Early Years Music Leader Trainee and

Apprenticeship programme (noted above), in the domain of music there continues to be inconsistent training and professional development opportunities for practitioners, leading to concerns relating to equity of provision.

Anecdotal evidence suggests that early years practitioners often feel wary and self-conscious about participating in musical activities (Rawstrone 2009). This is perhaps a reflection of the nature of early years training programmes in the UK, which seldom include music modules (Mackenzie and Clift, 2008). The DfES (2006: 43) drew attention to the scarcity of opportunities for professional development in music and sharing of expertise, among early years practitioners. Among their recommendations, they support the idea that 'training programmes be extended and developed for musicians wishing to work in early years settings' and that 'joint professional development be made available for musicians, nursery practitioners and other early years workers to share skills and practice'. Clark *et al.* (2003) report that six focus groups comprising early years professionals and artists stressed the importance of training that included separate as well as collaborative models.

The time is right for development of training pathways for a new type of professional, whom Young (2005a: 300) suggests may be labelled as 'early childhood performance arts specialists'. This training would equip professionals with a wide repertoire of specialised skills and knowledge for work within early years settings that could include improvisatory arts work with very young children and their parents or carers and skilful facilitation of interactive arts activities that are embedded in ongoing play, as well as the alternative format of adult-led, whole-group activities.

Summary

The first part of this chapter summarised a rapidly growing body of evidence supporting the view that all children are musical. Even very young infants exhibit sophisticated musical responses and pre-school children demonstrate musical behaviours that are organised, active and embedded in informal play. Given this evidence, it is incumbent upon early years practitioners and music providers to consider how musicality might most effectively be supported, not least because of the benefits that may be derived in relation to transferable skills and creativity, but also for the sheer joy and life-enriching experiences that music offers.

The second part of this chapter put forth the argument that early years practitioners and music professionals now have the opportunity to develop innovative and evidence-based music education provision, within a current policy context that has placed a large emphasis on raising standards of early years education and care in the UK as well as promoting programmes that prioritise creativity. High-impact and sustainable early years music provision will involve family and carer participation, multi-modal informal arts activities and collaboration between early years practitioners and musicians. Such collaborative initiatives need to be well resourced and underpinned by consistent and excellent professional development training pathways for early years practitioners and musicians alike. Furthermore, those in positions of responsibility within early years settings have the possibility of enhancing these environments by taking account of the potential impact of background music.

Ultimately, it is the creative musical potential of our children that should be a central focus for early years music education. There can be no more compelling rationale for the prioritising of research, training and sharing of good practice in this domain.

Further reading

Hallam, S. (2009) 'The power of music: Its impact on the intellectual, social and personal development of children and young people'. Online. <http://www.ioe.ac.uk/Year_of_Music.pdf> (accessed 04/01/2010).

Pound, L. and Harrison, C. (2003) *Supporting Musical Development in the Early Years*. Buckingham: Open University Press.

References

Arts Council of England (2005) *Reflect and Review: The arts and creativity in early years*. London: Arts Council of England.

–– (2007) *More Than Potato Prints: Making the most of the arts in early years settings*. Birmingham: Arts Council of England.

Bond, A., Burgess, S., Lowson, O. and Roberts, S. (2002) *First Steps Evaluation*. Hereford: Youth Music.

Clark, A., Heptinstall, E., Simon, A. and Moss, P. (2003) *The Arts in the Early Years: A national study of policy and practice*: London: Arts Council of England.

Creech, A. (2009) 'The role of the family in supporting learning'. In S. Hallam, I. Cross and M. Thaut (eds), *The Oxford Handbook of Music Psychology*. Oxford: Oxford University Press.

Custodero, L.A. (2002) 'The musical lives of young children: Inviting, seeking, and initiating'. *Zero to Three*, 25, 4–9.

Department for Children, Schools and Families (DCSF) (2008) *Statutory Framework for the Early Years Foundation Stage* (Ref. 00267-2008BKT-EN). Nottingham: DCSF.

–– (2009a) *Learning, Playing and Interacting: Good practice in the early years foundation stage.* Qualifications and Curriculum Development Agency.

–– (2009b) 'Standards Site: Early Years Foundation Stage'. Online. <http://nationalstrategies.standards.dcsf.gov.uk/earlyyears> (accessed 07/11/2009).

Department for Education and Skills (DfES) (2002) *Birth To Three Matters: A framework to support children in their earliest years.* London: DfES Publications.

–– (2003) *Every Child Matters: Change for children.* Nottingham: DfES Publications.

–– (2006) *Making Every Child's Music Matter: Music Manifesto report no. 2.* London: Music Manifesto/DfES Publications.

Dolgin, K.G. and Adelson, E.H. (1990) 'Age changes in the ability to interpret affect in sung and instrumentally presented melodies'. *Psychology of Music,* 18, 87–98.

Duffy, B. (2003) 'Fresh thinking'. *Nursery World,* 2 October.

Evangelou, M. and Sylva, K. (2003) *The Effects of the Peers Early Education Partnership (PEEP) on Children's Developmental Progress.* Report no. RR489. Nottingham: DfES Publications.

Gentile, D. (1988) 'An ecological approach to the development of perception of emotion in music'. University of Minnesota. *Dissertation Abstracts International,* 59(5-B), 2454.

Godeli, M.R., Santana, P.R., Souza, V.H. and Marquetti, G.P. (1996) 'Influence of background music on pre-schoolers' behaviour: A naturalistic approach'. *Perceptual and Motor Skills*, 82, 1123–1129.

Hallam, S. (2006) *Music Psychology in Education.* London: Institute of Education, University of London.

–– (2009) 'The power of music: Its impact on the intellectual, social and personal development of children and young people'. Online. <http://www.ioe.ac.uk/Year_of_Music.pdf> (accessed 04/01/2010).

Kalmar, M. (1982) 'The effects of music education based on Kodaly's directives in nursery school children'. *Psychology of Music,* Special Issue, 63–68.

Kastner, M.P. and Crowder, R.G. (1990) 'Perception of the major/minor distinction iv: Emotional connotation in young children'. *Music Perception,* 8(2), 189–201.

Love, A. and Burns, M.S. (2007) 'It's a hurricane! It's a hurricane! Can music facilitate social constructive and sociodramatic play in a pre-school classroom?'. *The Journal of Genetic Psychology*, 167(4), 383–391.

Mackenzie, K. and Clift, S. (2008) 'The MusicStart project: An evaluation of the impact of a training programme to enhance the role of music and singing in educational settings for children aged three to five years'. *International Journal of Music Education*, 26(3), 229–242.

McPherson, G. and Davidson, J. (2006) 'Playing an instrument'. In G. McPherson (ed.), *The Child As Musician: A handbook of musical development*. Oxford: Oxford University Press.

Mullen, P. (2002) *We Don't Teach, We Explore: Aspects of community music delivery*. Online. <http://www.worldmusiccentre.com/uploads/cma/mullen teachexplore.PDF> (accessed 27/12/2009).

Parncutt, R. (2009) 'Prenatal development and the phylogeny and ontogeny of music'. In S. Hallam, I. Cross and M. Thaut (eds), *The Oxford Handbook of Music Psychology*. Oxford: Oxford University Press.

Pound, L. and Harrison, C. (2003) *Supporting Musical Development in the Early Years*. Buckingham: Open University Press.

Qualifications and Curriculum Authority (QCA) (2000) *Curriculum Guidance for the Foundation Stage*. London: Department for Education and Employment/ QCA.

Rawstrone, A. (2009) 'Nursery equipment: Music – beat it!', *Nursery World*, 30 April.

Rieber, M. (1965) 'The effect of music on the activity level of children'. *Psychonomic Science*, 3(8), 325–326.

Roberts, P. (2006) *Nurturing Creativity in Young People: A report to government to inform future policy*. Department for Culture, Media and Sport/Department for Children, Schools and Families.

Shehan Campbell, P. (1998) *Songs in Their Heads: Music and its meaning in children's lives*. New York: Oxford University Press.

Southgate, D.E. and Roscigno, V.J. (2009) 'The impact of music on childhood and adolescent achievement'. *Social Science Quarterly*, 90(1), 4–21.

Steel, A. (2009) *Teaching expertise: EYFS – where to start*. Online. <http://www. teachingexpertise.com/articles/eyfs-where-to-start-3285> (accessed 12/11/ 2009).

Suzuki, S. (1977) *Nurtured by Love*. New York: Exposition Press.

The Sage, Gateshead (2009) 'Early years training programme'. Online. <http://www.thesagegateshead.org/l_and_p/practitionersandtraining/earlyyearstrainingprogramme> (accessed 04/01/2009).

Trehub, S. (2006) 'Infants as musical connoisseurs'. In G. McPherson (ed.), *The Child As Musician: A handbook of musical development*. New York: Oxford University Press.

–– (2009) 'Music lessons from infants'. In S. Hallam, I. Cross and M. Thaut (eds), *The Oxford Handbook of Music Psychology*. Oxford: Oxford University Press.

Trevarthen, C. (2001) 'Infant intersubjectivity: Research, theory and clinical applications'. *Annual Research Review, Journal of Child Psychology and Psychiatry*, 42, 3–48.

Trevarthen, C. and Malloch, S. (2002) 'Musicality and music before three: Human vitality and invention shared with pride'. *Zero to Three*, 23, 10–18.

Welch, G.F. (2005) 'The musical development and education of young children'. In B. Spodek and O. Saracho (eds), *Handbook of Research on the Education of Young Children*. London: Lawrence Erlbaum Associates.

Young, S. (2003) 'Time-space structuring in spontaneous play on educational percussion instruments among three- and four-year-olds'. *British Journal of Music Education*, 20(1), 45–59.

–– (2005a) 'Changing tune: Reconceptualizing music with under three year olds'. *International Journal of Early Years Education*, 13(3), 289–303.

–– (2005b) 'Music corner'. *Nursery World*, 13 January.

–– (2008) 'Early childhood music education in England: Changes, choices and challenges'. *Arts Education Policy Review*, 109(2), 19–26.

Chapter 13

Music in the primary school

Jessica Ellison and Andrea Creech

The role and benefits of music in the primary curriculum

There can be little doubt that music has the potential to enrich primary pupils' learning experiences. Music is an activity that is universally accessible, providing opportunities for the personal, social, artistic and cognitive development of children of all cultures, ages and abilities (Crncec *et al.*, 2006). In addition to its role in developing musical skills many claims have been made by researchers, policymakers and practitioners regarding the benefits of music education in relation to developing transferable skills, creativity and critical thinking (see Chapters 1 and 12). Positive psychologists argue that involvement in creative activities such as music promotes personal well-being and happiness, considered to be the optimum psychological condition for motivation for learning (Csikszentmihalyi, 2002; Seligman, 2004). In this vein, it has been suggested that creative musical activities encourage discovery, exploration, experimentation and invention, thus contributing to children's development and engagement in all areas of the curriculum (Geoghegan and MacCaffrey, 2004). However, research evidence concerned with music education during the early years of primary schooling also cautions that short-term interventions may not support sustained developmental gains (Jones and Zigler, 2002) and may draw attention away from high-quality programmes that are of sufficient duration and intensity to have a positive impact on children. Hence, the importance of coherent and consistent approaches to music in the primary years, with built-in potential for sustained progression.

In addition to strong evidence relating to cognitive benefits of involvement with music (reported in Chapter 1), much research demonstrates positive effects of music participation on children's personal and social development. Ofsted (2009) corroborated this, reporting that in three-quarters of primary schools visited the impact of music on pupils' personal development was judged as good or outstanding. These compelling arguments in favour of a commitment to excellent provision for music in primary schools would appear to have had an impact on policy and perceptions of head teachers. All of the primary head teachers interviewed by Ofsted (2009: 21) expressed support for this view, indicating that they saw music as 'an essential part of a broad and balanced curriculum' that had the potential to impact positively on pupil confidence, concentration and social skills. The government's primary strategy, *Excellence and Enjoyment* (DCSF, 2003: 36) similarly emphasised the value of music education and went even further, promising to extend music provision beyond the statutory entitlement provided by the National Curriculum 'to include instrumental, vocal taster and foundation sessions for all pupils'.

Yet, in practice, music has generally not been found to be given high priority in UK primary schools. Less than half the schools observed by Ofsted (2009) were accessing the 'Wider Opportunities' initiative laid out in the *Excellence and Enjoyment* document, despite the high profile accorded to this programme of funding (see Chapter 17). The Qualifications and Curriculum Authority (QCA) reported that only 5 per cent of primary schools made music their main subject focus for developing the curriculum in 2004–05, declining to just 3 per cent in 2005–06 (QCA, 2005). Overall, the QCA estimated that just 4 per cent of primary curriculum time was devoted to music. Furthermore, there is some evidence (Hallam *et al.*, 2009b) that music is a subject that is often covered by either teaching assistants or visiting specialist teachers, allowing classroom teachers to avail themselves of planning, preparation and assessment (PPA) time. Thus, even where there were potential opportunities for sharing of good practice in classroom music teaching, teachers were unable to benefit. Some explanations for this evident anomaly, whereby music is valued in rhetoric but not always in practice, will be explored later in this chapter.

An historical perspective on music in UK primary schools

It was only in 1988, with the introduction of a standardised National Curriculum across England, Wales and Northern Ireland, that there was a clear definition of the content, breadth of study, levels of attainment and progression expected within music at Key Stages 1 and 2 (primary years). Previously, responsibility for the music curriculum had been within the remit of head teachers and staff, overseen by school governors (see Chapter 2). Swanwick (1992) suggests that prior to 1988 'the actual structure and status of the music curriculum . . . [was] not markedly dissimilar' to what was proposed in the National Curriculum. Reporting on an enquiry into music in schools, carried out between 1985 and 1987, Swanwick (1992: 3) found that music was part of the curriculum in all of the 60 participating schools and that 'music was . . . quite highly valued, certainly by heads and other teachers'. Despite this, two-thirds of teachers described inadequate resourcing for music and many indicated that 'music as a subject seemed to languish in status'. As noted above, this discordance between values and practice is a theme that is evident within the context of current provision.

There have been many influences on what is prioritised in general classroom music content and standards. From the 1900s, these have ranged from a heavy emphasis on sight-singing and aural training to more creative, rather than re-creative, activities. Other areas of interest included folk songs, Sol-Fa singing based on the approach advocated by the Hungarian Zoltan Kodaly, elementary school percussion bands in the style of Carl Orff, and music and movement, following the principles of Jacques Dalcroze (Rainbow, 1989). Facets of musical development that have been evident in primary music provision have included opportunities for music listening and appreciation, instruction in musical concepts, form and language, creative composition, and the inclusion of popular music of the time (Rainbow, 1989; Green, 2002). These musical and social influences could be considered to have helped form the basis of the current National Curriculum (DCSF, 2010). As Plummeridge (1996: 4) suggests 'the National Curriculum does at least ensure that musical studies, as part of a liberal education, will from now on be available to all pupils'. He did acknowledge, however, the crucial role played by teachers in the development of appropriate curricula, content and implementation, for music education.

Towards the end of the first decade of the twenty-first century the primary curriculum has undergone further scrutiny. Rose (2009), in his review of the primary curriculum, advocates a move towards broad subject areas, one of which would comprise art and design, dance, drama and music under the umbrella of 'Understanding the Arts'. Specific musical learning outcomes are specified (Table 13.1), including appraising, listening, performing and composing. Overall, however, music is subsumed within an area that emphasises active participation in the arts, creativity and cross-curricular applications, providing teachers with a framework representing a 'national entitlement with full scope for teachers to shape how it is taught' (Rose, 2009: 14). While music is positioned as an enrichment activity, there is little emphasis on the powerful transferable benefits of active music making that have been evidenced elsewhere in this book (see Chapter 1). 'Drama is . . . a powerful arts subject which also enhances children's language development . . . as well as personal development. . . . Similarly, dance is a performing art which is equally at home in physical education, and both are enriched by music' (Rose, 2009: 16). Clearly there is a danger here that music will disappear altogether from primary classrooms where teachers have more confidence, expertise or resources to support alternative art forms to music.

Table 13.1 Understanding the Arts (from the Rose review, 2009)

Early (Years 1 and 2)	Middle (Years 3 and 4)	Later (Years 5 and 6)
Children should be taught:	*Children should be taught:*	*Children should be taught:*
To explore a wide range of media and materials to create artworks, improvise and depict imagined worlds, and model the real world through the arts;	To use their senses and the world around them to stimulate and develop imaginative ideas that inform their creative work individually, and working with others;	To work individually with others to use each art form by itself and in combination to create and to perform for different audiences;
To try out a range of tools and techniques with a range of materials for artistic purposes;	To explore how the arts can evoke and express feelings and ideas, and how this can be enhanced through combining the arts;	About the diverse roles of the arts within the cultures of their locality and the wider world;
To explore movement skills and create movement patterns in response to stimuli;	To explore alternative approaches to develop and refine performances and communications using ICT where appropriate;	To select and use appropriate ICT tools and techniques to develop and refine their ideas across the arts;
To use role-play to engage and empathise with characters, situations and events from known stories and stories they create together;	To create and present work in a variety of digital forms;	To listen carefully, developing and demonstrating musical understanding and increasing aural memory;
To sing songs and play musical instruments with expression and control, listening and observing carefully;	About the role of the arts in their life, their locality and wider society;	To perform by ear and use notations and ICT to support creative work;
To listen and observe carefully, taking account of simple instructions;	To listen carefully, recognise and use repeated patterns and increase aural memory;	To compose their own instrumental and vocal music and perform their own and others' compositions in ways that reflect their meaning and intentions;

To experiment with designs, shapes, colours and sounds, using ICT where appropriate; To choose and record images and sounds using ICT.	To perform with control and awareness of audience and what others are playing or singing; To recognise different musical elements and how they can be used together to compose music; How to compose and perform simple melodies and accompaniments; To recall, plan and explore sounds using symbols and ICT.	To describe, appraise and compare different kinds of music, using appropriate music vocabulary.

Current provision for music in primary schools in England

The most recent report from the Office for Standards in Education (Ofsted, 2009) provides a salutary message regarding the current provision for primary school music in England. Based on observations carried out between 2005 and 2008 in a representative sample of 84 primary schools, Ofsted judged the achievement and teaching in music to be good or outstanding in about half of the schools. This compares with Ofsted (2005) where it was reported that the achievement of pupils was good or better in around three-fifths of schools, while the quality of teaching was good or better in nearly three-quarters of schools. Although a number of sources have indicated a gradual improvement in the quality of music provision in primary schools (QCA, 2005; Ofsted, 2005), the more recent Ofsted report (2009) would suggest that the quality of primary school music provision in England, overall, may in fact be declining. While it is laudable that half of the schools visited were found to be engaging in high-quality music provision, this raises questions about the other half, and suggests significant issues relating to equity of music provision in primary schools.

Among those schools where the music provision was judged by Ofsted (2009) to be of a high quality, the music curriculum was inclusive, with strategies in place for supporting the personal and musical development of every pupil. Outstanding provision generated benefits that were evident across the curriculum and throughout the whole school. Schools with successful music programmes shared some notable characteristics. First and foremost, quality of provision was attributed to strong subject leadership, supported by commitment to excellence in music among the senior management of the school. Subject leaders required sufficient time to monitor and prepare work across the school and to support class teachers. Where this time was available the quality of provision was invariably enhanced. Although it was noted that generally music lessons were most effective in schools where a specialist music teacher was deployed, any potential lack of skills among non-specialist teachers was mitigated by support, challenge and professional development offered by subject leaders. Thus, where general classroom teachers were found to deliver outstanding music lessons, strong subject leadership was always in evidence. Indeed, variability in the quality and extent of subject leadership was found to be more salient in contributing to teaching and learning outcomes than whether or not music was the responsibility of specialist teachers.

The importance of subject leadership underpinned by commitment to music on the part of the head teacher has been a recurring theme in evaluations of primary music provision since 1978 when the Her Majesty's Inspectorate (HMI) survey of primary education in England reported 'a high correlation between standards at primary level and the effective use of the curriculum coordinator' (cited in Holden and Button, 2006: 24). Since that time a number of reports have repeatedly reinforced this view, acknowledging the difficulties that classroom teachers face in fulfilling the expectation to be expert in all areas of the curriculum (see Holden and Button, 2006: 24, for a review). The overarching message has been that music provision improves in contexts characterised by effective leadership by a specialist music coordinator, whole-school support and a committed head teacher prepared to allocate resources to music (DfES, 2006).

In this vein, improvement in music at Key Stages 1 and 2 was attributed by the QCA (2005) to clear leadership with priorities set for curriculum and staff development, careful consideration of the ways that time for music was allocated and used, and care given to effective teaching of musical skills. Experienced subject leaders were found to contribute to raising standards in music when their role also extended to supporting whole-school or key stage developments and ensuring good quality information at transfer from Key Stage 1 into Key Stage 2. Where subject leaders had insufficient time to fulfil these roles effectively, the overall provision suffered. Furthermore, subject leaders in music were found to be vulnerable to a sense of isolation, which hampered effective practice. This was alleviated where pyramid networks of support were in place (QCA, 2005), where subject leaders engaged in frequent dialogue with local authority Music Service instrumental teachers and where they were supported in accessing professional development opportunities (Ofsted, 2009).

A second notable characteristic shared by the schools where music provision was found by Ofsted (2009) to be excellent was the use of local authority Music Services to support the music curriculum. Partnerships with music services, especially those with a focus on Key Stage 2 whole-class instrumental teaching, reportedly made a significant contribution to broadening the music provision. Indeed, no other partnerships were found to have the same impact. This is further evidence that the Wider Opportunities initiative (Chapter 17), in particular, has contributed to raising the status and emphasis on music in the curriculum (QCA, 2005). However, effective partnerships were found to be dependent on sufficient, sustained dialogue between specialist instrumental teachers and classroom teachers. Without this, involvement in Wider Opportunities programmes may have limited impact.

A third characteristic of successful music provision was effective assessment practice that supported progression. While pupils generally did enjoy music and were found to benefit in terms of personal development in many schools, they did not always demonstrate the musical progression that might have been expected, particularly in Years 5 and 6. The least effective teachers did not communicate clear outcomes to pupils in relation to separate components of music. Specific areas for development were not identified, nor were pupils aware of when they had either not met or exceeded expected outcomes. Thomas (1997) suggests that these weak assessment practices may be at least in part accounted for by poor explanation in the National Curriculum with regards to how to develop children's musical skills and understanding in a systematic way. The interpretation of the National Curriculum is another area where generalist class teachers thus benefit from strong subject leader support (Box 13.1). Indeed, this is essential if children are to be facilitated in systematic progression through their primary music education.

Box 13.1 Subject leader support for effective assessment practices

The subject leader in an outstanding primary school ensured that every teacher was able to use the class computer to record pupils' work as a regular part of lessons. She was then able to access all the records and, through careful selection, created a portfolio for each year which she used to develop a shared understanding of expectations about progress for each year group.

(Ofsted, 2009: 18)

Assessment that is aligned with progression in music is embedded in effective teaching (Asmus, 1999) and is underpinned by accurate and clear communication of musical concepts, presented in a coherent manner (see Chapter 9). Chiodo (2001: 18) adds that music will only be valued as an integral part of the curriculum when 'music teachers can demonstrate each student's achievement of a sequential curriculum of musical skills and knowledge based on . . . national standards'. The least effective music lessons observed by Ofsted (2009) comprised many tasks with few links, leading to insufficient consolidation of learning. In these lessons there was often too much teacher talk and not enough demonstration, and activities were not differentiated, tending instead to be geared towards middle-ability groups. Conversely, highly effective lessons included creative and imaginative use of a varied repertoire, strategies for allowing pupils to engage with music at different levels and activities that had progression at their core (Box 13.2).

Box 13.2 Effective music lessons comprising a diverse repertoire, differentiated activities and embedded progression

Rounds are used musically so that pupils are encouraged to listen to the other parts rather than closing their ears to keep their own part going. Only when two parts are secure is a third part added. In outstanding work, pupils perform with understanding of the musical style. Slow, plaintive worship songs are sung with great expression and meaning, a good tone and musical shape to the melodic line. Up-tempo worship songs create a tangible sense of uplift. An African farewell song was unaccompanied in two parts and included one pupil who confidently 'called' each of the call-and-response sections during the performance. The rest of the pupils added dynamics as they followed the teacher's direction to improve and develop the overall effect of the song. All pupils were utterly focused and very supportive of the pupil who took the solo part.

(Ofsted, 2009: 10)

Despite some problematic practice, Ofsted (2009) did report that in three-quarters of schools music evidently had a positive impact on the personal development of pupils. However, *most* schools did not maximise the potential benefits of a strong music programme, suggesting that there was scope for widening the impact of music. For example, the pupils who might have benefited the most were not always identified for inclusion in extra musical opportunities (Box 13.3).

Box 13.3 Maximising the powerful influence of music

The best schools visited were giving attention to the progress made by boys. In one school, for example, there were many more girls than boys in the school choir, so the school formed an all-boys choir and timetabled this to rehearse in curriculum time each week. As a result, about a third of the boys in the school are now involved, gaining much enjoyment and showing more positive attitudes towards singing and music.

(Ofsted, 2009: 10)

Training for teaching music in the primary school

In the UK during the early 1990s, it was acknowledged that many primary teachers felt ill-equipped and insecure at the prospect of having to teach music, and that very few teachers in primary schools had any qualifications in music, even at a comparatively modest level. Music has been found to be one of the most difficult foundation subjects to cover at Key Stages 1 and 2 (QCA, 2005). Teachers lack confidence in teaching music, particularly if they are non-specialists (Hargreaves *et al.*, 2002) and there is an urgent need for continuing professional development (CPD) or better initial training to address specific musical skills and musical vocabulary. Many class teachers need support if pupils are to reach the standards expected of them at the end of Key Stage 2 (aged 11) (Ofsted, 2005; Holden and Button, 2006). Furthermore, there is evidence that it is during the very earliest years of formal education that children will benefit from experiences that awaken and stimulate their interest in music (Geoghegan and MacCaffrey, 2004). Thus, teachers of early years Foundation Years (see Chapter 12) and Key Stage 1 require training and encouragement if they are to deliver a well-defined and organised music curriculum which will equip children with basic musical literacy that will underpin progression through Key Stage 2.

Provision of adequate training and support for classroom teachers and subject leaders in music is challenging. The standards for teacher training require newly qualified teachers to have 'a secure knowledge and understanding of their subjects/curriculum areas and related pedagogy to enable them to teach effectively across the age and ability range for which they are trained' (TDA, 2007: 9). As music is positioned under the umbrella of the performing arts, it is possible that trainee teachers may have no direct experience in teaching music. Further, as Hennessy (2000) points out, music in primary training is not only disadvantaged by having little time in the curriculum but also because there may be little or no access to experience of music in teaching practice. Indeed, Barnes (2005) surveyed primary initial teacher education students, revealing that:

> *72 per cent reported never having seen composition happening in their schools during 12 weeks of school experience. 69 per cent had not seen examples of composition classes by their third and final school experience. 45 per cent of music specialists in the third year of their BA, QTS course had not even seen musical instruments being used in school during their whole training.*
>
> (Barnes, 2005: 4)

Similarly, 178 Key Stage 1 teachers who participated in additional music training generally indicated that they had received little or no training in music during their initial teacher training. Several of these teachers reflected that they had embarked on their teaching careers with minimal enthusiasm and little confidence for teaching music. Teachers who had prior musical experience indicated that they lacked knowledge relating to how to apply their musical skills at Key Stage 1 level (Hallam *et al.*, 2009b).

An alternative to developing the skills of existing teachers is to employ specialist music teachers to teach the music curriculum. There has been a longstanding debate as to whether primary school music is best taught by music specialists or non-specialist class teachers (Wheway, 2006; Hennessy, 2000). Mills (1989) warned that children valued music less if it was not taught by their own class teacher as part of their whole curriculum, going on to suggest that:

> *generalist teaching allows greater opportunity for music to take place as the need arises . . . because a class teacher has knowledge of individual children which a visiting specialist teacher cannot hope to match. A class teacher can use a child's success in music as a catalyst for progress elsewhere.*
>
> (Mills, 1989: 127)

However, these ideals may be problematic in practice. Overall, Ofsted (2009) found that primary schools where music was delivered by a specialist teacher were those with the most consistently high quality learning and teaching outcomes. As noted above, some lessons delivered by class teachers were judged as outstanding, but these invariably were where the class teacher was supported by a strong subject leader.

Hennessy (2006) addressed the issue of equity, arguing that:

> *where a school values music and has had the foresight (or luck) to appoint teachers with confidence in their abilities to teach music then the musical life of the school is healthy, permeates the whole community and sits alongside and within other subject areas as a full member of the curriculum.*
>
> (Hennessy, 2006: 23)

The issue of equitable access to high-quality music provision was also noted by Hallam *et al.* (2009b), where research concerned with music at Key Stage 1 revealed an extremely uneven and inconsistent level in the quality of provision. Even neighbouring schools, feeding into the same secondary school, were found to differ significantly, suggesting that there was little in the way of networks of support. This uneven provision may have accounted for some of the diversity in terms of interest in music, found among the Year 7 pupils in the local secondary schools. Thus, in the absence of primary music specialists (who, according to Miliband, 2004, are rare in the UK) or strategies to develop subject leadership in primary music, access to an enriching music curriculum may be compromised.

Although there are clearly difficulties associated with training for teaching music in the primary years, there are also clear action points that may contribute to enhancing the quality of music provision. As noted previously in this chapter, nurturing subject leadership has been shown to impact greatly on the wider benefits of music for pupils, teachers and the whole school. One significant strand of support for subject leadership is CPD. The value of music CPD has been found to be significant.

Rogers *et al.* (2008) evaluated the Singing Schools programme, a professional development initiative that supported classroom teachers in delivery of music at Key Stages 1 and 2. The intervention lasted for one year, and involved 16 primary schools across three local authorities in England. This sustained programme of support proved to generate demonstrable benefits for teachers and their pupils (Box 13.4).

Box 13.4 The Singing Schools programme

The Singing Schools programme was delivered by the Voices Foundation, a national music education charity that supports whole-class vocal teaching in primary schools. The programme, based on the principles of the Hungarian Kodaly approach, aimed to provide training and support for every teacher in each school, irrespective of prior training or experience. This involved providing teachers with an accessible planning and teaching programme, setting high but realistic expectations, providing resources and advisory teacher support and encouraging teachers to develop confidence in their competence and ability to adopt innovative teaching approaches. Evaluating the programme, Rogers *et al.* (2008: 496) reported that many generalist teachers had developed the skills they needed to teach music in the primary school: 'Through engaging with the programme, staff developed knowledge of musical concepts, rhythm, pulse and pitch and practical singing skills. . . . Participation generally had a positive impact on teacher confidence in relation to teaching music and singing.'

The programme took a whole-school approach, whereby all teachers and teaching assistants were involved in the training, which took place during twilight sessions. Music coordinators received an additional five days of training, enabling them to offer high-quality 'in-house' support. The whole-school approach, coupled with a tangible commitment from senior staff to enhancing the quality of music teaching across the whole school, was found to be integral to the success of the programme:

> *All the classes have taken this on board. It is a whole-school thing. Previously when I've been on singing courses it has been difficult to come back to school and feed it through to the staff. But here everyone had the training, including the teaching assistants. Everyone took to it and everyone enjoyed doing the training.*
> (Music coordinator)

A further key factor contributing to the success of the programme was the role of specialist advisory teachers who observed classroom teachers and provided feedback in relation to developing strategies, ideas and skills in music. Although some teachers were evidently anxious about being observed, this feedback was seen as supportive and helpful and was generally valued.

Finally, the joy of music making was shared by whole school communities who engaged in the Singing Schools programme. Indeed, music performance and celebration of song were highlighted as important contributing factors to the successful outcomes:

> *We had a very enjoyable singing celebration. The children all took part in that and enjoyed one another's efforts and applauded one another. We haven't done that before, had an afternoon together, simply singing songs.*
> (Head teacher)

(Rogers *et al.*, 2008: 490–492)

For many schools, the level of resourcing required for programmes such as that described in Box 13.4 may be prohibitive. However, a programme of training funded by the EMI Music Sound Foundation demonstrated that even one day of intensive support from a music specialist had the potential to impact considerably on practice in Key Stage 1 classrooms (Box 13.5). Although the evaluation of this training demonstrated much further scope for professional development, there was nonetheless an evident positive impact for pupils and teachers. A notable outcome was that the training helped heads of music in the local secondary schools to understand the diversity of music provision among their feeder primary schools, while in the primary schools themselves the training supported teachers in raising the profile of music within their schools.

Box 13.5 EMI Music Sound Foundation additional training for delivery of music at Key Stage 1

The EMI Music Sound Foundation sponsored a programme of professional development in music for Key Stage 1 teachers. The training was carried out in 22 local authorities, representing rural and urban areas of the UK, between September 2007 and July 2008. Twenty-seven secondary arts colleges were recruited to take part. Heads of music from each of the secondary schools identified clusters of their feeder primary schools. Each of these feeder primary schools was given the opportunity to take part in the project. One hundred and sixteen primary schools were recruited, each sending at least one Key Stage 1 teacher to a day of music training delivered by an experienced teacher-trainer. In total, 162 classroom teachers, 12 teaching assistants and four music specialists participated in the training.

Classroom teachers completed questionnaires before the training – and again at the end of the school year, after having had the opportunity to implement new ideas and classroom music strategies. Teachers completed six 'case study' assessments of pupils in their classrooms before and after implementation of the project who represented 'low', 'medium' and 'high' ability groups in music. Five teachers were visited and interviewed, and videos were made of their classroom music practice. The teacher-trainer who had delivered the training was also interviewed. Participants evaluated the training day, and head teachers and heads of music in the participating arts colleges completed questionnaires at the end of the project.

One full day of training was given in each local authority, delivered by an independent music consultant who provides music education courses for teachers throughout the country. The day was divided into four sessions, which covered: (1) 'exploring sounds' (descriptive skills); (2) rhythm skills; (3) singing and pitch; and (4) 'exploring resources' and individual planning advice.

The training impacted positively on teachers' enjoyment and enthusiasm for teaching music. The greatest impact was in terms of their improved confidence and a sense of empowerment that they could meet the requirements of the National Curriculum for Music. Pupils' attitudes towards music were perceived to have been enhanced. They enjoyed singing more, were more confident, had developed a range of skills and strategies for composing, performed well, and had improved their listening skills. The lower-ability children seemed to benefit the most, particularly in relation to concentration and motivation in music classes. Pupils in all three ability groups were judged to have improved significantly in terms of their ability to sing in tune. For the average and high-ability groups, two of the most significant areas of development were composition and improvisation skills, where relatively large increases were noted. The head teachers indicated that the main benefit of the training had been increased musical knowledge, skills, and enhanced confidence among their Key Stage 1 teachers. Almost all of the head teachers reported that the training had made a difference in their school and that it had helped to raise the status of music. The impact was sufficiently great that they indicated that they would continue to invest in music.

> *The training has enriched our curriculum throughout the school. . . . the training supported increasing medium-term planning and more effective delivery of music.*
>
> (Head teacher)

> (Hallam *et al.,* 2009b)

Ways forward: Challenges to music educators in the primary school

Some important themes have been highlighted in this chapter. First, the evidence in favour of prioritising high-quality music curricula is compelling. Indeed, it would seem that most primary head teachers recognise the value of music. The challenge is to ensure that head teachers, their staff and school governors are aware of the active steps they may implement in order to ensure that the potential benefits of music are maximised within their school communities.

It is clear that strong subject leadership is central to raising standards of primary music provision. In fact, the evidence cited in this chapter suggests that the 'subject specialist versus classroom teacher' debate could become nearly redundant, were schools to nurture strong leadership in music, supported with adequate resources. A real commitment to subject leaders would involve providing time for planning, monitoring, assessing and supporting classroom practice across the school. It would also mean ensuring that classroom teachers could avail themselves of opportunities to work alongside the subject leader, rather than depending on subject leaders to relieve them of teaching duties during PPA time. The leadership argument is not new – indeed, it seems tedious and rather wearisome to raise it yet again. But it is a crucial factor that cannot be ignored if schools and policymakers are serious about creating music programmes where pupils have the opportunity to achieve their potential in relation to musical skills, transferable skills and creativity.

This chapter, read in conjunction with Chapter 17, draws attention to the precious resource that exists in the UK, in the form of local authority Music Services. Partnerships among Music Services and primary schools have been found to have significant impact on the quality of music provision when they are sustained and offer the scope for ongoing dialogue between Music Service teachers and classroom teachers. Sustained partnerships offer opportunities for classroom teachers and their pupils to develop their identity as musicians, within the classroom context. Again, those in a position to effect change in relation to music provision in their schools need to explore the potential for developing partnership work.

All pupils have an entitlement to the musical, social, cognitive, personal and creative benefits that high-quality music provision promises. It is in the hands of policymakers and senior management of primary schools to ensure that proper support structures and networks are in place which ensure that this entitlement is not just an ideal. Coherent and consistent music provision must be coupled with leadership and commitment to taking full advantage of all that music has to offer. The exemplary practice in schools where music has been judged as outstanding demonstrates that while there may be risks associated with prioritising music, these are invariably far outweighed by the benefits.

Further reading

Hallam, S., Burnard, P., Robertson, A., Saleh, C., Davies, V., Rogers, L. and Kokatsaki, D. (2009a) 'Trainee primary-school teachers' perceptions of their effectiveness in teaching music'. *Music Education Research*, 11(2), 221–240.

Holden, H. and Button, S. (2006) 'The teaching of music in the primary school by the non-music specialist'. *British Journal of Music Education*, 23(1), 23–38.

References

Asmus, E.P. (1999) 'Music assessment concepts'. *Music Educators Journal*, 86(2), 19–24.

Barnes, J. (2005) *The Brain-based/Mental and Physical Well-being Argument for Music in the Primary Curriculum*. Canterbury: National Association of Music Educators (NAME).

Chiodo, P. (2001) 'Assessing a cast of thousands'. *Music Educators Journal*, 87(6), 17–23.

Crncec, R., Wilson, S. and Prior, M. (2006) 'The cognitive and academic benefits of music to children: Facts and fiction'. *Educational Psychology*, 26(4), 579–594.

Csikszentmihalyi, M. (2002) *Flow*. London: Rider.

Department for Children, Schools and Families (DCSF) (2003) *Excellence and Enjoyment: A strategy for primary schools*. London: DCSF.

–– (2010) *National Curriculum*. Online. <http://curriculum.qcda.gov.uk> (accessed 15/01/2010).

Department for Education and Skills (DfES) (2006) *Making Every Child's Music Matter: Music manifesto report no. 2*. London: Music Manifesto/DfES.

Geoghegan, N. and MacCaffrey, J.M. (2004) 'Impact of music education on children's overall development: Towards a pro-active advocacy'. In M. Chaseling (ed.), *Proceedings of the XXVI Annual Conference, Australian Association for Research in Music Education (AARME)*. Sydney: AARME.

Green, L. (2002) *How Popular Musicians Learn*. Aldershot: Ashgate.

Hallam, S., Creech, A., Rinta, T. and Shave, K. (2009b) *EMI Music Sound Foundation: Evaluation of the impact of additional training in the delivery of music at Key Stage 1: Final report*. London: Institute of Education, University of London.

Hargreaves, D., Miell, D. and MacDonald, R. (2002) 'What are musical identities and why are they important?'. In R. MacDonald, D. Hargreaves and D. Miell (eds), *Musical Identities*. Oxford: Oxford University Press.

Hennessy, S. (2000) 'Overcoming the red-feeling: The development of confidence to teach music in primary school amongst student teachers'. *British Journal of Music Education*, 17(2), 183–196.

–– (2006) 'Don't forget the teachers'. *Times Educational Supplement, The Teacher*, March 24.

Holden, H. and Button, S. (2006) 'The teaching of music in the primary school by the non-music specialist'. *British Journal of Music Education*, 23(1), 23–38.

Jones, S.M. and Zigler, E. (2002) 'The Mozart effect: Not learning from history'. *Journal of Applied Developmental Psychology*, 23, 355–372.

Long, M. (2007) 'The effect of a music intervention on the temporal organisation of reading skills'. Unpublished PhD, Institute of Education, University of London.

Miliband, D. (2004) 'Excellence and enrichment: New frontiers in music education'. Music for Life conference, London, 3 March.

Mills, J. (1989) 'The generalist primary teacher of music: A problem of confidence'. *British Journal of Music Education*, 6(2), 125–138.

Office for Standards in Education (Ofsted) (2005) *The Annual Report of Her Majesty's Chief Inspector of Schools 2004–05*. London: Ofsted.

–– (2009) *Making More of Music: An evaluation of music in schools 2005–08* (No. 080235). London: Ofsted.

Plummeridge, C. (1996) *Music Education: Trends and issues*. London: Institute of Education, University of London.

Qualifications and Curriculum Authority (QCA) (2005) *Music: 2004–05 Annual Report on Curriculum and Assessment*. London: QCA.

Rainbow, B. (1989) *Music in Educational Thought and Practice*. Aberystwyth: Boethius Press.

Rogers, L., Hallam, S., Creech, A. and Preti, C. (2008) 'Learning about what constitutes effective training from a pilot programme to improve music education in primary schools'. *Music Education Research*, 10(4), 485–497.

Rose, J. (2009) *Independent Review of the Primary Curriculum* (No. 00499-2009DOM-EN). Nottingham: Department of Children, Schools and Families (DCSF).

Seligman, M. (2004) *Authentic Happiness*. New York: Free Press.

Swanwick, K. (1992) *Music Education and the National Curriculum*. London: Tufnell Press.

Thomas, R. (1997) 'The music national curriculum: Overcoming a compromise'. *British Journal of Music Education*, 14(3), 217–235.

Training and Development Agency (TDA) (2007) *Professional Standards for Teachers: Qualified teacher status*. London: TDA.

Wheway, D. (2006) 'How is workforce reform affecting music in many primary schools? A timely snapshot'. *The National Association of Music Educators*, 17, 4–6.

Chapter 14

Music in the secondary school

Hilary McQueen and Susan Hallam

At the beginning of the twenty-first century there was considerable concern about the place of music in the secondary school curriculum. Students showed declining interest in music as they progressed through secondary school and there were problems with the number of students taking GCSE music (Harland *et al.*, 2000). Some suggested that music should be removed from the school curriculum with a refocusing on extra-curricular activity (Sloboda, 2001). These concerns were not new. In the early twentieth century music was a minority subject in secondary schools, although alive and well in the community. It was taught by classically trained musicians who aimed to pass on that form of knowledge to the uninitiated, as 'guardians of a sacred flame' (Paynter, 1982: 33). Music accounted for about 1 per cent of examination entries in 1926, and in the 1940s there was only one music examiner in the country for the School Certificate, compared with twenty-six for Latin (Crabtree, 1947). The inspection of music in secondary schools in 1911 indicated that some schools did not see music as having relevance for future employment, unless teaching, and therefore they did not include the subject in the curriculum. Technological advances in gramophones and radios also offered greater opportunities to listen to music rather than to sing or play it (Cox, 1993). Between 1922 and 1929 inspectors were critical of the lack of aural training and the variable quality of song choice in schools but they commented positively on extra-curricular activities, such as orchestras and brass bands. These have received similar positive comments in the most recent Ofsted report (2009).

Following the 1944 Education Act (HMSO, 1944), the School Certificate, and later the General Certificate of Education (GCE), were developed for pupils in grammar schools. In music this led to more theoretical and essay-type assignments rather than practical work, and a focus in the classroom on teaching the basics of music theory, and music appreciation through listening to recorded music (Paynter, 1982). Practical music beyond singing, recorders and percussion instruments tended to be extra-curricular, such as choirs and ensembles. These remained activities for the minority, although they offered beacons of achievement at school events and were supported by the increase of peripatetic teaching of instruments in schools (Pitts, 2000). Despite this, overall, music was considered to be the 'Cinderella of school subjects' (Mainwaring, 1941: 206) with singing and learning to read music dominant features of the music curriculum.

Throughout this period there had been debate over the nature of the music curriculum. This continued into the 1960s, with increasing reference to the possibility of the inclusion of popular music and practical work. The Newsom Report *Half our Future* (1963) was critical of music education, referring to it only being timetabled for one period per week, with an emphasis on singing, which alienated adolescent boys in particular. The report also drew attention to the low take-up of the subject at the end of the third year (now Year 9) as an exam option. A further report by the Schools Council (1971) *Music and the Young School Leaver: Problems and opportunities* expressed concern over the adequacy of the curriculum, suggesting that 'many teenage pupils, especially those in the 14–16 age group, are indifferent and even hostile towards curriculum music'. Innovative practice began to emerge through the work of the North-West Regional Curriculum Development Project which had been set up in 1967 (Cox, 2002; Rudd, 1972). The report *Creative Music and the Young School Leaver* (NWRCDP, 1974), called for more creative music sessions in school, using simple instruments. Creativity and aesthetic experience were promoted as essential to a music curriculum (Cox, 2001). Despite this, what went on in classrooms was slow to change, generally catering for the needs of the few with music skills (e.g. Small, 1975), although there were examples where popular music was introduced. For instance, Farmer (1976) introduced pop music into his teaching of the Certificate of Secondary Education (CSE), some of his pupils forming a reggae group, and visiting a recording studio and a record company.

By the end of the 1970s, a broader model that could provide the basis for the curriculum had been suggested: CLASP, an acronym formed from the musical elements of composition, literature studies (musical knowledge), audiation, skill acquisition and performance (Swanwick, 1979). The model found favour among teachers as well as having an influence on curriculum development (Plummeridge, 2000). During the 1980s, Paynter's encouragement of active music making and the CLP components of Swanwick's model – composing, listening and performing – were influential in the development of the National Curricula for music which were established in England, Wales and Northern Ireland. In Scotland, guidelines were issued for education 5–14, music being included within the 'Expressive Arts'. Scotland did not set out specific outcomes for each age group but rather expected children to develop at their own pace (SOEID, 1992). The curriculum for the remainder of the UK shared common themes, that for Key Stage 3 for Wales providing an example:

> Pupils should be given opportunities to build on the knowledge, understanding and skills acquired at Key Stage 2. They should be taught how to perform, compose and appraise music, focusing their listening (in all musical activities) on the musical elements. The repertoire chosen for performing and listening should include music of varied genres and styles, from different periods and cultures, composed for different media and various purposes. It should extend pupils' musical experience and include examples taken from the European 'classical' tradition from its earliest roots to the present day, folk and popular music, the music of Wales and other musical traditions and cultures. The repertoire for performing should be progressively more demanding and chosen in the light of the pupils' needs, backgrounds and stages of musical development. Pupils should be given the opportunity to work as a class, in a smaller group and as individuals, to reflect on and discuss their work and plan how to improve it, and to use ICT.
>
> (QCAAW, 2000)

In 2005, the National Curriculum in England was reviewed at KS3, with the principal aim of reducing the amount of prescribed content to give teachers more time and space to support personalised learning – broadly understood as the tailoring of what is taught and how it is taught to the needs of the individual pupil. The government's Key Stage 3 strategy (DCSF, 2009) includes four key principles: having high expectations for learners, supporting progression, fostering engagement, and transformation for teachers through staff development. The strategy requires that, across all areas of learning, opportunities should be provided for learners to develop skills relating to information processing, reasoning, enquiring, creative thinking and evaluating (DfES, 2005). Practical music making provides opportunities for the development of all of these skills. Five key concepts form the foundation of the music curriculum (QCDA, 2007): (1) integration of practice; (2) cultural understanding; (3) critical understanding; (4) creativity; and (5) communication with development achieved through: performing, composing and listening; reviewing and evaluating, and range and content.

Developments in other parts of the UK differ. In Wales, the National Curriculum remains subject-based. Syllabuses have been revised to identify the skills for each subject and the range of contexts, opportunities and activities through which these skills should be developed and applied. The performing, composing and appraising terminology has been retained (DCELLS, 2008). Scotland continues to include music as one of the Expressive Arts, the new curriculum focusing teaching on helping pupils to become successful learners, confident individuals, responsible citizens and effective contributors, supported by the Assessment is for Learning (AifL) programme (Curriculum for Excellence, 2009). In Northern Ireland the curriculum is set out as 'Areas of Learning', with music placed within the arts, the stated aims being 'personal and life-skills' (Northern Ireland Curriculum, 2009).

Music teaching in practice

While the National Curriculum provides a structure for teachers to work within, the finer detail of how to deliver it depends on teachers' approaches, and, in turn, to a large extent on what they consider is appropriate or feasible. The way that secondary music teachers put into practice curriculum elements such as performing, experiencing different musical genres (including Western classical), learning staff notation and using technology (QCDA, 2007) is inevitably influenced by their beliefs and principles and practical constraints or opportunities (Cain, 2007). Teachers may also need to develop their own skills and knowledge so that they become familiar with, for example, a wider range of musical material and the ability to use recording equipment as well as computer software and hardware. Mackrill suggests that familiarity with and competence in using music technology gives teachers 'a distinct advantage' (2009: 61). Personalising learning, which aims to foster deep educational experiences (Hargreaves, 2006) also offers challenges. Deep experience requires music to contribute in a holistic way to a child's development through cross-curricular activity, and personal and skills development. This might also be achieved through informal pedagogies, such as Musical Futures, and might also include finding ways to nurture those who have well-developed practical skills within a more collective musical context (Philpott, 2009).

The quality of provision

In its review of music in secondary schools for the year 2001–02, Ofsted concluded that music lessons displayed some of the best and worst practice across all subjects, with too much variability in quality. Some lessons were described as unimaginatively taught and out of touch with pupils' interests. Schools were berated for having low expectations, with too great a focus on teaching examination content. Accommodation was generally felt to be unsuitable and there was a need to make better use of space. The most recent report (Ofsted, 2009) also raises similar concerns. Slightly less than half of the schools visited had good or outstanding provision and in about 14 per cent of provision was perceived to be inadequate. Generally, lessons were practical and included a range of experiences but there was perceived to be a lack of challenge. Insufficient links were made between different activities, and students were not given enough opportunities to deepen their understanding. The curriculum generally included opportunities for students to perform and compose in a variety of musical styles, although these were rarely related to the work of established composers or performers and they tended to be focused on students' demonstration of their knowledge of musical devices and structures, with insufficient listening to examples of how these devices are used in the wider context. Appropriate breadth in the curriculum was ensured, for instance, through the use of gamelan, Indian music and samba in addition to Western classical music, although there was little exploration of music in its cultural context. Schools generally had a set of keyboards and a range of percussion instruments, and in the better provision there were bass and rhythm guitars, drum kits and/or electronic drum pads. However, schools did not always make best use of these instruments and there was insufficient use of ICT. Inspectors noted that resources within schools were not always able to keep pace with the quality of equipment which students saw and sometimes used outside school (Ofsted, 2009).

The most effective teaching occurred in extra-curricular activities and instrumental lessons where, in the best examples:

- the teaching had a clear musical learning focus
- teachers had high expectations
- there was an emphasis on quality, and students knew what to do to improve
- teachers made excellent use of demonstration
- the work was related to real-life musical tasks
- questioning was effective
- students felt that everyone was treated as a musician.

(Ofsted, 2009)

However, the range of extra-curricular provision varied widely, and frequently did not match the interests and abilities of the students.

Box 14.1 Example of a song-writing project

A Year 9 class of 24 pupils spent the summer term on a song-writing project. Working in self-selected groups, they composed, performed and then recorded the song, using voices, acoustic and electronic instruments and equipment, together with computer software. In the final sessions they produced a CD, using the department's resources, and they designed and produced the covers for the CDs. Most of them were not continuing to study music after this project ended, but they were enthusiastic about the high quality of their songs and recordings. They enjoyed using the full range of resources and many were surprised and delighted to go through all the processes which professional composers and performers use. This gave them an understanding of, and interest in, the musical and commercial aspects of the music industries, which they discussed easily and confidently. Although students talked about their enjoyment and sense of achievement, the progression rate was affected, in this school at least, by what the inspector considered to be their lack of traditional musical skills, such as being able to read music.

(Derived from Ofsted, 2003)

Box 14.2 Learning reggae music

Year 9 students were learning about reggae. Reggae music was playing as they entered. They were quickly set the challenge of playing air-guitar to a backing track which used reggae off-beat rhythmic patterns. The teacher watched students carefully as they responded, mentally noting those who did this well and those who found it more difficult. The class discussed what it felt like to play the rhythm and what role the guitar player had in a reggae group. They listened to other examples. As they explored the way of life and background to the evolution of reggae, the teacher referred frequently to a student who had been to Jamaica. The laid-back feel of the music became a central thread of all the discussion. This was skilfully used to improve the quality of a class performance of the reggae piece played at the end of the lesson (the same piece heard at the start). The teacher matched students to different instrument parts, using her knowledge of them, reinforced through observing the air-guitar task.

(Ofsted, 2009)

Take-up of music at Key Stages 4 and 5

Although attainment in GCSE Music is higher than in other subjects (see Chapter 9), there continues to be concern about the small number of pupils taking GCSE (8 per cent in 2008) and GCE A level (1.3 per cent) compared with other arts subjects (Ofsted, 2009). It is difficult to make comparisons with performance in Scotland where the examination system differs considerably (SQA, 2008, see also Chapter 9). The lack of take-up does not seem to indicate that students dislike music. Lamont *et al.* (2003) found high levels of enjoyment of music at KS3. Students seem to enjoy music even when the school's provision is considered no better than satisfactory. They welcome the opportunity to work practically and make music with their friends and peers and believe that music increases their self-esteem, particularly through performing to others (Ofsted, 2009; Hallam *et al.*, 2009). They and their teachers value the role of music in the curriculum for its musical and extra-musical benefits (Lamont *et al.*, 2003).

Some have argued that it is the quality of teaching which influences the poor take-up of music at KS4 (Ross, 1995; Harland *et al.*, 2000; Bray, 2000). Certainly, there are wide differences in uptake between schools (Little, 2009) and some evidence that the lack of authenticity and poor links with music outside school is an issue (Bray, 2000; Lamont *et al.*, 2003). Where the Musical Futures programme has been implemented, uptake at KS4 has increased – suggesting that when pupils feel that they can meet the practical requirements of GCSE they are more inclined to opt for music (Ofsted, 2006; Hallam *et al.*, 2008, 2009). There seems to be a general perception that music is a highly specialist subject at KS4 and above, and only accessible for those with considerable instrumental skills (Lamont *et al.*, 2003; Wright, 2002). Indeed, some music teachers discourage pupils who do not have instrumental skills from taking music at KS4 (Ofsted, 2009). Paradoxically, students who have high-level instrumental skills and pursue music outside of the school curriculum may see no need to continue with it at KS4, unless they wish to pursue a career in music (Little, 2009). The perception of music in the wider community may also be a factor, as music is perceived to have little value in career terms (Lamont *et al.*, 2003; Hallam *et al.*, 2009) and parents sometimes discourage their children, particularly boys, from taking it (Button, 2006; Hallam *et al.*, 2009).

Musical Futures

The inclusion of more popular and contemporary music styles in the curriculum has been a source of debate for over half a century. Finding a way to ground music education in a more learner-centred way has proved elusive, perhaps because music teachers have traditionally experienced a more formal training themselves and popular music has been viewed as a motivating means to a more traditional end – as a way to tap into the affinity young people have for 'their' music, and build on it. Recently, there has been a focus on the way that informal learning, generally associated with more popular styles, can be used in the classroom through purposive listening and requiring students to copy a CD track (Green, 2002b, 2008). This kind of informal learning is a key part of the Musical Futures approach and is designed to devise new and imaginative ways of engaging young people, aged 11–19, in music activities. Two key elements driving the development of the programme were the importance of informalising the way that music is taught and personalising the nature of the opportunities on offer. The four key strands of the Musical Futures programme are:

- **Informal music learning at KS3**: Informal learning principles, drawn from the real-life learning practices and processes of popular musicians, are integrated into classroom work, enabling students to learn alongside friends, through independent, self-directed learning. Teachers act as facilitators and musical models. They spend time standing back, observing and assessing the needs of their pupils, and offering help, support and guidance, based on objectives that pupils set for themselves.
- **The whole curriculum approach**: This strand is a scheme of work for Year 8 pupils, aiming to provide musical pathways for pupils who have not previously experienced sustained musical engagement. Strategies include providing extra support for the teacher, bringing informal learning processes into schools, making tangible connections with students' musical lives outside school, achieving a balance between what children already know that they want to do and new un-tried experiences, moving school music beyond the classroom confines and involving students in real musical activity, in authentic musical situations and environments.
- **Numu (www.numu.org.uk)**: This is an 'interactive web space' developed by Synergy.TV for creating music, publishing, marketing and promoting, which allows students to develop skills in accordance with their strengths and apply them to a real-life situation with a global audience.
- **Personalising extra-curricular music**: This strand is a guide for personalising extra-curricular music projects so that they complement the curricular work in schools and enhance students' musical progression.

A survey undertaken in 2008 revealed that about 700 secondary school music teachers were either using or planning to use the Musical Futures materials. The majority of these made use of the informal music learning approach, although about a quarter either used or planned to use the whole curriculum approach or Numu with a smaller number using or planning to use the model for Personalising extra-curricular music. The approaches were most often used with Year 9 groups, least frequently with Year 7, and typically over the course of an entire academic year (Hallam *et al.*, 2008).

Evaluations of the pilot project (Ofsted, 2006) and its implementation more widely (Hallam *et al.*, 2008, 2009) taking account of the perceptions of teachers, students and members of schools' senior management teams have shown:

- improved motivation and enjoyment of music lessons
- more positive attitudes towards music
- enhanced confidence and self-esteem
- development of a wider range of musical skills (listening, instrumental, composition, performance, understanding of different genres)
- an increase in independent learning through informal group work
- enhanced transferable skills (teamwork, organisational, support for others)
- more productive working relationships with teachers
- increased opportunities for all students to demonstrate and fulfil musical potential
- increased attainment and take-up at KS4
- improved on-task behaviour
- increased participation in extra-curricular activities.

Independent, practical learning, where students were allowed to take control and have choice, increased motivation and led to more practice and enhanced learning outcomes. Getting students to set targets for each lesson assisted in focusing work, and students were able to identify areas where they had made progress and also where they needed to improve. Having to perform in front of peers was also motivating as students did not want to lose face. Overall, the approach provided a break from more academic classes, was fun, made them feel good and reduced stress. Teachers reported:

- increased confidence in relation to facilitating student learning in a range of musical genres, teaching instrumental skills and teaching music in general
- enhanced effectiveness and enjoyment of teaching music
- the acquisition of a wider range of teaching skills which would be sustained in the long term
- that their expectations of pupils were exceeded
- increased awareness of pupils' musical interests out of school and more personalised teaching.

The programme was viewed by teachers as challenging but not difficult to implement. It encouraged them to concentrate on how children learn rather than on how they delivered the curriculum. It facilitated the giving of formative feedback, encouraged the use of peer assessment and made summative assessment of the work of individuals easier because of the group work. The increased motivation, enthusiasm, and success of students was rewarding for teachers. In some schools the benefits extended beyond music, enhancing student motivation more broadly and also providing more opportunities for public performance.

The implementation of the programme raised some issues. While the increase in the numbers of students wishing to continue music into KS4 was welcome, some schools did not have the capacity to teach them and selection processes had to be operated. In some schools, GCSE was seen as providing an inappropriate form of assessment – and BTEC examinations were preferred. In part, this may reflect the lack of development in the implementation of the programme from popular music to other genres. Some students raised concerns about not being able to read music, and some teachers commented on the difficulties of supporting students who lacked technical skills on an instrument. Indeed, schools were increasingly recognising the need to develop instrumental skills earlier. The focus on popular music and related instruments seemed to be more attractive to boys than girls, and some groups – for instance, those on the autistic spectrum and those with fears of performing – found the programme particularly difficult. Many of the students commented on the importance of groups being able to work productively together and, while some were able to resolve difficulties emerging in group work issues, this was not always the case (Hallam *et al.*, 2009).

While teachers reported that the teaching was exhilarating it was also exhausting and required total commitment. To provide additional support for the learning process, some schools had recruited Year 12 students to act as mentors, a scheme which was very successful. Alongside issues relating to the need for more staff to provide support for students, there were problems relating to space for group work, time to enable students to work productively, access to and maintenance of instruments, and the problem of noise during examination periods in those schools where the music department was located near to non-music activities.

For successful implementation, the senior management team in the school needed to be committed and supportive, particularly as the learning process often appeared chaotic to other staff, seeming to have the potential to lead to a loss of control and subsequent poor behaviour. Despite this, the approach was recognised by senior managers as offering a way to meet the needs for personalising learning and developing a range of transferable skills in students. It thus had the potential to influence teaching across the whole curriculum.

> ## Box 14.3 Example of a project preparing for Musical Futures work
>
> Morpeth High School has adopted a 'Learning to Learn' programme. In Year 8 all pupils come off timetable for one day every fortnight – for a project day, which they follow for six months before moving on to another project. The music department developed a project called 'Rock Factory', which was designed to engage pupils who had not previously engaged with the music department. The aim was to enable pupils to leave the projects as good learners, knowing how to access help and support. The project operates on a rock-band model, where pupils have tasters on drums, guitars, keyboards and mics, and then decide which instrument they want to pursue. This is supported by peripatetic teachers who help out in the lessons. The music room has a dedicated gig space with stage and lights, where pupils regularly perform. They start with the same song ('Wild Thing'), and are then given a range of ten songs to choose from. Throughout the process they focus on their learning skills – Why was/wasn't something successful? How can they help themselves improve? In Year 9, pupils follow the Musical Futures informal learning model. The teacher has found that the pupils who took part in Rock Factory in Year 8 bring those skills and passions into the informal learning in Year 9 and become peer coaches and leaders.
>
> (Derived from Musical Futures, 2009)

The role of the secondary school music teacher

Each musical genre has its own distinctive 'language'. This applies even to those sharing as their basis the Western tonal system. Musicians trained in one genre have to acquire new skills to learn to play and teach in another genre. As most secondary music teachers have been trained within the Western classical tradition this may limit their in-depth knowledge of other genres, including popular music. Being able to play and teach popular instruments may be outside their current expertise. Consequently, teachers are likely to be more comfortable developing the skills of students who share knowledge of similar musical genres (Hargreaves and Marshall, 2003; Hargreaves *et al.*, 2007). This preference may be reinforced, because in secondary schools the success of a music department tends to be judged by senior staff in terms of generally positive examination results at GCSE and the success of public concerts and other performances. This allows teachers to work to their strengths while also meeting the needs of senior management within the school. As a result, schools may not see the need to improve the music curriculum more generally at Key Stage 3. Indeed some head teachers may have little knowledge of what is going on in the classroom (Ofsted,

2009). The combination of teacher preferences and school pressures may explain why the most effective teaching seen in secondary schools occurs in extra-curricular activities and instrumental lessons. About 75 per cent of extra-curricular lessons and instrumental lessons were graded as good or outstanding in the most recent Ofsted report (2009). However, the range of extra-curricular provision varies widely and does not always match the interests and abilities of the students. Rather, it tends to reflect the interests of individual teachers.

The need for schools to present a strong musical tradition to parents and others in the community can lead to considerable pressure on teachers to manage large numbers of peripatetic instrumental lessons and extra-curricular activities to enable high-profile musical events to take place within the school (Ofsted, 2009). This requires music teachers to take on a managerial role. Most teachers have good partnerships with their local authority Music Service, the main providers of instrumental tuition and regional ensembles. Participation in authority-wide groups enriches the curriculum for many students and offers opportunities to participate in a wider range of ensembles and perform in national and international venues. These experiences also contribute substantially to success at GCSE and A level (Ofsted, 2009). However, facilitating the arrangements for extra-curricular and performance opportunities places an additional burden on music teachers, who are recruited primarily for their musical and teaching skills, not those relating to management.

The challenges faced by secondary school music teachers are not new. They have existed since music was first included in the school curriculum. In many ways the provision of music at Key Stage 3 is meeting the needs of students more successfully now than ever before, in part because there is general consensus that the school music curriculum has to be practical in nature and that the tasks which students are asked to undertake must have relevance.

The inclusion of opportunities to engage with a wide range of different genres in the curriculum inevitably puts pressure on teachers – because gaining high levels of expertise in any musical genre requires considerable time. There are relatively few opportunities for professional development, and the recent Ofsted report (2009) indicated that teachers were either unaware of national initiatives or had given limited thought to their impact on practice. In order to provide high-quality musical experiences across a range of genres, teachers need to work collaboratively with others, including professional musicians and instrumental teachers, making use of the different skills of each.

Endnote

The Musical Futures approach has demonstrated that it is possible to increase take-up of music at Key Stage 4, although this brings with it challenges, in terms of:

- capacity
- providing appropriate accommodation and resources
- ensuring that provision is made for students with expertise and interest in different genres
- offering opportunities for entry to alternative examinations to GCSE
- providing opportunities for professional development for teachers
- facilitating the inclusion of professional musicians and instrumental teachers in working with students within the curriculum.

These are not insurmountable, provided that the music teacher has the full support of senior management in the school.

Music also provides opportunities for the development of a wide range of transferable skills. The students participating in the Musical Futures programme emphasised how it had improved confidence, and supported the development of skills relating to independent learning, teamwork and performance. This was recognised by senior staff who viewed music as being able to take the lead in pedagogical developments. Music is also recognised as being a vehicle for promoting the inclusion of at-risk students, although the contribution that it can make to students' personal development has not, as yet, been fully exploited (Ofsted, 2009). This is a challenge for the future.

Further reading

D'Amore, A. *Resource Pack* (Second edition). London: Paul Hamlyn Foundation. Online. <http://www.musicalfutures.org/c/Teacher+Pack> (accessed 17/01/2010).

Evans, J. and Philpott, C. (2009) *A Practical Guide to Teaching Music in the Secondary School.* London: Routledge.

Office for Standards in Education (Ofsted) (2009) *Making More of Music: Improving the quality of music teaching in secondary schools.* London: Ofsted.

Price, D. (2006) *Personalising Music Learning.* London: Paul Hamlyn Foundation.

References

Bray, D. (2000) 'An examination of GCSE music uptake rates'. *British Journal of Music Education,* 17(1), 79–89.

Button, S. (2006) 'Key Stage 3 pupils' perception of music'. *Music Education Research,* 8(3), 417–431.

Cain, T. (2007) 'The National Curriculum for Music'. In C. Philpott and G. Spruce (eds), *Learning to Teach Music in the Secondary School: A companion to school experience* (Second edition). London: RoutledgeFalmer.

Cox, G. (1993) *A History of Music Education in England (1872–1928).* Aldershot: Scolar Press.

–– (2001) 'Teaching Music in Schools: Some historical reflections'. In C. Philpott and C. Plummeridge (eds), *Issues in Music Teaching.* London: RoutledgeFalmer.

–– (2002) *Living Music in Schools 1923–1999: Studies in the history of music education in England.* Aldershot: Ashgate.

Crabtree, C.M. (1947) 'School Certificate Music II: Music in a test-tube'. *Music in Education,* 11, 12–14.

Curriculum for Excellence (2009) *Expressive Arts.* Online. <http://www.ltscotland.org.uk/curriculumforexcellence/expressivearts/index.asp> (accessed 20/01/2010).

Department for Children, Education, Lifelong Learning and Skills (DCELLS) (2008) *Music in the National Curriculum for Wales.* Cardiff: DCELLS.

Department for Children, Schools and Families (DCSF) (2009) *Key Stage 3 National Strategy.* Online. <http://www.standards.dcsf.gov.uk/studysupport/impact/ks3/> (accessed 20/01/2010).

Department for Education and Employment (DfEE)/Qualifications and Curriculum Authority (QCA) (1999) *The National Curriculum for England: Music.* London: DfEE/QCA.

Department for Education and Science (DfES) (2005) *Key Stage 3 National Strategy – Leading in Learning: Exemplification in music.* London: HMSO.

Farmer, P. (1976) 'Pop music in the secondary school: A justification'. *Music in Education,* September/October, 217–219.

Green, L. (2002a) 'From the Western classics to the world: Secondary music teachers' changing attitudes in England 1982 and 1998'. *British Journal of Music Education,* 19(1), 5–30.

–– (2002b) *How Popular Musicians Learn: A way ahead for music education.* Aldershot: Ashgate.

–– (2008) *Music, Informal Learning and the School: A new classroom pedagogy*. Aldershot: Ashgate.

Hallam, S., Creech, A., Sandford, C., Rinta, T. and Shave, K. (2008) *Survey of Musical Futures: A report from the Institute of Education, University of London for the Paul Hamlyn Foundation*. London: Institute of Education, University of London.

Hallam, S., Creech, A. and McQueen, H. (2009) *Musical Futures: A case study investigation, an interim report from the Institute of Education, University of London for the Paul Hamlyn Foundation*. London: Institute of Education, University of London.

Hargreaves, D.H. (2006) *A New Shape for Schooling*. London: Specialist School and Academies Trust.

Hargreaves, D.J. and Marshall, N.A. (2003) 'Developing identities in music education'. *Music Education Research*, 5(3), 263–273.

Hargreaves, D.J., Purves, R.M., Welch, G.F. and Marshall, N.A. (2007) 'Developing identities and attitudes in musicians and music teachers'. *British Journal of Educational Psychology, 77*(3), 665–682.

Harland, J., Kinder, K., Lord, P., Stott, A., Schagen, I., Haynes, J., with Cusworth, L., White, R. and Paola, R. (2000) *Arts Education in Secondary Schools: Effects and effectiveness*. Slough: National Foundation for Educational Research.

Her Majesty's Inspectorate (HMI) (1985a) *The Curriculum from 5–16*. London: HMSO.

–– (1985b) *Music from 5–16: Curriculum Matters 4*. London: HMSO.

Her Majesty's Stationery Office (HMSO) (1944) *Education Act*. London: HMSO.

–– (1988) *Education Reform Act, Chapter 40*. London: HMSO.

House of Commons, Children Schools and Families Committee (2009) *National Curriculum: Fourth report of Session 2008–09, Volume 1*. London: HMSO.

Lamont, A., Hargreaves, D.J., Marshall, N.A. and Tarrant, M. (2003) 'Young people's music in and out of school'. *British Journal of Music Education*, 20(3), 229–241.

Little, F. (2009) 'An exploration into the uptake rates of GCSE Music with a focus on the purposes of music in school'. Unpublished EdD thesis, University of Durham.

Mackrill, D. (2009) 'The integration of ICT in the music classroom'. In J. Evans and C. Philpott (eds), *A Practical Guide to Teaching Music in the Secondary School*. London: Routledge.

Mainwaring, J. (1941) 'The meaning of musicianship: A problem in the teaching of music'. *British Journal of Educational Psychology,* 1(3), 205–214.

Musical Futures (2009) Online. <http://www.musicalfutures.org> (accessed 17/01/2010).

The Newsom Report (1963) *Half our Future.* London: HMSO.

Northern Ireland Curriculum (2009) *The Arts: Music.* Online. <http://www.nicurriculum.org.uk/key_stage_3/areas_of_learning/the_arts/> (accessed 20/01/2010).

North West Regional Curriculum Development Project (NWRCDP) (1974) *Creative Music and the Young School Leaver.* Glasgow: Blackie.

Office for Standards in Education (Ofsted) (2003) *Music in Secondary Schools: Ofsted subject reports series 2001/02 (HMI 811).* London: Ofsted.

–– (2006) *An Evaluation of the Paul Hamlyn Foundation's Musical Futures Project (HMI 2682).* London: Ofsted.

–– (2009) *Making More of Music: An evaluation of music in schools 2005–08.* London: Ofsted.

Paynter, J. (1982) *Music in the Secondary School Curriculum.* Cambridge: Cambridge University Press.

Philpott, C. (2009) 'Personalising learning in music education'. In J. Evans and C. Philpott (eds), *A Practical Guide to Teaching Music in the Secondary School.* London: Routledge.

Pitts, S. (2000) *A Century of Change in Music Education: Historical perspectives on contemporary practice in British secondary school music.* Aldershot: Ashgate.

Plummeridge, C. (2000) 'The evolution of music education'. In A. Kent (ed.), *School Subject Teaching: The history and future of the curriculum.* London: Kogan Page.

Qualification, Curriculum and Assessment Authority for Wales (QCAAW) (2000) *Music in the National Curriculum Wales.* Cardiff: HMSO.

Qualifications and Curriculum Development Authority (QCDA) (2007) *Music: Programme of Study and Attainment Target.* Online. <http://www.qca.org.uk/curriculum> (accessed 20/01/2010).

Ross, M. (1995) 'What's wrong with school music'. *British Journal of Music Education,* 12(3), 185–201.

Rudd, A. (1975) 'Local curriculum development'. In A. Harris, M. Lawn and W. Prescott (eds), *Curriculum Innovation.* London: Croom Helm/Open University.

Schools Council (1971) *Music and the Young School Leaver: Problems and opportunities* (Working Paper 35). London: Evans and Methuen Educational.

Scottish Office Education and Industry Department (SOEID) (1992) *Curriculum and Assessment in Scotland. National Guidelines, Expressive Arts 5–14.* Edinburgh: HMSO.

Scottish Qualifications Authority (SQA) (2008) *Course Report 2008.* Edinburgh: SQA.

Sloboda, J. (2001) 'Emotion, functionality, and the everyday experience of music: Where does music education fit?' *Music Education Research*, 3(2), 243–254.

Small, C. (1975) 'Towards a philosophy, Part 2: Metaphors and madness'. *Music in Education,* July/August, 163–164.

Swanwick, K. (1979) *A Basis for Music Education.* Windsor: NFER-Nelson.

Wright, R. (2002) 'Music for all? Pupils' perceptions of the GCSE Music examination in one South Wales secondary school'. *British Journal of Music Education*, 19(3), 227–241.

Chapter 15

Music in further education colleges

John Conlon and Lynne Rogers

Further education: a context

Further education (FE) provision is generally included in what is known as the 'post-compulsory' sector – that is, education and training provision that 'normally' happens beyond school leaving age. The post-compulsory sector includes specialist and general further education colleges, adult education colleges and sixth form colleges. Although the sector is sometimes characterised as 'post-16', which implies that all people being educated are older than 16, successive education and training initiatives where schools and colleges share resources and education provision, such as school/college compacts, technical and vocational education initiatives (TVEIs) and most recently the new 14–19 diplomas, have meant that the reach of the sector has often extended to younger students, aged 14 upwards.

The post-compulsory sector comprises 429 colleges in the UK: 356 in England; 22 colleges and two FE institutions in Wales; 43 in Scotland, and six in Northern Ireland (AoC, 2009a). Colleges across the UK vary considerably in size, numbers and type of students and the range of programmes and services offered. In Wales some colleges are primarily vocational, some run mainly academic programmes, and some offer both types of provision. In Wales, colleges account for 80 per cent of all post-16 qualifications and provide learning experiences for almost 300,000 people. In Scotland the majority of enrolments at FE level are for vocational courses, e.g. Scottish Vocational Qualifications (SVQs).

In England most colleges offer both vocational and academic programmes, and the 356 colleges comprise: 233 general further education colleges (GFE); 93 sixth form colleges; 16 land-based colleges; four art, design and performing arts colleges and ten special designated colleges. Of the specialist art, design and performing arts colleges only Hereford College of Arts offers FE courses in music: BTEC National Diploma in Music and BTEC First and National Diploma in Performing Arts (with a singing study option) and a Contact course for students with learning disabilities.

In Northern Ireland the six area-based 'super' colleges were formed by the merger of 16 FE colleges in 2007. The new colleges are of similar size and it is hoped that this will secure their long-term viability in the six regions. The range of courses provided cover essential skills, vocational and academic programmes at levels 2 and 3 and higher education programmes.

Many colleges have strong community links (see Box 15.1) and good relationships with industry, the sector skills councils, local employers, businesses and professional organisations (Ofsted, 2009). This can be particularly important in relation to music education and training where collaborative projects with local community organisations, access to work placements and creative apprenticeships add an extra dimension to provision. Across the country some colleges, such as Liverpool Community College, have made substantial investments in purpose-built performing arts venues that include spaces for music education.

Box 15.1 Collaboration between FE and the local community

Ofsted (2009) offers an example of collaboration between FE and the local community in which an 'Arts Depot' is incorporated within an FE college. The Arts Depot is a fully functioning community arts centre and has two equipped theatres, an exhibition gallery with opportunities for multi-media projections and displays, rehearsal studios for music, dance and theatre, and a disability arts and education forum. The result is what Ofsted describes as a 'model' of a shared-use arts space in which students 'behave and work to professional standards'. According to Ofsted this 'unique venue' helps students develop 'realistic' creative knowledge and skills more comprehensively than they would have done if they had studied exclusively in a college environment. Both the venue and the learning provision help to motivate young people, some of whom have previously been disaffected or disengaged.

While music education provision in general is not necessarily targeted at disaffected young people, it is worth noting a defining feature of post-compulsory education which specifically and purposely targets young people who have underachieved or been excluded from school. In this respect, music provision in colleges can play an important role in re-engaging young people who may have been 'written off' by other education or training providers.

This 'instrumental' role of the arts in education, particularly music, is well documented. Ofsted (2009) offers an example of a sixth form college where students who had underachieved at school were supported by a skilful tutor towards achieving a first diploma qualification in music. The report emphasises the role of the tutor, who designed and delivered music learning programmes that not only reflected individual learning needs within the group, but also created a 'buzz and excitement of performing' that helped the students to focus on the performance aspects of the course, and (from the students' perspective) the less attractive theory elements.

Whatever the expectations or intentions of students, there is comprehensive access to music education across the post-compulsory sector – but it is not a universal entitlement. Some colleges, such as Newcastle, offer an extensive range of music learning programmes (see Box 15.2), while others, such as Buxton, offer no award-bearing music courses.

Box 15.2 Newcastle College – a GFE college with an extensive range of provision

Newcastle College has established itself as one of the UK's leading providers of music, performing arts and media. It has created a £21 million, 'state of the art' academy which provides a wide range of study opportunities in music, acting, dance, media, technical production, and entertainment management. Music provision at Newcastle includes numerous study programmes in music technology, music production, music business, and advanced music programme production and performance, plus BTEC national diplomas, and summer schools for adults in performance, production and performing arts, and creative apprenticeships.

Breadth of music provision within FE

In the UK, the music industry – of which live performance accounts for 45 per cent – contributes £6 billion to the economy (CCSkills, 2009). There are just over 100,000 people employed in the music industry nationally, in occupations such as performer (both instrumental and vocal), composer, arranger, lyricist, publisher, recording artist, record manufacturer and retailer, educator, education officer, producer, technician, and sound engineer.

In England there are over 530 music and music-related qualifications on offer – from entry stage through to level 8. In England, Wales and Northern Ireland qualifications are mapped against the qualifications and credit framework (QCF), which shows both the complexity of learning, expressed as a level, and the duration of learning, expressed as qualification title (award, certificate and diploma). Of the music qualifications on offer (excluding doctorate-level qualifications), two are at entry level, 55 at level 1, 62 at level 2, 117 at level 3, 20 at level 4, nine at level 4/5, 80 at level 5, 112 at level 6, and 73 at level 7. Qualification types include GCSEs and GCE A Levels; BTEC first, national and higher national vocational diplomas; creative apprenticeships; graded examinations; associate, licentiateship and fellowships; professional awards; foundation degrees; degrees, and the new creative and media diploma at foundation, higher and advanced levels. Not all the qualifications are available, or on offer at the same time and some have a limited (or no) take-up.

In Scotland, qualifications are mapped against the Scottish qualifications and credit framework. Level 8 qualifications are the most complex (doctorate level), whereas those at level 1 are often initial, or 'entry into learning' qualifications.

Some GFE colleges offer qualifications within the range of levels 1–6 (entry to degree level), but the majority of qualifications on offer fall within the level 2–3 range (GCSE to A level/National Diploma). Graded music examinations are also offered by some colleges on a fee-paying basis, as are a range of music learning opportunities that are classed as 'leisure' or 'personal interest' courses and do not fall within the QCF. For instance, City Lit – a special designated adult education college in London – offers a range of courses in music, including music appreciation, opera in focus, instrumental ensembles, choral singing, instrumental or vocal tuition, music production courses, and rock, pop and soul singers' workshops.

Music learning provision reflects the occupational roles within the economy, and provision in post compulsory education is more extensive than in primary and secondary phases, both in terms of the number of study options on offer and the range of music or music-related subjects and qualifications available. Provision ranges from learning opportunities in music making (performance), through to courses covering DJ mixing skills, sound engineering and musical instrument making. Music study opportunities may be offered as discrete courses, covered by a specific examination such as GCSE Music, or be offered as a constituent element of a broader-based qualification such as BTEC Performing Arts.

In 2007 (the latest year for which full statistics are available) 458,000 students gained music qualifications in England across all phases of compulsory and post-compulsory education. Of these, 343,000 achieved graded examinations levels 1–3; 78,000 achieved GCSE, AS or A level and 37,000 gained vocational qualifications from entry level to level 5 (CCSkills, 2009). The exact numbers of students gaining music qualifications while studying at FE, sixth form and adult education colleges is not known. However, it can be assumed that a fair proportion of the 78,000 students achieving GCSE and GCE A level were studying in a post-compulsory college, as were nearly half of the 37,000 students studying for vocational qualifications, such as BTEC.

Perhaps the biggest growth in provision within the post-compulsory sector over recent years has been the expansion of music 'foundation degrees', which are validated by universities, but offered within FE or adult education colleges. Foundation degrees are work-based learning degrees that are delivered by colleges and universities working in partnership with employers. They are two years in duration and all foundation degrees have a built-in 'top-up' or progression route to an honours degree – that is, students continue their studies for an additional year to gain an honours degree. Foundation degrees are offered in England, Wales and Northern Ireland. Within England, Foundation Degree Forward (2010) lists 190 foundation degrees in performing arts, of which over 80 are focused on music. These include music, music business, music theatre, music production, popular music, commercial music, music management, music technology, music and sonic arts, applied music practice, and digital music creation. Box 15.3 provides an example of a college offering foundation degrees.

Box 15.3 Foundation degrees at Northbrook College

Northbrook College, based in Worthing, offers four foundation degrees: music composition for media, music production, music business and management, and music performance. Although the foundation degrees are offered within the college, they are actually validated by the University of Brighton and, in line with other foundation degree progression routes, on successful completion students can enrol on a BA (Hons) top-up programme, which is also validated by the University of Brighton.

The music foundation degree courses at Northbrook consist of modular, project-based units and are advertised by the college as preparation for 'a successful career in the music industry'. Resources and facilities at Northbrook are comprehensive – it has its own record label and a recording studio complex, which includes: 30 soundproofed studios, along with sampling and synthesis facilities; acoustics and keyboard resources; dedicated music computers; and industry and research standard software packages.

(Northbrook College, 2010)

The quality of provision in FE

In general, the quality of provision within post-compulsory education is well regarded. The Association of Colleges (2009a) reported that three-quarters of people say their local college has a good reputation for the quality and range of courses it provides.

There are no specific nationwide data on student satisfaction with music education provision but, in relation to music, Ofsted (2009) commented on how the best work seen in college courses arose from students developing very good work-related skills specific to the relevant industries. This enabled students to develop good communication and teamwork and the ability to work across different disciplines. An example of good practice during induction is given in Box 15.4.

Box 15.4 Good practice identified by Ofsted

All new students on BTEC music performance, stage management and music production courses starting in September 2007 took part in a multidisciplinary, cross-course, collaborative project based around a performance of Pink Floyd's *The Wall*. This large-scale, all-embracing assignment was carefully designed to address a wide range of assessment criteria for all participating students and to expose them very early on in their course to the rigours, frustrations and demands of industry. Students worked in small creative teams, but had individual briefs that modelled a professional contract with clear deadlines and technical expectations. Three performance stages were used in sequence, and students had the opportunity to explore theatrical, choral and instrumental elements in performance. Throughout the project the sense of teamwork was very strong and students experienced directly the interdependent component parts of such a complex piece of performance work.

As they worked on rehearsing and preparing for public performances, students undertook related contextual studies and reflective work on the specific characteristics of stadium rock concerts of the 1970s and 1980s. They studied the music, tablature and lyrics of the piece and kept critical logs of the entire project. The realistic working environment ensured that students learned to work alongside each other very quickly, to put all their work in a direct professional context with realistic practical, legislative and budgetary consequences, and learned at first hand the structure of a complex production process.

(Ofsted, 2009: 18–19)

Music qualifications: innovation and rationalisation

The most recent innovations in music education, training and qualifications have been made by Creative and Cultural Skills (CCSkills) – the relevant Sector Skills Council. These take the form of creative apprenticeships and the 14–19 Creative and Media Diploma, a new qualification route that could prove highly influential in the development of music education.

CCSkills is the Sector Skills Council for advertising, crafts, cultural heritage, design, music, literature, and performing and visual arts. It is committed to reform and rationalisation of the existing qualification structure across the cultural and creative sectors, including music qualifications. CCSkills (2009) claims the qualifications ecology within the sectors is extraordinarily complex and that the complexity is a result both of an historic failure of the sectors to engage with and debate the qualifications structure, and the increasing popularity of creative subjects for young students studying in further, or higher education. They also express a concern that education and training provision for the sectors does not always align with that needed by employers, who are confused by the plethora of qualifications and the complexities of the language of skills policy (CCSkills, 2009).

In 2008 the National Skills Academy (NSA) for creative and cultural skills was formed by CCSkills as a response to the need both to develop a unified strategy for education and training across the creative and cultural industries, and to bring coherence to the types and forms of education and training provision within the sectors. The NSA is a network of creative and cultural businesses and education providers in England. It works with 20 'founder colleges' across England which have committed to developing young peoples' vocational education and training routes to employment or higher education. Each of the founder colleges offers the new 14–19 Creative and Media Diploma and provides education and training for creative apprenticeships (see Box 15.5 for an example of a founder college). The NSA is also building a new 'centre of excellence' for technical theatre and live music training, located in the Royal Opera production park in Essex, which is due to open in late 2011.

Box 15.5 Gateshead College – an example of a founder college

Gateshead College, in the North East of England, was rated 'outstanding' by Ofsted in January 2009, receiving Grade 1s across all six areas of inspection. This result places the college in the top 4 per cent of colleges in the UK. The college has developed strong partnership links with The Sage, Gateshead, Dance City, Live Theatre, the Newcastle and Gateshead Arts Forum, and the Northern Cultural Skills Partnership. Ofsted describes the college as offering an excellent variety of education and training opportunities, ranging from entry level programmes through to degrees, including courses covering music performance and technology, art and design, digital multimedia and games design, media production, acting, musical theatre and dance. Gateshead College has made a capital investment in the creative and performing arts by building a 200-seat theatre venue, with state-of-the-art production studios, rehearsal studios and teaching resources.

In partnership with its founder colleges, the NSA is leading a review of existing qualifications, which are differentiated by those that only 'relate' to the sector and those that provide 'work-ready candidates for employment' (CCSkills, 2009). While both the NSA and CCSkills recognise that there are qualifications in post-compulsory colleges that are intrinsically valuable to high numbers of students, they remain committed to developing a skills-match strategy, with a qualifications structure that achieves a better fit between vocational qualification provision and employers' needs (CCSkills, 2009). As part of the process of rationalisation, the NSA is mapping the occupational skills used within the music industries, with a view to informing the content and relevance of music qualifications. At the time of writing, the consultation period for the mapping exercise has ended and there is expectation that the occupational standards for music will be drafted during 2010.

The creative and media diploma

The 2005 White Paper *14–19 Education and Skills* (DfES, 2005) set out a series of major reforms for the 14–19 curriculum, together with the introduction of diplomas, including a creative and media diploma. The introduction of the diplomas for 14–19 year olds, comprising a suite of qualifications, or 'lines of learning', was an important aspect of the Labour government's reform of education for young people. Seventeen lines of learning were planned, and the first five were rolled out in 2008. At the time of writing, the future of these is unknown, under the newly elected Liberal-Conservative coalition government.

Music education is covered by the creative and media diploma, which was one of the first lines to be developed and is already available at levels 1 to 3. The level 1 qualification, entitled 'foundation', is equivalent to five GCSEs grades D–G; the level 2 qualification, entitled 'higher', is equivalent to seven GCSEs grades A*–C, and the level 3 qualification, entitled 'advanced', is equivalent to 3.5 GCE A levels. The diploma was developed jointly by the three relevant sector skills councils – Skillset, representing the creative media industries (the lead organisation in the diploma development partnership), Skillfast-UK, representing fashion and textiles, and CCSkills. According to Skillset, the aim of the diploma is to provide a fully rounded education that combines classroom study with 'learning by doing in a practical environment'. It provides students with vital life skills and develops their 'readiness for the workplace' (Skillset, 2009).

It is the phrase 'readiness for the workplace' that is key to why the new diplomas have been developed. Although resonant of the Tomlinson report (Tomlinson, 2004) and the Nuffield review of 14–19 education and training (2007), both of which proposed the development of a new, overarching diploma, the new 14–19 diplomas are fundamentally different. They do not replace GCSEs, A levels and vocational qualifications – as recommended by both reports – but sit alongside them, sometimes embracing other qualifications and yet also competing with them to provide another study option for young people. New lines of learning currently being developed for 'academic' subjects, such as the humanities and social sciences, are now on stream, but essentially the first five 14–19 diplomas have a clear and intentional vocational bias.

The creative and media diploma is usually a two-year course. It has six elements: principal learning, additional and specialist learning, functional skills, personal, learning and thinking skills, work experience, and a student project.

Principal learning

This element of learning is compulsory and covers the creative and media sectors at the appropriate level. Students are encouraged to sample and engage with creative processes, conceptual ideas and practical skills across a range of creative and media-related disciplines, before choosing at least two disciplines to study in depth. The learning outcomes are projects that demonstrate understanding of two or more disciplines and result in something tangible, for example a music soundtrack with promotional art work or video.

Additional and specialist learning

This element comprises a range of study options chosen by the student in order to either broaden their education, or deepen their understanding of, or skills in, a creative discipline. At level 3, the diploma development partnership recognise that the opportunity to specialise may be important, particularly where students may need to demonstrate a level of skill, or attainment in a sector or discipline in order to progress into higher education or training in that field (CCSkills, 2009). Students may decide to deepen their knowledge and understanding by, for example, learning about music sound technology, or develop their musical skills by taking graded examinations. They have the option also to include a subject or discipline outside the music sphere that will help them to gain a place to study at higher education level or to enter employment.

Functional skills

To gain the diploma, students are required to demonstrate success at English, mathematics, and information and communications technology at the appropriate level of achievement for the stage of learning. In some cases this may mean learning sessions covering functional skills.

Personal, learning and thinking skills

At each stage of progression, from levels 1–3, students are expected to demonstrate incremental and increased use of skills such as teamworking, creative thinking and self-management. Learning in this area is linked to the projects, coursework and work experience undertaken and is reflective of the life skills considered important not only for study at higher levels, but also in relation to creative and work practices within the creative and cultural industries.

Work experience

As with many forms of study at both the compulsory and post-compulsory phases of education, the diploma has a work-based element, which is a mandatory component of the qualification. The minimum work-experience expectation is ten days, linked ideally to the sector in which the student wishes to work, or the creative or cultural discipline they wish to study. For students following a music pathway this could result, for example, in a placement at a commercial record label, or a community recording studio.

Student project

The final element of the diploma is a 'free choice' project in which the student can choose the topic and determine the outcome. In some respects the student project is synoptic in that it is meant to represent and provide evidence of the product of learning while on the diploma course. Music students, for example, could opt for promoting and producing a music performance within their college, or at an external venue.

The diploma qualification

A defining feature of the diploma is the absence of a single examination or awarding body responsible for awarding the qualification. Hence the diploma award could be regarded as a 'badge' that signifies success via many combinations of study, linked to a 'menu' of component qualifications. For example, students are not only able to choose which awarding body qualification they will work towards, but are able also to 'assemble' a diploma tailored from a range of component 'sub-qualifications' drawn from several qualification providers. It is possible therefore to choose a principal learning component from one awarding body, the functional skills component from another and an additional and specialist component from yet another. While this 'pick and mix' feature is regarded as a strength of the new qualification (in so far as it expands the choice of the student) it also places an increasingly important emphasis on initial assessment and diagnostic services within colleges, as the potential for students to make the right choice of component qualifications will be predicated on their ability to make informed decisions.

The Qualifications and Curriculum Development Agency (QCDA) approves awarding bodies to provide qualifications for the creative and media diploma. These include, for example, Edexcel/BTEC, Oxford Cambridge and RSA Examinations, City & Guilds, and the University of the Arts, London. QCDA has also set up an online Diploma Aggregation Service to help students and tutors choose the right combination of component qualifications and track success and achievement. On successful completion of the required number of elements, students will be awarded the diploma in the form of a transcript showing the individual units, or qualifications that make up the final diploma.

Roll-out of the diploma

Ninety-five per cent of GFE colleges in England are involved in delivering the new diplomas across all lines of learning (AoC, 2009a), but the actual number of delivery centres for the creative and media diploma – and more specifically music – is not known. The NSA intends to survey colleges in order to establish take-up of the creative and media diploma, and it may be that the numbers at this stage of the roll-out will be comparatively low. If this is the case it should be remembered that the introduction of BTEC qualifications in 1984 was a 'slow burn' process; it was many years and several incarnations before they became fully established.

The diploma development partnership anticipates revisions to the creative and media diploma before the final versions are agreed and stress the development of this qualification is an iterative process; it may be that the content and structure may be revised and possibly extended to include other disciplines (CCSkills, 2009). The NSA will be working with its founder colleges in order to ensure that the creative and media diplomas are fit for purpose and meet the needs and expectations of employers and higher education.

Creative apprenticeships

Creative apprenticeships provide an alternative, work-based, vocational training route to employment in the creative and cultural industries. They lead to a level 2 or level 3 qualification and are targeted at young people who want to engage immediately with the world of work, as opposed to studying full-time at college.

NSA founder colleges have committed to develop and provide training pathways for a range of creative apprentices, including those focused on the music industry. Up to 1,125 new apprenticeship places will be created to train 16–24 year olds for a career in the creative and cultural industries, and the NSA has secured funding to manage an 'Apprenticeship Service', which will be available from April 2010. One of the aims of the creative and cultural apprenticeship programme is to tackle the predicted skills crisis in the sectors. By 2017 it is estimated that the theatre and live events industry will face a 30,000 skills shortage in offstage and backstage staff. At present, creative apprenticeship covers six career paths, three of which have a potential music orientation. The six career paths are music (live events and promotion), music business, technical theatre (including sound production), costume and wardrobe, cultural and heritage venue operation, and community arts management.

Challenges and issues

While the successes of music education within the post-compulsory sector should be recognised and celebrated, there are issues of concern that warrant consideration.

Access to music education can depend on where students live. There are inequities in provision across the UK that mean some people will not be able to enrol on an FE music course that will lead to a qualification, or result in progression through the different levels of learning. As previously stated, despite there being 530 music and music-related qualifications available throughout England, not all colleges offer award-bearing music qualifications. Often, music education provision has been developed in, or close to, urban conurbations, or cultural centres. Some rural areas have a limited cultural infrastructure and virtually no music performance venues. This can be problematic for young people who may wish to follow a music career, not only in terms of access to music venues and education, but also in terms of them finding a music-related work placement should they be fortunate enough to access the 14–19 creative and media diploma and opt for a music pathway.

Despite the potential of the creative and media diploma to impact on music learning within compulsory and particularly post-compulsory education, the success of the entire diploma initiative will be dependent upon a long-term commitment from government. At a policy level, support for the diplomas is inconsistent across the three main political parties and their lifespan may be determined by whichever party is in power.

At an education policy level, the diplomas have been criticised because they sit alongside academic qualifications, as opposed to embracing and replacing them. The Nuffield Review Group argues that as long as academic qualifications in the form of GCSEs and GCE A Levels exist, the diplomas will fail in the trajectory to become the qualification of choice (Nuffield 14–19 Review, 2007).

At the delivery level, there are concerns that the higher diploma is too difficult for the teenage target group (AoC, 2009b). Despite 83 per cent of colleges (out of 133 responses) reporting student satisfaction with the new diplomas, colleges found the diplomas to be a logistical nightmare, and a quarter had still to find a solution to timetabling problems.

In relation to learning content, there are concerns about the balance between the breadth and depth of the diplomas (O'Donnell and Lynch, 2009). Is the broad range of the diploma a strength – in that it offers learners a range of skills and experiences, or is it a weakness – in that topics are not covered in sufficient depth to enable the development of particular specialisms? This may become particularly problematic when students opt to study an advanced level diploma (level 3) with the intention of pursuing progression routes to higher education.

The issue of government funding for the post-compulsory sector is once again on the agenda, with possible reductions forecast. If this happens, music education provision could be in jeopardy. Much music provision in FE involves music technology. In some colleges students have access to industry-standard facilities, specialist equipment, instruments and studios, with an expectation that resources will be available to students beyond the end of a 'normal' college working day. Music technology equipment has to be maintained and is an expensive commodity to replace should it become obsolete, or be broken or stolen. In many colleges, maintenance of equipment necessitates one or more music technicians. While Ofsted (2009) recognises that technicians can be an excellent source of expertise, they are an additional financial overhead not necessarily associated with other subjects or learning programmes. Furthermore, music rehearsal and performance spaces require additional capital expenditure compared with other subjects and do not always translate well to general purpose teaching spaces. The 'fitness for purpose' of some music education spaces is also an issue. Without doubt, some FE colleges have made substantial financial commitments to providing first-rate music rehearsal and performance spaces, but not all colleges are able, or willing to commit funds for this purpose. A review of FE in Wales reported that the provision for music technology and recording was often not as good as that for other elements of performing arts courses, particularly in relation to soundproofing (Estyn, 2003).

Relevant too is the decline in some of the traditional means of production and distribution within the music industry, as the move towards digitisation creates a need for new skills and places new demands on those wishing to train for the profession. It also necessitates expenditure on appropriate digital technologies by colleges as they attempt to 'stay ahead of the game' and deliver education and training that truly reflects the employment profiles of a dynamic and ever-changing music industry.

The commitment to and innovations in FE music learning opportunities over the recent past, including capital build projects, should be recognised and applauded. In some areas of the country, music education is not only recognised regionally, but nationally and, increasingly, internationally. The range of courses on offer is impressive – from first point of entry to degree level.

Learning is provided in some centres to industry standards, in partnerships between colleges and either commercial or community organisations, but the extent to which FE can attempt to meet the perceived needs of the music sector and mirror the investment made by it, should be questioned. For example, the investment in new technology made by the music industry is driven by potential profit margins, and is not justified in terms of educational benefit. A commercial studio can invest substantial sums in one recording artist with the prospect of a phenomenal financial return: not so an FE provider. College managers have to make investment decisions based on the realities of central government funding, through whatever channel this is directed. They have to consider the cost–benefit to a college in terms of the scale of investment, learning provision, student demand and outcome. What may be essential 'kit' to a music department, may not necessarily be considered essential to a college, and attempts to keep up with an ever-changing music industry may be forlorn. Music education is provided on the basis that it meets the education development needs of individual students, as well as being a preparation for employment. Music education also plays an important role in engaging young people who may have given up on education.

While the introduction of the creative and media diploma has faced criticism, it represents an attempt to resolve one of the historical challenges of music education in terms of its rationale and purpose. The diploma seeks to reflect the realities of the creative and cultural industries, including the music industry, which, increasingly, is characterised by portfolio employment skills. The prospects for young people who wish to become involved in the music industries increase in proportion to the range of skills they can offer, their flexibility and their willingness to train and re-train.

The challenge for FE reflects one that it has often faced and successfully addressed – how to ensure that relevant and meaningful music education provision is made available to all who wish to study, and is safeguarded from the vagaries of government funding.

Useful links

Creative and Cultural Skills www.ccskills.org.uk

Diploma Information 14–19 yp.direct.gov.uk/diplomas

References

Association of Colleges (AoC) (2009a) *College Key Facts Summer* 2009. London: AoC.

–– (2009b) *Diploma Survey Report: Results, analysis, conclusions and recommendations*. London: AoC.

Baker, M. (2008) 'Tories would scrap some diplomas'. BBC News, 19 September 2008. Online. <http://news.bbc.co.uk/1/hi/education/7625483.stm> (accessed 18/02/2010).

Creative and Cultural Skills (CCSkills) (2009) *Sector Qualifications Strategy for the Creative and Cultural Industries*. London: CCSkills.

CCSkills, Skillfast-UK and Skillset (2008) *Diploma in Creative and Media Companion Document*. London: Creative and Media Diploma Development Partnership.

Department for Education and Skills (DfES) (2005) *14–19 Education and Skills*. White Paper. London: DfES.

Estyn (2003) *Quality and Standards in Post-16 Education and Training in Wales: A review of further education inspection cycle (1997–2002)*. Cardiff: Estyn.

Foundation Degree Forward (2010) Online. <http://www.fdf.ac.uk> (accessed 26/03/2010).

Northbrook College (2010) Online. <http://www.musicatnorthbrook.com/> (accessed 26/03/2010).

Nuffield 14–19 Review (2007) *The New 14–19 Diplomas, Issue Paper 1*. Online. <http://www.nuffield14-19review.org.uk/> (accessed 06/01/2010).

O'Donnell, L. and Lynch, S. (2009) *National Evaluation of Diplomas Gateway 2 Lead Consortium Survey Research Brief DCSF-RBX-09-12*. London: Department for Children, Schools and Families (DCSF).

Office for Standards in Education (Ofsted) (2009) *Identifying Good Practice: A survey of college provision in arts and media*. London: Ofsted.

Pring, R., Hayward, G., Hodgson, A., Johnson, J., Keep, E., Oancea, A., Rees, G., Spours, K. and Wilde, S. (2009) *Education for All*. London: Routledge.

Skillset (2009) *What is the Diploma in Creative and Media*? Online. <http://www.skillset.org/qualifications/diploma/vision/> (accessed 10/12/2009).

Tomlinson, M. (2004) *14–19 Curriculum and Qualifications Reform*. Annesley: Department for Education and Skills (DfES).

Chapter 16

Music in universities and conservatoires

Helena Gaunt and Ioulia Papageorgi

Overview of university and conservatoire provision

The last two decades have seen unprecedented change in how people create, perform and listen to music. Cultural diversity and diasporas, burgeoning cross-arts collaboration, technological sophistication, and personalisation of consumption have contributed to the transformation of the music industry as a whole and its place in contemporary cultures (Clayton, 2009; Leadbeater, 2009; Kenyon, forthcoming). The leading role of the traditional concert hall is also changing. There is no doubt that live performance continues to attract audiences, but the contexts in which this may happen are increasingly diverse, and music shared informally or formally via the internet has sparked a quantum shift in the ways people can participate. As 'listeners', we are bombarded with choice – how much of a recording do we want, shall we include documentation of rehearsal and behind the scenes activity or sign up to a whole package of merchandise and tweeting? (See, for example, www.plushmusic.tv.)

Not surprisingly in this context, at the same time the most reliable feature of musicians' careers is their unpredictability. Highlighted by Rogers (2002), this is now a commonplace observation. While some musicians may follow familiar paths – DJ, classroom or instrumental teacher, solo artist, academic, orchestral musician, or radio producer – many more will combine several types of work, and may spend considerable time inventing new ways to create and present music. As Kenyon suggests: 'You feel that all bets are off, and no rules apply' (Rogers, 2002: 2).

Nevertheless, in a number of fields, including classical music, competition for tenured employment in highly specialised organisations such as orchestras continues to grow (ALCARM *et al.*, 2002). With more member countries of the European Union, and easy dissemination of work opportunities, (see for example www.musicalchairs), standards are extremely high, and posts in the UK are increasingly held by musicians from overseas. In addition, orchestral musicians are needing to acquire broader expertise as musicians in society. For example, 95 per cent of London Symphony Orchestra (LSO) musicians are now involved in their Discovery (learning and participation) programme, and many of them view this work as complementary to their work on the concert platform, indeed as something which informs performance.

At the same time the music industry also embraces phenomena such as *X Factor* which underline the ways in which celebrity status may be achieved without prior sustained development of musical skill, the critical role of the media, and the allure of a 'star' culture. There is a stark contrast between the experience of these musicians and the lives of most professional musicians, whose work is intense but brings relatively little financial return or recognition (Wills and Cooper, 1988). It is also increasingly being argued that the culture of celebrity and of unprecedented access to the stars through YouTube, Spotify, Bandstock, tweeting, etc. are if anything having a negative impact on both artistic quality and the role of music in society:

> Michael Jackson died and it was dull after just a few hours. Amy Winehouse was a cartoon, her beehive and boyfriends eclipsing her talent. . . . Simon Cowell is an entire record company in one man. A music machine, manipulating light entertainment, selling pap to the nation and telling us it's pop. But we know it's not. Pop is life-changing, culture-shifting, wondrous stuff.
>
> (Sawyer, 2009)

There is no doubt that professional music practices are continuing to diversify and that these are stimulating wide-ranging debate about the fundamental qualities of music and their value and purpose in society.

Not surprisingly then, the concept of a musician within contemporary higher education (HE) has similarly grown and diversified. Currently in the UK, music is offered as a degree programme in about 100 higher education institutions (HEIs), eight of which are conservatoires with a specialist status (QAA, 2008). Until 1992, the majority of programmes focused on Western classical music. Since then many programmes have evolved which focus on other musical genres (popular, jazz, world and national musics), contemporary applications and uses of music (music technology, screen music, multimedia applications of music), as well as music business and music industry management.

Conservatoires traditionally have offered the most obviously vocationally focused programmes. These too are beginning to diversify. Whereas 20 years ago most only focused on classical music training, nearly all now offer jazz at undergraduate and postgraduate level, and three offer undergraduate courses in popular music. Folk music has become an established undergraduate pathway at the Royal Scottish Academy of Music and Drama (RSAMD), Trinity Laban offers a BA in music theatre, and the Royal Welsh College of Music offers MAs in musical theatre and arts management. The Guildhall School offers an MMus in leadership which has arisen out of 25 years of work exploring artistic innovation and community outreach. Birmingham Conservatoire and the Royal Northern College of Music (RNCM), the two most closely allied with universities, have the broadest range of programmes on offer, with digital arts in performance and popular music at undergraduate level in Birmingham, and an undergraduate pathway in music education with qualified teacher status (QTS) available at the RNCM. Increasingly the potential of cross-arts work embedded in music programmes is being considered: Trinity became Trinity Laban, bringing music and dance into one conservatoire, and dance was added as a third performing arts discipline at the RSAMD alongside music and drama in 2009.

The Quality Assurance Agency for Higher Education (QAA) statement (2008) details disciplines in music as follows:

- musical performance, composition and improvisation
- musicology, music theory and analysis, organology, and ethnomusicology
- music technology and acoustics
- music aesthetics and criticism, and music psychology
- music pedagogy, music therapy and music in the community.

Increasingly, programmes now incorporate elements from several areas, seeking to balance depth of engagement with issues of employability. Several programmes even combine music with a humanities discipline, such as a language or cultural studies. In particular, technology (whether involved in the creation, production, recording or marketing and dissemination of music) is a significant component in a large proportion of undergraduate programmes. Of 1,382 courses on offer via UCAS for 2010, 71 per cent fall into this category. Popular music has also recently grown hugely as a discipline, with 237 courses on offer for 2010 (UCAS, 2009).

Postgraduate programmes offered are less diverse in range, but tend to allow for individually driven areas of focus in study. There is a considerable increase in numbers of programmes dedicated to music education and teacher training. Interestingly, the overall number of postgraduate programmes in music is slightly more than those offered in a humanities discipline such as history, although history has more than double the number of undergraduate programmes (see Table 16.1).

Table 16.1 Numbers of programmes offered by universities in music, compared with other subject areas (in 2010)

Subject category (as defined by UCAS)	Undergraduate courses (including foundation courses)	Postgraduate courses (including Masters, Doctoral and short courses)
Music	1,382	741
Medicine (including complementary, sports and veterinary medicine)	319	1,651
Marketing	1,384	2,614
Law	1,483	897
Psychology	1,819	850
Languages	4,528	2,491
History	2,814	648
Silversmithing	13	

Source: UCAS, 2009

Note: Conservatoires in the UK for the most part are not members of UCAS, and so are not represented in these statistics. (The exceptions are the Royal Welsh College of Music and Birmingham Conservatoire.)

Skills, student progression and music in the context of the Bologna process

In keeping with the considerable debate around the kinds of musician that university departments and conservatoires are aiming to produce, concepts of key skills and competencies which students need to develop are broadening. As well as being driven by the dramatic changes taking place in the music industry, these have been underpinned by the changing higher education context as a whole:

> *The range of courses offered in UK HEIs fosters and encourages well-informed, reflective, versatile, innovative and open-minded musicians with a raft of transferable skills.*

> (QAA, 2008: 14)

In recent years, important developments in the UK and in the rest of Europe have set the grounds for ensuring consistency in music education provision across universities in the UK, and a common framework for comparable degrees across all European universities. These include the publication of the QAA Benchmark Statement for Music in 2002, the Bologna Declaration of 1999, and the Erasmus programme for higher education and HE/FE students, teachers and institutions, established in 1987 by the European Commission programme.

QAA benchmarks

The first subject benchmark statement for higher education programmes in music was published by the Quality Assurance Agency for Higher Education in 2002 and updated in 2008 (QAA, 2008). This has marked an important development in the provision of music education in the UK, supporting comparability in curriculum design, intended learning outcomes, teaching methods and assessment.

One important aim of the curriculum structure in music is to prepare students to take responsibility for their learning and prepare graduates to enter the workforce with the necessary skills to pursue a career in music – or any other domain:

> Through this process, students take on increasing responsibility for their own learning. The acquisition of independent learning skills is a key element of 'graduateness', enabling students to continue their learning beyond HE and into their future careers, whether in music or in other areas of work.
>
> (QAA, 2008: 21)

The skills that music graduates are expected to have mastered by the end of their courses are divided into 'subject-specific' and 'generic/transferable' areas. Subject-specific skills are defined as: aural/analytical skills, performance skills, composing skills, knowledge-based skills, and technological skills. Generic/transferable skills are defined as: intellectual skills, communication and interaction skills, personal management skills, and imagination/creativity skills.

Clearly the balance of skills acquired, or considered desirable, varies between fields within music. Research in higher education has also shown that it may vary with gender, level of prior experience and musical genre specialisation (Burt-Perkins and Lebler, 2008; Lebler *et al.*, 2008; Creech *et al.*, 2008a; Papageorgi *et al.*, 2010b). Box 16.1 discusses some relevant research.

Box 16.1 Developing performance expertise in higher education – the 'Investigating Musical Performance' project

The 'Investigating Musical Performance: Comparative studies in advanced musical learning' project (funded by ESRC Teaching and Learning Research Programme, 2006–08) investigated how advanced musicians develop performance skills and processes of learning. A total of 244 undergraduate and portfolio career musicians representing four different musical genres (classical, popular, jazz and Scottish traditional) took part in the study and provided data through the completion of a specially designed self-report survey, semi-structured interviews and focus groups.

One area of investigation was how musicians perceive and rate their expertise and performance skills. Findings showed that there was a gap between the skills that musicians aspired to obtain (their 'ideal' skills) and their self-assessed competence (their 'perceived' skills). Musicians rated the importance of certain musical skills in becoming a successful performer higher than they rated themselves on the same skills. This was particularly evident with females. This may suggest that women need more support, especially in the early years of their studies. An alternative explanation would be that females reflect on their own development more successfully and are better at identifying where they need to improve, so perhaps male students need more support in developing metacognitive skills and realistic self-assessment strategies.

Differences according to gender

Male musicians felt that the drive to excel musically was particularly important in becoming successful, while female musicians emphasised the importance of developing coping skills. Interestingly, they rated their coping skills significantly lower than males, which may relate to the fact that female musicians seem to cope less effectively with the demands of performance, and experience higher levels of negative musical performance anxiety (Wesner *et al.*, 1990; Fishbein *et al.*, 1988).

Differences according to musical genre specialisation

Classical musicians considered the drive to excel musically and technically, as well as notation and analytical skills to be the most important skills contributing to their musical development. Musicians from popular, jazz and Scottish traditional genres reported that non-notation music skills were more important. This is not surprising, given that popular, jazz and folk musicians rely more heavily on skills such as improvisation, memorisation and playing by ear, while classical music has been associated with reading notation and mastering the Western musical canon.

(Papageorgi *et al.*, 2010b)

The Bologna process

Currently, 46 European countries are participating in the Bologna process, which aims to create a 'European higher education area' by 2010 (EACEA P9 Eurydice, 2009). This development has important implications for the employability of music graduates. A unified European higher education system with comparable degree structure and assessment methods will, for example, encourage the mobility of music students, graduates and educators, and increase the employability of UK graduates in Europe. Consequently, students and educators also have an unprecedented opportunity to contribute to the exchange and development of cultural practices and ideals.

In music, the 'Polifonia–Erasmus Thematic Network for Music' was established in 2004 (www.polifonia-tn.org), aiming to implement, monitor and further develop tools and approaches relevant to the Bologna process, with a particular focus on establishing 'Polifonia/Dublin descriptors' for learning outcomes in music, programme comparability and quality assurance. The project is also addressing issues related to the 'Education and Training 2010' Agenda of the Lisbon Strategy, such as improving institutional governance, embedding research within all three cycles of performance programmes, and strengthening links to the music profession.

The Erasmus programme

The Erasmus programme currently enables more than 180,000 students to study and work abroad each year. It also enables mobility of teachers and enterprise staff for training and professional development.

Such exchanges of students and teachers can have many benefits – enrichment of the internal culture of an institution, curriculum development, and the enhancement of artistic development (AEC, 2008). Educational experiences abroad may catalyse musical and professional development, broaden perspectives of the world and its cultural diversity, foster the development of intercultural social skills and promote self-reliant individuals and learners. Such experiences can therefore be a key part of professional preparation, promoting flexibility as a musician in different contexts, and often opening up new horizons and opportunities. Capitalising on Erasmus, a collaborative Masters programme in 'New audiences and innovative practice' has recently been developed, with a particular focus on stimulating artistic innovation (www.jointmusicmasters.org).

Pedagogy: Teaching, learning and assessment methods

The QAA statement for music (QAA, 2008) recognises that music pedagogies in higher education in the UK need to reflect the characteristics of a wide range of repertoires, genres and learning outcomes. In keeping with changes in higher education more generally, programmes are often adopting a much more diverse set of learning and teaching methods than previously. For example, systematic aural training can be supported at an individual student's own pace, using software such as Aurelia. Lecture demonstrations or lecture recitals may now replace the more traditional delivery of a written paper in seminars or for assessment. A growing awareness of the impact of peer learning has led, for example, to an emphasis on collaborative creative projects driven by students' own ideas, and on chamber music or small band playing. Interestingly the focus on one-to-one tuition has changed little within performance programmes, especially in conservatoires, although in many institutions these are being complemented by group classes or performance platforms to stimulate peer interaction. In many places there is greater emphasis on the interaction between higher education and the professional world, so important in supporting learners through the transition from student to professional life. This is supporting the move away from teacher-oriented education towards a more student-centred approach generally.

Similarly, assessment methods are becoming more varied, with an emphasis on including both formative and summative approaches (QAA, 2008). Alongside more traditional written examinations, performance assessments and dissertations, examples include:

- Peer assessment – where students rate their peers' work against agreed criteria
- Self-assessment – ascertaining students' ability to reflect critically on their work and identify strengths and weaknesses
- Reports on placements – where students have to reflect constructively on their experiences, which may then be moderated by a placement mentor/coach
- Reports on empirical work – assessing students' ability to conceptualise and plan a research project, as well as collecting and analysing data or gathering evidence and reporting findings using appropriate academic conventions
- Viva voce examinations – assessing ability to draw on knowledge and present convincing arguments in response to questions in a live situation.

An example of development of assessment processes in a conservatoire is shown in Box 16.2.

Box 16.2 Peer assessment in a popular music programme

In a Popular Music Bachelors programme at the Queensland Conservatorium in Australia, peer assessment has been adopted as an integral part of major assessments. All students become members of assessment panels which review the compositions and tracks submitted, produce written feedback and determine a mark against established criteria. The process requires commitment and vital skills of critical analysis and constructive feedback. Consequently, being an assessor is then in itself specified in the learning outcomes of the programme and given credit. Although time-consuming, students build powerful skills as reflective practitioners, and research has shown that assessment achievement levels are in no way compromised by including students on the panels.

(Lebler, 2007)

It is clear, however, that within the climate of rapid pedagogical shifts, it is imperative that educators focus on ensuring that teaching and assessment methods offer an appropriate match, both for intended learning outcomes and the learning styles and needs of individual students.

Learning environments and the transition from student to professional life

There is no doubt that now, more than ever, the transition from student to professional life for performing musicians demands resilience and a broad array of skills. Research is showing that forging a career requires tenacity, artistic imagination, personal confidence, the ability to recognise opportunities and to generate work from these, as well as refined musical skills (Creech *et al.*, 2008b). It also indicates, however, that students are not always well placed to meet these challenges. The development of their own musical interpretative skills and artistic voice (Burwell, 2005) may be inhibited. The dangers of a halo effect (Abeles *et al.*, 1992) or of falling into spoon-fed learning in the context of one-to-one apprenticeship can be that students fail to develop independence as learners or the key skills of effective reflective practice and so struggle to formulate realistic professional goals and the specific steps needed to achieve them (Gaunt, 2008, 2010a). Conservatoire students in particular tend not to be adept at transferring their high-level skills to other contexts – from playing to teaching others to play, for example (Mills, 2006). Within musical performance education, it is necessary to consider how one-to-one tuition, which has been premised on apprenticeship (Schön, 1987; Kennell, 2002), can most effectively evolve to meet the needs of contemporary students – perhaps through overtly modelling this learning environment as creative collaboration (John-

Steiner, 2000; Sawyer, 2007) and strengthening the practice of mentoring interactions within the relationship (Megginson and Clutterbuck, 2006; Renshaw, 2009; Garvey *et al.*, 2009). Developments of this kind should help to align institutional learning environments more closely with what research suggests most effectively enables students to flourish and realise their potential. These include inspirational teaching, promoting a positive learning environment, facilitating academic, professional and personal development, fostering a supportive community of learning, allowing the development and pursuit of personal interests and promoting student independence as learners (Lizzio *et al.*, 2002; Papageorgi *et al.*, 2010b). The key features of ideal learning environments articulated by conservatoire and university music department students (Papageorgi *et al.*, 2010b) are shown in Box 16.3.

Box 16.3 Key features of ideal learning environments articulated by music students

Motivating and inspiring students

You're seeing one of your teachers play, which is always great, you realise that they're not just dry and dusty academics; they're actually really hip, and then you're seeing one of your friends playing with them and really upping their game because they're playing with someone who is a considerable way on in their musical journey. So that sort of thing is really healthy.

(conservatoire student)

Facilitating networking and bringing musicians together

Networking is the biggest thing that I've been introduced to. Just the sort of contacts that . . . Like playing today's gig: I've never had a chance to play a gig like that, on my own back.

(conservatoire student)

Broadening musical minds and developing students' interests

Especially as a drummer, I find that I'm doing a lot of playing that I haven't done before. Previously I was in a rock band, but since I've come here I've done a lot more pop, R&B and stuff like that. So I'm concentrating on a lot of different genres that I wouldn't have done if I hadn't have come to the pop course.

(conservatoire student)

Facilitating entry into the active music scene

The fact that it's not difficult to go out and play jazz means that you have a motivation. . . the fact that there are loads of people into

---

> *jazz in Leeds (due to the institution) means that the venues make money putting on jazz gigs and you have an audience.*
>
> (conservatoire student)

Being progressive

> *It certainly has a distinctive character. . . there is a tension between the two ideals here. It's trying to break away from the older colleges, which is great, it's a forward-looking institution . . . because we are accepting that there is other music than just the canon, though the canon is important.*
>
> (conservatoire student)

Fostering a positive learning environment

> *This informality . . . these integrated networks are a welcome by-product of the conservatoire as a hub.*
>
> (conservatoire student)

Fostering personal development as well as professional

> *You're learning through experience . . . and I think it's good preparation for the real world – what I've learnt is how to manage your own time, how to use it productively, how to basically manage yourself. It's not just music – it's about myself as well, socially and emotionally.*
>
> (university music department student)

Cultivating supportive communities of learning

> *There's a sense of personal concern, which I think is one of the important things about York – on the whole, most people know each other and there's a good relationship between the staff and the students, so that means you do have this feeling . . . that there are people guiding you and watching you, so you're not just cast out into a kind of open sea!*
>
> (university music department student)

> (Papageorgi *et al.*, 2010b)

Implications and challenges

In keeping with the diversity and pace of change within the cultural context of music as a whole, higher music education currently reflects similar potential and tensions. For example, in classical music the culture of young celebrity, and the demands of the recording industry for ever-increasing technical perfection and homogeneity in sound (Lawson, 2003; Leech-Wilkinson, 2009) mean that instilling flawless technique in students, and the pressure to produce the next marketable young star are strong. These aims at times rub against the support of individual artistic exploration or the development of a broader set of professional skills.

At the same time, our understanding of what may constitute excellence in music is extending. Excellence as a creative collaborator across the arts, as music leaders or as portfolio musicians are different from, but equal to, the excellence of solo artists or ensemble musicians. This poses significant challenges for universities and conservatoires. How can they best support multiple areas of excellence, and enable individuals to forge focused paths within them? How much should programmes focus on a single area of excellence or on several to create multi-skilled musicians? How best can the intense hours of research or personal practice needed to achieve professional standards be combined with exploring new territories? What constitutes core skills and what should be areas of choice? How best can cross-fertilisation with other programmes and with the creative and cultural industries be effectively implemented?

Another consideration for programmes with large elements of practical music making has been the increasing need to support specific components of physical and psychological health. Managing repetitive strain injury, performance anxiety, and issues of stamina and everyday stress are important areas of research and consideration within programmes (Williamon, 2004). This is highlighting the embodied nature of making music, the significance of the relationship and flow between player and instrument, both physically and psychologically, which then extends to the relationship between artistic collaborators, and between them and their audiences. The contribution which this makes to what is variously referred to as 'presence in performance (Rodenburg, 2007), flow (Csikszentmihalyi, 1990), or improvisatory skill (Dolan, 2005; Gaunt *et al.*, 2009), has encouraged several institutions to explore more systematically connections in the training and education of musicians, actors and dancers (see for example RSAMD, Trinity Laban and the Guildhall School). Further research and pedagogical development is needed in this area.

In addition, with the current significance being attributed to the arts and participative music in making connected communities, there is a particular demand for people with skills as music educators, leaders and animateurs (www.musicmanifesto.co.uk). Some programmes provide opportunities to build relevant skills through working in formal and informal educational contexts and across musical genres. These may be linked to the education and outreach programmes of professional ensembles and cultural organisations. An example is shown in Box 16.4.

Box 16.4 Student development of educational skills within the LSO 'On Track' programme

Students from the Guildhall School work alongside musicians from the LSO on their 'On Track' programme, playing and performing with a range of children who already learn orchestral instruments. This enables them to develop skills through first-hand experience, coached by more experienced players and animateurs whom they see as strong role models, and to work to their strengths as performers. In turn the students provide a younger role model and coach for the youngest musicians, and often stimulate the LSO musicians to reflect on their own practice within this educational field. The environment proves successful, particularly in the initial stages of building awareness of the demands of educational work. Considerable further development is then needed for the students to be able to work effectively in a range of contexts, and where they might take a stronger leadership role.

Full-time music teachers and musicians with skills as animateurs or instrumental teachers to complement their role as performers, creators and producers are vital in making sure that music education has a workforce which is 'fit for purpose'. Yet relatively few currently undergo significant development of these skills while in a university or conservatoire. There are surprisingly few programmes offering substantial training and development of this kind beyond classroom QTS courses. Notable exceptions include the Key Stage 2 Music CPD programme offered by Trinity Guildhall and the Open University (www.ks2music.org.uk). There is no doubt that this is an area which needs urgent development. Although many musicians are learning skills 'on the job' and through short CPD courses, higher education has an important part to play in providing an appropriately skilled workforce.

In response to these issues, many universities and conservatoires have extended programmes to take a more holistic view of musicians and equip students with a range of generic skills as well as the discipline-specific expertise. In undergraduate performance programmes, for example, health and well-being, project management and entrepreneurialism often feature, as shown in Box 16.5.

Box 16.5 A BMus year 1 module at the Royal College of Music Professional skills: Healthy body, healthy mind, healthy music

The module introduces students to fundamental principles of physical and mental health that are integral to performance success. Stemming from recent research in the College's Centre for Performance Science, as well as contemporary evidence from the fields of medicine, psychology and exercise science, the seminars provide students with an informed backdrop

---

against which they can make the most of their educational and professional opportunities. Individual seminars include: 'It'll be alright on the night . . . right? (Optimising the psychology of performance)' and 'Sex, drugs and rock-n-roll (The effects of drugs on performance)'. Alongside the seminar series, students experience Alexander Technique group taster sessions. They are also offered individual fitness and hearing assessments.

(Royal College of Music, 2010)

There is a danger, however, that programmes are consequently becoming overloaded. More fundamental consideration needs to be given to how best to support musical and professional development of musicians in the twenty-first century. As well as the subject content addressed, how can approaches to learning and teaching and assessment be used to catalyse the development of deep learning, and the flexibility, imagination and confidence to apply those skills in contemporary professional contexts? Essential points of focus must now be: (1) approaches that stimulate students' autonomy as learners and their ability to evolve an individual professional path (Bennett and Hannan, 2008; Creech *et al.*, 2008b; Gaunt, 2010b); (2) peer collaboration and support, as these underpin innovation and can benefit students' confidence and professional achievement (Papageorgi *et al.*, 2010a; Lebler, 2007); and (3) ways of embedding work experience and networking through, for example, work placements and professional mentoring.

To achieve this, there are a number of challenges for the sector. Closer collaboration is needed between music providers in the sector, building on synergies and areas of complementary expertise. More substantial professional development is needed for teachers in music in higher education, in relation to both individual practice and curriculum design. This may be especially the case in conservatoires, where pedagogical professional development has not traditionally been a priority. Some initiatives are already in place, with institutions introducing induction programmes for teachers and, for example a specialist pathway within the 'Teaching and Learning in Higher and Professional Education Postgraduate Programme' (www.ioe.ac.uk/study), and a European initiative as part of the Polifonia project. However, considerably more remains to be done in this area, to make pedagogical professional development more widespread, to build stronger connections between practitioners and the research base, and to foster dynamic communities of learning within music departments and conservatoires as a whole.

While not all courses will necessarily be vocational, the fundamental purpose of programmes will benefit from continual review in the light of the pace of change in music. Recent developments in the field of musicology offer an interesting example, where the notion of the score as the fixed text is gradually transforming, with a growing interest in performance studies.

The Research Centre for Musical Performance as Creative Practice, funded by the Arts and Humanities Research Council is one example of a project which is demonstrating the potential for university departments, conservatoires and industry partners to collaborate in addressing important contemporary research questions in this field (www.cmpcp.ac.uk).

Finally, with the increasingly diverse vocational potential and unpredictable work patterns for musicians, part-time study, short courses and distance learning are likely to become more important in enabling musicians to acquire and update the full range of skills they need to maintain a successful career.

Further reading

Jorgensen, H. (2009) *Research into Higher Music Education: An overview from a quality improvement perspective.* Oslo: Novus Press.

PALATINE: The Higher Education Academy Subject Centre for Dance, Drama and Music, established in 2000 to support and enhance learning and teaching in performing arts higher education across the UK. The website features events, funding opportunities, reports and resources. <http://www.palatine.ac.uk> (accessed 25/02/2010).

Tuning Working Group of the Polifonia Project (2007) *Handbook on Curriculum Design and Development in Higher Music Education.* Association of European Conservatoires. Online. <http://www.polifonia-tn.org> (accessed 18/01/2010).

Welch, G. and Papageorgi, I. (2008) 'Investigating musical performance: How do musicians deepen and develop their learning about performance?' TLRP: Teaching and Learning Research Briefing (No. 61).

Useful links

The European Association of Conservatoires www.aecinfo.org/mundus musicalis

The Centre for Musical Performance as Creative Practice www.cmpcp.ac.uk

The Royal College of Music www.health.rcm.ac.uk

The Institute of Education www.ioe.ac.uk/study/masters/PMM9_TLH9IM.html

Lectorate Lifelong Learning in Music & The Arts, Prince Claus Conservatoire, Groningen and the Royal Conservatoire of the Hague www.jointmusic masters.org

Trinity Guildhall www.ks2music.org.uk

Musical Chairs www.musicalchairs.info

Music Manifesto www.musicmanifesto.co.uk/research/details/music-manifesto-report-no-w/109085

Plushmusic www.plushmusic.tv

Polifonia - Erasmus Thematic Network for Music www.polifonia-tn.org

Quality Assurance Agency www.qaa.ac.uk/academicinfrastructure/benchmark/honours

UCAS www.ucas.com

References

Abeles, H.F., Goffi, J. and Levasseur, S. (1992) 'The components of effective applied instruction'. *Quarterly Journal of Music Teaching and Learning,* 3(2), 17–23.

ALCARM, Lewis-Crosby, A. and Moon, R. (2002) 'Knowing the Score 2'. Association of British Orchestras. Online. <http://www.abo.org.uk/information/publication> (accessed 04/12/2009).

Association Européenne des Conservatoires (AEC) (2008) *Higher Music Education: A global perspective.* Online. <http://www.aecinfo.org/mundusmusicalis> (accessed 17/12/2009).

Bennett, D. and Hannan, M. (eds) (2008) *Inside, Outside, Downside Up: Conservatoire training and musicians' work.* Perth: Black Swan Press.

Burt-Perkins, R. and Lebler, D. (2008) '"Music isn't one island": The balance between depth and breadth for music students in higher education'. In *Proceedings of the 17th International Seminar of the Commission for the Education of the Professional Musician.* Spilamberto, Italy: International Society for Music Education.

Burwell, K. (2005) 'A degree of independence: Teachers' approaches to instrumental tuition in a university college'. *British Journal of Music Education,* 22(3), 199–215.

Clayton, M. (2009) 'The social and personal functions of music in cross-cultural perspective'. In S. Hallam, I. Cross and M. Thaut (eds), *The Oxford Handbook of Music Psychology.* Oxford: Oxford University Press.

Creech, A., Papageorgi, I., Duffy, C., Morton, F., Haddon, E., Potter, J., De Bezenac, C., Whyton, T., Himonides, E. and Welch, G. (2008a) 'Investigating musical performance: Commonality and diversity amongst classical and non classical musicians'. *Music Education Research*, 10(2), 215–234.

–– (2008b) 'From music student to professional: The process of transition'. *British Journal of Music Education,* 25(3), 315–331.

Csikszentmihalyi, M. (1990) *Flow: The psychology of optimal experience.* New York: Harper & Row.

Dolan, D. (2005) 'Back to the future: Towards the revival of extemporisation in classical music performance'. In N. Bannan and G. Odam (eds), *The Reflective Conservatoire: Studies in music education.* Aldershot: Ashgate.

Educational, Audiovisual and Culture Executive Agency (EACEA) P9 Eurydice (2009) *Higher Education in Europe 2009: Developments in the Bologna process.* Brussels: EACEA.

European Commission (2009) 'The Erasmus Programme'. Online. <http://ec.europa.eu/education/lifelong-learning-programme/doc80_en.htm> (accessed 24/11/2009).

Fishbein, M., Middlestadt, S.E., Ottati, V., Strauss, S. and Ellis, A. (1988) 'Medical problems among ISCOM musicians: Overview of a national survey'. *Medical Problems of Performing Artists*, 3, 1–8.

Garvey, R., Stokes, P. and Megginson, D. (2009) *Coaching and Mentoring: Theory and practice.* London: Sage.

Gaunt, H. (2008) 'One-to-one tuition in a conservatoire: The perceptions of instrumental and vocal teachers'. *Psychology of Music,* 36(2), 215–245.

–– (2010a) 'One-to-one tuition in a conservatoire: The perceptions of instrumental and vocal students'. *Psychology of Music,* 38(2), 178–208.

–– (2010b) 'Understanding the one-to-one relationship in instrumental/vocal tuition in higher education: Comparing student and teacher perceptions'. *British Journal of Music Education.*

Gaunt, H., Ford, B. and Noonan, I. (2009) 'Improvisation in music, drama and health'. Paper presented at The Reflective Conservatoire: Building Connections Conference, Guildhall School of Music & Drama, 28 February–2 March.

Hargreaves, D.J., Purves, R.M., Welch, G.F. and Marshall, N.A. (2007) 'Developing identities and attitudes in musicians and classroom music teachers'. *British Journal of Educational Psychology*, 77, 665–682.

John-Steiner, V. (2000) *Creative Collaboration.* Oxford: Oxford University Press.

Kennell, R. (2002) 'Systematic research in studio instruction in music'. In R. Colwell and C. Richardson (eds) *The New Handbook of Research on Music Teaching and Learning.* Oxford: Oxford University Press.

Kenyon, N. (forthcoming) 'Performance today: a snapshot and some trends'. In C. Lawson and R. Stowell (eds), *The Cambridge History of Musical Performance*. Cambridge: Cambridge University Press.

Lawson, C. (ed.) (2003) *The Cambridge Companion to the Orchestra*. Cambridge: Cambridge University Press.

Leadbeater, C. (2009) 'The art of with'. Online. <http://www.charlesleadbeater. net/home.aspx> (accessed 12/12/2009).

Lebler, D. (2007) 'Student as master? Reflections on a learning innovation in popular music pedagogy'. *International Journal of Music Education*, 25(3), 205-221.

Lebler, D., Burt-Perkins, R. and Carey, G. (2008) 'What the students bring: Examining the attributes of commencing conservatoire students'. Paper presented at the World Conference of the International Society for Music Education, Bologna, July.

Leech-Wilkinson, D. (2009) 'The changing sound of music: Approaches to studying recorded musical performance'. London: CHARM.

Lizzio, A., Wilson, K. and Simons, R. (2002) 'University students' perceptions of the learning environment and academic outcomes: Implications for theory and practice'. *Studies in Higher Education*, 27(1), 27–52.

Megginson, D. and Clutterbuck, D. (2006) *Techniques for Coaching and Mentoring*. London: Kogan Page.

Mills, J. (2006) 'Performing and teaching: The beliefs and experience of music students as instrumental teachers'. *Psychology of Music*, 34(3), 372–390.

Papageorgi, I., Creech, A., Haddon, E., Morton, F., De Bezenac, C., Himonides, E., Potter, J., Duffy, C., Whyton, T. and Welch, G. (2010a) 'Investigating musical performance: Perceptions and prediction of expertise in advanced musical learners'. *Psychology of Music*, 38(1), 1–36.

–– (2010b) 'Institutional culture and learning I: Inter-relationships between perceptions of the learning environment and undergraduate musicians' attitudes to learning'. *Music Education Research*, 12(2), 1-16.

Quality Assurance Agency for Higher Education (QAA) (2008) 'Music'. Online. <http://www.qaa.ac.uk/academicinfrastructure/benchmark/honours> (accessed 28/08/2009).

Renshaw, P. (2009) 'Lifelong learning for musicians: The place of mentoring'. Online. <http://www.lifelonglearninginmusic.org> (accessed 12/12/2009).

Rodenburg, P. (2007) *Presence: How to use positive energy for success in every situation*. London: Michael Joseph.

Rogers, R. (2002) *Creating a Land with Music: The work, education and training of professional musicians in the 21st century*. London: Youth Music.

Royal College of Music (2010) Online. <http://www.health.rcm.ac.uk> (accessed 14/02/2010).

Sawyer, K. (2007) *Group Genius: The creative power of collaboration*. New York: Basic Books.

Sawyer, M. (2009) 'Sounding off'. *Observer Music Monthly*, December.

Schön, D.A. (1987) *Educating the Reflective Practitioner*. San Francisco: Jossey-Bass.

UCAS (2009) Online. <http://www.ucas.com> (accessed 18/11/2009).

Wesner, R.B., Noyes, R. and Davis, T.L. (1990) 'The occurrence of performance anxiety among musicians'. *Journal of Affective Disorders*, 18, 177–185.

Williamon, A. (2004) *Musical Excellence: Strategies and techniques to enhance performance*. Oxford: Oxford University Press.

Wills, G. and Cooper, C.L. (1988) *Pressure Sensitive: Popular musicians under stress*. London: Sage.

Chapter 17

Music Services

Lynne Rogers and Susan Hallam

The context

Across England, Scotland, Wales and Northern Ireland, Music Services provide
a range of services in schools and specialist centres. This includes the provision
of instrumental and vocal tuition, ensembles, choirs and bands, advice and
guidance for schools, and professional development for teachers. The funding
for Music Services has varied over time and is vulnerable when budgets
are under pressure. This influences the nature and extent of what can be
provided. During the 1980s there were considerable cutbacks, and legislation
and financial restraints forced many local authorities (LAs) to devolve the
monies previously spent on instrumental tuition to schools (Rogers, 1995).
Despite this, a survey undertaken for the Performing Rights Society (1999)
by PricewaterhouseCoopers and MORI showed that Music Services had
increased access to teaching and were offering a wider range of instruments
and ancillary services than ever before. However, in-service education and
training (INSET), concerts, assistance with concerts and workshops had
become less accessible, and there was a significant decrease in the availability
of instrumental and vocal performance groups in schools. Despite the increase
in overall numbers of pupils receiving tuition, in only 27 per cent of schools
was demand being fully met. The principal providers of instrumental tuition
in counties and at secondary level were LA-supported Music Services, while
in London boroughs, unitary authorities and at primary level, the principal
providers were independent (i.e. individual private teachers). Parents were
bearing a much greater proportion of the total tuition fees and many were
experiencing difficulties with fee remissions systems which were variable
across the country. One in five schools did not spend its delegated money
buying in its local Music Service, leading to reductions in Music Service staffing
budgets. Despite this, schools (where levels of satisfaction were between 85

and 98 per cent) and, to a lesser extent, LAs perceived a good and improved quality of delivery of tuition. Overall productivity had improved, achieved by reducing full-time teaching posts in favour of part-time posts, increasing working hours for teachers, and introducing the teaching of larger groups and more pupils per hour. Travel rates paid to teachers were also reduced. In these circumstances, unsurprisingly, teacher recruitment was reported as becoming more difficult.

The variability in provision across the UK continued into the late 1990s. The *Times Educational Supplement* (TES, 1998) survey of Music Services provision in 1998 showed that:

In England
- Schools in one in ten LAs had no access to a public music service.
- Fewer than one in ten pupils received regular instrumental lessons.
- Most LAs had cut back on full-time instrumental teachers.
- Two in three councils reported difficulties in recruiting instrumental teachers.
- Nine out of ten LAs charged for instrumental lessons.
- Average charges had increased by more than 40 per cent since 1995.
- Around one in ten pupils received subsidised lessons.

In Wales
- Access to Music Services was higher than in England and Scotland.
- About one in ten pupils received weekly lessons.
- The average charge was less than in England.

In Scotland
- Nearly one in six pupils had weekly lessons.
- The average charge was between that of England and Wales.
- More than a quarter of pupils had subsidised lessons.

Parents in Scotland had faced the steepest rise in fees, and more pupils in Scotland received subsidised instruction (27 per cent in Scotland, 14 per cent in England and 13 per cent in Wales). The overall number of pupils taking instrument or singing lessons had risen in Wales and Scotland, both nations having a better record than England (TES, 1998).

Music Services in Wales

In the mid-1980s, in several Welsh LAs, the proportion of pupils learning to play a musical instrument was more than twice the UK average. However, during the 1990s there was a significant contraction of LA Music Services due to the delegation of budgets to schools under local management of schools regulations and the reorganisation of local government, which created 22 unitary authorities to replace the eight county councils that had existed previously. Most of the newly created authorities were too small to be able to sustain Music Services. Many, but not all, made arrangements to pool resources with neighbouring LAs to provide a shared Music Service, but the level of resource nevertheless diminished.

By the late 1990s in many parts of Wales the opportunity to play a musical instrument was limited to pupils whose parents, or schools, were prepared to make a financial contribution to the cost of the lessons. In January 1999, the Secretary of State for Wales announced the establishment of the Music Development Fund (MDF) which was to provide funding, ring-fenced to support Music Services to enable them to create new music-making opportunities for young people and to facilitate longer-term, strategic planning. Social inclusion and the provision of enhanced opportunities were fundamental to the fund's rationale. The range of initiatives established included:

- rock and pop tuition
- world music workshops
- music therapy
- vocal tuition
- choral animateurs
- tuition on minority instruments
- the purchase of thousands of new instruments.

Throughout the five-year period of MDF funding the number of pupils and young people having access to music provision increased significantly, the range of musical activities increased in larger LAs, standards of performance rose, and smaller LAs consolidated a smaller range of activities. Many services successfully targeted disadvantaged young people and increased provision for pupils with learning difficulties (Estyn, 2006). However, subsequent reductions in funding had an adverse effect on the range of tuition and activities provided, because few LAs had invested the MDF in ways that would enable a sustainably legacy. In April 2005, resources previously allocated to the MDF were transferred to general funding for LAs, which led to Music Services receiving reduced monies and having to make further cuts, typically in the number of specialist tutors employed and the purchase and maintenance of musical instruments (Estyn, 2006). Most recently, the Minister for Children, Education, Lifelong Learning and Skills has established a review of music education for 3–19 year olds in Wales. The report, due in 2010, will:

- Review current provision for 3–19 year olds within the curriculum and through 'out of hours' activity, identifying strengths and areas for improvement in current practice.

- Map the present support given by LAs and other organisations.
- Identify how music provision might be strengthened, with a view to bringing greater cohesion between statutory music provision and instrumental/vocal tuition.
- Reflect on the extent to which music is being used to improve learners' health and well-being.
- Make recommendations for any improvement, taking into account the present constraints on public finance.

Music Services in Northern Ireland

Education and Library Boards were established in Northern Ireland in 1973. These took over and amalgamated the Music Services which had been started by most county education committees. Each of the five boards organises a Music Service as part of its non-statutory provision in support of education. The services provided differ across the boards, partly because of the geography of each area and partly due to historical development. All provide instrumental tuition, support for orchestras, ensembles and bands and most offer holiday courses. The services teach pupils from 65 per cent of all schools in Northern Ireland – 61 per cent of primary schools and 83 per cent of post-primaries (ETI, 2003). The Education and Library Boards' resources are determined by the Department of Education. As across the UK, barriers to access include the cost of lessons and differences in charging arrangements which contribute to inequality of access (ETI, 2003).

Music Services in Scotland

In 1996, local government reorganisation in Scotland led to the disaggregation of regional authorities and the restructuring of many LA services, including the provision of musical instrument instruction. The 32 unitary LAs continued to have control and responsibility for instrumental and singing instruction in schools, but as this provision was not a statutory requirement its funding, range and availability varied widely (SAC, 2003). Fees levied for local authority instrumental and singing instruction and for access to instruments were perceived as the greatest barriers to participation, along with cultural and gender factors.

In 2003, the then Scottish Executive (now the Scottish government) announced the launch of the 'Youth Music Initiative' (YMI) designed to expand the availability of free music instruction for pupils in Scottish schools. This followed on from the audit of youth music, the *What's Going On?* report that was commissioned by the Scottish Arts Council, Youth Music UK and the

Musicians' Union (SAC, 2003). The YMI aimed to ensure that every primary school pupil should have access to at least one year's free music tuition by the time that they reached Primary 6 (aged 9–11). It also identified a number of priorities and gaps in provision – including composition, primary school tuition and music technology – which were to be addressed. There were four main aims:

- to provide music-making experiences for all children
- to build the capacity of the music education sector to cope with extra demand
- to encourage more young people to participate
- to develop individual talent to its full potential.

LAs were successful in providing free music tuition to all children by the time that they were in Primary 6. The nature of projects varied across the LAs. For example, 218 projects were offered in year four of YMI. Of these projects:

Tuition type
- 101 delivered vocal instruction
- 144 delivered instrumental instruction
- 107 ensemble work
- 46 choral tuition
- 18 technology/recording
- 70 creativity/composition/inventing
- 43 Kodaly tuition
- 34 another type of tuition.

Musical genre
- 112 delivered tuition through Scottish traditional music
- 95 delivered tuition through jazz/blues
- 101 through world music
- 105 through rock/pop
- 138 through Western classical music
- 34 through another genre of music.

(SAC, 2008)

In 2009, in an effort to raise the status of instrumental music, the Educational Institute of Scotland, the country's largest teaching union, published a *Charter for Instrumental Music* (EIS, 2010) which aims to promote and support music education in Scotland. This included a call for greater recognition for Scotland's 750 instrumental music teachers, with a proposal that they be registered with the General Teaching Council for Scotland, putting them on the same footing as classroom teachers.

Music Services in England

As with Wales and Scotland, the creation of the new unitary authorities had a major impact on Instrumental Music Services (IMSs). Some newly created authorities worked collaboratively to retain existing provision; some developed independent IMSs; and some bought services from other IMSs or independent providers. The abolition of the Inner London Education Authority (ILEA) in 1990 had a major impact on instrumental music tuition in the capital, as decisions about the provision of Music Services became the local responsibility of the constituent boroughs. Prior to this, the ILEA had devolved to schools a sizeable proportion of their overall budget with which heads could determine priorities. Where schools chose to buy in tuition for instrumental or vocal music from the central resource, the ILEA supplemented the cost by 50 per cent. On devolution, the government funded the 'Centre for Young Musicians', until subsequently, its operation was fully devolved to the 'Foundation for Young Musicians', a charitable and limited company. While this central provision for ensemble work and tuition for talented pupils was maintained, tuition in schools, which depended on head teachers making music a priority, declined, perhaps because many of the boroughs did not have a 'key' LA person to develop a coherent music strategy.

By the late 1990s the longer-term implications of a continuing decline in public funding for IMSs across the country had become apparent:

- Access to tuition was mainly restricted to those able to pay.
- Opportunities to play in groups, orchestras, bands and choirs, had declined.
- Instruments traditionally perceived as less attractive or very expensive (e.g. bassoon, double bass) became rarities, with serious implications for group activities.
- In geographical areas which were not centres for artistic and musical activity, there was increasing difficulty in attracting teaching staff because of the lack of full-time employment opportunities or a career structure.
- There was a gradual decline in the number of those pursuing music as a career – the number of instrumental and class music teachers and those able to play professionally.
- Over time there was a decline in those suitably qualified to work in the media, arts, and recording industries.
- There was a decline in the benefits to the individual through enhanced self-development and the acquisition of transferable skills.

(Hallam and Prince, 2000)

The Department for Education and Employment (DfEE), in its consultation on 'fair funding', feared that this decline would continue, and set up Music

Standards Fund (MSF) grants to address the issue. The first tranche of money was distributed in March 1999 and the government has continued to support Music Services since then. In 2006–07 the MSF was increased to enable all young people to be able to learn a musical instrument – the 'Wider Opportunities' programme. The additional funding was allocated on a pupil-weighted formula and was devolved to schools. Some schools did not use the additional funding for music at all, while others utilised it to support the statutory National Curriculum entitlement. Following this, the government ring-fenced the MSF. The current position is that funding is distributed to LAs, which are responsible for ensuring the quality and value for money of the provision purchased, decisions being made in consultation with their Schools' Forum, with priority being given to Key Stage 2 (7–11 year olds).

Surveys of Music Service provision in England were undertaken for the government in 1999, 2002, 2005 and 2007, the last focusing on the Wider Opportunities initiative. The first survey, which took place in 1999 (Hallam and Prince, 2000) was undertaken to explore the nature of provision at that time. A follow-up survey in 2002 (Hallam and Rogers, 2003) aimed to establish a robust database which could be used to provide a baseline for wider opportunities in primary music, prepare the way for changes in MSF allocations, enable national benchmarks to be established and complement the 'Music Services Guidance' as a tool for self-evaluation, development and target setting. The survey in 2005 (Hallam *et al.*) monitored progress since 2002, provided information relating to children's ethnicity, special educational needs (SEN) and eligibility for free school meals, and identified five different types of Music Service. These are outlined in Table 17.1.

Table 17.1 Types of music provision in England (adapted from Hallam *et al.*, 2005)

Type of provision	Main characteristics
Type 1: LA Music Service (71% of sample) **1a** with time allocated to schools for instrumental and vocal tuition (53% of sample) **1b** with central control for all music provision (17% of sample)	All primary, junior, special and secondary schools have a free entitlement for instrumental tuition according to the number on roll. Additional instrumental lesson time over the free entitlement is sold to schools via service level agreements. Schools buy in instrumental and vocal tuition on an hourly rate (varying); this charge may be passed on to families by the schools. The Music Service employs full-time, part-time, and hourly paid teachers. Schools are allocated time for instrumental and vocal provision; central control is held for ensemble provision, curriculum support and extra events.

1c with budget for music provision delegated to schools (1% of sample)	The Music Service may offer festivals, live music concerts, taster sessions. Curriculum support (including advice on curriculum delivery), INSET, and support for individual teachers, are offered. Remissions policy for children on free school meals is in place.
Type 2: LA Shared Music Service (7% of sample)	One Music Service provides service for two or more LAs. Provision is as for Type 1a and 1b.
Type 3: Partnership between LA and independent provider(s) (9% of sample)	Some or all of the instrumental/vocal service is provided by one or more independent providers. The LA retains responsibility for ensemble provision, curriculum development and Wider Opportunities. Music teachers are recruited by the independent provider and are employed or self-employed. A small central team employed by the LA is responsible for ensemble provision, special events and curriculum support. Individual tuition: families charged directly by the independent provider. Ensemble provision: families charged by the LA. Schools are allocated free time based on roll number, and may purchase extra time over their free allocation.
Type 4: Private company limited by guarantee, or independent charity (11% of sample)	The services of a 'Music Service' are delivered by one or more independent providers. Festivals, workshops, live music concerts and taster experiences are offered to schools. Curriculum development, curriculum delivery, advice and IT support are available.
	Instrumental/vocal tuition is typically provided by a team of self-employed peripatetic teachers. Schools may buy in coaching for in-house ensembles, and area ensembles are provided through music centres. Families are charged directly by the independent provider for tuition and ensembles. Financial help for pupils may be available via remission schemes for tuition, ensembles, instrument hire and residential courses.

Type 5: Responsibility for music provision devolved entirely to schools (2% of sample)	MSF budget devolved entirely to schools, who take individual responsibility for music provision. The LA does not offer any music provision, there is no formal recognised alternative independent provider.

Over the period of the surveys, there was an improvement in the information that Music Services collected in order to monitor and evaluate their performance. By 2005, the best services were able to provide detailed descriptions of the nature of the composition of their pupil population, the standards that they reached, staffing and finance data. Between 2002 and 2005, a further 16 new Music Services were established.

In 1999 most Music Services provided tuition for between 4% and 10% of their school population. By 2005, 8.4% of the school population was receiving tuition, 13% in KS2, 8% in KS3 and 5% in KS4. On average 3,428 pupils were learning in each Music Service, with a range from 85 to 16,741. In 2009, the numbers of young people accessing instrumental tuition through Music Services was projected to rise to 1.5 million from 400,000 in 2002, and between 2008 and 2011, some 2 million young people will have had the opportunity to learn a musical instrument.

The data available in 1999 indicated that 40% of children learning were boys. This reduced to 32% in 2002, reverting to 40% in 2005, the increasing availability of tuition in guitar and drumming seeming to be more attractive to boys. In 2002, 7% of pupils on the SEN register at Stage 2 or above received tuition close to the average proportion of pupils in the school population. In 2005, overall, 9.1% of the children learning to play an instrument were in receipt of additional support in relation to their SEN. In 2002, 57 Music Services were able to provide data regarding ethnicity, indicating a predominance of white children. By 2005, a substantial proportion of minority ethnic groups were receiving tuition (27%), while 12% of pupils receiving tuition were in receipt of free school meals. These data contradict the frequently held perception that Music Services only cater for white middle-class pupils and indicated that substantial proportions of children from ethnic minorities, eligible for free school meals or with SEN do learn to play an instrument.

In 2005, 76% of primary schools and 88% of secondary schools were reported to be receiving specialist music tuition, an increase from 69% of schools overall in 2002. Also in 2002, 38% were taking advice on resources, appointments and preparation for or follow-up for inspections. By 2005, this had risen to 82%. In 2002, 30% were taking advantage of support for curriculum development. This had risen to 82% in 2005. Similar rises were reported in relation to curriculum delivery, from 25% to 78%, and IT support, from 18% to 60%. In the 2005 survey, the number of categories of support for schools was extended beyond that of 2002, and high proportions of Music Services were offering a wide range of services. The range of instruments which children played in 2005 demonstrated an expansion, with children being able to access world musics, folk music, and more popular musical instruments (drums, guitar) in addition to the classical Western instruments. The range of ensemble provision reflected these changes.

The survey undertaken in 2005 was the first where Music Services were able to provide reliable information about the standards attained by pupils. This demonstrated that a small number of pupils were attaining extremely high standards, well beyond what might be expected for their age. There was no change in the percentage of staff reported to be on full-time contracts between 2002 and 2005 (22%), little change in the percentage of part-time and hourly paid staff, and no difference in the level of staff qualifications.

Boxes 17.1, 17.2 and 17.3 provide examples of the kinds of activities that Music Services are engaged with.

Box 17.1 Example of a community Music Service in London

The Barking & Dagenham Community Music Service (CMS) operates in a deprived area of London, with an increasing proportion of the population from minority ethnic groups. The aim of the CMS is to 'provide opportunities for every young person to develop through music and positively impact on the five outcomes of *Every Child Matters'*. The service is placed within the local authority's Quality and School Improvement Service and has 54 members of staff. It provides instrumental/vocal tuition, ensemble experience, curriculum support, vocal and instrumental workshops, and adult music classes. It also organises an annual programme of live music concerts. There are high levels of participation and access. Estimates for the year 2008–09 indicated that 35 per cent of the school population would access CMS services. An Advisory Group meets three times a year and includes representatives from the council, schools, colleges and the LA. Feedback is sought from stakeholders and service users through surveys and the advisory group. Tuition is free at the point of delivery. Schools are charged for whole-class instrumental and vocal teaching (WCVIT) and the DCSF KS2 music grant is used to subsidise the costs. Schools are allocated a core entitlement of instrumental tuition for all other tuition, based on pupil numbers, which is charged at a subsidised hourly rate. Many schools request and receive additional tuition to the core. Ensemble, workshop and playing day provision is provided free of charge. CMS has strong partnership links with professional associations, including the London Symphony Orchestra/ Guildhall School of Music & Drama/Barbican Campus and other London arts and commercial organisations, as well as integrating WCVIT, Musical Futures, Building Schools for the Future and Sing Up.

Box 17.2 Example of an urban Music Service

Bolton has a well-established music tradition, fostered through the commitment of the LA to the Music Service, the voluntary sector including the Schools Music Association, the Bolton Symphony Orchestra, the Bolton Chamber Orchestra and a wide range of other music, theatre and choral societies, in addition to a strong youth culture of rock bands and privately run music studios that provide high-class recording facilities. Forty primary schools buy in curriculum support from Bolton Music Service, which provides an ongoing INSET programme for class teachers, while 77 schools buy in instrumental/vocal tuition, which is free for the first 30 minutes. More than 1,900 children have weekly instrumental/vocal lessons. All children in each school participate in a music session, at least once a fortnight, led by specialist teachers from the Music Service. 'Music live', a presentation to the whole school (KS1/KS2) is given by teams of teachers, while 'Listen in', a concert performance for all schools, is given by a chamber group from the Music Service free of charge, supported by the Standards Fund. The Wider Opportunities programme provides 100 whole-class programmes in a range of instruments, including combinations of strings, djembes, clarinets, brass, samba, steel pans, African song, recorders, glockenspiels, ocarinas and harp. All programmes last for a full school year and are delivered by combinations of Music Service staff and class teachers. A Wider Opportunities handbook is provided for all programmes, including activity banks with cross-referencing to the National Curriculum, teacher planning, record keeping and termly evaluation. Schools are offered a free pilot year and then buy in the programme thereafter. A musical instrument hire scheme is now established to enable more children to continue with tuition after Wider Opportunities. Performance projects with the Hallé (2006–08) have increased the impact of Wider Opportunities across the borough. The Music Service provides all secondary schools with transfer information on all Year 6 pupils receiving instrumental/vocal tuition. This information includes instrument, standard of pupil, and whether the pupil owns an instrument, enabling secondary schools to make informed decisions about purchasing time for instrumental/vocal tuition for the following year. Secondary subject focus groups share good practice on baseline assessment and a working party developed a 'Music Passport' which was piloted in 2006–07. The Wider Opportunities programme operates in special schools and a new Music Outreach programme is being developed. The Wider Opportunities programme has also been implemented in some secondary schools. Music technology support is available and the service delivers the LA secondary music subject leadership programme, and offers a wide range of CPD opportunities. The service is constantly developing new initiatives and work with new partners.

Box 17.3 Example of a small rural Music Service

North Somerset Music Service operates in a largely rural area, which is generally prosperous but with some very significant pockets of deprivation. The Music Service is by far the largest provider of musical opportunities, offering a diverse range of support to young people, schools and the community, including:

- instrumental/vocal tuition in every primary and secondary school
- free Wider Opportunities delivery in every school with KS2 pupils
- INSET for teachers
- in-class support and CPD for teachers
- newly qualified teacher support and training packages free to schools
- enrichment experiences for pupils, such as 'culturally unique workshops', music ICT workshops and vocal events
- festivals, whole-day events, summer residential courses, etc.
- bands, orchestras and choirs, through the 'Centre for Young Musicians'
- gifted and talented schemes
- KS3/4 network meetings and support.

A commercial ICT package is at the heart of the day-to-day management of the service and enables accurate records of provision, progress and trends to be maintained in order to respond effectively when necessary. The Music Service works successfully in partnership with Sing Up, the Creative Learning Agency, the two secondary schools which have relevant specialist status, and the Youth Service, and it benefits from collaboration with Wells Cathedral School. There are also extensive plans for further developments, including provision for lesson starter packages, workshops by composers, and a Numu web forum.

The Wider Opportunities programme

In 2001, the government pledged in the White Paper *Schools Achieving Success* that, in England, over time all primary school pupils who wanted to should have the opportunity to learn to play a musical instrument. Focusing on pupils at Key Stage 2 (ages 7–11), this built on and extended the statutory entitlement to music education provided by the National Curriculum and became known as the 'Wider Opportunities' programme. There are parallels with the Youth Music Initiative in Scotland. In England, a range of instrumental and vocal models were piloted and evaluated (Ofsted, 2004; Youth Music, 2004). Three common elements of the programme were:

- Taster sessions – a variety of live and hands-on musical experiences to stimulate interest and broaden musical perspectives

- Foundation activities – general musicianship experiences across a range of instruments and voice to develop disciplined musical skills, knowledge and understanding
- Specialist instrumental tuition – the opportunity to go on and learn a musical instrument, generally in a whole-class setting, including ensemble playing, composition and performance and specialist tuition in small and large groups. Ofsted (2004) recommended that the tuition phase should last for at least one year.

Evaluation of the pilot projects was extremely positive. Ofsted commented that the Wider Opportunities policy was 'leading to the significant transformation of music education for all pupils in KS2' (Ofsted, 2005). New musical traditions had been introduced into schools and more children wished to learn instruments. The quality of teaching was judged to be better than that in conventional KS2 sessions. Lessons were planned and taught by a combination of freelance and community musicians, Music Service tutors, classroom teachers and teaching assistants. This provided opportunities for CPD for all of those participating. Classroom teachers were able to learn instrumental skills from visiting musicians, while the musicians developed an in-depth understanding of the school context, classroom management and the wider music curriculum. Participating schools took advantage of a wide range of local specialist provision, including that from Music Services, voluntary and community music groups, a range of independent providers, Youth Music Action Zone resources, visiting composers, local orchestras, opera companies and bands. In some cases strong partnerships were also established with music industry bodies, including instrument makers and retailers (Ofsted, 2004; Youth Music, 2004).

A survey in 2007 showed that Music Services had made considerable progress in providing every child with the opportunity to play an instrument (Hallam *et al.*, 2007). Whole-class instrumental tuition was the most commonly reported strategy (72 per cent of LAs) followed by whole-class vocal tuition (40 per cent of LAs). Barriers to implementation included insufficient staff, lack of instruments, conflict with other priorities, timetabling difficulties, inadequate accommodation and the lack of expertise of primary school teachers. Factors supporting the initiative – in addition to the funding – were supportive head teachers and the high profile of music education. The Ofsted report *Making More of Music* (2009) confirmed the important role of LA Music Services in taking forward the government's commitment to enabling every pupil to have the opportunity to learn to play a musical instrument. The programme, at its best, was reported as having a considerable impact in raising expectations and standards, encouraging wider participation, and increasing classroom teachers' confidence and subject knowledge.

The most recent impact evaluation (Bamford and Glinkowski, 2010) reports that the programme has received widespread positive support from pupils, parents, teachers, head teachers and local authorities. In addition to enabling the children to acquire a range of musical skills it raised self-esteem and confidence, enhanced aspirations, and increased focus, empowerment and responsibility. During Wider Opportunity sessions the children were motivated, showed increased concentration and improved behaviour, had positive attitudes towards learning, showed respect for their instruments and enjoyed the lessons. The programme also raised the profile of music in the school, increased the level of musical activity, raised expectations, changed teachers' perceptions of some pupils, ensured that music was on the curriculum, enhanced the profile of the school, increased recruitment, enhanced the involvement of parents and families, encouraged schools to form networks and collaborate with each other, led to greater involvement in community initiatives, and in some schools provided a catalyst for change. Successful programmes built partnerships between the child, the family, the school and Music Services. The programme allowed talent to be identified, nurtured and developed, and challenged the value of individual lessons over group lessons. Celebratory events acted as powerful drivers for quality enhancement and were influential as advocacy tools. One aim of the programme had been to provide professional development for generalist primary teachers through paired teaching, but this was found to have not been consistently implemented. Although many Music Services made good use of the national training programme offered by Trinity Guildhall and the Open University, there were still issues related to shortage of staff.

Endnote

Music Services have undergone considerable change over the last decade. They have increased the number of students learning to play instruments and the number of schools having access to provision. They have widened the range of instruments, ensembles and services available and become more inclusive. They have always been vulnerable when public finances are under threat, despite the evidence of the benefits of active engagement with music (see Chapter 1). To justify their existence Music Services need to be able to provide hard evidence of the benefits that they can bring to the community, and that what they offer is value for money. They have made considerable progress to these ends. Challenges for the future include:

- having a clear vision of their role in the twenty-first century
- balancing competing demands (quality and quantity, access and progression)

- working in partnership with others
- diversifying sources of income
- developing the workforce to meet the changing needs of society
- enhancing systems for gathering and communicating information to facilitate advocacy in local forums.

Further reading

Bamford, A. and Glinkowski, P. (2010) *Wow, It's Music Next. Impact evaluation of Wider Opportunities programme in music at KS2*. Leeds: Federation of Music Services.

Hallam, S., Rogers, L. and Creech, A. (2005) *Survey of LEA Music Services 2005*. London: DfES.

Hallam, S., Creech, A., Rogers, L. and Papageorgi, I. (2007*) Local Authority Music Services Provision (2007) for Key Stages 1 and 2*. London: DCSF.

References

Bamford, A. and Glinkowski, P. (2010) *Wow, It's Music Next. Impact evaluation of Wider Opportunities programme in music at KS2*. Leeds: Federation of Music Services.

Department for Education and Skills (DfES) (2001) *Schools Achieving Success*. London: HMSO.

Educational Institute of Scotland (EIS) (2010) EIS Charter for Instrumental Music. Edinburgh: EIS.

Estyn (2006) *An Evaluation of the Use Made by Local Authorities and Schools of Resources Made Available by the Music Development Fund in Wales*. Cardiff: Estyn.

Education and Training Inspectorate (ETI) (2003) *Report on a Survey of the Music Services provided by the Education and Library Boards*. Northern Ireland: ETI.

Hallam, S. and Prince, V. (2000) *Research into Instrumental Music Services*. London: Department for Education and Employment (DfEE).

Hallam, S. and Rogers, L. (2003) *Survey of Local Education Authorities' Music Services 2002*. London: Department for Education and Skills (DfES).

Hallam, S., Rogers, L. and Creech, A. (2005) *Survey of LEA Music Services 2005*. London: Department for Education and Skills (DfES).

Hallam, S., Creech, A., Rogers, L. and Papageorgi, I. (2007) *Local Authority Music Services Provision (2007) for Key Stages 1 and 2*. London: Department for Children, Schools and Families (DCSF).

Office for Standards in Education (Ofsted) (2004) *Tuning In: Wider opportunities in specialist instrumental tuition for pupils in Key Stage 2: An evaluation of pilot programme in 12 local authorities*. London: Ofsted.

–– (2005) *Ofsted Primary Music Report 2005*. London: Ofsted.

–– (2009) *Making More of Music: An evaluation of music in schools 2005–08*. London: Ofsted.

Performing Rights Society/PricewaterhouseCoopers and MORI (1999) *Musical Instrument Tuition in Schools Survey*. London: PricewaterhouseCoopers and MORI.

Rogers, R. (1995) *Guaranteeing an Entitlement to the Arts in Schools*. London: Royal Society for the encouragement of the Arts, manufacture and commerce (RSA).

Scottish Arts Council (SAC) (2003) *What's Going On: A national audit of youth music in Scotland*. Scotland: SAC.

–– (2008) *Scottish Arts Council Report on the P6 Target Data Year Four (2006/07)* Edinburgh: SAC.

TES (1998) 'Councils sing the blues'. *Times Educational Supplement*, 31 July.

Youth Music (2004) *Creating Changes for Making Music*. London: Youth Music.

Chapter 18

The music studio

Andrea Creech

One-to-one teaching is established as a continuing core activity within instrumental (taken here to include vocal) learning. According to Lehmann *et al.* (2007: 185) 'most people who become proficient musicians do so only with the assistance of teachers'. Although there are differences by instrument, children often begin formal engagement with one-to-one learning at an early age, reflecting a view that 'the earlier the better is probably appropriate as a general guide to when children should start learning an instrument' (McPherson and Davidson, 2006: 331). At the same time, within our current social context it is likely that increasing numbers of adults over the age of 50 will engage with leisure and learning (Age Concern, 2008), including learning musical instruments. In the UK, much of this teaching and learning takes place within the context of private music studios, where instrumental teachers teach on a freelance basis.

The growing trend for musicians to develop musical portfolio careers, combining performing, composing, community music and teaching, has been discussed elsewhere in this book and indeed may be seen as a unifying theme. The private music studio forms part of a work portfolio for a great many musicians (Box 18.1).

Box 18.1 Private music studios as part of a portfolio career

A survey of 263 violin teachers in the UK (Creech, 2006) revealed that for 75 per cent of them teaching from private studios formed part of their portfolios. Of those who taught in private studios, many were also employed to teach within other contexts, including state schools (39%), independent schools (43%), music colleges or university departments (12%) and junior conservatoire programmes (11%). All of the teachers who responded to the survey also engaged in some other kind of musical work, including performing, coaching ensembles, facilitating creative workshops and composing.

It is thus extremely difficult to calculate just how many private instrumental teachers there may be in the UK, because this strand of work so often forms just part of a wider portfolio of musical activity. Indeed, the Musicians' Union (MU) surveyed their total membership, revealing that over 60 per cent of the 30,000 members said that teaching formed part of their portfolio careers (MU, 2009). Professional organisations such as the MU and the Incorporated Society of Musicians (ISM) hold registers of instrumental teachers, and these may provide the best indication of the numbers of musicians for whom studio teaching forms a major part of their work. The MU currently (2010) has 5,200 members registered with their teaching section (although there is no way to verify how many of these teachers operate from private music studios), while the ISM register of professional private music teachers has a membership of 987 (ISM, 2009).

A further indication of the extent of private music studio teaching is the number of pupils learning with private instrumental teachers. Based on a survey of 1,295 young people, Youth Music (2006) calculates this to be just under six per cent of the UK population of 7–19 year olds. This compares with the estimated ten per cent of young people in the same age range learning instruments through local authority Music Service provision (see Chapter 17).

Professional advice and support for music studio teachers

The ISM and the MU are professional UK organisations whose function is to provide advice and support for musicians, including private music studio teachers. In this vein, both of these organisations provide guidance on codes of practice, contracts, fees, child protection, insurance and various administrative matters. In addition, there are several organisations that variously represent particular instruments or teaching approaches (see list of useful websites at the end of this chapter). All of these organisations serve the important function of providing a forum where private music studio teachers (whose work is often isolated from other teaching professionals) are able to network, share resources and access professional development opportunities.

Working conditions for studio teachers

Studio teaching takes place in a variety of contexts. Instrumental teachers sometimes rent studio space within independent schools or other premises such as music shops, and they often operate private studios from their own homes. Others travel to their pupils' homes where the teaching takes place. Of the 1,295 pupils surveyed by Youth Music (2006) who had lessons with a private teacher, half reported that their lessons took place in the pupils' home, while half took place in the teacher's home or alternative private studio premises.

The majority of private studio teaching would seem to be undertaken on a one-to-one basis. The ISM (2009) reported that out of 824 private teachers surveyed in 2007 only eight per cent offered shared or group tuition. While there may be logistical barriers to group tuition within private music studios, there is evidence to suggest that group teaching may be effective, offering advantages in utilisation of time and resources, maximising fee income, encouraging competition and peer learning and building a sense of community through musical ensemble and social activities (Hallam, 2006). Kennell (2002) suggests that a combination of individual and group tuition may be most effective.

Private music studio fees are typically charged on an hourly basis, with hourly rates in the UK currently ranging between £9 and £70 (ISM, 2009). The majority of teachers who responded to the ISM survey charged between £20 and £35 per hour, with a median of £26. Some regional variations were found in fees, with teachers in London, the South East and South of England charging slightly more than teachers in other parts of the country. Qualifications and experience did not have an impact on teachers' earning power – there were no statistically significant differences in fees charged by instrumental teachers with higher levels of qualifications and more years of experience, compared with more inexperienced and less qualified teachers. This point is important, as it may have a bearing on studio teachers' motivation to engage in professional development, which will be discussed later in this chapter.

The typical hourly rates of pay, cited above, recompense the studio teacher for time and expertise. However, these fees must also include an allowance for holiday periods and cover a range of overheads which, according to the ISM (2009), might include:

- instrument maintenance and repairs
- instrument, property, car, health and public liability insurance
- private pension contributions
- income tax and national insurance contributions
- accounting and audit fees
- bank loan interest rates or mortgage
- music, books, stationery, recordings, advertising
- subscriptions to professional associations and periodicals
- secretarial, telephone and answering services
- time spent on lesson preparation
- time spent on updating pupils' records, marking, writing reports
- time spent on interviews with prospective pupils
- time spent on pupils' concerts and workshops
- studio lighting, heating and maintenance
- studio hire charges
- cost of transport
- time spent travelling, if tuition is given in pupils' homes.

In addition to the face-to-face teaching described above, studio teachers are increasingly developing web-based studios, where pupils may access instrumental tuition online. Bond (2002) predicted that teaching in the 'virtual world' will rapidly become an expected part of typical music studio practice. Although this development is reliant on interactive online learning environments that are accessible to teachers and pupils alike, the indications are that more and more studio teachers are incorporating 'virtual studios' into their practice. For example, a Google search for websites from the UK that included the phrase 'online guitar lessons' (guitar being the most popular instrument among 7–19 year olds, according to Youth Music, 2006), yielded several thousand results. These sites offer videos of lessons, downloadable music and backing tracks and a range of advice. While widespread interactive virtual learning in music may still be some way off, this is an area that is sure to impact on the future careers of studio teachers.

Roles and responsibilities

Private studio teachers have a range of roles and responsibilities. First and foremost effective practice in this area of work clearly requires musical competence, knowledge of one's instrument and understanding of teaching and learning. Moreover, the Association of Graduate Careers Advisory Services (2009) suggests that the occupational profile of a private music teacher includes qualities such as excellent communication skills, professional ethics, self-management and organisation, self-determination and a flexible, open-minded approach.

Pedagogy

There is relatively little research concerned specifically with the private music studio, despite a growing interest in instrumental and vocal pedagogy. This may be due to a continuing 'closed door' nature of much private instrumental teaching, as well as the fact that studio teachers do not benefit from the protection of a wider institutional framework and may thus be reluctant to participate as subjects of research. Much of the research that informs our knowledge of pedagogy within the private studio has been carried out within teaching contexts that are located within institutions, such as schools, music colleges and university music departments, where it is likely that institutional factors will impact on issues relating to objectives, curriculum and assessment. Nevertheless, research that has included private music studio teachers (e.g. Creech, 2006) suggests that teaching and learning within the private music studio shares many salient features with that taking place elsewhere.

Differing models of one-to-one teaching have been identified, the most pervasive and prevailing one arguably being the master-apprentice model, characterised by transmission of knowledge within a didactic approach. This contrasts with the mentor-friendly model, describing a teaching approach that is closer to facilitation (Lehmann *et al.*, 2007).

Within the current UK context, discourse around teaching and learning generally is heavily influenced by the idea of personalised learning, which includes responsibility for target-setting and tracking progress, providing access to an extended curriculum, supporting wider needs and providing high-quality teaching and learning experiences that are aligned with individual needs (DCSF, 2009). Private studio instrumental teachers are not impervious to this personalised learning agenda. Many also teach for Music Services and will be aware of the National Standards for Instrumental Teachers, endorsed in 2005 by the Federation of Music Services (FMS, 2009). These standards charge instrumental teachers with responsibility for respecting their pupils' social, cultural, linguistic, religious and ethnic backgrounds and for setting challenging teaching and learning objectives that take account of each individual's background and interests. In a similar vein, the ISM (2009) stipulates that its private teacher members should take responsibility for providing a 'varied and balanced course of study appropriate to the age and ability of each pupil, with regard to both technique and repertoire', that they should provide performance opportunities, that they are expected to be aware of pupils' wider musical interests and that it is their responsibility to plan appropriate assessment and progression routes for individual pupils. Likewise, Crozier (2009) states that teachers must be sensitive to the needs of their learners, enabling them to become musically independent. Considered overall, this framework of responsibilities implies a level of responsiveness to individual pupils that would require a teaching approach closer to the mentor-friendly model than the master-apprentice model.

Wherever individual teachers and their pupils are on the transmission–facilitation continuum, research suggests that lesson time will be likely to be comprised of teacher talk and gestures, teacher modelling and pupil performance (Colprit, 2000). Effective instrumental teaching by master teachers was found by Duke and Simmons (2006) to include setting goals for students, conveying information clearly and effecting change (see Chapter 6 for a detailed discussion of factors involved in the development of expertise). Hallam (2006) summarises evidence that individual instrumental lessons are often dominated by unidirectional teacher talk and focused on technique more than on musical considerations. Detailed analysis of 23 videotaped violin lessons with pupils aged between 8 and 16 bore this out (Creech, 2006). Very often the pupils listened passively to teachers and responded to direct instruction relating to technique, in a cycle of 'teacher instruction – pupil response – teacher feedback'. Although interaction patterns did vary, whether or not the setting was within an institution (six of the lessons) or a private studio (17 lessons) did not seem to be an obvious contributing factor.

Interpersonal communication

In instrumental tuition, teacher–pupil relationships and teacher–parent communication have been found to make a significant contribution to effective teaching and learning (see Box 18.2). This is recognised by the ISM (2009), whose code of practice for private instrumental teachers specifies that teachers should 'initiate and maintain good communications with parents . . . as well as with pupils, and to communicate clearly and openly at all times'.

Teacher–pupil relationships

Irrespective of the pupil attainment levels, relationships with teachers have been found to have a significant impact on outcomes for the instrumental learners. For example, pupil motivation in one-to-one music tuition has been found to be underpinned by teachers who are relatively uncritical, encouraging and enthusiastic during the initial stages of learning (Hallam, 1998). In contrast, during later stages of musical development, knowledgeable criticism from teachers and other experts is prioritised and the relationship between teacher and pupil has been seen to migrate towards the master-apprentice model. In the context of very advanced learners, although pupils begin to develop autonomous learning strategies, the master exerts considerable power, critiquing students' performances and facilitating their transition into the professional music world (Manturzewska, 1990). Throughout these stages, inspiring and sustaining pupil motivation may be a particular challenge within private music studios where pupils do not necessarily benefit from the motivational influence of peer groups, noted earlier in this chapter.

Teacher–pupil relationships in the context of instrumental lessons have been found to be heavily influenced by a number of factors, including teachers' past relationships with their own teachers (Morgan, 1998) and student personality characteristics (Schmidt, 1989). Inevitably, some teacher–pupil matches will be better than others but, in accordance with the ISM code of practice (2009), professional instrumental teachers have the responsibility for setting minimum standards of interpersonal behaviour and applying them consistently.

Box 18.2 The influence of teacher–pupil interpersonal interaction on teaching and learning outcomes

Creech (2006) researched the contribution of interpersonal interaction to teaching and learning outcomes among 263 violin teachers and their pupils. Seventy-five per cent of these teachers taught in private music studios, with pupils of all ages and levels of ability. Their teaching experience ranged from one year to over 30 years; 50 per cent had over 15 years of experience. Several teaching methods and approaches were represented; 177 teachers (67%) taught by 'no specific method', 49 (19%) taught by the Suzuki method, and the remaining 37 (14%) taught by a range of other specific methods. Some teachers had more than one pupil who participated in the research. In total, 337 pupils and their parents took part in the study, thus making it possible to examine interpersonal interactions among 337 teacher–pupil–parent trios.

Pupil–teacher accord, associated with the quality of responsiveness, was found to have a positive effect on pupil enjoyment, satisfaction, motivation, self-efficacy and self-esteem. Conversely, for each of these outcomes a negative effect was found for pupil–teacher reticence, suggesting that psychological remoteness within pupil–teacher relationships may in fact have a detrimental effect on learning, while mutual respect, common purpose and the establishment of child-centred rather than teacher-centred goals holds the potential for the achievement of positive outcomes. There was some evidence that pupil–teacher influence had a small but positive impact on musical attainment. This supports the view that in constructive and productive learning partnerships the pupil benefits from being allowed an active voice.

The survey results suggested that interpersonal interaction influenced outcomes for teachers as well. In particular, teacher 'sensitivity to pupils' contributed to enhanced teacher self-efficacy and professional satisfaction. Teacher leadership, commitment and confidence (aspects of the interpersonal quality of control) each bore significant positive correlations with these outcomes. At the heart of this finding is the challenge of responsive leadership, whereby effective instrumental teachers combine authoritative guidance with responsiveness to individual pupil needs and circumstances.

Teacher–parent relationships

Music education research, to date, has provided much compelling evidence that teacher–parent communication, particularly during the early years of instrumental learning, is linked to musical achievement (Creech, 2009b; Davidson *et al.*, 1996). Private music studio teachers must forge good relationships with pupils and their parents, not only to support effective teaching and learning but also to negotiate the practical and administrative aspects involved in a business relationship. This may be another challenge that is particularly salient for private music studio teachers. Although the teachers in the study carried out by Creech (2006) evidently recognised the importance of communication with parents, for many this was an area that provoked much interpersonal conflict (Box 18.3).

Box 18.3 Teacher–parent interactions

Creech (2006) studied the interpersonal interactions among 337 teacher–pupil–parent trios, in the context of learning the violin (see Box 18.2 for details of the sample). There was some ambivalence in relation to communication with parents: 70 per cent of survey respondents agreed that parents should follow the teacher's advice, yet 60 per cent agreed that parents should share in the decision making, while 50 per cent agreed that they found it hard to be patient with parents who did not follow the teacher's advice.

Teachers frequently attributed problematic issues to the parents, characterising parents as a hindrance to positive outcomes. 'Parents are the main reason their children cease to be pupils of mine' (teacher, female aged 20–29). 'It's never the kids, only the parents that can upset me' (teacher, female aged over 60).

Nevertheless, teachers acknowledged the important supportive role parents play in accomplishing positive outcomes. 'I like to see the parents regularly so we can make sure that we are all striving towards the same goals' (teacher, female aged 40–49).

Sensitivity to the goals and priorities of both pupils *and* parents was found to be associated with greater professional satisfaction and self-efficacy among teachers. Furthermore, confident and responsive teachers empowered parents to help their children learn, which supported persistence and positive attitudes towards learning.

Within the context of the private music studio, answers to the questions 'What do you expect from me?' and 'What do I expect from you?' need to be made clear, among teachers, pupils and parents alike. During the crucial early years of learning, parents play a significant role in sustaining pupil commitment and enthusiasm for the subject, facilitating learning with resources as well as behavioural, cognitive and personal support. Where there is disagreement regarding teacher–parent roles and responsibilities, the outcomes may be negative for all concerned, including breakdown in teacher–pupil and teacher–parent relationships and low personal and professional satisfaction.

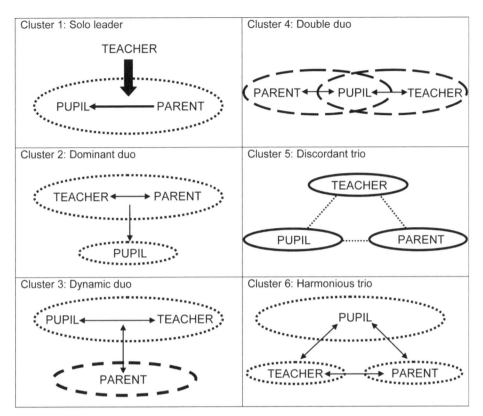

Figure 18.1: A model of interpersonal interaction among violin teachers, pupils and parents (Creech, 2009a)

Creech (2009a) proposed a model of interpersonal interaction among violin teachers, pupils and parents (Figure 18.1). While no single type of interaction consistently produced the best outcomes for teachers, pupils and parents alike, overall the most effective teaching and learning outcomes were found among those classified as 'harmonious trios' representing a parent–professional–child partnership characterised by reciprocal communication and mutual respect among all three participants (Box 18.4). These findings support the view that pupils function best when they perceive the adults as both caring and supportive of autonomy and when they are able to engage in ongoing mutual interaction with adults who continue to have a stake in their development and to act as their advocate.

Box 18.4 'Harmonious trio' case study

(Private music studio teacher with over 30 years' experience, pupil aged 15, lesson in teacher's home)

This teacher took a holistic approach, with concern for nurturing pupils' personal potential:

> *Very often I have ended up teaching therapeutically. . . . It is not up to me to say you can't possibly progress any more. . . . There may be reasons that are blocking the child's progress . . . psychological or emotional reasons, not just to mention mental and physical ability. Ideally, I see myself as a teacher who is sympathetic to the circumstances of each pupil.*
>
> (teacher)

Experience had given the teacher confidence in communicating proactively with parents:

> *I will say 'Trust me, I am your teacher . . . allow me to use [my musical knowledge] wisely'. . . . Thirty years ago I couldn't have spoken to the parent of a teenager in the same way and received respect.*
>
> (teacher)

The pupil–teacher relationship was characterised by positive accord, with the pupil exerting influence within the learning partnership:

> *We have had discussions about which pieces are the best for me, but it has mostly been left up to my decision. . . . You do end up developing a negative attitude towards the instrument if you are restricted in what you can play. . . . Having more responsibility and choice makes you more positive about it.*
>
> (pupil)

The pupil was an independent learner but at the same time was receptive to and appreciative of his father's support:

> *It did help to have him there, in some ways. . . . It was quite helpful to have proper notes made that you could follow. But it's not always the best way to have someone constantly watching over you. You've got to have a certain amount of independence.*
>
> (pupil)

His father was a loyal source of support, having in the past spent many years attending lessons and listening to practising as well as continuing to attend every one of his concerts. 'We travel, we make sure that we go to all the concerts with him'. The father felt comfortable approaching the teacher

---

to discuss violin-related matters and continued to communicate with the teacher about his son's progress. 'I would expect that to happen if there was a problem that wasn't being addressed by Matthew [his son] himself.'

There was a sense that, while tolerating the teacher's more holistic approach, the father had perhaps steered the lesson objectives in the direction of the examination curriculum:

A teacher will have a style, their methods. . . the child has to adapt to the teacher, but also the teacher must adapt to the child. . . . At Matthew's age there is a working relationship, and both parties – she has learnt – there is an interplay between them. . . . In my son's case, he likes examinations. He likes to have that aim.

(father)

Pupil and father considered music to have had a tremendous positive impact on their family life. 'It has dramatically changed our life. . . . it brings the family together' (father).

Teaching and learning objectives

The objectives pursued by those offering instrumental lessons within private music studios are related to the roles and responsibilities of studio teachers, noted above. While there has not been a great deal of research specifically concerned with teaching and learning objectives within the context of the private music studio as opposed to institutional settings, some evidence suggests that these objectives are diverse.

Professional private music teachers (ages of pupils not specified) were found by Ward (2004) to rate the encouragement of spontaneity and personal choice among their pupils as the least important aspects of performance teaching. However, a wider range of objectives was reported by Creech (2008). It is likely that as the concept of personalised learning, discussed above, becomes more embedded in instrumental teaching, music studio teachers and their pupils will pursue a range of objectives, across the spectrum illustrated in Box 18.5.

Box 18.5 Teaching and learning objectives

Two hundred and sixty-three UK-based violin teachers were asked to describe their teaching objectives (see Box 18.2 for details of the teachers). Qualitative open questions relating to teacher objectives were coded into categories that ranged from task-specific (musical skills) to holistic (personal development) objectives. The most frequently stated objectives (41% of teacher respondents) related to instilling in pupils enjoyment of music, a lifelong interest, enthusiasm and love for the instrument. Furthermore, 24 per cent of teachers stated that their objectives were related to the personal development of their pupils, including achieving personal potential, providing a stress-free activity, providing encouragement, self-expression and self-fulfilment. While 30 per cent of teachers stated that their objective was to establish musical skills in their pupils, only 9 per cent claimed to aspire to high musical standards. Social skills (14 per cent of teachers) and cross-curricular transferable skills, including the development of concentration, memory, discipline, confidence and independent learning (13 per cent of teachers) were also reported as objectives.

Competing demands

Private music studio teachers are particularly vulnerable to pupil drop-out, because their livelihoods are directly dependent on pupils choosing to continue learning. Thus, an understanding of the competing demands made upon pupils in relation to homework and extra-curricular activities is relevant.

Private music studios are contexts where pupils engage in an out-of-school pursuit that has been identified as an enriching activity (DfEE, 1998). Such activities encourage the development of the pupils' own interests outside of the formal curriculum. For many pupils, the primary purpose of engagement in musical enrichment activity is not to attain high levels of musical expertise. Instead, enjoyment of music, developing friendships and social networks and enhancing transferable skills such as self-confidence and self-esteem are often considered more important outcomes (Creech, 2006). For some pupils, competing activities offer similar benefits. For others, the high level of commitment, in terms of time and resources, makes sustained engagement with instrumental learning difficult (Box 18.6). Where resources are limited, parents are likely to disrupt involvement behaviour which may in turn impact on pupil engagement (Grolnick, 1997). In this vein, Hurley (1995) found that those who dropped out viewed violin study as demanding too great a time-cost for the (perceived) relatively small rewards it offered.

Box 18.6 Competition for resources

One hundred and thirty-one parents of violin pupils aged 5–17, all of whom learnt with private music studio teachers, completed questionnaires exploring their attitudes to their children's extra-curricular instrumental lessons (Creech, 2001). Ninety-four per cent reported that their children participated in other activities that included sports, dance, drama, visual arts and languages. Twenty per cent of the children took part in a minimum of three extra-curricular activities, in addition to homework.

Parents described juggling many commitments and activities and identified time commitment as a difficult issue which in many cases had not been anticipated.

Where it has boxed me in is the amount of time that music takes up, for something that is just supposed to be fun, and a sideline, and a hobby. There's the practice, there's orchestra, there's chamber music, there's their lessons – it's absolutely huge. . . . I don't know anybody who'd be as committed as a parent of a child doing an orchestral instrument. . . . So I find that very tiring . . . and that's the only regret I have, the amount of time for what will probably happen in the end – they'll go off to college and do something totally different.

Pupils transferring from Key Stage 2 to Key Stage 3 (primary to secondary) were found by Hallam *et al.* (2005) to be the most vulnerable to drop-out from instrumental learning (Table 18.1).

Table 18.1 Drop-outs from local authority Music Service instrumental lessons, by Key Stage

Key Stage	Music Services' responses	Drop-outs		
		Range of numbers	Average (mean)	Total
KS1	62	0–61	12	713
KS2	80	0–765	153	12,215
KS3	78	0–1230	129	10,023
KS4	77	0–256	39	2991

Source: Hallam *et al.* (2005)

While individual music studio teachers will be aware of a variety of factors that impact on drop-out among their own pupils, these may be similar to the reasons for drop-out from instrumental lessons accessed through Music Service provision, found by Hallam *et al.* in 2005 (Table 18.2).

Table 18.2 Reasons for dropping out from local authority Music Service instrumental lessons

Reason for dropping out	Music Services' responses	Percentage of drop-outs	
		Range	Average (mean)
Loss of interest	47	1–86	27
Competing demands from schoolwork	47	1–87	14
Cost of tuition	44	1–30	10
Competing demands from other extra-curricular activities	44	0–29	8

Lack of space or time to practise	33	0–20	6
Lack of progress	39	0–16	6
Lack of support from family	37	0–30	6
Dislike of instrument	34	0–20	4
Peer group pressure	32	0–10	3
Relationships	31	0–10	3
Lack of interest in the type of music being taught	31	0–9	2
Lack of opportunity to perform with others	22	0–5	1
Dislike of examinations	24	0–5	1
Other reasons	36	2–76	17
No reason	14	1–86	27

Source: Hallam *et al.* (2005)

While some of these reported reasons for giving up are outside of the control of private music studio teachers, others may be mitigated by actions such as developing activities that will sustain interest, adjusting the demands for practising, responding to pupil musical genre preferences and raising awareness of interpersonal issues. (See Chapter 6 for a full discussion of strategies for developing sustained engagement.)

Professional development

Continuing professional development poses particular challenges for private music studio teachers. As has been suggested, these musicians often balance complex portfolio careers which involve a wide range of demands, deadlines and responsibilities. It may be very easy, within this context, for teaching to become a mechanical routine and for the value of continuing professional development to become obscured. It may also be difficult for portfolio musicians to prioritise their professional development, because training that contributes to one area of their career development could leave scarce resources (time or money) available for development in other areas of their work. A very tangible problem is that in pursuing professional development activities freelance studio teachers incur a double financial cost of losing a day's pay to take up a day's training, as well as funding the training itself (Broad *et al.*, 2007). Nevertheless, the fact that music studio teachers may have few opportunities for sharing of ideas with other teachers or benefiting from feedback from colleagues is a salient issue, which often makes professional development opportunities attractive for studio music teachers. As noted above, enhanced qualifications are not linked to enhanced pay for studio teachers. Thus, the motivation for professional development must be related to professional satisfaction more than financial reward.

It must be remembered that private music studios are situated within a wider, rapidly changing environment with new developments and initiatives on local, national and international levels. As discussed earlier in this chapter, for many the private music studio forms part of a wider portfolio of work. This often includes teaching within formal contexts such as Music Services, where instrumental teachers are now expected to conform to national standards that stipulate 'they take responsibility for their own professional development and use the outcomes to improve their teaching and their pupils' learning' (Standard 4, FMS National Standards for Instrumental Teachers, FMS, 2009). Increasingly, therefore, teachers recognise the importance of keeping abreast of the latest thinking, and refreshing and enriching their professional skills and knowledge.

Just as in other areas of music education, such as community music (Chapter 19), in recent years there has been expansion in terms of the professional training that is available for instrumental teachers. However, much of the available training targets the needs of instrumental teachers in the employment of Music Services, where there is an increasing focus on whole-class instrumental and vocal teaching approaches. There are few accredited training opportunities for instrumental teachers who work outside of formal institutions, although some courses, including higher education, are now offered in the UK (Box 18.7).

Box 18.7 Accredited professional development routes for private music studio teachers

The Associated Board of the Royal Schools of Music were pioneers in the area of accreditation for private music studio teachers, implementing in the 1990s the Certificate of Teaching (CT ABRSM) for instrumental teachers, now held by over 2,000 instrumental teachers worldwide. The only entry requirements for this qualification are that candidates are aged 21 or over, have at least one year of teaching experience and teach a minimum of five pupils on a regular basis. Thus, the course is clearly geared towards meeting the potential professional development needs of music studio teachers for whom teaching forms part of a wider portfolio of work.

The ISM recognised the need for accredited professional development within higher education, for private music studio teachers. Working collaboratively with Reading University in the 1990s they established the Music Teaching in Professional Practice (MTPP) postgraduate qualification (Diploma leading to MA), designed to meet the needs of instrumental and vocal teachers.

Summary

The private music studio is an enduring feature of many professional musicians' portfolio of professional practice. The true extent of teaching in the UK taking place within this context is unknown, but indications suggest that it may approach the level of instrumental teaching taking place through the auspices of local authority Music Services.

Partly because of the portfolio nature of the careers of many private music studio teachers, these musicians cannot fail to be aware of the changing pedagogical approaches and professional values and practices that are stipulated in more formal institutional contexts. To this end, many private music studio teachers access professional development opportunities, despite considerable costs to themselves and little promise of financial recompense in terms of increased earning power.

The challenges of managing complex interpersonal relationships with pupils and parents are salient, particularly within the wider context of a complex portfolio career. Teachers have the responsibility to manage all of the business aspects entailed by a private music studio, as well as responding to diverse pupil and parent objectives and needs. In order to ensure the sustainability of their private music studio practices, teachers need to consider flexible approaches which take account of the many competing demands and aspirations that pupils bring to their learning.

The working conditions of private music studio teachers are often precarious, with relatively low rates of pay that do not reflect professional qualifications. One route that undoubtedly offers music studio teachers opportunities for diversification and enhanced learning outcomes is the development of web-based interactive resources, whereby teaching may take place in 'virtual studio space'. Another route is the development of group teaching approaches, incorporating these into more traditional one-to-one teaching models. To this end, it is imperative that private music studio teachers continue to access professional development. In light of the contribution these teachers evidently make to the corpus of out-of-school enrichment activities, it would be a far-sighted move if funding streams could be developed to support professional development activities, perhaps under the auspices of professional organisations that represent private music studio teachers.

Further reading

Creech, A. (2009) 'The role of the family in supporting learning'. In S. Hallam, I. Cross and M. Thaut (eds), *The Oxford Handbook of Music Psychology*. Oxford: Oxford University Press.

Hallam, S. (2006) *Music Psychology in Education*. London: Institute of Education, University of London.

Useful links

Association of Teachers of Singing www.aotos.org.uk

British Double Reed Society www.bdrs.org.uk

British Flute Society www.bfs.org.uk

British Suzuki Institute www.britishsuzuki.org.uk

Clarinet & Saxophone Society of Great Britain www.cassgb.org

European Guitar Teachers Association www.egta.co.uk

European Piano Teachers Association www.epta-uk.org

European String Teachers Association www.estastrings.org.uk

Incorporated Society of Musicians www.ism.org

Musicians' Union www.musiciansunion.org.uk

National Association of Percussion Teachers www.napt.org.uk

References

Age Concern (2008) *The Age Agenda 2008: Public policy and older people*. London: Age Concern. Online. <http://www.ageconcern.org.uk/AgeConcern/Documents/AA_2008_Report.pdf> (accessed 04/01/2010)

Association of Graduate Careers Advisory Services (2009) *Occupational Profile: Music teacher, private/peripatetic*. Online. <http://www.prospects.ac.uk> (accessed 30/12/2009).

Bond, A. (2002) *Learning Music Online: An accessible learning program for isolated students*. Adelaide: National Centre for Vocational Education Research.

Broad, S., Duffy, C. and Gardiner, R. (2007) *A Sound Investment: Workforce development in music education* (No. RES004). Edinburgh: Scottish Arts Council.

Colprit, E.J. (2000) 'Observation and analysis of Suzuki string teaching'. *Journal of Research in Music Education*, 48(3), 206–221.

Creech, A. (2001) 'Play for me: An exploration into motivations, issues and outcomes related to parental involvement in their children's violin study'. Unpublished MA dissertation, University of Sheffield.

–– (2006) 'Dynamics, harmony and discord: A systems analysis of teacher–pupil–parent interaction in instrumental learning'. Unpublished PhD thesis, Institute of Education, University of London.

–– (2008) 'Interpersonal dynamics and teacher objectives in instrumental teaching'. Paper presented at the Research Commission, International Society of Music Education, Porto, Portugal, 13-18 July.

–– (2009a) 'Teacher–parent–pupil trios: A typology of interpersonal interaction in the context of learning a musical instrument'. *Musicae Scientiae*, XIII(2), 163–182.

–– (2009b) 'The role of the family in supporting learning'. In S. Hallam, I. Cross and M. Thaut (eds), *The Oxford Handbook of Music Psychology*. Oxford: Oxford University Press.

Crozier, R. (2009) *Associated Board of The Royal Schools of Music: Why professional development?* Online. <http://www.abrsm.org/?page=teachers/courses/UKIreland/profDev.html> (accessed 30/12/2009).

Davidson, J., Howe, M., Moore, D. and Sloboda, J. (1996) 'The role of parental influences in the development of musical performance'. *British Journal of Developmental Psychology*, 14(4), 399–412.

Department for Children, Schools and Families (DCSF) (2009) *Standards Site: Personalised learning*. Online. <http://nationalstrategies.standards.dcsf.gov.uk/personalisedlearning> (accessed 30/12/2009).

Department for Education and Employment (DfEE) (1998) *Extending Opportunities: A national framework for study support*. London: HMSO.

Duke, R.A. and Simmons, A.L. (2006) 'The nature of expertise: Narrative descriptions of 19 common elements observed in the lessons of three renowned artist-teachers'. *Bulletin for the Council of Research in Music Education* 170, 7–19.

Federation of Music Services (FMS) (2009) 'Federation of music services national standards for instrumental teachers'. Online. <http://www.thefms.org/teachers-parents-children/teachers-and-professional/resources/national-standards> (accessed 31/12/2009).

Grolnick, W. (1997) 'Predictors of parent involvement in children's schooling'. *Journal of Educational Psychology*, 89(3), 538–548.

Hallam, S. (1998) *Instrumental Teaching*. Oxford: Heinemann.

–– (2006) *Music Psychology in Education*. London: Institute of Education, University of London.

Hallam, S., Rogers, L. and Creech, A. (2005) *Survey of Local Authority Music Services 2005*. London: Department for Education and Skills.

Hurley, C.G. (1995) 'Student motivations for beginning and continuing/discontinuing string music instruction'. *The Quarterly Journal of Music Teaching and Learning*, VI(1), 44–55.

Incorporated Society of Musicians (ISM) (2009) Online. <http://www.ism.org> (accessed 30/12/2009).

Kennell, R. (2002) 'Systematic research in studio instruction in music'. In T. Colwell and C. Richardson (eds), *The New Handbook of Research on Music Teaching and Learning*. New York: Oxford University Press.

Lehmann, A.C., Sloboda, J.A. and Woody, R.H. (2007) *Psychology for Musicians: Understanding and acquiring the skills*. New York: Oxford University Press.

Manturzewska, M. (1990) 'A biographical study of the life-span development of professional musicians'. *Psychology of Music*, 18(2), 112–139.

McPherson, G. and Davidson, J. (2006) 'Playing an instrument'. In G. McPherson (ed.), *The Child as Musician: A handbook of musical development*. Oxford: Oxford University Press.

Morgan, C. (1998) 'Instrumental music teaching and learning: A life history approach'. Unpublished PhD thesis, University of Exeter.

Musicians' Union (MU) (2009) Online. <http://www.musiciansunion.org.uk> (accessed 30/12/2009).

Schmidt, C.P. (1989) 'Applied music teaching behaviour as a function of selected personality variables'. *Journal of Research in Music Education*, 37(4), 258–271.

Ward, V. (2004) 'Good performance, music analysis and instrumental teaching; towards an understanding of the aims and objectives of instrumental teachers'. *Music Education Research*, 6(2), 191–215.

Youth Music (2006) 'Our music: Musical engagement of young people aged 7–19 in the UK'. Online. <http://www.musicmanifesto.co.uk/assets/x/50283> (accessed 30/12/2009).

Chapter 19

The role of music leaders and community musicians

Andrea Creech

What is 'community music'?

Community music is an elusive concept. In the UK this term has come to be associated with collaborative music making outside of formal educational contexts, although it also includes music education outreach work within schools. Guided by the principles of access to music making for all, equality of opportunity, participation and inclusiveness, community music initiatives encompass workshops and musical activities in a wide range of community settings, facilitated by musicians representing diverse musical genres and interest areas.

The latter part of the twentieth century saw huge growth, in the Western world, in opportunities for organised music making within formal educational settings. The domain now identified as 'community music' emerged from this musical climate, taking music playing, teaching and learning outside of formal contexts. Community music initiatives were heavily influenced by the community arts movement of the 1970s, characterised by an ethos of democracy and empowerment (Higgins, 2007). Since that time there has been, across the UK and elsewhere, an explosive growth of community music outreach initiated by arts and community agencies (Swanwick, 2008).

In order to grasp fully the complexity and scope of community music, it is important to recognise that in the UK this sphere of music making has developed within a social climate where ideas of multidisciplinary practices – integrating social, educational, medical and therapeutic theory and practice – have been dominant. Furthermore, the principles of community music may be seen as a backlash against pervasive specialisation and professionalisation of music and an acknowledgement of the rapidly growing evidence that everyone, regardless of social, educational, psychological or medical aspects, has the capacity to communicate through music (Hallam and MacDonald, 2009).

Recognition of community music

The magnitude and value of community music in the UK was formally recognised in 1999 with the establishment of Youth Music, the national charity committed to nurturing the musical development and expanding the musical horizons of young people aged 0–18 (Youth Music, 2009). Youth Music oversees the allocation of funding to community music initiatives, guided by five objectives: (1) access for those with the least opportunity; (2) breadth of musical styles and cultures; (3) UK-wide coverage; (4) development of 'Music Leaders'; and (5) quality of provision. In particular, support is directed towards 'Youth Music Action Zones' across England and Wales – areas where young people experience social and economic deprivation. Another priority area is support for early years music provision, discussed in Chapter 12. In addition, in line with their commitment to development and quality, Youth Music dedicates resources to the continuing professional development of music practitioners. Swanwick (2008) reported that Youth Music had funded training and created employment for over 6,000 Music Leaders. Furthermore, with a substantial grant from the National Lottery and partnership funding from other sources, Youth Music had 'made an input into music education in 99 per cent of local authorities and many other agencies' (Swanwick, 2008: 13).

Who are community musicians?

Just as a definition of 'community music' is problematic, so too is describing a 'typical' community musician. Musical activities in the UK may be found within an enormous range of community settings, both inside and outside of institutions such as schools, music centres, community centres and places of worship. The diversity of people leading these activities has been found to be wide-ranging, reflecting a rich social fabric (Finnegan, 1989).

Sound Sense, a UK professional organisation for community musicians, lists 'confident, accomplished musical skills in whatever tradition(s) you're comfortable with' as the first key characteristic of a community musician (Sound Sense, 2006). Community musicians, in line with this criterion, comprise a diverse population, potentially representing any genre of music and any level of accomplishment. Other key attributes of community musicians, according to Sound Sense, are excellent interpersonal and teamwork skills, an understanding of the social and musical cultures one is working within, good administrative skills and knowledge of bureaucratic structures that support community music activities. Notably, Sound Sense does not include facilitation skills, teaching qualifications or leadership qualities in the person specification.

The pedagogical and leadership skills noted above are reflected in the label 'Music Leader', which in the UK has come into common parlance in the community music world. This professional badge has become prevalent largely as a result of the implementation of the MusicLeader support service for music practitioners and project managers, funded by Youth Music (MusicLeader, 2009). Notwithstanding the connotations of the term 'Music Leader', Swanwick (2008: 14) notes that 'these musicians may or may not have any teaching background, professional training or qualification'. Recent case study research which evaluated the professional development needs of ten Music Leaders found that the majority (nine of them) regarded themselves first and foremost as musicians, spending many hours engaging in developing their musical performance skills, which were rated highly by the evaluation team (Davies *et al.*, 2007). This finding would seem to chime with Swanwick (2008: 13) who describes Music Leaders as a group of professionals who 'would rather see themselves as musicians, wishing only to communicate their ways of making music to others'. Interestingly, the self-perceived musician identity contrasted with the majority view of the young people who participated in their musical activities, which was that Music Leaders were 'teachers' (Davies *et al.*, 2007).

Community and outreach work can now be considered part of many musicians' portfolio careers, irrespective of their particular musical genre (see Chapter 16). The Association of British Orchestras (ABO) lists 38 orchestras and opera companies holding ABO full membership whose musicians engage in music education, community and outreach programmes (Harvey, 2005). The summary of community and outreach work demonstrates that these musicians facilitate musical activities with people of all ages and backgrounds, in a wide range of settings which include hospitals, community centres, factories, adult day centres, early years settings, supermarkets, hospices and prisons. The nature of the activities is similarly diverse, including creative music projects, demonstrations and performances, family days and 'have-a-go' taster sessions. Many of the ABO members have set up partnership programmes with youth services and health care providers. In addition, much of the community and outreach work documented by the ABO involves multi-modal work with composers, music animateurs, dancers, visual artists, writers, designers and actors (Box 19.1).

Box 19.1 Community music education outreach work: LSO Discovery

Between September 2008 and July 2009, some 495 workshops, 127 concerts and 109 Continuing Professional Development (CPD) events took place, coordinated by 'LSO Discovery' – the London Symphony Orchestra's (LSO's) education and community programme – many involving the 'LSO On Track' partnership with the Barbican Campus, the Guildhall School of Music & Drama and ten East London local authority (LA) Music Services. These activities were organised under the broad categories of 'Celebrate and Inspire' (e.g. 'Lite of Spring' and 'Take a Bow', involving LSO musicians working together with instrumental pupils from the Music Services and Music Service tutors), 'Everybody Play' (bespoke workshops in schools, summer camp and KS1 and KS2 concerts supported by visits to schools by LSO musicians), and the 'Next Generation' scheme (nurturing the talent of 21 gifted young musicians from the ten Music Services).

In addition, a number of smaller initiatives have been implemented, including the 'Mastering Auditions' series (masterclasses involving LSO musicians, students from the Guildhall School of Music & Drama and pupil and tutor observers from the Music Services), 'Youth Fusion' (Fusion Orchestra roadshows as well as school-based events where gifted and talented pupils work with LSO musicians), 'Urban Sounds' (led by Guildhall Connect creative music student ensembles) and the Barbican World Music Schools concert. Finally, the LSO 'On Track' partnership supports a CPD programme for KS2 teachers from the ten partner East London boroughs.

The community and education outreach activities offered by LSO Discovery offer unique opportunities to bring together music education providers and performers of an international standard – all within a coherent framework, grounded in the community of East London. The potential for raising aspirations and enhancing musical opportunities among young musicians and developing progression routes in music is great. Great potential also exists for developing CPD opportunities and broadening the professional skill base among Music Service providers and among LSO musicians.

Feedback from participants, across all of the strands of the programme, has been consistently positive, in particular emphasising the opportunities to participate in musical excellence, learn new skills, become inspired and enthused and gain confidence.

> I really love music. It gives me the chance to express my feelings. Since I was 3, I was always day-dreaming about being somewhere which is about music or dance.
>
> (young musician participant, from LA Music Service)

> *Your work reminds me of all that is good in the world and all that we should aspire to for our children.*
>
> (Music Service Head)
>
> (Hallam *et al.*, 2009)

Many community musicians, however, work independently as freelance musicians, outside the framework of formal arts organisations such as those holding membership of the ABO. Ten case study Music Leaders who participated in research carried out by Davies *et al.* (2007) were selected as a representative sample in respect of musical genre and experience, including two from each of the five network MusicLeader Areas (London, North East, North West, West Midlands and Yorkshire). All but one were freelance community musicians, providing a broad range of music making, including samba, hip hop, rock, vocal, choral, classical orchestral, beginner woodwind, early years music technology, and improvised percussion. There were several problems associated with freelance status, one being chronically low pay and another being an evident lack of mutual understanding between employers and Music Leaders regarding what a reasonable partnership code of practice should be, particularly when opportunities were project-based or one-off sessions. Partly because their CPD was typically self-funded, the Music Leaders prioritised CPD relating to musical skills and had generally accessed little training relating to initiating and organising projects, despite recognising their own development needs in relation to project management.

A further problem identified in the Music Leader research (Davies *et al.*, 2007) that potentially impacts on all community musicians delivering short-term project-based activities, irrespective of their employment status, related to progression and integration of informal with formal learning. Short-term project work allowed little scope for Music Leaders to develop an awareness and knowledge of the young people's wider musical contexts or previous musical experiences, making signposting of progression routes problematic. Furthermore, despite Youth Music's intention that 'the activities and projects supported by the available funding . . . complement music in the National Curriculum' (Swanwick, 2008: 13) the Music Leader research participants had little knowledge of key national music strategies and generally regarded knowledge in this area as the responsibility of others. For young people, then, formal and non-formal learning was not always joined up.

The community musician's role

Community musicians (here taken to encompass Music Leaders engaged in community and outreach work) pursue a range of objectives in their work, which at any point in time may be classified as educational, personal growth, community development, therapeutic, social or celebration objectives (Mullen, 2002). It is unlikely, as the practical examples in this chapter will illustrate, that these objectives are ever discrete. Rather, an emphasis on one area such as personal growth may have implications for other areas, such as skill acquisition or community development. In this vein, while many people may be motivated to engage with community music programmes by a desire to learn a particular musical skill, they may experience wider benefits that then contribute to the motivation for sustained engagement.

Although Mullen includes educational objectives within the community musician's brief, he rejects the relevance of teaching per se within community music contexts on the grounds that 'teachers and teaching are not necessary for creative music making' (Mullen, 2002: 2). However, Mullen's critique is founded on an (arguably) outdated view of teaching as didactic and authoritarian, whereby the teacher's role is to act as an agent of social control. A contrasting view is put forth by Koopman (2007) who argues that experienced teachers, acting within facilitation or coaching models, possess the expertise that is required to most effectively initiate, organise and guide musical encounters. Koopman acknowledges that many musical processes are learnt informally, but cautions that to deny the relevance of teaching within community music settings is to 'deprive large groups of children and adults of excellent opportunities to develop their musical abilities. Don't let us waste the chance to offer them music education rather than short-lived musical kicks' (Koopman, 2007: 161).

The debate between Koopman (2007) and Mullen (2002) seems to focus on a question relating to the role of facilitation versus the role of direction, within community music settings. It is clear that in some settings the community musician's role arguably involves some didactic strategies, as in the case of large ensemble conductors and choral directors. Indeed, didactic styles of musical leadership formed the mainstay of the portfolio of work carried out by three of the Music Leader participants observed by Davies *et al*. (2007). However, Finney (2006, cited in Swanwick, 2008) advocates a process-based rather than product-based approach to musical development. Mullen concurs, proposing that the community musician's role is to convene the group, to clarify and to act as a guardian of the process. The focus on process rather than product is encapsulated by the mission of organisations such as the St Albans Rehearsal Orchestra (SARO, 2009) whose purpose is enjoyable music making in the context of rehearsals only, with no performances.

Facilitation is described as the method of delivery for community music workshops (Higgins, 2008), involving open dialogue among participants and an emphasis on creativity, expression, spontaneity and cooperation. Specific aspects of a process-directed and facilitative community music pedagogy include authentic learning oriented to the prior experiences of participants and embedded within specific cultural and social contexts (Koopman, 2007). Koopman suggests that effective music facilitators employ strategies that promote learning how to learn and self-regulation, active participation, modelling and social interaction. Higgins (2008) adds that the generous giving of oneself and encouragement of others within the context of non-hierarchical, democratic music workshops are characteristics of good facilitation practice. The diversity of community music is such that aspects of these various approaches are likely to be relevant in differing contexts, although the overarching principle of process rather than product may be said to be a predominant feature of community music.

Community music participants: Who are they?

As discussed elsewhere in this book, during childhood, adolescence and early adulthood the development of musical skills is dependent on opportunities for engagement in music, the support of family and school, and wider socio-cultural factors. As noted above, the vital role that community music initiatives play in providing access to music participation is championed by Youth Music, which provides a range of support for musical development among young people who may otherwise become disengaged from music very early on. Swanwick (2008: 13) reported that 'Youth Music has reached more than 1.4 million young people, making over 1800 funding awards and distributing finances totalling £66 million'.

Adults are more likely to participate in community music when they have actively engaged in musical activities during childhood. Re-engagement is evidently attributable to factors which include personal motivations, musical motivation, social motivation or expressing spirituality (Hallam and MacDonald, 2009). The social, emotional, physical and creative value of adult participation in music has been well documented. A body of evidence suggests that music can provide a source of enhanced social cohesion, enjoyment, personal development and empowerment (Hillman, 2002; Sixsmith and Gibson, 2007). Hays and Minichiello (2005) found music to be closely related to their older participants' sense of identity and well-being, while Pieters (1996) found evidence of cognitive benefits. Direct health benefits have also been suggested, with lower mortality rates evident among those who make music or sing in a choir (Byrgen et al., 1996). This evidence highlights the importance of widening access to music making among young people, thereby increasing the chance that they will later re-engage with music and reap the benefits to be derived from music participation.

While community music programmes seem to reach adults who have engaged with music earlier in their lives, in the UK little attention has been paid to the potential impact of participation in community music in the lives of older 'novices' – those who missed out on opportunities and support for music during their formative years. Indeed, within our current social context where extraordinary demographic transitions are underway (Age Concern, 2008), where the numbers of old people suffering from depression is increasing and where there is an accepted need for initiatives that support older people's well-being and productivity (Jamieson, 2007) an opportunity exists for initiatives that make it possible for community music making to effect a significant contribution to the quality of life of older people – novices and experienced music makers alike. To this end, the Music for Life Project, carried out by the Institute of Education, University of London and the Guildhall School of Music & Drama in partnership, under the auspices of the New Dynamics of Ageing strand of the Economic and Social Research Council, is currently researching how participation in community music can enhance older people's social, emotional and cognitive well-being. The research is also addressing issues of barriers to participation, as well as pedagogical matters that impact upon delivery of the music sessions (see Chapter 10).

The impact of community music

As noted above, the objectives and outcomes of engagement with community music are diverse and sometimes unexpected. The following illustrative example (Box 19.2) demonstrates how one workshop has the potential to create a safe space where educational objectives as well as personal growth and fun social interaction are in evidence. Here, young people experiment with music, express themselves, develop concentration and persistence, acquire new skills and experience peer learning within a framework of guided facilitation.

Box 19.2 Introduction to playing instruments: 'Re-Creation' music workshop

It is Saturday morning in December, at a church hall in the North East of England. A community music 'Re-Creation' music workshop is underway, introducing young people, aged 10–12, to playing instruments. This one-hour session forms the first part of a series of song-writing workshops. Two Music Leaders are facilitating, and have arrived early to set up, bringing a drum kit, guitar and keyboard. The session begins with a variety of warm-up

---

activities intended to build confidence, improve physical and musical cooperation and anticipation skills, and develop vocal and ensemble skills. The group is quickly making music, guided by the facilitators who use strategies such as repetition, demonstration, rote learning and adding layers to create a group performance. The facilitators are consistently encouraging and there is a real sense of engagement among the young people, who persist with mastering complex individual parts that involve controlling rhythm, pitch and pulse. The young people take turns in singing vocals, playing the drum kit, guitar and keyboard as backing in group performances that, in the context of a first encounter with these musical instruments, are impressive.

> I felt that the less confident children were given help and suggestions by me or the rest of the group as encouragement. It was a small group, so they relaxed quite early on as they got to know each other's characters quickly, and I felt that most members of the group were relaxed enough to contribute freely – there was a lot of discussion. . . . There was a lot of laughter, which suggested that the group were enjoying themselves and feeling relaxed. . . . Everybody swapped round and played all the instruments. . . . they were able to ask questions and make suggestions without feeling inhibited.
>
> (Music Leader)
>
> (Davies *et al.*, 2007)

Box 19.3 is a second example of a community music workshop. Here, the emphasis is placed squarely on personal development through the creative mediums of art and music.

Box 19.3 A community musician describes his 'badge of identity' workshop

My 'badge of identity' workshop . . . has its objectives located in sustainability, relevance and empowerment. In short, the 'badge of identity' workshop is designed so that the participants create an artefact that reflects who they are. Materials for construction have been selected beforehand and typically include fabric, photographs, natural substances (leaves, stones and earth), paper, wood, metal and trinkets. As each individual completes her/his art object, they are asked to write a haiku poem to accompany their creation. Through quiet reflection the participants reinterpret their work into a tight structure of syllables, words and lines. The art-objects plus the haikus are then exhibited within the workshop space, creating a gallery that can be walked through.

As facilitator, I explain that the artefacts are to be used as 'scores' in order to generate musical ideas. Breaking down into smaller units such as duos, trios and quartets, the participants interpret the art-objects through music. After all of the art-objects have been considered musically, each group shares their creation through musical performance. The act of 'performing' somebody's badge of identity can be a profound experience for both the musicians and those who created the badges. The performers experience an unexpected responsibility in the gift-giving of the musical response. Those to whom the art-object had 'originally' belonged have the unusual sense of listening to an interpretation of themselves. This can be, and often is, a moving experience, as personal aspects of one's life – missed family, significant moments, times gone by, etc. – are relayed back through music and lyrics. Through group and individual transformations, both musically and personally, the workshop allows participants to experience a sense of the unconditional welcome and an open invitation to invent.

(Higgins, 2008: 329)

In contrast to the workshop examples offered in Boxes 19.2 and 19.3, the following example of community music practice in the UK (Box 19.4) illustrates the benefits that may be derived from an established community music centre (operating as a registered charity) where, for the past 21 years members of a rural community in South West England have met weekly, participating in wind bands and choir. Questionnaires relating to the experience of participation in the centre were completed by all of the 150 young people, aged between 5 and 25, who currently participate. Focus group interviews were also carried out, exploring the social and musical outcomes.

Box 19.4 Community music centre

This well-established music centre in the South West of England provides a context for young people to participate in weekly ensemble activities – primarily wind bands and choirs. The members of this musical community are united by their interest in making music. The centre operates a policy of inclusiveness, and everyone who wishes to join is welcomed. Accordingly, the musical benefits are clear, evidenced by participants' reports of enhanced technical skills, ensemble skills, sight reading, musical awareness and access to music that they had not previously heard. Peer learning was found to be a particularly powerful and valued influence. Musical development was inextricable from the palpable social benefits that included trust, social bonding and confidence building. These social benefits acted as strong incentives for sustained engagement with the musical activities.

(Blandford and Duarte, 2004)

The far-reaching community benefits of sustained community music initiatives noted in Box 19.4 are elaborated by Higgins (2007) in his account (Box 19.5) of 12 years in the life of the Peterborough Community Samba Band (PCSB). Here, the benefits may be seen in terms of musical outcomes, community development and personal development.

Box 19.5 The Peterborough Community Samba Band

The PCSB was founded in 1993: 'just before 7:30 p.m. on a Thursday night, I sat nervously, not knowing if there would be any attendance at all' (Higgins, 2007: 285). Emily, the first person to arrive, turned out to be a participant for whom the following 12 years of active engagement in music would be transformative. PCSB 'made the biggest impact of anything I've done I think. I can't imagine me not doing it now. It's such an intrinsic part of who I am. It's not just something that I do'.

The original adult group soon grew and created a junior offshoot known as the Samba Sizzlers, facilitated by Emily. Parents with teaching experience were enlisted as helpers, thus initiating a network of parents who were able to support the group in a number of organisational ways. Parents soon began to engage musically as well and stepped in when younger members were absent. One previous member, now an adult, recalled, 'It was a social thing from quite early on and I gained lots of friends. Then my parents got involved in the organisation and families started socialising out of the group'. Another past member attributed samba as part of the reason she has 'a great relationship with my parents as we do this as a family'.

(Higgins, 2007)

Continuing professional development for community musicians

This chapter has demonstrated how the notion of 'community musician' encompasses many different people from diverse backgrounds, with differing interests and pursuing a wide range of objectives. The evidence presented here also illustrates the proliferation of community music initiatives around the UK. Issues of training, quality assurance and evaluation of work in this area have been addressed by Youth Music, which has established Music Leader networks across the country that support the professional development of community musicians (Box 19.6).

Box 19.6 Evaluation of professional development needs of Music Leaders

Ten Music Leaders participated in case study research, over the course of one year. The Music Leaders were each given £500 to fund continuing professional development of their choice. Alongside this, each Music

---

Leader's professional practice was observed twice by an evaluation team, the first time at the beginning of the year, prior to the CPD, and the subsequent occasion at the end of the year, following engagement with CPD. Following the observations, the Music Leaders engaged in lengthy (60–90 minutes) self-reflective interviews. The observations were recorded on digital video, and copies of these recordings, together with feedback, were supplied to each Music Leader, who later provided further reflective comments on their practice. In addition, all of the Music Leaders provided monthly diaries documenting their ongoing professional development. All of the Music Leaders were found to demonstrate significant and sometimes dramatic improvements in practice. This was attributed to engagement in the research process itself, and specifically to the opportunities to receive feedback and to engage in reflection on practice.

(Davies *et al.*, 2007)

Alongside a plethora of short- and medium-term CPD opportunities for community musicians, formal accreditation is now being offered by a number of institutions. The UKPASS online system for application to UK postgraduate programmes (UKPASS, 2009) lists four Masters-level qualifications in community music (University of Edinburgh, Liverpool Institute of Performing Arts, Leeds College of Music and York University). In addition, the Guildhall School of Music & Drama offers the 'Guildhall Artist Programme in Leadership' and the Royal College of Music offers a 'Postgraduate Diploma in Creative Leadership', both aimed at developing Music Leader skills to a high level. Community Music London, in partnership with the University of Westminster offers a foundation degree in Community Music Practice, while the University of Sunderland, in partnership with Gateshead College and The Sage, Gateshead, offers a BA(Hons) in Community Music. Many other first and postgraduate music degree programmes around the country include community music options or modules in their course specifications.

Thus, in response to the rapid expansion of community music and the demand for high-quality leaders in this area, many professional development opportunities are now available. The challenge may be to preserve the inclusive ethos of community music and to sustain a focus on processes rather than products. This is a challenge that can surely be met by those with a commitment to providing access to high-quality, inspirational and life-enhancing musical opportunities for all.

Summary

Community music is a complex and wide-ranging area of practice that has expanded at an exponential rate during the last 20 years. Although much community music takes place within informal contexts, many formal institutions now engage in community music education outreach work, sending musicians into formal contexts such as schools to facilitate creative projects and support engagement with more formal activities such as schools concerts. In this vein, much community music is reliant on partnership working among musicians and other artists and also between musicians and professionals in other domains such as education, health and social care.

The overarching ethos of inclusiveness guides community music practice, both in terms of those who participate and those who facilitate community music initiatives. Accordingly, community music is guided by the principles of access to high-quality music making for all, widening participation, breadth of musical genre and social context.

The proliferation of community music has led, increasingly, to formal recognition of this area of arts work. The value of community music has been enshrined in the aims and objectives of agencies such as Youth Music as well as in the mission statements and work of many flagship artistic institutions such as the London Symphony Orchestra.

Professional musicians from all backgrounds and representing all musical genres can now expect that community music will comprise a part of their portfolio careers. Opportunities for professional development and formal accreditation have rapidly appeared, in response to the growth in community music and the demand for quality control in this area. It is no longer feasible for most musicians to focus exclusively on musical skills. Rather, the demands of community music are such that leadership, facilitation, knowledge of pedagogy, interpersonal skills and administrative skills are all equally important.

The future of community music holds exciting possibilities. It is still relatively early days to evaluate the potential far-reaching consequences of a movement that brings together the objectives of personal and social development, creativity and informal learning with a commitment to musical excellence. One potential pitfall is the short-term nature of many projects and workshops. There may be a significant gap between claims that are made in relation to musical and social benefits and what is actually achievable, within these types of activities. This is not to decry the value of community music, nor is it meant to deny the creative and inspirational nature of many projects and workshops. Rather, it is intended to flag up the importance of developing sustainable, long-term musical initiatives that can really impact on our communities in meaningful and demonstrable ways.

Further reading

Hallam, S. and MacDonald, R. (2009) 'The effects of music in community and educational settings'. In S. Hallam, I. Cross and M. Thaut (eds), *The Oxford Handbook of Music Psychology*. Oxford: Oxford University Press.

Swanwick, K. (2008) 'The "good-enough" music teacher'. *British Journal of Music Education*, 25(1), 9–22.

References

Age Concern (2008) The Age Agenda 2008: Public policy and older people. Online. <http://www.ageconcern.org.uk/AgeConcern/Documents/AA_2008_Report.pdf> (accessed 04/01/2010).

Blandford, S. and Duarte, S. (2004) 'Inclusion in the community: A study of community music centres in England and Portugal, focusing on the development of musical and social skills within each centre'. *Westminster Studies in Education*, 27(1), 7–25.

Byrgen, L.A., Konlaan, B.B. and Johnasson, W.E. (1996) 'Attendance at cultural events, reading books or periodicals, and making music or singing in a choir as determinants for survival: Swedish interview survey of living conditions'. *British Medical Journal*, 313, 1577–1580.

Davies, A., Davies, V. and Creech, A. (2007) *Music Leader Evaluation Project*. London: Youth Music.

Finnegan, R. (1989) *The Hidden Musicians: Music-making in an English town.* Cambridge: Cambridge University Press.

Hallam, S. and MacDonald, R. (2009) 'The effects of music in community and educational settings'. In S. Hallam, I. Cross and M. Thaut (eds), *The Oxford Handbook of Music Psychology*. Oxford: Oxford University Press.

Hallam, S., Creech, A. and Shave, K. (2009) *LSO and Barbican Campus Music Partnership Project*. London: LSO Discovery.

Harvey, F. (2005) *Education Programmes of ABO Orchestras and Organisations: Current and recent projects, plans and new initiatives*. London: Association of British Orchestras.

Hays, T. and Minichiello, V. (2005) 'The contribution of music to quality of life in older people: An Australian qualitative study'. *Ageing & Society*, 25(2), 261–278.

Higgins, L. (2007) 'Acts of hospitality: The community in community music'. *Music Education Research*, 9(2), 281–292.

–– (2008) 'The creative music workshop: Event, facilitation, gift'. *International Journal of Music Education*, 26(4), 326–338.

Hillman, S. (2002) 'Participatory singing for older people: A perception of benefit'. *Health Education*, 102(4), 163–171.

Jamieson, A. (2007) 'Higher education study in later life: What is the point?' *Ageing & Society*, 27, 363–384.

Koopman, C. (2007) 'Community music as music education: On the educational potential of community music'. *International Journal of Music Education*, 25(2), 151–163.

MusicLeader (2009) *About MusicLeader*. Online. <http://www.musicleader. net> (accessed 28/12/2009).

Mullen, P. (2002) We Don't Teach, We Explore: Aspects of community music delivery. Online. <http://www.worldmusiccentre.com/uploads/cma/ mullenteach explore.PDF> (accessed 27/12/2009).

Pieters, J.M. (1996) 'Psychology of adult education'. In A.C. Tuijnman (ed.), *International Encyclopedia of Adult Education and Training* (Second edition). New York: Elsevier Science.

St Albans Rehearsal Orchestra (SARO) (2009) 'St Albans Rehearsal Orchestra'. Online. <http://www.saro.org.uk/index.html> (accessed 04/01/2010).

Sixsmith, A. and Gibson, G. (2007) 'Music and the wellbeing of people with dementia'. *Ageing and Society*, 27(1), 127–145.

Sound Sense (2006) 'Sound Sense - Supporting Community Music'. Online. <http://www.soundsense.org> (accessed 28/12/2009).

Swanwick, K. (2008) 'The "good-enough" music teacher'. *British Journal of Music Education*, 25(1), 9–22.

UKPASS (2009) *Online Application Service*. Online. <http://www.ukpass.ac.uk> (accessed 29/12/2009).

Youth Music (2009) 'Youth Music: Music Is Power'. Online. <musicispower. youthmusic.org.uk> (accessed 28/12/2009).

Chapter 20

Where now?

Susan Hallam and Andrea Creech

The UK has much to be proud of in relation to its music education. Provision is arguably the best in the world – and it makes a major contribution to the strength of the creative industries, which continue to play a crucial role in the UK economy.

The key to its success is the regular provision of general music classes and extra-curricular instrumental tuition in primary and secondary schools, on a weekly basis, delivered by well-qualified and enthusiastic teachers, supported by extensive opportunities for learners to participate in a wide range of different types of musical groups in schools or music centres. Historical analysis shows that when these fundamentals are not in place musical activity disappears, along with all the benefits which it brings, intellectually, personally and socially (see Chapter 1).

Early years and primary schools

Attaining high levels of expertise in music takes considerable time, and the foundations for this need to be developed early. Young children have a natural proclivity for music and are 'open-eared' (not prejudiced against particular kinds of music), curious and imaginative. They can enhance their creative skills in music and develop interests in a wide variety of different musical genres if given opportunities to do so. Other benefits include the enhancement of listening and language skills and motor coordination. Musical performances also provide schools with opportunities to engage parents in their child's education (particularly those who might normally be reluctant to visit the school) and members of the wider community. There is some debate over whether structured or unstructured musical opportunities are more valuable for very young children in the early years, but what is certain is that children's responsiveness to music will decline where their environment is bereft of musical activities. Thus, in order to maximise the potential benefits to be derived from music, children need high-quality, creative musical opportunities early and often.

There are ongoing issues with the quality of music provision in some early years and primary school environments (see Chapters 12 and 13). To ensure equality of opportunity and to maximise the wider benefits of musical activity:

- Music needs to be taught or strongly supported by those with high levels of musical expertise.
- The foundations for reading musical notation need to be established early.
- All children need to be given the opportunity to learn to play a musical instrument.
- Schools need to have strong partnerships with Music Services.
- Children need opportunities to participate and perform in musical groups which meet regularly.
- Children need opportunities to work with community musicians on specific short-term projects which inspire and challenge them, and to receive appropriate preparation and follow-up work.
- Children need opportunities to explore and develop musical ideas, facilitated by creative music professionals who have knowledge of effective teaching and learning approaches.
- Music in formal settings should include music from children's own homes and cultural backgrounds.
- Children and their parents/carers need to be facilitated in sharing musical activities and integrating these activities into daily life.

Secondary and further education

At secondary level and beyond, students identify with specific musical genres. They may be reluctant to engage with particular types of music which they feel are not 'cool'. Increasingly, young people wish to establish their independence. Learning activities which support this and relate to 'real life' tend to be well received (see Chapters 14 and 15). In secondary and further education, students need opportunities to:

- engage in musical activities with which they can identify (usually popular music)
- personalise their learning, developing their own specific skills and creative styles

- develop musical understanding of, and experiment with, a wide range of different types of music
- develop instrumental skills and musical literacy related to specific genres
- be inspired and challenged by visiting musicians in specific projects where appropriate preparation and follow-up work is available
- participate in a wide variety of musical groups in schools and music centres, locally and nationally
- use technology in creative and innovative ways to support a positive musical self-concept.

This means that teachers in schools and colleges need to develop deep knowledge of the musical skills that each individual student has and their aspirations for the future.

Higher, professional and continuing education

Professional musicians increasingly have 'portfolio careers', performing, composing, writing and teaching. The nature of the professional work available has changed considerably and this presents challenges to universities and conservatoires. As students progress through their programmes of study they need to be given opportunities to explore a range of career trajectories and be provided with the support that they need to implement them.

The nature of the portfolio career also means that musicians tend to be isolated. They have few opportunities for engaging in ongoing professional development and as most are self-employed they have to finance any such activities themselves. Networks need to be established to enable sharing of ideas and good practice.

Currently, the only recognised teaching qualifications are those relating to teaching in schools (PGCE, Cert Ed) or Further Education (PGCE, Diploma in Teaching in the Lifelong Learning Sector). Typically, these require attendance full-time (one year) or part-time (two years), although there are opportunities for gaining qualified teacher status (QTS) through employment-based routes – but these normally require class teaching experience. The nature of the portfolio career means that these qualifications are inappropriate and unnecessary. An accredited qualification is required which is recognised as rigorous and meaningful across the sector which is appropriate for those engaged in teaching, coaching, providing workshops, and so on. A possibility for this might be a 'Passport to a Portfolio Musical Career', based broadly on the 'Preparing to Teach in the Lifelong Sector' (PTTLS) qualification, which is currently a prerequisite for specialists who wish to teach in the further or lifelong learning sectors. PTTLS equips specialists with introductory pedagogical skills and the knowledge needed for becoming effective coaches, facilitators and teachers in their subject area. Known as a 'passport to teaching module', it involves approximately 30 learning hours that comprise work-based mentoring, observation and development of a portfolio of continuing professional development (CPD). A 'Passport to a Portfolio Musical Career', providing accreditation for a skills base that would include knowledge of appropriate teaching and learning approaches for diverse contexts, how to address issues of inclusivity, motivation, progression and assessment, could be embedded in programmes currently offered by conservatoires, universities, further education colleges, or private companies. It would need to be accredited by national bodies – Training and Development Agency for Schools (TDA) or Standards Verification UK (SVUK), for instance – so that it was widely recognised. Over time it might become a statutory requirement for those engaged in leading musical activities with children, young people and throughout the lifespan.

There is also a need for a greater focus on CPD for those working in schools. Ofsted (2009) commented that music teachers tend not to take advantage of opportunities to update their skills and frequently are unaware of current developments. The training related to the Wider Opportunities programme has been taken up by many teachers but there are still issues about the lack of musical expertise in generalist primary teachers, in schools where there is no specialist teacher to offer support, and in secondary school teachers in relation to world and popular musics and the use of technology. The budgets that schools have available for the CPD of their staff are typically constrained and music is not always given priority (Hallam *et al.*, 2005). Head teachers need to offer support for music that goes beyond rhetoric.

Lifelong learning

Participation in making music is a lifelong activity, although individuals may reduce their level of activity when focusing on the development of a career or family issues. Typically, as retirement approaches re-engagement takes place with subsequent benefits for health and social and emotional well-being. Given the positive outcomes of musical participation, a number of issues need to be addressed. First, provision of activities locally is patchy, and the quality of provision is uneven and may not meet the needs of everyone. Barriers to participation include access, transport, ill health and competing demands – looking after young children or a partner, for instance. Some people may be reluctant to take initial steps to become involved. Overall, providers – local authorities (LAs), for instance – need to:

- take steps to encourage engagement
- ensure that relevant and interesting activities are available
- ensure that the musical activities on offer are appropriate for the local community
- ensure that the quality of teaching is high and that staff have received appropriate training
- maximise opportunities for group activities
- address issues relating to mobility and transport
- develop outreach programmes that are relevant to local communities
- improve access to information about opportunities for participation in music
- recognise older learners' prior experience
- acknowledge that older learners continue to have aspirations and a desire to meet challenges in the context of participation in music.

Music for all

Much progress has been made in recent years in providing opportunities for active engagement with music of children and young people with special educational needs (see Chapters 3 and 17). There has also been an increased focus on young people at risk and those already in custodial institutions. Youth Services may provide space for young people to practise and develop their technical skills, including mixing, recording and producing. The informal nature of youth work is often more appropriate for disaffected young people than mainstream schooling. The quality of work in such circumstances has been reported as 'good' overall, but some Youth Services did not have the resources or partnerships with schools and colleges to deliver high-quality opportunities (Ofsted, 2009). There is the potential for Music Services to work collaboratively with Youth Services to deliver tuition and opportunities for group activities.

There has also been recent attention on supporting children who live in deprived areas. Youth Music Action Zones have focused on communities across England and Wales where there are high levels of social and economic need. Currently, 21 of these Zones are in operation, drawing on expertise from the public and the voluntary and private sectors, and covering a wide range of musical genres and activities. One strand of activity is the Youth Music Mentors programme, which aims to improve the life chances of young people through music-based mentoring in one-to-one, peer group and work-based contexts (Box 20.1).

> **Box 20.1 Positive outcomes from the Youth Music Mentors programme**
>
> *Before, I didn't really have anything in my life. I was a confused little person wandering in a big world. Music gives you something to look forward to. I've got to know loads of different people and its opening a whole new world.*
>
> (Dee, 17, Southampton)
>
> (Youth Music, 2009)

Boxes 20.2 and 20.3 provide examples of how young people's sustained engagement in music, facilitated through Youth Music Action Zones, had direct and significant positive implications for local communities.

> **Box 20.2 More Music's 'Friday Night Project'**
>
> More Music, (Lancashire's Youth Music Action Zone) is a community music organisation based in the West End of Morecambe. Their 'Friday Night Project' has made hugely significant gains in helping change the lives of disadvantaged young people in the area – those who are at risk of offending, drug and alcohol abuse and other challenging issues. The project engages them in positive activities, with the aim of building confidence and self-esteem. Activities include MC-ing, DJ-ing, lyric writing, music production, studio recording and live performance. Not only does this provide young people with the opportunity to learn new musical skills, it also gives them a creative medium for self-expression. Back in 2006, More Music had to employ a local security firm to protect staff and participants from a gang of local young people aged between 12 and 18. This particular group used to spit at, verbally and physically abuse staff and participants alike, vandalise the building and fire air pistols and snooker balls through office windows at employees. More Music responded to this problem head on, and took on the challenge of organising workshops that would engage this group of young people, giving them a sense of ownership of the project and More Music as a whole. Initially they worked very closely with the local police (who provided physical support in and around the sessions), with Signposts (who provided youth workers and a neutral building to work in) and with outreach workers to promote the project on the streets. The first term of sessions proved to be demanding, with violence used against staff, vandalism and extreme alcohol- and drug-related incidents. During the second term the sessions were moved into the 'Hothouse', More Music's own building, where project leaders began to build relationships and trust with the young participants, offering them a safe, non-judgemental and welcoming environment.

Three years later the project is well established within the local community, with the young people performing regularly at local community festivals. The Lancashire Constabulary has reported a significant drop in crime and antisocial behaviour in the West End of Morecambe during session hours. The police have also identified a sizeable reduction in inter-estate violence. Many of the young people have crossed over into More Music's mainstream activity, and the number of sessions has been increased, with a satellite project in another run-down area of Morecambe recently being launched. The approach taken by More Music ensures that young people are given wide and varied opportunities to develop their musical, personal and social skills in a safe and supported environment. This approach involves combining contemporary music and youth work within a partnership framework and has given the young people a sense of stability and trust within their unstable lives and social networks. It has also seen all participants grow in confidence and connect positively to the community around them, as well as significantly reducing risk-taking behaviour. Through community performance the young people have been able to demonstrate how they can make a positive contribution to society.

(Youth Music, 2009)

Box 20.3 Music making for young people who have been excluded from school

The Saint Christopher's 'Music Maker' youth project is based in a community centre on the Holme Wood Estate in Bradford, a place where many young people experience economic disadvantage while dealing with other complex social issues. The Music Maker project reaches young people aged between 8 and 18 and takes place in various settings, including primary and secondary schools, after-school clubs and the Saint Christopher's youth project itself. The young people, many of whom have no previous experience with music making, are encouraged to explore the basics of music making and composition through experimenting with the equipment and technology available. Many of the young people enjoying the project are at various stages of exclusion from their schools. The staff at the schools have quickly realised the positive effects that the Music Maker project has had on their pupils – many become less disruptive and more focused. Three pupils who had previously been excluded were welcomed back to school having worked hard, with the help of the Music Maker project, to earn their place back with their friends and peers at school. Musically, the young people who joined the project have each found an area of music making that they enjoy. Many of them would not have had the chance, due to economic restrictions, to enjoy music making. Some have gone on to form bands and purchase instruments with the help of their parents.

The wider community has expressed their gratitude to the project: the after-school clubs provide young people with a positive activity to enjoy. The young people themselves have also said how much they enjoy hanging out at the project, many of them seeing the youth project as a second home. The benefits of the Music Maker project are far-reaching and diverse. For example, one participant who had recently been permanently excluded from school went on to become a trainee Music Leader and to study for two A levels at her local college. She says 'Music Maker has changed my life and I wouldn't miss it for the world'.

(Youth Music, 2009)

There are also three 'In Harmony' projects which have been inspired by the success of the Venezuelan 'El Sistema' project. This originated from a project that sought to use the orchestra as a safe, social and empowering space, rather like a second or alternative family, to sustain and develop the well-being of children. Playing in a symphony orchestra is expected to develop a child's sense of loyalty and commitment, responsibility, self-esteem and self-confidence, teamwork and leadership. The orchestral structure enables opportunities for more than 100 young musicians to perform in a single ensemble – a dynamic and complex interaction of individuals playing both leading and supportive roles, and opportunities for smaller ensembles such as brass groups, percussion ensembles, string orchestras and wind bands. Examples of the three projects are given in Boxes 20.4, 20.5 and 20.6. The projects are also innovative in that they are run by groups of organisations rather than single organisations. The UK projects aim to enthuse and motivate at-risk children, families and communities so that children can improve their skills, attainment and 'life chances', families can improve their well-being, and communities can improve their cohesion and mutual respect and can champion social justice. The programme harnesses and develops a mix of musical, creative, social, personal and life skills that are of value to all children – and could be life-changing for the most vulnerable and at-risk.

Box 20.4 In Harmony Liverpool

Led by the Royal Liverpool Philharmonic, In Harmony Liverpool is being delivered in partnership with Faith Primary School, resident-led West Everton Community Council, Liverpool Music Support Service and Liverpool Hope University. The aim is to have a significant positive impact on the well-being, confidence, aspirations and attainment of children at Faith Primary School and in the West Everton community. Faith Primary School is the only school in West Everton, which is one of the most deprived areas of the country. Every child at Faith is making music every day of the week, working with a team of highly skilled musicians.

Student volunteers from Liverpool Hope University support the team. Eighty-one children, including the school's Reception class and 11 members of staff, including teachers, teaching assistants, the head teacher and the school secretary, are participating in the daily music activities. The instruments include violins, violas, cellos and double basses. The weekly music programme includes:

- Shake Up and Sing, singing and movement every morning to get children focused for school, with many opportunities for children to conduct and lead songs for the rest of the school
- whole school singing on Monday afternoons
- instrumental lessons every Monday and Thursday mornings on violin, viola, cello and double bass for all children and all school staff
- West Everton Children's Orchestra rehearsals every Friday afternoon at Liverpool Phil at the Friary
- musicianship sessions every week for every class, including tailored music-making sessions for children at Early Years Foundation Stage.

Instrument practice clubs are run every lunchtime and after school. In addition to this core programme, the children, staff, parents and the local community attend concerts at Liverpool Philharmonic Hall, including full symphony orchestra and smaller ensembles, and the whole school has participated in the Phil's extensive schools' concert programme. Additional programmes are planned for the school holiday periods, while maintaining regular instrumental tuition and orchestra rehearsals. One hundred people, including children and community members from West Everton visited the Southbank in April 2009, with front row seats for a performance by El Sistema's main youth orchestra, the Simon Bolivar Youth Orchestra. This was inspirational for the West Everton children, who bowed and plucked along with their imaginary violins and cellos.

(Derived from In Harmony, 2009. Please note that this programme may have developed and changed since this information was accessed.)

Box 20.5 In Harmony Norwich

In Harmony Norwich is led by Norwich & Norfolk Community Arts in partnership with Larkman Primary School, Catton Grove Primary School, Mile Cross Primary School, Earlham Early Years Centre, the University of East Anglia and the Chamber Orchestra Anglia.

The delivery of In Harmony Norwich is:
- Targeted at the Larkman, Mile Cross and Catton Grove areas of the city, three established areas of deprivation.

- Based in the three key Primary schools for these areas, Larkman, Catton Grove and Mile Cross Primaries, and built on strong partnerships with these schools.
- Takes the form of a mixture of in-school and after-school provision. In school, all Reception and Year 1 children in these schools will get between one and one and a half hours of provision per week, mixing instrumental tuition with general musicianship sessions.
- After school provision takes place at each of the three school locations, from Monday to Thursday. This is currently prioritised for Year 1 children, and around 25 places are offered at each school for older children across the other year groups. These sessions start with choir and general musicianship, followed by group instrumental lessons. Thursday is the 'ensemble' session, bringing together the different instrument groups, and also offering a chance to mix the children in the different after school groups.
- Each year we work with a new Reception class and children going up to Year 2 access the programme through the after school sessions.
- Working with Violin, Viola, Cello, Double bass and Percussion as key instruments, in addition to singing, which everyone does. Year 1 and older children have already selected their instrument of choice, whilst Reception children make this choice in the Summer term. Instrumental lessons start in the second half of term, having worked on our polystyrene practice instruments for the first half.
- Parents, teachers and Teaching Assistants are also getting involved, some of them learning alongside their children.
- Musicians from the Chamber Orchestra Anglia come along every month to work with the children and perform for them, with the whole orchestra getting involved in big performances, such as the project launch days in March 2009.

The project started with 150 children, parents/carers, teachers and community members attending a special performance given by the Simon Bolivar Youth Orchestra at the Royal Festival Hall in April 2009, something that has inspired the children in their learning over the last year.

(Derived from In Harmony Norwich, 2010)

Box 20.6 In Harmony Lambeth

Lambeth Music Service and its major partners, Southbank Centre and Amicus Horizon, are implementing the In Harmony programme on the Lansdowne Green Estate in Stockwell, including children from two primary schools. Several hundred children aged 4–8 have the opportunity to be involved in the developing musical community through singing, movement and an opportunity to play an instrument and perform in an orchestra. The wider community are engaged in supporting the orchestras and choirs, forging a sense of community between the schools, the central estate, surrounding estates, families and community leaders. Youth workers, volunteers and Family Support Services will ensure that children and families get the support they need to benefit from the opportunities. The project includes musicianship classes, instrumental lessons, playing in ensembles, holiday music courses, support for public events, pre-school music sessions, mentoring from the guest musicians from the London Philharmonic Orchestra and inspiring performance and composition opportunities, in collaboration with Southbank Centre's Learning and Participation department. Children from surrounding schools and estates are able to join the programme by attending after-school sessions, and those who already learn appropriate instruments can join the ensembles. The children have had the opportunity to sit with the players of the London Philharmonic Orchestra during a rehearsal of *In the Hall of the Mountain King,* and have heard a variety of live performances by string players in several different settings – duos, trios, quartets – from their teachers and the LPO, a klezmer band, and English folk settings (with Bellowhead). As time goes on, more weekly sessions will be added, up to five per week. A software company is turning the musical teaching material into an animated, interactive online resource. This is for children and parents to use at home and in designated practice areas, and a local charity with experience in providing laptops for children and managed learning environments is conducting a feasibility study and fundraising, to provide families with access to online resources. The early years resources include chiffon scarves, large blue circles of material (ponds) which children can hold on to in a circle and play musical games – (including bouncing a frog puppet while singing in Turkish), and the worlds' largest scrunchie which can be held by up to 15 children in a circle, to help them feel pulse and movement. The children are enjoying the sessions and are developing quickly as musicians. The schools' leadership teams and the estate management are very supportive of the project, and the parents and families have demonstrated their support.

(Derived from In Harmony, 2009. Please note that this programme may have developed and changed since this information was accessed.)

Technology, change and musical traditions

Technological developments have had – and continue to have – an impact on all areas of musical activity. They have not simply been tools for furthering musical innovations, but are driving change in all kinds of ways, influencing instrumentation, the range of sounds that can be created, removing limitations relating to instrumental technique, the processes of composition and notation, and access to music to listen to.

The impact of technology on education has also been profound, with some instruments becoming 'endangered' while requests to play others have increased dramatically. There is a danger that some musical traditions will die out altogether and it may be that efforts will need to be made to ensure that these are sustained in the long term – brass bands, for instance, classical music and folk music. Young people, in particular, unless they are introduced to a range of different musical traditions early (when they are still 'open-eared') can become intransigent in their reluctance to engage with any music other than their preferred genre. Given the ease of access to different musics and the facility to mix them – on iPods, for instance – there are opportunities for individuals to listen to a wider range of music more easily than ever before. There has been a tendency for the media to restrict the type of music played on any radio channel to that which is perceived to be of interest to particular groups of listeners. This was not always the case. Historically, a wider range of music was played, familiarising listeners to a range of genres. Musicians themselves draw on a wide range of musical influences in both composing and performing, so it might be timely for those with responsibility for producing and marketing music programmes to reconsider their strategies. When presented with classical music in sporting contexts, introducing TV or radio programmes, or providing background for adverts it becomes familiar and loses its 'stigma' and its 'classical' nature is not problematic. These practices could be adopted more widely.

Assessment

Assessment has very powerful effects on learning (see Chapter 9). In primary schools, musical assessment undertaken by teachers is problematic because generalist teachers tend to lack sufficient expertise, while in secondary schools teachers are under pressure to assess too frequently, with inadequate attention to issues of progression (Ofsted, 2009). GCSE Music may not be entirely appropriate for young people engaged in making popular music, and several schools adopting the Musical Futures programme have changed to enter their pupils for BTEC examinations. Overall, examination bodies have responded well to the need for different types of examinations to meet changing needs. A particular challenge, however, is going to be the assessment of instrumental progress where children are taught in very large groups.

Transitions

Through a lifetime of engagement with music, learners and professionals (including teachers) will experience a range of transitions as they develop and maintain their expertise. Transition routes have become increasingly individualised and frequently involve elements of individual choice, taking many forms, with varying degrees of impact. As individuals experience transitions they have to adapt to different: (1) learning environments, teachers and facilitators; (2) pedagogical practices; (3) peer and friendship groups; (4) expectations of performance and types of assessment; (5) skill requirements; (6) ways of thinking about learning; and (7) ways of thinking about self and identity.

Ofsted (2009) commented on the lack of continuity in all aspects of the music provision that was observed, and on how this negatively affected the progress that learners were making and seriously diminished the impact of additional opportunities. Better continuity was needed within primary schools so that pupils had a consistent quality and quantity of music education. Pupils commented frequently that music was better or worse because of a change of teachers as they moved up a year. Pupils exhibit wide variation in musical skills when they transfer to secondary school. This can create particular difficulties for secondary school teachers. Ofsted (2009) reported that continuity between primary and secondary schools was virtually non-existent, effective partnerships between secondary and primary schools were rare, and virtually no information was shared at the point at which pupils transferred to other schools except, at most, some information about which pupils learnt to play musical instruments (Ofsted, 2009). A musical 'passport' which gave a detailed account of the musical activities of each student – which they could update and use wherever it was appropriate – might help overcome some of these difficulties. Indeed, given the typically long-term nature of the acquisition of musical expertise, such a document could provide the basis for a portfolio of continuing professional development which would then form part of the 'Passport to a Portfolio Musical Career', proposed earlier in this chapter. Some secondary schools have recognised the need for better continuity and have developed links with primary schools so that they know the pupils through sharing work. Ideally, links should be sustained over considerable periods of time, perhaps through shared concerts and teaching, but a single project towards the end of Year 6 can be useful, particularly if the work is jointly planned and discussed. These kinds of links also familiarise secondary school teachers with the nature of work going on in primary schools.

Personalised learning

The key to providing a successful music education for everyone is to adopt an individualised approach, allowing everyone to have some control over their learning and its direction, and providing opportunities to exercise autonomy and shape their future. Indeed, developing autonomy and self-direction might be argued to be one of the aims of education. The 'Teaching and Learning in 2020 Review' (DfES, 2007) focused on a pedagogy of personalised learning with nine key features: (1) high-quality teaching and learning; (2) target setting and tracking; (3) focused assessment; (4) intervention; (5) pupil grouping; (6) the learning environment; (7) curriculum organisation; (8) the extended curriculum; and (9) supporting children's wider needs. In practice, however, little seems to have changed in schools as a result of this (Sebba *et al.*, 2007), although in music there would seem to be more possibilities for successful implementation. In an international project, 'Developing Visions of the School of the Future' which brought together 70 students from 12 countries to generate ideas (British Council, 2009) some of the young people's ideas resonated with thinking and current practice in music education. The students ideas – some of which have already been adopted in music education, to at least some extent – stressed the importance of technology, relevance and flexibility in relation to learning and teaching, for instance:

- Challenge should be seen as normal and not to be feared.
- Learning should take place in and out of school and include multimedia, visits, trips, exchanges, field work, work experience and project work.
- Classes should be small and based on levels of expertise, with flexibility, choice and learning of academic and non-academic skills.
- Assessment should enable students to feel confident about what they have achieved and to see how to improve.
- Parents should be educated on how to support learning, with clearer and better communication between parents and teachers.

To develop personalised learning in music, greater cooperation and partnership working between different agencies and groups of musicians is needed to generate the level of flexibility required.

Working together

The Music Manifesto launched in 2004 (DfES) attempted to broaden the scope of music education and encourage greater integration between schools and other stakeholders such as broadcasters, conservatoires, the music business and music itself. The second Music Manifesto report, *Making Every Child's Music Matter* (DfES, 2006: 7) recommended that everyone involved in music education should work together to provide the framework and focus needed to deliver a universal music education offer to all children, from early years onwards, where they could take an active part in high-quality music making. The report argued that this meant putting the child at the heart of music education, providing the right opportunities, in the right way and at the right time. This requires that schools and music providers connect their music provision more meaningfully with young people's own interests, passions and motivations. The report suggested greater collaboration between different providers. Since then there have been examples of such collaboration – for instance, the music partnership projects (see Chapter 19) where professional orchestras, other providers and local authority Music Services are working together.

Collaborative working is not always easy. Hallam (2010) suggests a series of factors that are important for effective partnership working. These are set out in Box 20.7.

Box 20.7 Effective partnership working: The important factors

Strategic and delivery functions

Partnerships fulfil two main functions: strategic and delivery. Where organisations are involved in both strategic planning and delivery it is important that the commitment to and understanding of the partnership exists at all levels of the organisation(s).

Leadership

Partnerships require leadership. Leadership can be provided by one or more people acting on their own behalf or as representatives of an organisation. In sophisticated models, different people are empowered to lead at different times, according to their skills and expertise and the needs of the partnership.

Membership

Having the appropriate membership is critical to a partnership's success. At the strategic level, members must have access to the appropriate decision makers, budget holders and policymakers, or have sufficient authority vested in them to make decisions or to commit funding. The combined authority of the partnership may give it a level of influence greater than that held by any one individual partner.

Aims

The reason for the existence of the partnership needs to be clear, as does its aims and objectives.

Clarity of roles

Members of the partnership need to be clear about their roles and responsibilities within the partnership. This clarity cannot be assumed. Different people understand different things and make assumptions.

Trust and time

The extent to which the above issues can be discussed within the partnership will depend partly on relationships, values and the amount of trust that exists between the partners. Time is required for these issues to be discussed. Each time a new person joins the partnership the issues may need to be revisited.

High-quality experiences

The partnership must achieve something. All of the above is of little importance if the activity is not effective at the delivery stage. The experiences of the young people and the music educators whom the partnership is seeking to support must be high-quality, and fit for purpose. Continuing Professional Development needs must be identified and met.

Senior managers

Many of the same issues of context and clarity of communications, leadership and roles and responsibilities apply equally at the delivery stage. When projects take place in a school or involve young people of school age the importance of decision makers, budget holders and policymakers still applies. The role of senior managers is critical but is one that is often overlooked.

Young people

Young people themselves need to be able to contribute at all stages.

Planning, monitoring, evaluation and feedback

There needs to be sufficient time for planning, ongoing monitoring, evaluation and feedback so that the value for money and the impact of the partnership will not be diminished.

(Hallam, 2010)

Local authority music plans (LAMPs)

Local authorities have a role to play in encouraging closer collaboration through local authority music plans (LAMPs) which are designed to broaden the music offered to children and young people in a local authority area. LAMPs, as they develop, should become the basis of a comprehensive, inclusive and coherent music plan for young people, enabling LAs to audit and identify music provision as a whole in their area and progression routes. All LAs are expected to include reference in their LAMPs to the Arts Council England 'Regularly Funded Organisations', the work of community musicians, Youth Music-funded projects, Youth Music Action Zones and anyone involved in music education in and out of school. In time, as LAMPs develop, it is anticipated that information will be made accessible to young people and their parents or carers who should be consulted as part of their preparation.

Sustainability of music education

Music has the potential to develop a wide range of transferable skills in those who engage with it (see Chapter 1) including those which are particularly desired by employers – for instance, teamwork, leadership, independent working and creativity. Despite this, music is still perceived by many people as lacking in relevance for future employment. The musical community needs to take steps to change this perception and promote musical skills as useful preparation for a wide range of employment opportunities. This is particularly important in times of economic difficulty. To this end, a key skill that needs to be emphasised in the training of portfolio musicians is one of advocacy. Musicians themselves need to raise and sustain awareness within their own communities of the considerable benefits that music participation offers in respect of health, personal, social and emotional well-being.

Notwithstanding the wide-ranging benefits of music that have been outlined in this book, it is perhaps most fitting to conclude by celebrating the rich musical diversity that is evident across the UK. The wider benefits of music making are indeed impressive and should not be ignored. However, the value of music in its own right must not be forgotten. The UK has a plethora of opportunities in place for individuals and communities to access the deeply enriching and rewarding experience of participation in music. The music education opportunities that now exist across the UK represent a most valuable resource that must be preserved and developed as part of any long-term strategy relating to quality of life for all.

References

British Council (2009) 'Developing visions of the school of the future'. International conference, Budapest, March.

Department for Education and Skills (DfES) (2004) *Music Manifesto: More music for more people.* London: DfES.

–– (2006) *Making Every Child's Music Matter* (Music Manifesto Report No. 2). London: DfES.

–– (2007) *2020 Vision: Report of the Teaching and Learning in 2020 Review Group.* London: DFES.

Hallam, R. (2010) 'Effective partnership working in music education: An interim overview'. Paper at the 20th World International Society for Music Education (ISME) Conference, Beijing, August.

Hallam, S., Rogers, L, Creech, A. and Preti, C. (2005) *Evaluation of a Voices Foundation Primer in Primary Schools.* London: DfES.

In Harmony (2009) <http://www.inharmonyengland.com> (accessed 20/02/2010).

In Harmony Norwich (2010) <http://www.norcaarts.co.uk/programmes-and-projects/In-Harmony.cfm> (accessed 19/05/2010).

Office for Standards in Education (Ofsted) (2009) *Making More of Music: An evaluation of music in schools 2005–08.* London: Ofsted.

Sebba, J., Brown, N., Stewart, S., Galton, M. and James, M. (2007) *An Investigation of Personalised Learning Approaches Used by Schools.* London: DfES.

Youth Music (2009) *Music is Power.* Online. <musicispower.youthmusic.org.uk> (accessed 20/02/2010).